THE LAUGHTER OF TRIUMPH

William Hone and George Cruikshank,
the author and the artist

'The Freeborn Englishman'
From *A Slap at Slop*, 1821

The Laughter of Triumph

WILLIAM HONE

AND THE FIGHT FOR THE FREE PRESS

Ben Wilson

Satire's my weapon; but I'm too discreet
To run a-muck at all I meet,
I only wear it in a land of Hectors,
Thieves, Supercargoes, Sharpers and Directors.

Alexander Pope

faber and faber

First published in 2005
by Faber and Faber Limited
3 Queen Square, London WC1N 3AU

Printed in England by Mackays of Chatham, plc.

A CIP record for this book
is available from the British Library

ISBN 0–571–22470–9

2 4 6 8 10 9 7 5 3

For my parents, Marney and Chris

Contents

Acknowledgements

My first and deepest thanks must go to Vic Gatrell, whose special paper at Cambridge, 'The Politics of Laughter', inspired my love of visual culture and introduced me to William Hone's trials and satires. Vic's knowledge of satire is second to none, and his enthusiasm contagious: his classes were the only things that got me out of bed before 9 during four years at university. Thanks also to the Master and Fellows of Pembroke College, in particular Michael Kuczynski, Dr Jon Parry and the late Dr Mark Kaplanoff, whose long, long lunches kept my spirits up.

And to Rowan Pelling, who introduced me to Clare Conville, the very best of agents. Clare's sharp mind, inexhaustible patience and great company kept me going during the writing of this book; thanks, Clare, for the bottles of champagne and lunches of lobster which, along with your friendship, encouraged me to write when I would otherwise have given up.

I would also like to thank, for many and different reasons, Hattie and Chris Pask, David Maxwell, James Rivett, Elisa Lodato, Patrick Walsh, Matthew Hook, Matthew Wilson and all friends and family who tolerated my absences. I am a Luddite when it comes to computers, so special thanks go to Andrew Singleton and Ross Monro for technical advice. The staff of the Rare Books Room of the British Library have been consistently helpful and cheery. I am indebted to Finbar McDonnel for help with the cartoons. Fred Hodder read an early draft and his suggestions were incorporated; for such original comments and peerless companionship all his friends miss him dearly.

I am grateful for the unfailing help from everyone at Faber, especially the people I worked with most closely, Lesley Felce and Lucy Owen. Walter Donohue has been the best of editors; his commitment to the book, generosity and insights contributed so much to the writing. He has made the process of writing what it should be: tremendous fun. I have enjoyed every moment working with him, especially when it coincided with lunch.

William Hone: Comicality and Seriousness

Public opinion can never exist as a power in the State, unless there exist also persons who expose to hatred and contempt those Ministers and those laws which they conceive to be detrimental to the interests of the community.

Yellow Dwarf, 1818[1]

If I cannot do a thing in my own way, I never can do it at all.

William Hone, in a letter to Francis Place, 1824[2]

In October 1842, Charles Dickens accompanied George Cruikshank to a funeral at Abney Park Cemetery, Stoke Newington, on a day he described as 'muddy, foggy, wet, dark, cold, and unutterably wretched in every possible respect'. They were going to pay their respects to William Hone. Dickens had met Hone for the only time a few weeks before when he had travelled to the old man's home in Tottenham. The meeting had been arranged by their mutual friend George Cruikshank, the illustrator of books written by both Hone and Dickens.

'God knows it was miserable enough,' wrote Dickens, 'for the widow and children were crying bitterly in one corner, and the other mourners – mere people of ceremony, who cared no more for the dead man than the hearse did – were talking quite coolly and carelessly in another; and the contrast was as painful and distressing as anything I ever saw.'

The novelist was moved and affected by the gloomy scene. But what made it worse was the dark comedy that often accompanies an awkward English funeral. Dickens found eccentric George Cruikshank's behaviour and appearance irrepressibly funny, especially in stark contrast to the sombre rituals of a nonconformist funeral. It was for Dickens, 'a scene of mingled comicality and seriousness . . . which has choked me at dinner ever since'.

Now, [Cruikshank] has enormous whiskers, which straggle all down his throat in such weather, and stick out in front of him, like a partially unravelled bird's-nest; so that he looks queer enough at the best, but when he is very wet, and in a state between jollity (he is always very jolly with me) and the deepest gravity (going to a funeral, you know), it is utterly impossible to resist him, especially as he makes the strangest remarks the mind of man can conceive, without any intention of being funny, but rather meaning to be philosophical. I really cried with an irresistible sense of his comicality all the way . . .

When Cruikshank was dressed in the black cloak and hat of chief mourner, Dickens almost had to leave the room because the sight was too much. It soon became obvious that, as early as his last rites, William Hone had slipped from the memories even of his closest friends; his obsequies quickly degenerated into farce and petty quarrels.

The mourners went into the parlour, where, as Dickens recalled, there was

an independent clergyman present, with his bands on, and a Bible under his arm, who, as soon as we were seated, addressed us thus in a loud voice:

'Mr C–, have you seen a paragraph respecting our departed friend, which has gone the round of the morning papers?'

'Yes, sir,' says C–, 'I have,' looking very hard at me the while, for he had told me with some pride coming down that it was his composition.

'Oh!' said the clergyman, 'then you will agree with me, Mr C–, that it is not only an insult to me, who am the servant of the Almighty, but an insult to the Almighty, whose servant I am.'

'How is that sir?' said C–.

'It is stated, Mr C–, in that paragraph, that when Mr H[one] failed in business as a bookseller, he was persuaded by *me* to try the pulpit, which is false, incorrect, unchristian, in a manner blasphemous, and in all respects contemptible. Let us pray.' With which . . . and in the same breath, he knelt down, as we all did, and began a very miserable jumble of an extemporary prayer.

At that instant Dickens was 'really penetrated with sorrow for the family' and Cruikshank was 'upon his knees and sobbing for the loss of an old friend'. But the moment of poignancy was ruined when George muttered through his tears 'that if it wasn't a clergyman, and it wasn't a funeral, he'd have punched his head'. 'I felt', poor Dickens had to admit, 'as if nothing but convulsions could possibly relieve me . . .'³

Charles Dickens attended the funeral curious to witness the last rites of a man who had once been known in every home in the land, but died forgotten. At the height of his career, William Hone's name was synonymous with the fight for the liberty of the press. His journalism, famous throughout the world for its venomous attacks on a hated government, had exploited and defied censorship with intelligence, verve and humour. Hone achieved celebrity at the age of thirty-seven, defending himself from an ostensible charge of blasphemous libel in three trials held over three days in December 1817. In reality they were show trials to vindicate the government's aggressive campaign against the press. Hone's performances in court were, as E. P. Thompson wrote, 'some of the most hilarious legal proceedings on record'; it was also a pivotal moment in the history of the British press. [4]

In 1842, Dickens was thirty years old, a former parliamentary reporter and author of five novels. By this time, the British press was one of the freest and most intrusive in the world, boasting a power over every act of government; in turn, it was flattered by politicians as the 'Fourth Estate'. Many bemoaned its licentiousness, but few could deny its influence and constitutional liberties. Meeting the old man in Tottenham must have been a reminder to Dickens of how recent these things were. In 1809, when Hone began his career in journalism, Jeremy Bentham wrote that the freedom of the press existed in a 'sort of abortive embryo state'.[5]

'We have laws to prevent the exposure of unwholesome meat in our markets, and the mixture of deleterious drugs in beer,' Robert Southey, Poet Laureate and Tory journalist wrote. 'We have laws also against poisoning the minds of the people, by exciting discontent and disaffection.' No formal censorship had existed in Britain since 1695, when the laws which required books to be licensed prior to publication lapsed. From henceforth, the state could only punish writing after it had been published. Blackstone wrote in his *Commentaries* of 1769, 'The Liberty of the Press is, indeed, essential to the nature of a free State; but this consists in laying no previous restraints upon publication, and not in freedom from censure for criminal matters when published.' Control of the press had been neither comprehensive nor routinely effective; it had often been allowed to lapse for long periods. But the discretionary powers ministers possessed to regulate the press and arrest critical writers were as oppressive as the extinct licensing laws; the administration's attitude to the press and its policies in this period certainly deserve the name censorship. The definition of 'criminal libel' rested solely with the government; what it considered dangerous or 'unwholesome' was the only criterion for a decision to prosecute. The vagueness of the law benefited the state and left writers in a permanent state of unease. As Bentham wrote, it was impossible to know what constituted a criminal publication at the time of writing; journalism that could be defined as illegal was neither more nor less than 'Any thing which any body at any time may dislike, for any reason' – or more accurately, that which men in power decided to prosecute. For those who believed that Britain was the freest country in the world, one which tolerated forward-thinking and unorthodox philosophical, theological and scientific books, the existence of laws which punished free discussion was shameful. When the government chose to act, the libel laws were discriminate, efficient, and savage in their operation.[6]

Hone's experiences at the hands of the Home Secretary, Lord Sidmouth, and Lord Chief Justice Ellenborough showed just how vindictive the state could be in silencing the press. In 1817, the year Hone reached his maturity as a political commentator, the Whig MP Henry Brougham told the Commons: 'Every man who rises in a meeting, or sits at his desk, to attack the measures of his majesty's ministers, now knows he does so with a halter about his neck.'[7] Ministers could not punish every writer that offended them; but they could make examples of a few prominent journalists: none knew this better than Hone. He was swept off the street, subjected to legal harassment, financial penalties and the plots of government spies; long before he was brought to trial, his health had been ruined, his newspaper closed and his family reduced to poverty. The government knew that poor writers such as Hone could not afford a barrister and that they would be silenced, if not by the law, by months or years of protracted legal proceedings. The power of arbitrary arrest and indefinite imprisonment was effective in itself, and often there was no need for the government to bring an accused writer to court at all. Even if an offending writer was called to trial, it was on sure ground; a journalist was judged by a Special Jury, one comprising men of the so-called 'better sort' – wealthy merchants, civil servants or clergymen – vetted by the government. The odds were stacked in favour of the ministry in trials of this kind. When Hone took the defendant's stand, it was in the knowledge that the government rarely lost.

When most writers avoided confrontation with the state's over-whelming advantages, William Hone stood forward; his career as a political journalist was a personal avowal of the liberties of the press. This he did in and out of court to the risk of his health, livelihood and the safety of his large family. His three trials engrossed the country, and Hone became a popular hero. Laughter was his primary weapon; he deployed satire with ruthlessness and intelligence to lacerate his ene-mies and destroy censorship. His famous collaborations with George Cruikshank defied the state's powers with glorious contempt and had lasting consequences for the way the press was regulated in Britain. His career showed that laughter had a *legitimate* political role; it was a fun-damental freedom for a people shackled by repressive laws.

The courage, skill and humour Hone showed as a defendant and journalist endeared him to the British people, who delighted in his stand against injustice as well as in the rich vocabulary of contemptu-ous epithets and nicknames he levelled at his enemies. Certainly, few espoused the press's cause with comparable bravery. Yet within two decades of the trials his death went almost unremarked; the memories of the bitter conflict between the government and the press had faded from popular consciousness. The brief obituary in *The Times* said that his trials 'may be considered one of the *cause célèbres* of this country'; but they were already buried in obscurity. Today the name William Hone, one of the most important men in the history of the British press, meets no recognition from the public or even from journalists. [8]

When it was first published in 1874, Cruikshank and the Reverend Dr Thomas Binney, the nonconformist minister, challenged the veracity of Dickens's account of Hone's obsequies. Cruikshank said that his friend's writing 'partakes more of the character of fiction than of reality'.[9] His portrayal of the funeral became notorious, even for people who had never heard of William Hone, because it seemed to raise serious questions about the reliability of Dickens as a reporter. Many said that the novelist had distorted the funeral as an excuse for a humorous contrast between solemnity and farce; that even his supposedly factual reportage were merely practice for fiction. But if Dickens embellished his description for comic effect, it is a fitting epitaph for a man once famous for combining serious journalism with joyous humour.

Hone was famous throughout the country for his defence of the free press, but he was also noted as a genial and amusing man, a recognisable figure in the world he inhabited: Fleet Street, the Strand and Ludgate Hill, the centre of national journalism and publishing. The proprietor of several bookshops and publishing companies during three decades, his premises were the haunt of many notable figures of the time, and drew great crowds of Londoners when his famous satires came off the press. The customer or visitor would have found a man who conversed with 'perfect freedom, familiarity, and bonhomie'. Hone was big in every respect – hearty and good-natured, but also a formidable physical presence. 'He was rather corpulent, dressed very plainly, and his lofty forehead, keen eye, grey and scanty locks, and a very expressive countenance, commanded respect,' a friend remembered of the journalist in middle age.[10] In cartoons he was often caricatured as a John Bull figure, a formidable and bulky man with a mischievous glint in his eye. But the large frame was prone to breakdown and illness, just as his cheerful demeanour gave way to depression, or what he and his contemporaries called 'hypochondria'.

The world rarely knew of his personal crises however. Laughter was Hone's defining characteristic as a public writer and private man. He described himself as a man 'with a lively conception of wit, and an irresistible propensity to humour'. Even when he was in prison, Hone never lost his eye for comic detail and delight at the farcical. He was a popular London personality, and it was remembered that 'he loved the society of men of talent, and, being gifted with great humour, joined the foibles of the day'. His small circle of intimates comprised William Hazlitt, Charles Lamb, George Cruikshank and the brothers John and Leigh Hunt. They all found him a relaxed, intelligent and amusing companion, and appreciated his 'extraordinary powers of language and argument'. *The Times'* foreign correspondent, Henry Crabb Robinson, was introduced to him at Lamb's house in Islington, and wrote in his diary that evening: 'The conversation of Hone, or rather his manners, pleased me. He is a modest, unassuming man.' Many were as surprised as Robinson that the journalist who famously never baulked from hard words, offensive epithets, or satirical invective was such a pleasant, self-effacing, and generous companion. [11]

Hone was close to William Hazlitt for much his life, and it was said that he was the only person who could lift the essayist from the brooding reticence and splenetic temper which made him seem so formidably severe. The two writers drank together in the Southampton Arms on Chancery Lane, often in the company of dissolute George Cruikshank. It was from the wainscoted backroom of this tavern that they worked together on one of the most successful satirical collaborations in publishing history. Hone was one of the few people who made Hazlitt feel truly comfortable; his jokes and laughter were infectious, and raised the darkest mood of his friends. During his adolescence Hone had suffered long periods of depression. A friend wrote to him, 'Laugh! laugh, you dog, 'tis the best cure in the world for the hyps [hypochondria] . . .' Hone learnt that lesson early in his life. [12]

John Hunt once described Hone as a 'coarse' man. Self-educated and coming from a poor background, he extolled the virtues of the common man against the luxury, corruption and affected politeness of refined society. He was a bulky, shabbily dressed man who never dissimulated his opinions. He laughed aloud and without shame whatever miseries assailed him throughout his life. Hone's humour was of the earthy, unrefined and lusty variety. Conduct books criticised laughter as boorish and unbecoming a civilised society. 'Having mentioned laughing,' Chesterfield wrote to his son in his famous book of advice, 'I must particularly warn you against it: and I could heartily wish that you may often be seen to smile, but never heard to laugh while you live. Frequent and loud laughter is the characteristic of folly and ill manners: it is the manner in which the mob express their silly joy at silly things; and they call it being merry.' He also criticised 'the disagreeable noise that it makes and the distortion of the face that it occasions'. European and American tourists wrote of the coldness of the English, their awkward and artificial refinement which silenced loud laughter. These were the kind of stilted manners Hone detested. As he commanded a friend, John Childs, one Christmas: 'Take of the good before you, stir your fire, laugh not withstanding Chesterfield, take of the good again, let your lungs ring out Wassail and the lungs of your young ones and guests ring Wassail* till sides and cheeks ache with merriment and laughter.'[13]

The Hone household was a happy place. John Childs played an important role in the family Christmas festivities, sending a gift of a turkey every Christmas. Hone wrote a letter of thanks in 1819, describing the jollity of life with the Hones: '. . . I received from you what, in London, we call an Alderman in Chains[†] – this was reserved for our Christmas day dinner when we, that is, my wife and our seven young ones, played our many parts, and drank your health, and carolled away till our eighth little one in my wife's care crowed herself so hoarse that we were obliged to adjourn our mirth.' At another time he described his home life as 'one of rude merriment – a noisy carnival'.[14]

If laughter was essential for the soul, it was also, for Hone, a weapon that was deployed in his journalism to shame, level and humiliate his political enemies. During his trials, he made a crowd of over a thousand men and women hoot with laughter at the pompous old judge, the fearsome Lord Ellenborough. It was, Hone believed, a fundamental freedom that could never be repressed by censorship or punishment. A pungent vein of humour runs through his journalism. For all the government's efforts to silence and punish its critics, it could not prevent the crowd from expressing its contempt with laughter: the liberty to mock the country's august rulers, to make them laughing stocks, was worth more than grave and measured attack. It vented public indignation, sating a desire for revenge against corrupt and cruel politicians. And it was regarded with solemn disapproval by the state; during his trials, the prosecution asserted that something as disrespectful as laughter would 'burst asunder the bonds of society'. Hone's contempt for ministers and the royal family was relished by much of the country, but genuinely feared by his enemies. The Tory *Quarterly Review*

* Taking of the 'good' requires no explanation; 'Wassail' was the Viking custom of taking enormous festive toasts from horn-shaped cups.
† An 'Alderman in Chains' was London slang for a turkey garnished with a string of sausages, which resembled a plump city dignitary enjoying the regalia of office.

realised the threat from a man 'who appears to possess talents above the ordinary class, and effrontery much above these talents'.[15]

William Hone was stigmatised as a danger to the state and the corrupter of public morals. The government was driven to censor the press because it believed that the people were gullible wretches predisposed to violence, who would inevitably rise up in revolution when they read reformist journalism. Hone's mockery was considered foremost in the threats to society; his jokes were taken deadly seriously. 'I call upon Mr Hone, who was once, I know, a friend to his King and Country, and to true Religion, to reflect upon the mischief his publications are now disseminating!' demanded an anxious contributor to the *Loyalists' Magazine*. 'I ask him, whether, as a tradesman, he would be enriched by that riot and rebellion for which his satires are preparing the way? . . . Then why, for a mere pelf, sacrifice his conscience – his sense – his religion – his country?'[16]

Hone went out of his way to stress his moderation and social responsibility. But his compulsion to expose abuses and advocate political reform sprang from his instinctive revolt at injustice. 'In society Mr Hone was a cheerful companion, and his heart was never closed to the complaints of his fellow creatures,' according to his obituary. He was renowned for his generosity and compassion, which he often put before the needs of his wife and large family. Even when his books were selling in the hundreds of thousands, and he was the most popular journalist in the country, he lived in penury. He explained his gloriously dismissive attitude to money in a letter to a friend:

Property is encumbering in some forms. In the shape of *money* it is confounded annoying. If you have it, you naturally divide it with some destitute and distressed fellow creatures, and then divide the remainder till the quotidian is invisible. And if you have it in the shape of a *house* you as naturally let in some shelterless devil as a tenant, upon whom you haven't the heart to levy a distress for rent.[17]

Hone deserved the words that the MP William Smith used to describe him to the House of Commons in 1817: 'a gentleman and a man of humanity'. There was a story told of a wealthy London merchant who stopped in the street one day and took off his hat for a moment to mop his brow. Suddenly a coin landed in the upturned hat. The surprised plutocrat looked up to see Hone walking the other way, absent-mindedly distributing his coins to those he believed had a greater need for them than himself. For a few years in his middle age, Hone received an advance of £10 a week from the publisher Thomas Tegg for a book he was writing. It was not a lot of money, but enough to get by. One day Hone met another writer who stopped him with a long litany of woes. 'Tell me no more,' Hone said, reaching into his pocket. 'Here, take this; it will at least assist the family for a time.' He continued on his way, called in on Tegg, and cheerfully told his publisher what he had done. Tegg was furious. 'Remember the old saying, Mr Hone, "Be just before you are generous".' The shrewd (and very wealthy publisher) was right; the victims of Hone's generosity were his wife and children, who had much to complain about his reckless attitude to money and obsessive journalistic crusades, which although they made his name, scarcely provided enough for them to live on. [18]

The money always disappeared, and Hone went through several hard-earned fortunes in his lifetime. He could have said with Edward Gibbon: 'my purse was always open, but it was often empty.' In his last years Hone was reduced to begging money from literary societies, and his family were destitute when he died. It was left to people like Dickens to raise money for the impoverished Hones.

But financial considerations were secondary to his charitable nature. 'I know no distinction between public and private life,' he said during his trials. 'Men should be consistent in their conduct; and I have endeavoured so to school my mind that I might give an explanation of every act of my life.'[19] Before he became a journalist, Hone was an energetic social reformer, campaigning for the abolition of the notoriously cruel and inefficient Poor Laws and instigating an investigation into the sadistic practices and squalid state of private lunatic asylums. As a journalist he believed that the press existed to defend those people without a voice, the marginalised and abused victims of society; that public opinion was the only check on arbitrary government. One of his most remarkable pieces of journalism was an investigation into the calculated injustice that led to the execution of a young domestic servant. In it, Hone aimed to provoke the disgust of compassionate members of society so that public opinion, passionately expressed and cogently argued, would force the state to purge itself of noxious abuses.

This investigation, an exhaustive exposé of the miscarriage of justice that condemned Eliza Fenning to death, was one of Hone's finest and most enduring triumphs as a journalist. His demolition of the Crown's evidence against Fenning and his revelations of the subsequent efforts to alter the judicial record, coupled with a poignant tale of human suffering, was one of the first detailed criminal investigations conducted by a journalist. Hone's ability to construct a rational and technically complete survey of legal malpractice was a victory for the press, proving that journalists could match, and surpass, the sophisticated arguments of the state. He believed that once the workings of the government were made transparent, the voice of public opinion would prevent further misgovernment, which at its worst condemned the innocent to death. As he wrote in 1817:

This should be the age of *discussion*; improvements are now proposed invariably by means of *the press*; and thanks to that mighty engine of life and energy, they are now *proposed to the whole community at once* ... It is to the MIDDLE CLASSES *now*, as at *other* times, in this country, the salvation of all that ought to be dear to Englishmen must be confided: it is amongst *this* class that the great improvement has been going on; it is from *this* class, now informed as no class in any country, at any time, ever were informed, that whatever of good may be obtained will proceed.[20]

The press should represent the articulate voice of educated, cultured and moral middle class people: the 'polite' or 'respectable', as he called them. This inevitably led to an involvement with national politics. As a political writer, Hone argued for parliamentary reform and the expansion of the franchise. The public was not, as MPs, ministers and Tory journalists maintained, a heedless mob that would automatically rebel when it read political journalism. When the voice of the people was heard in the Commons the government would be forced to comply with demands for social reform and the cruel edges of Regency society blunted. 'What is the end of legislation,' he once said in conversation, 'but to protect the weak against the powerful, the few against the many?'[21]

But when only a minority had the vote, when the Commons was dominated by MPs who were rewarded with handsome pensions and sinecures for supporting the government, the disadvantaged could never be defended from the inefficiencies or wanton cruelty of those whom Hone labelled 'the *soi-disant* guardians' of the country. They were too mired in corruption and blinded by the rewards of political office to be truly paternalistic overlords. 'It is with this nasty, dirty, filthy, money-getting spirit that our aristocracy have dirtied themselves,' he once said.[22]

Hone believed that humankind was 'held in bond to do justice, love mercy, and practise universal charity', and he was prepared to make sacrifices to live up to the ideal he preached in print. 'I am as destitute as any man in London . . .' he told the court of the King's Bench:

I have as true a relish for the comforts, as well as the elegancies of life, as most men in much higher ranks; but I have ever been independent in mind, and hence I am a destitute man. I have never written or printed what I did not think right and true; and in my most humble station have always acted for the public good, according to my conception, without regard to what other men do, however exalted their rank.[23]

In 1817 *The Times* wrote of the trials: 'Hone's whole defence, indeed, will be read with an interest, and will excite feelings, now and hereafter, which it far exceeds our powers to appreciate.'[24]

But the memory of Hone's defiance and humorous denunciation of his enemies is kept alive only in the pages of scholarly works. This is a pity. Hone's personal and political struggles are entertaining, inspiring, and, in terms of the history of the press, vital; he is seemingly the perfect subject for a popular biography. His entry in the *Dictionary of National Biography*, written by H. R. Tedder in 1885, said: 'Hone was a thoroughly honest and conscientious man, and deserves to be remembered for his sacrifices on behalf of the freedom of the press and cheap literature.' But what is left of the name, the warmth of character and the reputation in the public mind today?

The answer is very little, and that is because over ninety years have passed since a major non-academic biography has appeared. Parts of Hone's life are sparsely covered by the surviving sources. His fame, as great as it was for a few exciting years, was fleeting. We lose track of him for years on end when the trail goes cold. The life, as a whole, is impossible to recreate. Perhaps this explains the reluctance in writers to tackle a biography since Frederick William Hackwood in 1912. Many of Hone's letters and notes are extant in libraries and archives around the world, but as he said, 'I would never write a letter if I could help it, and with this habit, or infirmity, or vice, or whatever it be, I never can, and therefore will not pretend to, become a *good* correspondent.'[25] This failing denies posterity a full picture of Hone. It is a very recognisable flaw. Writing to his friend John Childs in 1819 in gratitude for the customary gift of a Christmas turkey, he apologised for the tardiness of his thanks: 'It was my *duty* to have done so before but – (now for a civil lie) – procrastination is the thief of time & I put off, I put off, even to this day, when finding my Conscience troublesome, that is, the burden of reproach greater than I could bear, I mustered courage to say "thank you" with my pen, – my heart & mind having done so as often as I thought of you.'[26]

Although he would pick up a pen to write to a friend with sighs of reluctance, Hone spent almost every day of his adult life writing for publication. He was often revealing about his private life and personality in articles and books, and there is the occasional detail of biographical information buried in the political reportage. Yet in almost every sentence the character of Hone shines through. The surviving drafts of his private letters show constant rewrites, changes of heart, scratchings out, and an obsessive reworking of sentences and phrases. The journalism, by contrast, is impulsive, wild, caustic, pugnacious. His anger at injustice and cruelty flashes out in spontaneous bursts of genuine revolt or frustration. A relish for comic incident and the satirical flourishes in his books, pamphlets and appearances in court reveal the humorous propensities that delighted the people who met him, from elevated people such as Queen Caroline and the Whig lords, writers such as such Charles Lamb, to the Londoners who visited his shop. The spontaneity of his journalism was intended to give his audience a sense of immediacy with the process of writing; he wanted them to read something which approximated to his voice, and the raw prose self-consciously aims to strip away any hint of artifice or sophistry. Hone could never be called a great prose stylist, but the words seem to spark from his mind with the ease and buoyancy of an instinctive journalist. Perhaps the self-confidence is deceptive, an illusion that masks hard graft; but the passion is never disguised, and it is plain to see why he was such a popular writer in his time.

His heart was in his public writings more than any other part of his life. Hone conducted his social and professional existence in the face-to-face world of Fleet Street, conversing with writers, politicians and customers over his shop counter or in London taverns, a mode of daily business that has left few traces. The jolly, personable William Hone was often precluded from an active social life by the pressure of work. He attended debates in parliament, researched articles, investigated his stories and wrote seven days a week, often hearing the bells of St Paul's Cathedral chime the early hours of the morning. In the heat of a campaign he would live off cold tea and stale bread, seemingly unable to take his mind away from writing. He talked of his 'stay at home habits and literary indulgences' that were 'ill calculated to the formation of friendships', admitting, 'while I have been known to all the world, I am without any personal friends', beyond a handful of intimates. Hone was a modest man, who kept much of his private life hidden from the prying eyes of his contemporaries or biographers.

This is why he has been forgotten. It is a sad neglect: this was the man who stood against the government – 'literally deserted', as he said, by his political allies and colleagues. He is the forgotten hero of the British press. Hone's career in journalism saw the most significant events in the struggle for a press free from political control. His style and wit as a writer and defendant made him one of the most popular journalist in Regency Britain, and they are as fresh today. Hone found pomposity or self-importance hard to affect, and even in the formal atmosphere of the court of the King's Bench he fought with the same spirit of impudent defiance which characterised every aspect of his life. His trials will always be exciting, for he attempted to win his case with laughter, an entertaining but risky strategy. It was typical of William Hone that he dared defend himself from a charge of criminal libel – in a show trial that had implications for the future of the press – by declaring that he intended 'to laugh his Majesty's Ministers to scorn; I have laughed at them and ha! ha! ha! I laugh at them now and I *will* laugh at them, for as long as they are laughing stocks! Were there any poor witless men less ridiculous than these Ministers, my persecutors . . .?'

William Hone 1780–1842 by G. Patten

Cast of Characters
in order of appearance

William HONE, 1780–1842.

Francis PLACE, 1771–1854. Journeyman leather breeches maker; tailor of Charing Cross; leading metropolitan reformer.

John BONE (dates unknown). Secretary of the London Corresponding Society, state prisoner, philanthropist.

Sir Francis BURDETT, Bt., 1770–1844. Reformist MP for Westminster. Lord Holland said that he had a 'great good nature and a generous feeling of indignation against oppression in every form'. He was a popular hero, notwithstanding his patrician pride and 'frigid hauteur'.

Thomas, Lord COCHRANE, later 10th Earl of Dundonald, 1775–1860. Captain in the Royal Navy (1800–1814); MP for Westminster, 1807–14 and 1815–18; commander of the Chilean, Brazilian and Greek navies during the independence movements of the 1820s; rear-admiral in the British navy, 1832.

Edward Law, 1st Baron ELLENBOROUGH, 1750–1818. Lord Chief Justice (1802–18).

William COBBETT, 1763–1835. Sergeant major in New Brunswick (1785–91); editor of the *Weekly Political Register* from 1802; author and editor of many books including *Parliamentary History* (1806; later *Hansard's Parliamentary Debates*), *State Trials* (1809), *Rural Rides* (1830), *Advice to Young Men* (1830); MP for Oldham in the reformed parliament. He was, according to Marx, the 'inveterate John Bull'.

James Henry LEIGH HUNT, 1784–1859. Poet, essayist and editor of the Sunday *Examiner* newspaper; friend and supporter of John Keats, Percy Shelley and Lord Byron.

John HUNT. Co-founder and proprietor of the *Examiner* with his brother, Leigh.

Henry BROUGHAM, 1st Baron Brougham and Vaux, 1778–1869. Barrister, co-founder of the *Edinburgh Review*; Whig MP; Queen Caroline's lawyer; educational reformer; Lord Chancellor (1830). 'There goes Solon, Lycurgus, Demosthenes, Archimedes, Sir Isaac Newton, Lord Chesterfield, and a great many more in one post-chaise,' Samuel Rogers wrote.

GEORGE, 1762–1830. Prince of Wales, Regent (1811–20), King (1820–30). 'He understands how a shoe should be made, or a coat cut, or a dinner dressed and would make an excellent hairdresser but nothing else,' his wife waspishly commented.

Eliza FENNING, 1792–1815. Domestic servant, executed for attempted murder.

Sir John ('Black Jack') SILVESTER. Recorder of the City of London.

William HAZLITT, 1778–1830. Essayist.

Dr John STODDART, 1773–1856. Editor of *The Times* (1812–16) and founder of the *New Times*.

George CRUIKSHANK, 1792–1878. Caricaturist, illustrator and painter.

Robert SOUTHEY, 1774–1843. Essayist, historian and poet; Poet Laureate from 1813. Like Wordsworth and Coleridge, he was an early Jacobin who converted to Toryism, a cause he espoused in the *Quarterly Review*. He was the *bête noire* of the Romantics.

Henry Addington, 1st Viscount SIDMOUTH, 1757–1844. Speaker of the House of Commons (1789–1801); Prime Minister (1802–4); Home Secretary (1812–22). He was a pious churchman and the darling of the county gentry; he called himself the last of the 'port wine faction'.

Robert Stewart, Viscount CASTLEREAGH, later second Marquis of Londonderry, 1769–1822. Irish Chief Secretary (1797); President of the Board of Control (1802); Secretary of War (1805–6 and 1807–9); Foreign Secretary (1812–22). A famously weak and indiscreet orator, he amused the House of Commons with his malapropisms.

George CANNING, 1770–1827. Treasurer of the Navy (1804–6); Foreign Secretary, (1807–9); Ambassador to Lisbon (1814); President of the Board of Control (1816–20); Foreign Secretary and Leader of the House of Commons (1822–7); Prime Minister (1827). 'Brilliant wit, the most cutting personal satire, often mixed with buffoonery, but always delivered in elegant language, and with action particularly suited to it, these are his excellencies.' He was the self-proclaimed heir of William Pitt, and after the death of Charles James Fox, the unrivalled orator of the British parliament.

Robert Banks Jenkinson, Earl of LIVERPOOL, 1770–1828. Prime Minister (1812–27). 'He was much ridiculed, seldom being addressed by any other name than "Jenky" [in cabinet] . . . ; his manners were effeminate and cold, and were rendered still more unpleasing by an almost constant state of absence of mind either real or affected.' Liverpool was 'the grey man' of British politics.

John Scott, 1st Earl of ELDON, 1751–1838. Lord Chancellor (1801–6 and 1807–27). He 'neither liked nor understood politics'.

Sir Samuel SHEPHERD, 1760–1840. Solicitor-General (1813–17), Attorney- General (1817–19). Sir Walter Scott said that he was 'suave with a little warmth of temper'.

Charles ABBOTT, first Baron Tenterden, 1762–1832. Fellow of Corpus Christi, Oxford; puisne judge of the Court of Common Pleas (1816); judge of the King's Bench (1817); Lord Chief Justice (1818).

Thomas Jonathan WOOLER, 1786(?)–1852. Editor of the *Black Dwarf.*

CAROLINE Amelia Elizabeth, 1768–1821. Princess of Wales, Queen (1820); estranged consort of George IV.

Charles LAMB, 1775–1834. Poet, critic and essayist. Hone said that Lamb was the only man who knew him intimately.

Charles DICKENS.

PART I

'A momentary half-existence'

The Fatal Bookcase
Childhood, 1780–1800

From books you can gain more amusement than you can get from all the toys you have ever seen, and more instruction than you have had from all the people you have ever talked with. After you begin to read you will soon be able to understand many things which you now only wonder at, and speedily be convinced of this grand Truth, delivered by one of our greatest philosophers, that 'Knowledge is Power'.

William Hone, from a letter to his foster-child, John L'Ouverture, 1810

. . . I dedicate no inconsiderable portion of my time to other people's thoughts. I dream away my life in others' speculations. I love to lose myself in other men's minds. When I am not walking, I am reading; I cannot sit and think. Books think for me.

Charles Lamb

Hone felt that he was qualified to represent the views and interests of the middle classes. He had risen from an isolated, austere and unlearned background, educated himself, and made money and a name by personal sacrifices. Like many of his contemporaries, Hone received only the most rudimentary schooling; his achievements as a writer he saw as a vindication of autodidactic culture. His journalism displayed a wealth of knowledge and depth of reading, and he was convinced that self-education and improvement were a duty placed upon members of society before they had a right to claim a voice in the government of their country. Hone was always painfully conscious that his enemies saw him as a Grub Street hack, a ruffian who propagated ill-considered opinions and unreliable facts among a credulous public. The *Quarterly Review* called him 'a wretch, as contemptible as he is wicked' and 'a poor illiterate creature'.[1]

Hone was compelled to defend his journalism, arguing that he put as much effort into his work as most academics. When he was researching his scholarly work, *A History of Parody* in the 1820s, he told his public: 'I went daily to the British Museum, chiefly for the purpose of consulting the King's collection of pamphlets . . . I attended there every day as soon as the doors were open, nor left the reading or print room till they closed.'[2] The research gleaned in the British Museum or from his own extensive library enriched his more populist writing. Hone's political journalism was always set within its historical context, and the style derived much from the pamphleteers and political language of the seventeenth and eighteenth centuries. Even his satires stood within an ancient tradition of parodic literature. When called upon to defend himself in 1817, Hone's learning and knowledge of English literature rivalled that of his university-educated prosecutors. But he was always dogged by a sense of inferiority. As he said to friend from the world of academe: 'You dons at Cambridge, with letters after your names, scorn all poor fellows who have not been to school.'[3]

Notwithstanding the lack of a formal education, and the occasional feeling of shame it brought, Hone was always anxious to assert the honourable status of a self-taught writer. His life, he believed, was the story of victory over ignorance and superstition. 'Prone to inquiry from my childhood, and knowledge in other languages being to me as a "fountain sealed", I could only obtain it on my own,' Hone wrote in the 1820s, explaining his addiction to learning as a child: 'All books that fell in my way, no matter on what subject, I read voraciously, and appetite increased with indulgence.'[4]

He was born in Bath in 1780, but the family moved to the outskirts of London soon after. His father, a lawyer's clerk, had led a dissolute youth in the company of itinerant actors, before converting and settling down to a life of religious contemplation. Mr William Hone senior was a loving father but a very serious and humourless man. He avoided worldly pleasures and dedicated his life to his religion and his job. 'Humility and patience were his practise,' the son remembered. 'Temperate in personal requirements, and plain in dress, he often pointed out the Quakers as examples of uprightness in gait and in mind.' The Hones lived in a house to the west of Tottenham Court Road, in a suburban hamlet. 'All beyond Warren Street, which had been lately commenced,' Hone reminisced, 'was open meadow land

and dairy-farms as far as the eye could see . . .'

Until he was a teenager William would lead a very secluded life; his parents were terrified that he would be corrupted by urban vice. The spires of London were within sight, the sounds of the busy city ever-present, but its labyrinthine streets and alleys, its great buildings and crowds remained a mystery to the boy until he was much older. London was, for Mr Hone, modern Babylon; living on its threshold was as great a compromise he was prepared to make. Yet the sights and sounds of the city were impossible to escape. William could only watch as the diverse crowds of Londoners made weekend trips to the meadows and gravel pits near his house. The spectacle hinted of the unknown metropolis:

On Sundays London poured towards the country a populous tide of individuals . . . youths walking on crutches or with one crutch, girls suffering under disorders of the hip-joint, rickety children, with jointed iron-straps on their legs – at least one-tenth of the passers-by were crippled or diseased . . . [T]radesmen or respectable journeymen and their wives were profusely powdered. Men wore scarlet coats and long-flapped, figured waistcoats; cocked hats, with their hair behind in long or large clubbed pigtails, and the sides in large stiff curls; silver or plated buckles, curiously wrought or bespangled, on their shoes.

Sometimes Hone was allowed to stay with some cousins of his mother, who lived in Belsize, on the heights north of London. He built a tree house in an old mulberry tree, from which he could look down on the mysterious, unexplored city, and hear the hourly chimes of the clock of St Paul's Cathedral and the evening chapel bell of Lincoln's Inn. In later life, when he had the liberty to do so, Hone fell in love with London, its taverns, public buildings, narrow courts and its legends; he also became a famous city personality. As he once wrote, 'London is familiar to me, I know every street and turning in the city, have walked over half the metropolis when the land covered with houses and churches was green fields.'[5]

Hone was a Londoner through and through – if not by birth, certainly by emotional attachment – but his love of the city was conditional upon the ability to escape from the buzz and whirl of Fleet Street to the Arcadia of Islington, Pentonville, or Hampstead. From his boyhood adventures in the fields and groves of north London, he wrote, 'I derived a love for quiet and the country which has yearned in me throughout life, and has frequently detached me from alluring society and busiest occupations to bury myself awhile in rural solitude and nourish peaceful thoughts "far from the haunts of careworn men".' During his spells in prison, he would miss London's villages and fields more than any other freedom. In the 1820s, when the property developers were poised to build over these favourite spots, Hone wrote books which preserved the memories of the villages, woods and streams where he spent his youth as a memorial to a feature of London life that was about to be lost for ever.

'Nature was my first book,' Hone wrote. But when he learnt to read, his first love was supplanted by the written word. Before he was six, the boy was sent to the home of an old lady (a so-called 'dame school') to learn the rudiments of reading and writing. Mrs Bettridge's school was a joy: 'There, on low wooden benches, books in hand, sat her little scholars. We all loved her, I most of all, and I was often allowed to sit on a little stool by her side. I was happier there than anywhere.'

But one 'dark day', the child was not allowed to go to Mrs Bettridge's school; he was gloomy and tearful all day. He awoke the next morning, but was deprived of the chance to read once again: 'It was my first sorrow.' He was so anxious that a servant took him to see Mrs Bettridge in her basement apartments. She was on her deathbed. William remained with her, until he heard that John Wesley was coming to visit her. His father had spoken of Wesley – the founder of the Methodists – as 'the Old Devil', and Hone had 'a most terrific idea of this satanic personage'. The thought of actually meeting him was too much.

I turned and gazed in stupor at my poor Dame, until the sound of his footsteps startled me to attempt instant escape, but before I could reach the door I saw the black legs, and great silver buckles, coming down the stairs, and there came into the room a venerable man, his long, silvery hair flowing upon his shoulders, his countenance cheerful and smiling and ruddy as a youth's, and his eyes beaming kindness.

He knew that appearances could be deceptive, that this was no doubt 'Satan coming as an angel of light'. But John Wesley brought tranquillity to the old lady, and the 'room seemed illuminated by his presence'. Young William was overcome when they began to pray: 'my tears flowed, and then I dropped upon my knees weeping, but feeling happy, I knew not why'. When he came to leave, Wesley put his hand on the trembling boy's head and said, 'My child, God bless you, and make you a good man.' 'I wondered was this "the Old Devil"?,' Hone said. It was a formative moment in his life: 'From that hour I never believed anything my father said or anything I heard at chapel.'

His beloved teacher died a few days later, and Hone's education lapsed. William Hone senior promised, in recompense, to buy his son a copy of *The Pilgrim's Progress*. That book held a special place in the education of English children in the eighteenth century; it was intend-ed to make the young emulous of the Christian journey, and evangeli-cals such as William Huntingdon, Hone senior's favourite preacher, made it his aim to provide a copy for every child in the country. The Hone's meagre household library comprised the Bible, *Paradise Lost*, a few religious tracts and *Mrs Glasse's Cookery*; a new book was, for the boy, 'an event'. 'I eagerly awaited its coming home,' he remembered of the joyous day, 'and well recollect my emotions of heart when my father, eyeing me with affection, slowly drew from his pocket a good old woodcut copy of the famous "Pilgrim".'

The book lived up to the expectation of the bibliomaniac boy, but not the hopes of the pious father: 'The pleasure I derived from the work is indescribable,' Hone wrote. 'I read it continually, and read it repeat-edly. I read it without the least conception of the allegory, forgetting, too, that the narrative was a dream – I supposed it to be real and literal. I earnestly desired to become a man that I might travel and find the places described.' The book infested his imagination. On his first visit to London, his father took him to the Royal Exchange, and put the boy on his shoulders. Young William stared about at the exotic scene: the flags, the immense crowds, and, carved on pillars, lists of foreign lands with which the merchants traded. 'Father!' shouted the boy to the amazement of the businessmen, 'Vanity Fair! This is Vanity Fair!'

After the intoxication of first reading, Hone 'continually hankered for books'. But they were not so easy to come by; Mr Hone wanted to restrict his son's reading to inspirational religious books. William had to resort to devious means to satisfy his lust for reading. He saved his pocket money and toured bookshops, buying whatever he could afford. He plundered rubbish bins, hording the papers with which vict-uallers wrapped foodstuffs with the desperation of a drug addict: 'My desire for reading became distressing to myself and to those around me.' When he managed to get a non-religious book, he had to hide it from his parents and stop himself from talking about it lest, 'I should have betrayed feelings which I strove to conceal'. Reading had made him inquisitive and wilful; it had not taught him obedience, as his father had intended.

Hone went to school for a short while when he was seven; but once more, his education was cut short, this time because he caught small-pox. His parents thought that he was about to die, and he was only awakened from a feverish sleep by the shock of overhearing them dis-cuss funeral arrangements. Recovery was slow, and Hone was taught to write by copying exercises from the Bible. He would only return to school briefly, when he was twelve, but then it was back to the tedium of home instruction. Mr Hone would teach William for an hour at lunchtime, and for an hour after work. William could make nothing of his father's arithmetic lessons and 'home instruction became irksome'. The Hones were now living on a street near Red Lion Square, Holborn, which was more built up than Warren Street, but the mead-ows were still within sight. 'Every breeze that blew brought odours from the new-mown grass, and told of green fields,' he lamented.

The parents were still protective of their child, and he was prevented from exploring London, escaping to the tranquillity of the countryside, or visiting bookshops. 'Had I been at school,' he wrote, 'desires of this kind would have been diverted by my occupations in company with the other boys, and my advance in learning, in which I really delighted, would have reconciled me to confinement.' His younger brother, Joseph, did not share William's passions: 'He cared but little for read-ing, and I cared for little else,' he recalled. As so, this clever, lonely boy grew frustrated languishing at home with no means of satisfying his rampant curiosity. The lessons drawn exclusively from the Bible only exacerbated his frustration. 'I saddened into listlessness, wrote without care . . . I felt my faculties were wounded; they seemed benumbed . . . from that time I regarded the Bible as a book of hopeless or heavy tasks.'

Mrs Hone relented, and, unbeknownst to his father, William stole out and befriended local shopkeepers, who lent him books and pamphlets. He spent his days at a copperplate printer's workshop, learning the process of putting together illustrated books and prints. An old cobbler allowed him to study a store of ancient books, including Caxton's *Polychronicon* and Pynson's *Shepherd's Kalendar* – so-called 'Black Letter Books', with their primitive engravings and antiquated letter-types, which had survived from the fifteenth century, the dawn of printing. Hone fell in love with 'black letter lore' which he 'indulged without satiety' all his life. In *The Spirit of the Age* (1825), William Hazlitt wrote of Hone 'that his greatest vice is that he is fond of a joke and given to black-letter reading'. That famous sense of humour came later – Hone seems to have been a highly strung and serious-minded child – but the love of books, not just as pages full of words to devour, but lovingly crafted artefacts with a history, was firmly implanted in his mind.[6]

'Ardently seeking for truth,' he remembered of this time, 'I conversed with books rather than men, and hewed out principles as I could.'[7] Hone did not learn arithmetic or Latin, like other schoolboys, and he grew up a rather unconventional and lonely boy, his head filled with bits of folklore, snatches of history and a rudimentary knowledge of publishing. As he would have been the first to admit, deprived of the society of boys his own age and the discipline of the schoolroom, he entered adolescence with little experience of the world outside the compass of his reading. But, as it turned out, his early reading and isolation prepared him for his future career. Had he been to school and learnt as much as other boys he would have learnt no more than other boys; which is to say, how to be servile to authority, cringing in front of masters, emulous of the office worker, and with stunted intellectual ambitions. However in the early 1790s, with no prospects of entering the republic of letters, his dreams only made him unhappy and frustrated. When Hone was thirteen, it came as a hard shock that he would have to give up his private passion and 'earn means for my support among the realities of life'.

The reality of middle-class employment was not something that Hone was used to, nor particularly welcomed. 'I now began to think what station I should be likely to fill in life, and conceived myself doomed to be an attorney's copying clerk,' he wrote, speculating on the fate awaiting a poor, uneducated, but literate thirteen-year-old boy. 'This occupation I looked upon with horror. All persons whom I knew in that situation were thoughtless beings, weak, mindless, and scarcely paid for their labour.' He got his first clerical job in Southwark. Predictably, Hone spent all he earned, including his dinner money, at book auctions in Tooley Street.

'I became melancholy,' he remembered of this bleak time, 'and in the summer evenings stalked about the fields, anticipating and brooding over the hardships of my imagined destiny.' And it could hardly be said that he took to working life with alacrity. His next position was as a factotum to a solicitor in the City. Unfortunately, there was an unlocked bookcase in his office and the teenager was 'irresistibly attracted' to the books. His work suffered, and he made a vow to his employer that he would withstand all temptations and get on with his work.

'I promised and strove to amend,' Hone recalled; 'but the bookcase, seductively open, infatuated me; while daily resolving to read less and less, I heedlessly read more and more. Conscience did its office, and I determined to leave off reading entirely, after I got through the contents of the fatal bookcase. That period never came, for I was suddenly, and deservedly dismissed, with an imagination inflamed to intensity by the infatuating reading in which I had recklessly indulged.'

Hone senior had to employ his son as a clerk in his own office in an effort to instil into his son a sense of the discipline required of a worker. But this office had bookshelves as well, and the teenager managed to get through Plutarch's *Lives*, Pope's translation of Homer, Rollins' *Ancient History*, and as much of Swift's works as he could find. Under the influence of the other clerks, he also became 'play-house mad'; so great was his addiction to the theatre he sold his collection of books to afford his daily ticket. Such behaviour pained the father, who had once been led astray by theatres, for him the source of all depravity and evil. But worse was to come. Hone's reading led him to philosophy, and to many of the writers of the 1790s, that revolutionary decade. Fed on a diet of Socrates, Plato, Godwin and Holcroft, he 'imagined that with the culti-vation of the intellect, Christianity . . . would disappear and Reason become omnipotent. With the growth of these notions, I contrasted Scripture authority – treated its historical accounts as absurdities – ridiculed its sacred characters – and regarded Christianity and its doc-trines as impositions and childish dreams.' He openly called the Bible 'a fable-book' and he became 'a believer in all unbelief'.

But these feelings only came in early adolescence. Hitherto, William had been a pious and conservative young man, nicknamed the 'Young Methodist'. His political awakening was slow; but when it came, it was equally radical. The Hones did not read newspapers, and Hone was an unworldly young boy. In July 1789, the nine-year-old Hone was rolling his hoop through Holborn when a friend stopped him.

'There's a revolution in France,' the boy said.

'What's a revolution?' the unworldly Hone inquired.

'Why, the French people in Paris have taken the Bastille, and hung the Governor, and let loose all the prisoners, and pulled the Bastille down to the ground.'

'How do you know?' Hone asked.

'My father says so; he read it in the newspaper just now – and he says it's a revolution.'

'Revolution', the new word in Hone's vocabulary, clearly meant vio-lence and instability. The outcome was open prison gates, anarchy and lawlessness. England's version in 1688 had been almost bloodless, a preserving revolution that established the monarchy and parliament on stronger ground, and had guaranteed the liberty of the subject under the rule of law. The upheavals and executions on the other side of the Channel horrified the boy. The spread of revolutionary ideas to Britain, especially with the publication of Tom Paine's *Rights of Man* in 1792, threatened all that made the country peaceful and free. In that year he composed a single-sheet publication called 'The Contrast', which was divided into two, with a panegyric on English liberty by Joseph Addison on the left-hand side, and a description of continental slavery by James Theodore Middleton on the right. He included a poem he had written setting Addison and Middleton's arguments in the context of the 1790s. The twelve-year-old boy attacked Paine and the French Directory, the enemies of British liberty; one verse read:

> Come Britons unite, and in one Common Cause
> Stand up in defence of King, Liberty, Laws;
> And rejoice that we've got such a good Constitution,
> And down with the barbarous French Revolution.

It was published by the Association for Preserving Liberty and Property Against Republicans and Levellers, a society set up to answer revolutionary propaganda. The author was praised not for a precocious talent, but for a spirit of healthy loyalty.

But Hone's view of British constitutional history was not idealistic and unquestioning. At about the same time that he was penning patriotic poems, he found a loose page of a book in one of his trawls through rubbish bins for reading matter. It was part of a man's defence in court against injustice. Intrigued, the boy set out to discover what it was. He went into bookshops and showed the page to the proprietors. Most were baffled or irritated, and sent him on his way. At last, a bookseller identified it as a page from *The Trial of John Lilburne*. Hone, by 'patience, industry, and extraordinary management', selling his toys and boxes he made out of card, managed to earn half a crown and bought the book. (If he resented working for bread and lodging, a book was always worth the labour.)

Colonel John Lilburne was the leader of the Levellers during the last years of the Civil Wars and the early part of the Commonwealth. He argued that the Long Parliament, the army and Cromwell had betrayed the ideals of the fledgling British republic, executing Charles I only as a cynical means of establishing their own tyranny. He saw little difference between Stuart absolute monarchy and the Commonwealth government: the people were the losers whichever tyrant reigned. He published his attacks on Cromwell and the generals in defiance of censorship, and became a popular hero. When called to trial, his defence was a passionate demand for free speech and the liberty of public discussion. He was found not guilty. 'Since "The Pilgrim's Progress", no other book had so riveted me,' Hone remembered; 'I felt all Lilburne's indignant feelings, rejoiced at his acquittal, and detested

Cromwell as a tyrant for causing him to be carried back to the Tower, after the Jury had pronounced him to be free from the charge. This book aroused within me new feelings . . .'

And those new feelings, Hone tells us, were hatred of oppression and a belief in the rule of law and the freedom of the press as the safeguard of personal liberty. The story of 'Free Born John' Lilburne standing up against Cromwell on behalf of the people of England, risking his life to express his opinions, gained a hold over the boy. The constitutional freedoms he had extolled in his doggerel lines were the result of personal sacrifices made by people like Lilburne. The need to defend these privileges from the violence and mob rule of the French Revolution was clear in his mind; but the threat to freedom also came from the political heirs of Charles I and Oliver Cromwell. When William Pitt's government declared Paine's *Rights of Man* a seditious work, and successfully prosecuted booksellers and publishers who distributed it, it appeared that the English liberties he had extolled were merely ideals. The government's success cleared the way for many more prosecutions throughout the 1790s against reformist writers, publishers and activists. The London Corresponding Society, founded in 1792 by the cobbler Thomas Hardy to disseminate constitutional information, bore the brunt of the repression. In 1794, a year after Hone penned his loyal panegyric on English liberty, twelve members of the LCS and the Society for Promoting Constitutional Information were put on trial for high treason, accused of attempting to overthrow the constitution.

'The Question now, therefore is, whether Englishmen shall be Masters of their own Houses; whether they shall enjoy any of the comforts of society; in fact, whether they shall be allowed the Privilege of thinking, without the Penalty of Death.' So ran a manifesto published by the LCS. Its members were not revolutionaries and Jacobins, as the government alleged; their 'crime' was to have advocated universal manhood suffrage and annual parliaments and accused the government of wasting British blood fighting the French in a sinister campaign to restore the tyrannical Bourbons to the throne. They argued that the Gagging Acts, which shackled the press, the suspension of *habeas corpus*, which allowed the state unlimited powers of arbitrary arrest, the vast costs of war, and the unbounded power of the government, was more likely to goad the people to revolution than reformist tracts. The twelve reformers were acquitted, and Hone must have seen them as modern day Lilburnes, men who risked their freedom avowing the right of public discussion.

The government's failure to suppress it led to the temporary ascendancy of the LCS. In the summer of 1795 it attracted 150 new members a week, including the Cambridge mathematician William Frend, the journeyman Francis Place, who was to become the leader of reformist political organisation in London throughout the first three decades of the nineteenth century, and young William Hone. He believed that there must be some fatal flaw in the supposedly glorious constitution if it accused people of treason for expressing their opinions; the LCS revived the spirit of defiance and martyrdom in the cause of liberty reminiscent of his hero Lilburne, and it was natural that he should wish to be associated with such a movement. His early fascination with Lilburne looks forward to the time when he would have to stand trial to defend his own beliefs. The example of 'Free-Born John' held out hope and encouragement to him then. He owned a very rare bound copy of Lilburne's tracts, which had once belonged to the scientist, dissenting minister, and LCS defendant Jeremiah Joyce, who had read them in the Tower when he was imprisoned awaiting trial for high treason in 1794. The connexion between the stands of Lilburne, Joyce and Hone in the cause of liberty was embodied in the tangible form of a book – a treasured artefact redolent of martyrdom and bravery: 'For which reason,' Hone wrote in 1820, 'and because Lilburne was a man exceedingly after my own heart, I greatly prized the volume.'[8]

The senior Mr Hone was determined to stop such dangerous behaviour. At first Hone self-consciously treated his father's attempts to rein him in with the same contempt with which the LCS defied the state: 'I disregarded his admonitions, eluded his restraint, joined a society which kept me out late at night, and opposed my Father's remonstrances by questioning his right to control me. I became self-willed, and determined not to be swayed.'

But the government was persistent in its campaign to destroy popular political protest. On 29 October 1795, George III was attacked by a

mob which threw stones and dung at his coach; in the midst of the
melee a gunman took a shot at the King but missed. Later in the day, the
crowd attacked 10 Downing Street chanting, 'No war! No famine! No
Pitt! No King!' Ministers responded with the Treasonable Practices Bill
on 6 November and accused the LCS of plotting a revolution. The
Society was not trying to import French radicalism, but it was held up
as a scapegoat for widespread discontent at high taxes and the war. Six
days after the Bill was passed, the LCS marshalled some 400,000 people at a public meeting in London. This marked the end of the Society's
popularity. The Bill criminalised much of the LCS's activities; meetings of more than fifty people were outlawed; members came under
suspicion; and arrests of publishers and reformists followed. The government's attack on the reformists was successful, and the public began
to suspect organisations such as the LCS of republicanism and
Francophilia.

Mr Hone had no option but to remove his truculent son from the
danger, sending him to remote Chatham to continue his career as a
clerk. Here he was placed with a pious employer and a collection of
'respectable young men', his fellow clerks, all of them good Christians.
Hone, the rebellious atheist, was the black sheep of this happy community, and it was hoped that he would be taught religious devotion and
diligent working habits by his godly friends. But Hone flaunted his
dangerous opinions in front of these sober young men, and brooded on
ways to escape. Respite from his new friends could only be temporary:
'When we were not together, which was seldom, I took solitary walks,
and climbed the hills, or strolled in the woods.' Exile to Chatham failed
to redeem Hone's soul, and the same unresolved ambitions, unchanged
since his early adolescence, continued to plague his imagination.

'From the time I could read and use a pen', he wrote later, 'I have
been a lover of books and addicted to writing.' At the age of eighteen or
nineteen it seemed as if a life of clerical drudgery was to be his lot. The
only chance of fulfilling his literary and political ambitions was to enter
the book trade centred on Fleet Street and the Strand. Booksellers were
typically publishers of pamphlets and periodicals, and from such a
position within the trade it was possible for Hone to publish his own
journalism – perhaps his only chance of being a writer. Yet without a

large capital outlay to rent a property, buy a printing press and a stock of books, such dreams were vain; an unknown clerk would have stood very little chance of saving the necessary capital.

Salvation came in 1800, when he was twenty. He was back from his Chatham captivity, working as a clerk in the City and lodging with a Mrs Sarah Johnson in Lambeth. His father had preached at her local chapel when Hone was nine, and he had met the widow's only daughter, also called Sarah. 'The friendship of our parents continued,' Hone remembered; 'an attachment between the daughter and myself strengthened with our years.' He pulled off the double feat of marrying his childhood love and the only daughter of his well-to-do landlady. Sarah Hone rarely appears in Hone's journalism or extant letters. But through a long marriage she stood by her husband, tolerating the zealous political campaigns, which salved her husband's conscience but often prevented him earning enough money to put bread on the table. Sarah had to put up with much during forty-two years of marriage, but when we hear of her, she is either laughing with her husband or supporting his work. In 1820, after twenty years of marriage, Hone enthusiastically recommended marriage to the brother of one of his friends: 'It sharpens a man's capabilities, enlarges his powers of usefulness, and concentrates his mind to one object.' It was the closest he got to acknowledging Sarah's role in his success.[9]

At the age of twenty he was in love and at the beginning of a very happy marriage. The match brought another advantage to the young man. His mother-in-law gave him a loan of £100, with which he was able to escape the tedium of regular employment and set up his first bookshop, on Lambeth Walk. He began his career with the laudable but unrealistic intent of teaching the world to think, freeing South Londoners from the ignorance, superstition and slavery he believed they laboured under. Unfortunately, it was not as simple as that. Hone's early life was chequered with financial disaster and intellectual frustration. He plunged into a perilous trade at a young age, and with no connexions. It would take him some fourteen years of unremitting labour and crushing disappointments to rise to prominence as a writer and publisher.

As Hone was later to say, books 'have been the solace of my life'. He never stopped reading; his knowledge of books in European and classical languages was impressive (at some point he picked up a sound working knowledge of Latin and French, and an acquaintance with Greek); as a bookseller he had access to a vast range of literature, and he became ever more intimate with most of the great works of history and philosophy. In time his vast knowledge would enrich his journalism. But as a quixotic young man such a privilege was not good for business; he once described his choice of career as 'very unfortunate, I am too much attached to my books to part with them'.[10]

A Parcel of Nobodies

I am not for a King of shreds and patches . . . but, for the efficient magistrate, the constitutional King of England, – the abuse of his prerogative, by ministers, being checked, controlled, and guarded against by a fair representation of the people in Parliament.

Sir Francis Burdett

Give me the liberty of the Press, and I will give to the Minister a venal House of Peers – I will give him a corrupt and servile House of Commons . . . armed with the liberty of the press, I will go forth with that mightier engine; I will shake down from its height corruption, and bury it beneath the ruins of the abuses it was meant to shelter.

Richard Sheridan in the House of Commons, 1810

In July 1799 parliament passed an 'Act for the more effectual Suppression of Societies established for Seditious and Treasonable Purposes; and for better preventing Treasonable and Seditious Practices'. The Act was aimed specifically at the London Corresponding Society, which was named in the legislation as a body actively working 'to overthrow the Laws, Constitution and Government' of the United Kingdom. Within a few months, sixty-five leading members of the LCS and other reformist clubs were arrested and held without trial. For the next three years the *habeas corpus* act was continually in suspension. Publishers and journalists were arrested throughout the country, and Charles James Fox believed that there existed no such thing as the liberty of the press in Britain: 'One can hardly conceive how any prudent tradesman can venture to publish things which are disagreeable to ministers,' he told the Commons. Francis Place called this time Pitt's 'Reign of Terror'.[1]

The LCS had been all but defunct since 1798, the victim of government harassment and the fear of French invasion, which turned the public against allegedly disloyal organisations. The LCS leaders were easy targets at a time of panic; Place believed that the ministers 'had no specific charge with which they could go before a jury but alarmed as the people were it answered their purpose to make a pretended shew of danger'. The supposed revolutionaries were committed to gaol by the Privy Council; no incidences of treason, seditious publishing or illegal meetings were cited, no trial ever held; but the campaigners were not freed until 1801.[2]

The government had silenced its critics; the LCS had broken up; and throughout the early 1800s the war against France demobilised reformist agitation as popular anger focused on Napoleon and his allies. The reformers were stigmatised as Francophiles, Jacobins and Levellers; many now preferred to retire or seek new areas of political action. As Place insisted, the members of the LCS were 'none of them Anarchists, none of them hot headed revolutionists but sedate men who sought for representation through the government itself by such steps as might bring about the changes they wished by degrees, and not more rapidly than as instructed people could bear them'. It was a sad irony that journalists were gaoled and societies banned for advocating measures of constitutional reform that William Pitt himself had supported in 1780.[3]

The reformist networks were in disarray in the first years of the nineteenth century, the leading figures in gaol or scared into silence. Budding reformists and LCS men found new occupations. Francis Place, for example, built up his tailoring business in Charing Cross and taught himself mathematics. It was at this time that William Hone opened his first bookshop. Lambeth, situated on the edge of London and bordering open fields, was better known for its notorious pleasure gardens, frequented by prostitutes and the beau monde, than for its bookshops. The ambition of any political bookseller was to open a business on Fleet Street or the Strand to find the market, but such an undertaking was expensive. And the task was made harder by a growing family. In 1801 Sarah Hone gave birth to a daughter who was also named Sarah, and within the next four years she would produce three more: William (1802), Fanny (1803) and Matilda (1805). Hone did not mention his family much in his journalism, but he had a long and loving marriage to Sarah, who was to bear him twelve children in twenty-five years.*

Hone soon found that Lambeth was bereft of book lovers, and at the age of twenty-one, his first business failed. Preserved in his private papers is a poem he wrote on his twenty-sixth birthday: "W Hone/ Nothing to say/ Except "Good Day".'[4] His laconic anniversary scrawl expresses the paucity of information that survives from this time. The details are sketchy. In the next few years he would move his wife and daughter to a bookshop in St Martin's Lane, a more promising location than semi-rural Lambeth. But this venture was another disaster, and the Hone family returned to the home of Sarah's mother. In 1804 he published his first book since 1792, *Millington's Cookery*, an odd choice given his political and literary ambitions. A perplexed friend wrote to him: 'It appears to me unaccountable how such a subject ever popped into your head. I should have wandered over the wide field of literature and stooped to cull many fairer flowers in preference to going near the hedge to pick gross herbs and aromatic plants for real use.' In 1806, he was still trying to pursue something of a career as a publisher of domestic manuals, putting forth an edition of *Shaw's Gardener*. A concerned friend – one of the Godly Chatham clerks – put Hone's scant success down to atheism: 'I am afraid Providence does not think itself under any obligation to bestow undeserving favours on you – You don't go to Church.'[5]

Although the LCS had broken up as a national movement, its principles and ideals survived. Hone's connexion with its former members continued, and he was ready to join them as they sought new ways to challenge the old order and modify their political action to avoid the ire of the government. The organisation had never been monolithic in its aims or methods. Its leaders had been determined to educate the people before they encouraged them to demand constitutional change; they had ambitions for social reform as much as political. 'It induced men to read books, instead of wasting their time in public houses, it

---

* In addition to the children mentioned, Alfred was born in 1810, John 1812, Emma 1814, Charlotte 1816 (she died in 1817), Rose 1818, Samuel 1820, Ellen 1822 and Alice 1825. Sarah was a robust woman, producing her last child at the age of forty-four, and living until her eighty-fourth year.

taught them to respect themselves, and to desire to educate their children,' Francis Place wrote of the LCS debates and lectures. 'It elevated them in their own opinions . . . They were compelled by these discussions to find reasons for their opinions, and to tolerate others.'[6]

Place credited the LCS with having transformed British working-class culture by its efforts in the 1790s. His view was naïve and optimistic; a persecuted and barely legal organisation could not have this impact on the country. His view tells us more about the dreams of the founding members. In the 1800s, when the reformers were driven underground, the priorities of the London campaigners changed. New projects were sought that would shield the movement from charges of fermenting treasonable plots.

On 23 April 1806, William Hone and John Bone convened a public meeting at the Horn Tavern in Doctor's Commons near St Paul's to announce the foundation of a new reform campaign. Hone, fired with zeal and idealism, too young to have been involved fully with the conflict of the '90s, represented the rising generation of reformists. His partner was a veteran of the cause, an authentic LCS martyr. John Bone had been for a time its secretary; Place described him as 'an honest upright man, very religious, sedate and methodical but not well qualified for the office he filled'.[7] A poor manager he might have been, but it was not his fault that he presided over the society at the moment it had fractured and broken apart. In 1799 he was sent to Coldbath Fields Prison in Clerkenwell, a gaol known as the 'English Bastille' because of the high numbers of political prisoners and its filthy conditions. Upon his release, Bone went into voluntary exile in Antwerp.

Bone and Hone put before the public a scheme for a savings bank, insurance office and employment registry named Tranquillity. They were offering a radical and innovative solution to the problems of poor relief. The timing was apposite. A fierce debate was raging about the nature of poverty. In 1806 some 700,000 men, women and children were dependent on public relief at a cost of £4.2 million annually. Recent treatises argued that the mass of unemployed and homeless were not innocent victims: their distresses were due to fecklessness and irresponsibility. Incorrigible habits of idleness, alcoholism and sexual promiscuity – supposedly the defining characteristics of the poorer classes – were to blame, not personal misfortune, illness, the economic cycle or simple human incompetence (except in a few exceptional circumstances). The very name of Bone and Hone's scheme was a pointed criticism of the ways that the poor were being treated.[8]

This anxiety was thrown into sharp relief by Malthus's *Essay on Population*. A country's supply of basic foodstuffs, the economist argued, could not keep pace with rapid population growth; unless nature intervened to curb the soaring number of souls, famine would ensue. The hundreds of thousands claiming relief from the taxpayer, encouraged into parasitical dependence rather than a healthy state of self-reliance, were thus devouring the vitals of the nation. The indigent and unemployed – the incurably idle – preferred handouts to an honest day's labour; they were consuming the resources of the state and taking the wages of the industrious without producing a thing. The inevitable consequence, many were coming to believe, was national decline and natural disaster when all resources were exhausted. Public and private charity was seen as holding out inducements to opt out of work and enjoy a life of idleness and dissipation. The fear that indigence held certain attractions meant that many magistrates, Poor Law overseers and clergymen were concerned to make treatment of the poor as harsh and unsympathetic as possible, a powerful disincentive to sloth. Jeremy Bentham believed that the unemployed and vagrant should be actively coerced into productive labour. The only practical solution was the workhouse, where the indolent would be taught that hard labour was the only relief for an empty stomach. The Malthusian nightmare could be avoided if competition for food and shelter replaced charity. Poverty, it seemed, was becoming tantamount to a criminal offence.[9]

Budding reformists such as Francis Place and William Hone had experienced poverty and the misery of unemployment. Place's family had suffered privations as he struggled to make even the smallest living as a journeyman leather breeches maker in the years before he became a very wealthy tailor; Hone had lurched from bookshop to bookshop during the first years of his adult life. Both men were the opposite of idle or profligate, yet both had suffered. The stereotyping of the unfortunate poor as drunken cadgers stank in their nostrils.

The very poor seemed immoral and profligate in many cases

because the system of public relief was brutal and inefficient. The antiquarian Poor Laws required every parish to levy rates to feed and shelter their unemployed, elderly and ill. The indignity of applying to the parish for money crushed the spirits of respectable but unfortunate families; once a worker was compelled to seek help, he or she was condemned to a life of bare subsistence and humiliation. It became increasingly difficult to gather enough money to resume a trade or buy clothes respectable enough to satisfy prospective employers. Bone and Hone were sympathetic to the plight of unlucky families who had been reduced to begging from the parish; once hope of rehabilitation evaporated, the poor were more likely to descend into a vortex of dissipation, finding respite only at the gin shop or taproom. The reputation of the lower classes as drunken and feckless wretches was a consequence of a rickety and demoralising system, not necessarily the root of poverty. Bone and Hone attacked the dehumanising treatment of the indigent and the vast amounts of money 'which the present scheme squanders upon the most disgusting and squalid wretchedness – the offspring of its own negligence and prodigality'.

Tranquillity would replace the moribund Poor Laws. It was to be based in London as a prototype of a new system which would gradually extend out of the capital to become a national institution. Rather than cast themselves on their parishes in times of need, people – rich and poor – should invest small sums of money in Tranquillity every year. In times of sickness, unemployment, or when they were too old to work, the members of the society would receive annuities, temporary accommodation, education for their children, and training in skilled labour. Bone and Hone told the meeting at the Horn Tavern: '[Tranquillity] will receive the smallest sums that the industrious and economical of every class may be disposed to deposit, and which accumulating at compound interest will be returned to them in proportionate annuities, at the period when according to the present system, they would, if overtaken by poverty, be reduced to partake of eleemosynary support.'

Hone and Bone believed that the poor should not be stereotyped as indolent and irresponsible, nor should they be humiliated by subjection to 'the beggar-teasing caprices of parish controllers'. Tranquillity would discriminate between the deserving and undeserving: those who really wanted to better themselves would lay aside money to provide for illness, accident, unavoidable unemployment and old age. When all they had was the coercive and unsatisfactory Poor Laws to rely upon, the poor would continue to *seem* improvident and fatalistic; the more fortunate members of society had a duty to provide the lower orders with means of insuring themselves against the invisible hand of economic forces. As the two reformers implored on behalf of the poor: 'Let them be provided with opportunities and inducements to be virtuous, and if they are too depraved to avail themselves of them, let them suffer the whole weight of the censure.' The scheme put forward by Hone and Bone was truly innovative; its emphasis on individual contributions and sensitivity to misfortunes encountered at different times in the life cycle challenged the generality of the Poor Laws, whilst suggesting a more compassionate alternative to the harsh edge of utilitarian coercion.

Those who were encouraged to invest in Tranquillity would have a good return on their money if they met hard times. The society was to be based in a large complex of buildings on the outskirts of London, which would provide temporary accommodation, education for their clients' children, a labour exchange, a bank, trade schools and gardens for quiet contemplation. Significantly, it had a bar; the poor would be allowed the comforts of alcoholic refreshment and the responsibility to decide how much they wanted, not forced into abstinence, as most other Poor Law reformers piously decreed was the sure path to moral and material redemption. Tranquillity was a halfway house between poverty and re-entry into the world, where people could get their life in order and learn a new trade in an harmonious environment. The Poor Laws required people to return to their native parishes to claim relief. This stifled the free flow of labour and placed an intolerable burden on the poorest parishes, where help was most needed but poverty the greatest, Poor Law funds the lowest, and jobs scarce. Tranquillity's administrative arm would organise the 'free circulation of Services and Labour' throughout the capital, and eventually the country, liberating people from confinement in their native parishes, and the poorest parishes from a glut of claimants.

The Tranquillity scheme addressed many of the flaws inherent in the Poor Laws. Bone and Hone attacked a corrupt and cruel system with all the gusto with which the defunct LCS had attacked the state. The two men had found fertile ground to express reformist politics; the Poor Laws and the state they criticised had much in common: the same corruption and inefficiencies, the same contempt for the British people. Tranquillity also followed the LCS in seeking the improvement of the poorest classes. The Poor Laws required their claimants to suffer their poverty with meek gratitude and Christian fortitude only; it provided little in the way of education for children or training for adults. Tranquillity would be alive with activity and imbued with a spirit of self-betterment and self-education. John Bone was obsessed with personal cleanliness. The institution would boast a large public bath, free for subscribers and open to all on the payment of a small fee. The unfortunate poor would emerge from Tranquillity with a job if they were lucky, but certainly more confident, respectable, educated and clean than they would have been in the workhouse.

John Bone wrote that 'instead of teaching the Poor to rely entirely on charity, they should be taught the value of depending on themselves'. Tranquillity had to be wary of the criticism from Malthusians and utilitarians that charity made indigence attractive for lazy parasites. It was a private-subscription society built and maintained with the contributions of its members, so the unproductive poor could not claim an automatic right to a free and easy life among its orchards. But as Hone and Bone's manifesto made clear, their investors could not cover all the costs of such a scheme. The most important aspect, however, was that the poor should be the instigators of their own salvation: even a small contribution would mark out the industrious, moral and self-reliant from the work-shy and drunk. Help had to be forthcoming from the richer members of society, if not from the state itself, to subsidise the costs. Once a poor family has done everything in its power to insure against misfortune, '. . . Society is unjust if it does not make up the deficiency, not as a matter of Charity but of right'.

They canvassed support from among the charitably inclined Londoners, and got the backing of a number of city dignitaries. Tranquillity would allow the 'benevolent Opulent' to help the poor in the most efficient way, and, crucially, to 'extend their liberality to the unfortunate without wounding his delicacy'. Bone and Hone were always concerned that the unemployed should not be treated like help-less children; necessary relief should be a motivation for self-improve-ment, not enervating charity.

George Rose, MP, a close friend of George III and William Pitt, and formerly Paymaster-General and vice-president of the Board of Trade, was their most pre-eminent ally. Rose had been an active campaigner on behalf of the poor, and was the author of a recent book advocating some sort of alternative to the Poor Laws. Tranquillity was a radical solution to the problem, and a new way of looking at the causes and complexi-ties of poverty itself. But Hone and Bone needed the active support of the government before the help of people like Rose could be utilised. Poor people could only be persuaded to invest money if they were exempted by Act of Parliament from the legal obligation to contribute to their local Poor Rates. The government's support was essential if the bank was to inspire the confidence of investors. The idea was taken seriously by the 'Ministry of the Talents', the short-lived coalition head-ed by Lord Grenville, and the Whigs Charles James Fox and Lord Grey. Tranquillity established itself in the Albion Buildings, Blackfriars, and Hone and Bone worked throughout 1806 to get it on its feet. In early 1807, they began to advertise among the community to attract their first clients, publishing the rules and regulations of the sav-ings bank.

'It was very Quixotic,' Hone admitted later, '– we were mad; mad because we supposed it possible, if an intention were good, that it would therefore be carried into effect. We were not immediately dis-couraged, but we met with that trifling and delaying of hope which makes the heart sick.' The Whig ministers were supportive of the idea, but slow to act; their administration fell in March 1807, just as Tranquillity was poised to begin its work. 'I lost everything,' Hone remembered, 'even the furniture of my house,' which was seized to pay the debts. The self-appointed saviour of the poor was now himself a pauper.[10]

Hone was often reckless and naïve in pursuit of ideas he believed to be the answer to social evils. Risking his family's security in a project such as Tranquillity may have been laudable, but he did not consider the weight of opposition that had to be overcome; it did not even occur to him that an impecunious book dealer might not be the ideal candidate for a revolutionary and very expensive philanthropic scheme. He was an outsider with few contacts and no experience; the chances that the state would hand over the administration of poor relief to him and John Bone were slight. The two men were driven by deeply held convictions; as they wrote, it 'has long rendered it the duty of every individual in the community to present the best plan he could devise, to the Public'. But instinctive compassion and moral duty are no substitutes for an organised structure and, above all, influence with those in power. A good (and perhaps workable) scheme could never succeed when parliament was wedded to the Poor Laws, especially the regulatory influence it had over the lives of the poor. The workhouse system and coercion were, of course, features of nineteenth-century Britain, and it would be a long time before social security would be accepted as a duty of the state. Just as Hone's tendency to distribute his coins indiscriminately as he wandered the streets of London, regardless of who deserved them, drained his resources and deprived his family, Tranquillity was a stab in the dark, and it proved costly.

Yet the idea survived in the minds of reformers. In 1815 and 1816 Rose returned to the idea, and a new campaign got under way in an attempt to overhaul the Poor Laws. Savings and providential banks were set up in Bath, Edinburgh, Southampton and other towns throughout the country. Rose credited Hone and Bone's Tranquillity as the inspiration for all privately funded savings banks; they had pioneered a scheme, aspects of which were put into effect in more favourable circumstances and by men with the power to make a success of it.[11] A London providential bank was set up under the patronage of the Duke of Somerset, and with the support of two royal dukes, two other dukes, two marquises, nine earls, and two bishops. One of this institution's founding members praised Tranquillity as the model for all philanthropic projects, and thanked its creators for publicising the movement; he could not let the opportunity pass 'without noticing the obligations the nation are under to Mr John Bone', and by implication, Mr William Hone, who was after all the society's secretary. 'We hoped to throw a grain into the earth which might become a great tree,' Hone said, '– in other hands it has succeeded.'[12]

The author of *Modern London* (1804) said that the city manufactured news, providing the 'incessant reception and diffusion of all the fugitive history of our time'; it 'seems to discharge a part not unlike that of the heart in the circulation of the blood, or that which the brain performs the chief functions in the nervous and sensorial system'.[13]

London in the early nineteenth century was divided between the City – with its winding lanes, shops, home of the mercantile and business community – and the West End, a place of ordered squares, mansions, palaces, parks, neglected slums and the Houses of Parliament. As Charles Lamb wrote, the two poles of London 'meet and jostle in friendly opposition at Temple Bar'. The stretch of London from Charing Cross, along the Strand, up Fleet Street and Ludgate Hill to St Paul's Cathedral is a straight line that connects the fashionable West End with the hub of the City. From the fourteenth century until the 1980s this causeway from modish bon ton to the seamy metropolis thrived upon gossip, rumour and news. The politics of Westminster and high society scandals of St James flowed to the City along this line. Although writing much later in the century, T. H. S Escott's description of Fleet Street is relevant for this period: 'The entire thoroughfare between Ludgate Hill and Charing Cross is connected as by a whispering gallery with every point of social meeting in the capital, and, indeed, throughout the country.' A wonderful image: a murmur in Westminster magnified to a crescendo by St Paul's.

So it is hardly surprising that Fleet Street and the Strand were crowded with bookshops, print sellers, publishing companies and newspaper offices. It was the centre of news for not just London but the whole country. In *Modern London*, the author describes the seamless, unremitting progression of the crowd, 'so that the great thoroughfares of London appear like a moving multitude, or a daily fair'. The crowd came to Fleet Street to look at the displays of prints and satirical squibs that booksellers and publishers pasted on their windows, or to buy pamphlets and newspapers. The digestion of news took place among a crowd – in front of shops, in taverns, coffee houses, offices and barbers' shops. The scene outside Hannah Humphrey's print shop was described in 1802: 'The enthusiasm is indescribable when the next drawing appears; it is veritable madness . . . You have to make your way in through the crowd with your fists.' This shop, famous as the seller of James Gillray's caricatures, was in St James, but such scenes were reminiscent of Fleet Street. 'Where has Spleen her food but in London?' wrote Lamb. 'Humour, Interest, Curiosity, suck at her measureless breasts without a possibility of being satiated.'

The bookshop was at the centre of politics, journalism and literary culture. There were three varieties of bookseller. The first were publishing houses, selling books, pamphlets and prints which came from their own presses. The second type were wholesale dealers, which fed the country market with periodicals, reviews and works of general literature. The third and most numerous variety were the smaller retailers who sold an amorphous stock of antiquarian books, works issued from other firms, but who occasionally published their own comparatively cheap works. The Longmans firm exemplified the larger publisher–bookselling form. Its shop in Paternoster Row produced Hume's *History*, its own encyclopaedia, and the *Edinburgh Review* from 1802. John Murray in Fleet Street published the *Quarterly Review* and Byron's poems. Sir Richard Phillips's office in St Paul's Churchyard was the base for the *Monthly Magazine* and produced a range of cheap pamphlets and periodicals, as well as selling a large stock of books.

The daily newspaper press reproduced parliamentary debates, government pronouncements, crime reports and only a small amount of comment. Political and literary debates were conducted in the pages of journals and pamphlets published by booksellers. The small shops that lined the route from St Paul's Churchyard to Westminster were salons. Writers would come looking for employment; politicians would pay visits to have their speeches published; the crowd came to buy the latest pamphlets and cartoons. Many of the shops were tiny – Hone's famous Fleet Street shop, from which he operated in the 1810s, had a front just three feet across. Yet, whatever the size, they were the scenes of political and literary controversy, the purveyors of scandal and gossip, inundated with customers of all social classes when notable works came off their presses. The bookseller thus had a central role in London life, and the proprietor unique access to the public life of the capital.

'Near the middle part of the ever-crowded, noisy, tumultuous thoroughfare called the Strand, is the very focus – the hot-bed, the forcing-house – of the "Newspaper Press" . . . ,' wrote one of Hone's acquaintances in his reminiscences of London in the first decade of the nineteenth century. 'This literary manufacturing and news-mart may be almost regarded as exemplifying the perpetual motion . . . During the sitting of Parliament, and when warmly-contested party questions are under discussion, the activity and excitement in this region are only to be compared to a hive of bees, at the time of swarming.'[14]

The collapse of Tranquillity did not hold John Bone and William Hone back for long. In 1808 they took over 'The Old and Curious Bookshop' at number 331 on the Strand, directly opposite Somerset House and at the heart of national publishing.

Bone and Hone were still ensconced in the networks of reformers that had survived the repression of the late 1790s and the collapse of the LCS. 'The Old and Curious Bookshop' had a pedigree as a longstanding reformist centre; its former owner, Jeremiah Samuel Jordan had been imprisoned, first in 1792 for selling Thomas Paine's *Rights of Man* and again in 1798, and throughout his career had printed and distributed political books on behalf of the LCS and other reformist organisations. Bone and Hone's personal associations with political dissent, the battle against censorship and the remnants of the LCS membership were not concealed when they took over.

The beginning of Bone and Hone's business coincided with the time when the reform movement was beginning to emerge from the shadows and was gaining momentum. Their shop stood at the centre of the liveliest political area in Britain. Stretching from the City in the east to Kensington in the west, from Oxford Street down to the Thames, Westminster was one of the most important constituencies in the country. The majority of MPs were returned to parliament by a handful of wealthy voters (rarely more than a few hundred at best), but Westminster had 12,000 men, many of whom were middling tradesmen, artisans and shopkeepers, who were entitled to return two members to the Commons. Elections in London were therefore hard-fought and contentious; at a time of rotten boroughs, closed nominations and electoral corruption the seat was considered a barometer of public opinion, and the two MPs it returned were justified in saying that they represented popular sentiment. Charles James Fox had contested the seat in 1784, and he legitimised his demands for parliamentary reform on the grounds that he, alone among the leading statesmen, had been elected by the people and therefore spoke on behalf of public opinion. Westminster elections were rowdy, and nationally important.

Fox died in 1806 and at the by-election the reformists were disgusted at the election of Lord Percy after his father, the Duke of Northumberland, had won over the electorate with gifts of bread, beer and cheese; a popular constituency, it seemed, was just as susceptible to bribery and aristocratic influence as any rotten borough. At the general election in 1807, Francis Place and his old LCS connexions – 'some friends of the ancient constitution', as they styled themselves – were determined to restore Westminster's reputation as an independent constituency and the sole representative of national opinion.

Under Place's leadership, the Westminster Committee wanted to transform the constituency into a safe seat for reformist MPs and show the country a model of how politics could be conducted if there was a mass electorate. In 1793 it had been estimated that 307 English MPs were returned to the Commons on the nomination of just 154 aristocrats and wealthy individuals who owned constituencies. The small number of independent electors in the country were therefore utterly disillusioned by the political system; their votes counted for nothing when their MPs were swamped by the lackeys of a tiny electoral college. The Committee wanted to prove that the situation was not 'utterly irremediable': a free election in London could prove 'that there still existed a public in the country, and that all the noble virtues of their ancestors were not entirely eradicated'. They wanted to show that there could be such a thing as an election free from corruption and bribery. Two Westminster MPs, freely chosen by independent voters, would advance the interests of their constituents in parliament, holding the executive to account when it acted to harm their rights and livelihoods. They needed candidates who were immune from party influence and oblivious to the temptations of patronage: independent, stubborn and vocal gentlemen who would be heard above the babble of corrupt MPs. They sought a candidate 'best calculated to restore to them the purity of the constitution, and, by so doing, to stimulate and encourage the people at large to follow their example'.[15]

Sir Francis Burdett, a foxhunting squire, one of the richest men in the country, and a popular hero, who was nicknamed 'Old Glory' and the 'Champion of the People' by the mob, was the natural choice for the Westminster Committee. He had entered parliament in 1796 at the age of twenty-four when he leased the Duke of Newcastle's constituency of Boroughbridge in Yorkshire for six years at the cost of £4,000, but had immediately made his mark as a campaigner for popular rights, a peppery orator who stood aloof from party intrigue. He had risen to national prominence, and achieved huge popularity in London, between 1798 and 1800 campaigning with his political mentor, the veteran reformer and one of the twelve LCS defendants of 1794 John Horne Tooke, for reform of the appalling conditions in Coldbath Fields prison, where many LCS members were imprisoned. 'The best part of my character', Burdett had once written to his father-in-law, the banker Thomas Coutts, 'is a strong feeling of indignation at injustice and oppression, and a liberal sympathy with the sufferings of my fellows.'[16] This stubborn independence and instinctive revolt at the merest hint of tyranny made him the perfect candidate for Place's Westminster Committee. His impact on the public and politicians was captured by William Hazlitt in *The Spirit of the Age*: 'He is a plain, unaffected, unsophisticated English gentleman . . . All that he pretends to is common sense and common honesty; and a greater compliment cannot be paid to these than the attention with which he is listened to in the House of Commons.'[17]

Burdett's political views were similar to those of the moderate reformists. He believed that the rights of the people had been usurped by generations of venal politicians. The people's House of Parliament failed in its duty to represent the views of the country. Parliamentary seats were bought and sold on the open market; MPs owed their nomination to the Commons to their patrons, the borough-mongers who owned the constituencies, and not the free choice of voters. The power of ministers was determined, not by public opinion, not by the Crown, but by their ability to reward their parties with handsome emoluments known as 'places': sinecures, pensions and civil and military jobs.

Ministers remained in office as long as they could buy a following of MPs with the reservoir of patronage at their disposal.

The liberties, wealth and rights of the people, Burdett and the reformers argued, were trampled underfoot by a parliament safely insulated from the people they claimed to represent. Looking to the past, Burdett held up Magna Carta and the Bill of Rights as the high points of British history and the pillars of liberty. But the rights that had been wrested from the Crown by the people were under threat again. What was Magna Carta worth when members of the LCS and critical journalists could be held without trial? Who did the Commons represent but the wealthy few? Throughout history, absolute monarchy had been gradually weakened; the battle was now with parliamentary despotism. People like Burdett looked back to the mythical past, to the supposed Anglo-Saxon Constitution, when every man had the vote. The liberties and rights of the native Britons had been taken away by successive generations; ministers and sinecurists were modern-day Normans, who suppressed a manly race of freeborn Britons. The idealised past was a powerful rallying point, rich in symbols; the thousands of men named after Alfred the Great in the nineteenth century, including Hone's fifth child, testified the popularity of the Anglo Saxon myth in their parents' youth.

In 1802 Burdett had sought nomination for Middlesex, another constituency with a large number of voters, so that he could claim that his place in parliament was due to the free choice of a sizeable cross section of the public. However, in 1804 he was compelled to leave parliament when the local Tory sheriffs accused him of corruption and the election was declared void. Burdett lost the subsequent election. After six years of tedious political wrangles in Middlesex, a futile fight against entrenched corruption at the expense of £100,000, Burdett announced his retirement from politics.

The Westminster Committee saw him as the authentic voice of popular discontent, an indispensable advocate of parliamentary reform and the liberty of the press. For them he was 'frank, honest and manly . . . he *stands almost alone* the *devoted* and *intrepid friend of humanity, of England, its people,* and *its laws*'. He was too important to fall victim to the corrupt electoral system. Sir Francis announced that he was prepared to come out of retirement only if called to do so by the people: 'electors ought to seek representatives, not candidates solicit electors'. Place and the Committee put Burdett's name forward at the hustings and spoke and published on his behalf. They aimed to return the baronet 'free from every sacrifice and expense to himself, upon *independent principles, consonant to the genuine spirit of the constitution of England,* which declares that *elections shall be free*, and without corruption'. The Westminster reformers undertook to fight an election, which had cost over £50,000 in recent years, with a fighting fund of just £200.[18]

The 1807 Westminster election was an important moment in the history of parliamentary reform. The election was all about independence. The Westminster Committee wanted MPs who were free of party control and the scramble for profit and patronage. But, most importantly, they wanted to prove that the artisans, tradesmen and shopkeepers of London were responsible and independent.

Any kind of reform that would extend the franchise had been swatted away because it was assumed that 'ordinary' voters, unlike propertied gentlemen, were susceptible to cash inducements and specious demagoguery; they were unable to make a fully rational choice. In 1807 the imperative was to prove that there existed such a thing as reasonable and uncorrupted public opinion among the great body of the people.

The election of Burdett by a significant majority demonstrated that the common voter could come to a reasoned choice without being seduced by mob orators (Burdett stayed at home during the campaign) or bribed with cash and beer (the Committee spent just £780 during the campaign). The Committee had relied on political and constitutional arguments to win over the electorate, standing under the banner 'Purity of Election'. 'Not a single "agitator" interfered in the Election,' William Cobbett reported. 'It was carried on by the People themselves ... There were no appeals to the Passions, no revilings of any one. "You *know* Sir Francis Burdett, choose him if you will," was the substance of all that was said.' The ministerial candidate, the brewer John 'Colonel Narcotic' Elliot, and the Whig Richard Sheridan were left grasping at what scanty support they could find. The electors and their MP were incorruptible and independent – or so the Committee represented them. Such a thing was unprecedented, and a great victory for the reformists' case. Place wrote, mocking the shock that many felt at the outcome, 'What parcel of people who were nobody, common tailors, and barbers, and snobs,* to carry Westminster.'[19]

The Committee were initially prepared to support the candidature of James Paull, a wealthy merchant and former Whig MP as the second MP. But he was furious when Burdett, once a firm political ally, made the decision to stand as well; the 'Champion of the People' would steal his votes. They fought a duel on the eve of the poll, and both men were wounded in the leg. The Westminster Committee withdrew its support, turned against their former candidate with devastating effect: Paull attracted just 269 votes.† Instead, the London voters chose Thomas, Lord Cochrane to sit alongside Burdett as their second representative. The young lord, heir to the impoverished Earl of Dundonald, was already a national hero and one of the most famous men in Europe. As the Royal Navy's most successful officer since Nelson, he had fought the French navy from the West Indies to the Mediterranean, along the Bay of Biscay and the coast of Spain. Under his command was Lieutenant Marryat, who would later immortalise the exploits of his captain in adventure novels. In the twentieth century he was the inspiration for C.S. Forester's Hornblower. But Cochrane's actual achievements at sea rivalled anything that the novelists could imagine. As the commander of tiny brigs with scant armaments, he had captured French frigates several times the size of his own vessels with foolhardy bravery and low cunning. Captain Lord Cochrane harried enemy shipping, desecrating Napoleon's navy and in-shore infantry on the Spanish coast in daring attacks that wowed the English public, made him rich in prize money, and earned the part-epithet, part-compliment of '*Le loup des mers*' from the Emperor himself.

The Westminster Committee was dubious about the political worth of a man they believed nothing more than a simple sailor. 'Let those

* 'Snob', in this case, meant most accurately a cobbler, or more loosely a common city dweller. The *OED* cites Hone's *Every-Day Book* (1825) for the use of snob in this sense; later in the nineteenth century the word took the meaning we understand today.
† At the close of the poll, Burdett was far in the lead with 5,134 votes; Cochrane came second with 3,708; the losing candidates were Richard Sheridan (2,645), John Elliot (2,137), and James Paull (269).

who say so', he replied, 'give us a list of those who are actually unfit to represent you in parliament. – Such as Placemen, Pensioners and Fops – such as those who dash about in their curricles in Bond Street – they are a damn deal more unfit to represent you than such a man as I am.'[20] His straight-speaking contempt for the old corps of corrupt politicians and complete independence from any party endeared him to the Westminster electors, and in time the Committee came to see that he was capable of representing its reformist demands. He had a hatred of all forms of corruption and nepotism, and, as a military hero, his voice was influential. Place and his lieutenants would support him as enthusiastically as Burdett in subsequent elections, until he left to fight colonial rule as admiral of the South American navy in 1818.

The 1807 election was a triumph for the reformists. The persecuted men who had begun their political careers with the LCS, some of whom had served imprisonment as traitors, had re-emerged, now as a force in British politics with two MPs arguing their cause in parliament. They had at last shed the epithet of Francophilia with which the government had labelled them. Association with Sir Francis Burdett, the squire from the old English tradition, and Lord Cochrane, one of Napoleon's most feared enemies, helped dispel that image.

The membership of the Westminster Committee had been kept secret. This was done partly to avoid legal harassment, but mainly because its leading lights, such as Place, were prominent London traders whose business could be ruined if customers objected to their politics. The movement was fronted by Burdett and Cochrane in the Commons, a number of City politicians, and by Hone and Bone's bookshop on the Strand. They became the official booksellers, publishers, propagandists and the public face of the enigmatic Westminster reformers. The two men continued the work of keeping the public informed and equipped to demand political change, opening a public subscription to the Fund for Advertising in the Cause of Parliamentary Reform (an adjunct of the Westminster and Middlesex election committees) to subsidise the costs of publishing and distributing political pamphlets to the people. They also published the reform proposals of the veteran campaigner, Major John Cartwright, who had spent his life touring the country as an apostle of liberty and political rights.

Jeremiah Jordan had been close to Burdett, supplying him and Horne Took with books on prisons during their campaign against the abuses prevalent in Coldbath Fields. The new owners of the shop were determined to maintain the connexion. From the beginning of 1809 Bone and Hone were entrusted with publishing and circulating the MP's speeches. In that year the issue of corruption blew up in the most spectacular way. George III's second son, Frederick, Duke of York, commander-in-chief of the armed forces, was accused of selling commissions in the army through the agency of his former mistress, Mary Anne Clarke. Burdett took a prominent role in the House of Commons inquiry into this instance of how nepotism guided the government of the country. But rather than launch an independent attack on the government or simply join the Whigs, Burdett called a meeting to take instructions from his constituents and learn how best he could represent their opinions. Bone and Hone's book, *A Full Report of the Proceedings of the Electors of Westminster . . . at a public meeting held in Westminster Hall*, shows how reformist politics worked in London. The people at the meeting instructed their MP to use the Duke of York scandal as the starting point for an inquiry into the prevalence of corruption, and evidence of the need for the reform of an obviously decrepit political system. Other constituencies, they said, should have the same right as they had of electing representatives to parliament who would be as active as Burdett in 'preserving inviolate the Rights and Privileges of the People'.

Burdett took their advice, telling his constituents: 'An honest Parliament is wanting; a Parliament composed of individuals, who shall look not for place but to the people; and who, instead of scrambling for private advantage, shall apply themselves to the care of such as are public and universal. It is high time that we should turn our minds to the immediate consideration of Parliamentary Reform.' Hone and Bone's report of the meeting was worth far more than all the theoretical arguments in favour of constitutional revision; here was an illustration of how MPs *should* act – in perpetual consultation with the people they claimed to represent, taking the reasoned and cogent demands of their constituents to the floor of the Commons. It was a foretaste of what reform would bring to the government of the country, the way in which public opinion should be refined, debated and brought to attention, not just in London, but in every constituency.

The next pamphlet to come off the Bone and Hone press was *A Correct Report of the Speech delivered by Sir Francis Burdett . . . in the House of Commons . . . on the conduct of HRH the Duke of York.* This work did more than inform the public of Burdett's proposals however; its main interest was an instance of a threat to the freedom of the press. The daily newspapers, it was well known, were in the pay of ministers. Papers such as *The Times*, the *Morning Herald*, or the *World*, received sums of between £100 and £600 on the understanding that they followed the government line. In this case, they had censored Burdett's speeches and modified the government's defence, giving the people an account of the debate in 'a character very different from that [to] which they were really entitled'. Just as the Commons ignored the people, the daily press restricted their right to read full accounts of proceedings in parliament. As a political journalist, Hone would always refuse to accept official reports or government information without verifying the sources. His book reminded people that what liberty the press enjoyed was only superficial; newspapers were just as much in the government's pocket as MPs. The only truly independent sources of public information were the small bookshops that were not fed government bribes. It was from these private enterprises, rather than from the established newspapers, that the battle for the liberty of the press would be fought.

The success of the book in giving a verbatim account of the campaign against the Duke of York meant that Bone and Hone were entrusted with the job of publishing Burdett's next campaign. Following the scandal of open corruption, he introduced a bill to prevent the sale of parliamentary seats. Introducing the pamphlet, Bone and Hone wrote that their decision to publish the speech was motivated by the consciousness that public opinion, expressed by people in Westminster and elsewhere, was crucial for the success of reform: '. . . the people must decide the question. They must now speak their sentiments in language that cannot be misunderstood.'

In his speech, Burdett said that reform was needed to 'arrest the progress of destruction, for some stimulus to reinvigorate the Constitution, and save it from decay by extirpating the vile and loathsome canker of corruption, which, preying upon the vitals, palsies the energies and consumes the substance of the country.' His proposals were moderate: the extension of the franchise to householders; equal numbers of voters in all electoral divisions; general elections to be held on one and the same day in all constituencies; and the duration of parliaments to be three years rather than seven. Burdett argued that the rise of the press and public discussion turned people against corruption and parliamentary tyranny, making reform inevitable:

Can the people remain contented with such power? – Impossible. Believe me, Sir, the discontent that exists in this country arises principally from the certain knowledge the People now have of the corrupt state of this House, and their exclusion from that share in the Constitution to which they are by law entitled, that they are not fairly, nor indeed at all represented, – in fact, that the interests of this House are not identified with, but opposite to theirs. – Remove this defect, repair this great injury, and the advantages will be immediate and important.

Burdett's bill was defeated easily by the Prime Minister, Spencer Perceval, and his large following in the Commons. But the idea that public discussion and popular pressure would eventually achieve equitable reform would set the tone for the rest of Hone's political career. In 1809 the country was largely quiescent; reform would become a national issue from 1816, when Hone took a much larger role in educating and rousing popular opinion.

Between 1808 and 1810 Hone was the joint proprietor of a bookshop which was in the forefront of the battle to refine public opinion into an articulate demand for reform. Yet the link with the Westminster Committee was just one aspect of Hone's publishing and bookselling career. He was fully involved with the literary and intellectual world, and his bookshop became a haunt of many interesting early nineteenth-century personalities. As the seller of 'old and curious books', Bone and Hone catered for historians, authors, antiquarians and collectors. It was not merely a den of Burdettites, but a centre of learning and a meeting place for the London literati.

The first part of the shop's catalogue for 1809 advertised a stock of

2,708 books published in every century from the fifteenth to the nineteenth.* Heading the list were handsomely embellished maps, topolog-
ical surveys, architectural designs and folios of prints. There were
works of philosophy, *belles-lettres*, bibliography, anatomy, legal texts,
novels and classics in Latin, Greek, Italian and French from the preceding four centuries. Much of the stock was taken up with historical
works of political interest – from the British civil wars, the Commonwealth, Restoration, exclusion crisis, Revolution and other moments
of history. Naturally enough, a significant proportion of the books
were surveys of the Poor Laws from their beginnings in the sixteenth
century.

The publishing side of the business was not limited to Westminster
Committee propaganda. Members of the intellectual and fashionable
Burney family were customers; a note survives from Dr Burney ordering a collection of rare seventeenth century Dutch books.[21] Another
influential friend of the enterprise was Sir Richard Phillips, publisher
of the *Monthly Magazine* and proponent of the idea that popular
instruction and reformist politics were inextricably linked. The public
had to be educated before they could claim political influence, and he
dedicated his life to issuing literary works in cheap editions. In 1809,
Phillips introduced Hone and Bone to Thomas Northmore, the scholar of ancient British languages and fellow of the Society of Antiquities,
who wanted to sponsor a *Political Almanac*. The book would come out
in periodical form, and set the reform movement in its historical context – 'a *manual of liberty*', as Northmore called it. It would commemo-
rate great anniversaries, such as the signing of Magna Carta, the
Glorious Revolution, the Bill of Rights and the Act of Settlement, and
include biographies of the great heroes and theorists of English liberty
such as John Hampden, John Pym, Algernon Sidney, Colonel
Lilburne, John Locke and the first and third Earls of Shaftesbury.
Unfortunately, this plan to enlist historical education in the cause of
reform never materialised.[22]

Bone and Hone's bookshop was typical of the early nineteenth century; more than just a place to pick up books, it was part of city life, a

---

* The second half of the catalogue does not seem to have survived.

centre of news, gossip and learning, where people came together to discuss politics, history, literature and meet acquaintances. A Strand or Fleet Street bookseller was uniquely placed to meet all kinds of Londoner, from politicians like Sir Francis Burdett or eminent scholars such as Northmore, down to the occasional purchaser of cheap political tracts. Three examples of Hone's regular customers provide an insight into the colourful daily round of bookselling.

The first was Lumley Skeffington, a famous fop, who was at one time the leader of society fashion. He was described as 'well bred and good-tempered. His features were large, and he had a sharp sallow face, with dark curly hair and whiskers.' In the late 1780s and early '90s, he was a member of the Carlton House set, the companions of George, Prince of Wales, who scandalised society with their outrageous parties, vastly expensive lifestyle and extravagant clothes. Skeffington outdid all the dandies with his extraordinary fashions, and even the Prince deferred to his tastes. In 1809, he was at thirty-eight a fading relic of the hedonistic days of the 1780s, desperately clinging on to the foppish styles long since abandoned by the Prince and the rest of society. He retained his breeches with white ribbons on the knees, his silk stockings, the bright waistcoats and shiny top boots, and continued to wear rouge on his face until his death in 1850. When he wasn't perfecting his costume, Skeffington wrote plays for the London stage which were notoriously mediocre. Byron wrote,

> And sure *great* Skeffington must claim our praise,
> For skirtless coats and skeletons of plays . . .
> . . . five facetious acts comes thundering on,
> While poor John Bull, bewildered by the scene,
> Stares, wondering what the devil it can mean;
> But as some hands applaud, a venal few!
> Rather than sleep, why, John applauds it too.

He probably came to the bookshop to buy rare books and plays for his research. Hone's eldest daughter remembered this strange character leafing through old folios of prints, sighing over the portraits of young society beauties: 'The loveliest of the lovely!' or 'An Angel!'[23]

Another customer, Princess Olive of Cumberland, developed an obsession with Hone. As Mrs Olivia Serres, she was appointed land-scape painter to the Prince of Wales in 1806. However, in 1809 she seemed to have undergone a slight breakdown, at one time begging for money from the Prince, at another offering to lend him £20,000. From 1817 she also began to allege that her mother had been married to Henry Frederick, Duke of Cumberland, the rakish brother of George III – an unlikely story but one she maintained with utmost confidence. She asked Hone to inspect the documents and help vindicate her claims to royal blood. Hone complied and went to her house. He was shown into an upstairs room, where 'Princess' Olive was sitting at a round table. Hone joined her and, to his growing discomfort, she insist-ed that they read the documents together. As they poured over the papers, she edged her chair closer to his, and Hone began to realise he was being seduced. He moved his chair away, she got closer. According to Hone, there followed 'another edging of the chair – another retreat – and so on until we had fairly circled the table. With the prospect of other rounds in view, I started up, seized my hat and escaped, never more to examine the proofs of the Princess Olive's title to Royalty.'[24]

Lumley Skeffington and Olive Serres were among the more eccen-tric of Hone's clientele. He developed a more fulfilling friendship with another celebrity. Lady Augusta Murray married George III's son Prince Augustus (later Duke of Sussex) in Rome in 1793, when she was thirty and he an impressionable young man of twenty. The Royal Marriage Act of 1772 ruled any marriage contracted by a descendant of George II without the consent of the reigning monarch illegal. Augusta and the prince had two children together between 1794 and 1802, before they were separated by the ecclesiastical courts. She was pre-vented from styling herself Duchess of Sussex, and from 1809, the duke began proceedings to get their children taken into his custody. At this time of her life, Lady Augusta was living in poverty, surviving on a small royal pension granted her on condition she did not publish the Prince's love letters.

Lady Augusta was a frequent visitor to the shop. The books were laid out on the drawing-room floor so that she might make her choices in privacy and comfort. The Hones entertained her in their own apart-ments because she was a close friend, but also to prevent gossips reporting her frequent visits to one of Burdett's lieutenants. Sarah Burn, Hone's eldest daughter, recalled, 'She derived much pleasure in conversing with my father, often talked of the Duke in terms of deep affection, and would weep over the cruelty of their separation. Her carefully cultured, highly improved mind attracted the admiration of the literary and other talented persons of the day.' Her children played with Hone's, while the adults discussed politics and literature. She admitted that she had to keep her carriage away from the shop, lest the royal family stop her pension when they heard that she was a friend of an anti-government publisher. She once told Hone that her support for Burdett and reform was a patriotic duty.[25]

Hone at this time of his life was a friendly and welcoming book-shop owner, combining the things he loved most in the world – liter-ature and political campaigning. Customers found 'a short, stout, active man, with a keen eye, a well developed forehead, having a ten-dency to baldness, a slightly upturned nose, and a general look of cleverness'.[26] Women like Lady Augusta Murray were naturally drawn to him, appreciating his intelligent, amusing conversation and his charitable nature. Without being famous or influential, he was known as a genial bookshop proprietor always ready to discuss books or Westminster politics. It was certainly an interesting existence, and his social life seems never to have been dull, with a constant stream of scholars, politicians, notables and members of the public coming and going as they trailed their gossip, scandal and opinions down Fleet Street and the Strand. The Tranquillity project, failure though it was, had made him famous as a reformer and selfless philanthropist. He was entrenched within the network of London social reformers, and there is a hint that he was involved with the anti-slavery movement. This would account for the privileged responsibility he was given in 1810, that of adopting a young West Indian boy.

The child was welcomed to London by the abolitionists as the son of Toussaint L'Ouverture, the leader of the St Domingo slave revolt, one of the great heroes of the early nineteenth century. The standing that L'Ouverture had in Britain was captured in Wordsworth's sonnet lament-ing his death in 1802:

. . . Though fallen thyself, never to rise again,
Live, and take comfort. Thou hast left behind
Powers that will work for thee; air, earth and skies;
There's not a breathing of the common wind
That will forget thee; thou hast great allies;
Thy friends are exultations, agonies,
And love, and man's unconquerable mind.

Given his father's reputation, it was little surprise that John Toussaint L'Ouverture arrived in London to extravagant praise, bordering on religious fervour. 'Active and intelligent,' wrote Sarah Burn, 'he was in great danger of being ruined by "hero worship". Perceiving this danger, my father pitied the lad, and rescued him by bringing him home.' John was taken to Lambeth to live with Sarah Hone's mother, where he played in the garden with the youngest Hone children, Fanny and Matilda. Hone raised a subscription to provide for his education, and after a few months climbing trees in Mrs Johnson's garden with his foster-sisters, he was sent to school. 'We were all sorry when he left us,' Sarah Burn remembered. Shortly after this, when John was suffering a slight illness, Hone sent him some toys with an affectionate letter:

> 331 Strand
> Tuesday 23rd Octr. 1810
>
> My Dear John,
> . . . I hope you will soon let me have the still greater pleasure of lending you some books, for from books you can gain more amusement than you can get from all the toys you have ever seen, and more instruction than you have had from all the people you have ever talked with.
> After you begin to read you will soon be able to understand many things which you now only wonder at, and speedily be convinced of this grand Truth, delivered by one of our greatest Philosophers, that 'Knowledge is Power'.
> . . . Mr Bone and all friends beg to be remembered to you, and we all most certainly send you the best of good wishes for your health and improvement.
>
> I am, Dear John,
> Your True friend,
> William Hone.

It transpired that John was not the son of Toussaint L'Ouverture. However, the incident shows how highly regarded Hone was in liberal London society; a kindly man and committed philanthropist, he was the natural choice for the responsibility of bringing the boy up. There is a lot of Hone's character in the letter: his generous spirit and his belief in the power of literature. Unfortunately, nothing more is known of young John. There are no references to him in Hone's papers, which is not necessarily to mean that contact was cut off. Perhaps he found a home elsewhere, or, most likely, returned to St Domingo.[27]

'So determined have the English been, in guarding their persons and property against oppression,' wrote the author of *Modern London*, 'that neither their manners nor their laws will endure a blow with impunity, much less imprisonment and acts of greater violence . . . a blow given must be returned and the contest decided, or he that receives it is disgraced . . . Englishmen, in foreign countries . . . are regarded on some occasions as little better than barbarians, and on others as lunatics.'[28]

Twice in 1810 the people came out on to the streets. On the first occasion, London saw a battle between the mob and the army; on the second, a peaceful demonstration united Londoners of all social classes in a celebration of free speech. This marks the resumption of the conflict over the liberty of the press which was to run for over a decade. At this time journalists and politicians were under constant threat from imprisonment and excessive fines for even the most mild of political opinions. Censorship was a powerful weapon in the government's hand, and it exercised this authority frequently and successfully throughout the 1810s. The battle between the press and the government was to climax in 1817 with Hone's trials. The story begins in 1810.

When a House of Commons committee was investigating the Walcheren expedition, a serious naval debacle, Charles Yorke, First Lord of the Admiralty, invoked a clause excluding 'strangers' from the gallery. No journalist could report the full implications of the disaster. It gave rise to a fervent speech in favour of freedom of expression from Richard Sheridan, and an equally heated speech attacking it from William Windham. A debate was sparked on the freedom of the press, which spilled out of parliament to the streets. The British Forum, a

Westminster debating society led by another LCS man, John Gale Jones, displayed a notice outside parliament advertising a forthcoming discussion: 'Which was the greater outrage on the public feeling – Mr Yorke's enforcement of the standing order to exclude strangers from the House of Commons, or Mr Windham's recent attack on the Liberty of the Press?'

Gale Jones was arrested for thus insulting the dignity of parliament and sent to Newgate Prison. According to the Bill of Rights of 1689, parliament was given immunity from the censure of 'any court or place out of Parliament'. This privilege was supposed to protect MPs from the Crown in the aftermath of the Glorious Revolution. However, throughout the eighteenth century, parliament had defined 'any place' very loosely, and used the archaic terminology of the Bill of Rights to punish criticism of any sort. Parliamentary privilege had transformed from a recourse to defend MPs from outside threats to a weapon in their hands. According to parliament's interpretation, it could imprison any politician or journalist it liked without recourse to the courts.

As Richard Sheridan told the Commons, if Gale Jones could be arrested for a mildly sarcastic butt at Charles Yorke, it would effectively 'bar all public discussion, all consideration of politics outside the walls of Parliament'.[29] Political journalists would be, if not outlawed, subject to arbitrary imprisonment. Sir Francis Burdett went further than Sheridan, arguing that the arrest of Gale Jones was not just an unconstitutional act, but an example of parliament's exorbitant and unchecked power over the people of Britain. Parliament, he claimed, had the right to arrest people who were guilty of 'obstructing' parliamentary business; but the Commons descended into an arbitrary tyranny when it used its power to arrest people for expressing their opinion. 'Inflated with their high-blown fanciful ideas of Majesty,' Burdett wrote of his fellow MPs in William Cobbett's *Political Register*, 'they think Privilege and Protection beneath their dignity, assume the sword of Prerogative, and lord it over the King and the People.' MPs denied Burdett's accusations and defended their right to arrest and hold people without trial. 'Was it to be supposed that the simple act of arguing on the powers of the Commons was a crime?' the young MP teased them. 'Would not the House endure even the most abstract doubt of their powers!'[30]

But parliament believed that it possessed the privilege of arresting people who insulted its dignity. 'If the House of Commons can commit for no other offence than what are committed in our lobbies and our gallery,' stated an outraged MP, 'we would in fact have no more power … [than] any constable of the night, who has the power to put a drunk man in the watch-house. Is it to be that the powers of the House of Commons extend no further than that of a constable?'[31] The majority of MPs agreed. Not only could they arrest Gale Jones for mocking them, but they were also justified in voting Burdett's immediate arrest on the charge of breaching parliamentary privilege. At the end of an all-night debate, Burdett was committed to the Tower of London by 189 votes to 152 at 7.30 a.m. on Friday, 6 April 1810. The warrant was signed by Charles Abbott, Speaker of the Commons.

The document was dispatched to Burdett's house, 78 Piccadilly, delivered by Francis Coleman, Sergeant-at-Arms. But the criminal was at his Wimbledon retreat, and Coleman had to wait until the next day to make his arrest. Burdett read the warrant when he arrived home. 'If you bring an overwhelming force, I must submit,' he told Coleman; 'but I dare not, from my allegiance to the King, and my respect for his laws, yield a voluntary submission to such a warrant; it is illegal. You must leave my house.'[32]

If the prisoner would not come willingly, there was little the Sergeant-at-Arms could do except call out an armed force. But the delay between the issue of the warrant and the attempted arrest meant that news of parliament's decision spread throughout London. A weekend of rioting followed. On the Friday, 'not withstanding the wind and rain', thousands of men and women surrounded the Tower to stop Burdett being carried there; the government responded by moving cannon up to the main gate and sending an infantry regiment as reinforcement. The Thames was also lined with people lest their MP be transported by barge. When it became clear that Burdett was not going to accept his arrest, the crowd moved to Piccadilly.[33]

The streets and squares of the fashionable quarter were filled with marauding Londoners for three days. Few cabinet ministers' houses were left with window panes intact, and even 10 Downing Street was set upon. According to legend, when Lord Castlereagh's house was attacked, the minister had no option if he did not want to be recognised but to don a greatcoat and stone his own house. The rioters then decided, in time-honoured fashion, to celebrate Burdett's contempt of parliament with an 'illumination' – an occasion when mob rule decreed that every household put a lighted candle or lamp at the windows. As one eye-witness reported,

The mob called out for lights as they went along, as a mark of joy that Sir Francis had not surrendered himself. Consequently all the streets between Oxford Road, Swallow-street, Piccadilly, Park-lane, and down to the House of Commons were illuminated. Those that did not put up lights had their windows broken, but no light saved the windows of obnoxious individuals. St James's and Grosvenor Squares were in blaze. The west end of the town, at a little distance from it, seemed all on fire. . . . Patrols of horse were in the mean time, scouring the streets; the Foot Guards were in readiness . . . [34]

Troops arrived in force on Saturday afternoon, sent by parliament to carry Burdett to his prison. The crowd blocked the entrance to the house, and the soldiers were reinforced by the Guards and cavalry: 'Their appearance excited the most alarming ferment. Groans, boos, shrieks, and every exclamation of contempt and indignation, were thundered forth from all quarters. These expressions were succeeded by more dangerous symptoms, and showers of stones were hurled at the guards, with vengeful fury, from the populace, whose irritation seemed to increase every moment . . . [35]

London came under a heavy garrison. Regiments poured in from surrounding districts; Portman, Berkeley, Hanover and Soho Squares and Lincoln's Inn Fields were defended with cannon and howitzers – an arc of firepower ringing west London. A battery of sixteen guns was stationed in Green Park, aimed at Burdett's house. Throughout the night cavalry chased the crowds down streets and alleys; the rioters responded by erecting barricades to prevent a cavalry charge, and pelted the troops with fistfuls of stones.[36]

On Sunday morning a stream of people left the City and marched down Fleet Street and the Strand towards the West End. Burdett played up to his audience, going for his daily ride amidst the fighting, and attended the opera in the evening. Lord Cochrane and the

Westminster Committee went to his house to discuss how Burdett was to be protected. Place requested that the City authorities arrest any one attempting to take Burdett into custody. Cochrane turned up with a barrel of gunpowder and set to work mining the front of the house as a booby trap to repel an invasion. He had to be reminded that he was in Piccadilly, not fighting Napoleon, and that his fellow MP was reluctant to have his home blown to pieces.[37]

Early on Monday morning Burdett was teaching his son the principles of Magna Carta when he looked up and saw a constable peering through the window. This was a surprise to him, notwithstanding his knowledge that parliament had been trying to arrest him for three days, because the window was twenty feet above street level. Whilst the constable perched on a ladder to divert Burdett, soldiers broke into the house through a servant's window on the ground floor. Sir Francis was arrested in the act of reading Magna Carta, a brilliantly contrived climax to a stand against what most Londoners saw as an illegal arrest.[38]

The news spread with amazing rapidity. A huge crowd converged on Minories, to block the passage of the coach taking Burdett to the Tower. The army, however, anticipated them. The route was lined with infantry and the coach was escorted by 600 cavalrymen brandishing their sabres at the crowds. Burdett arrived safely at the Tower, the people kept at bay by a battery of cannon. It was estimated that 50,000 troops had been required to execute parliament's order. As he was taken to his cell, running battles began in the streets between the army and the protesters.[39]

Sir Francis languished in the Tower whilst his case was heard in several courts, culminating in the Lords, which upheld the decision of the lower House. He was freed only when parliament's jurisdiction ended with its prorogation on 22 June.

The Westminster Committee planned a triumphal procession to escort Burdett home. A huge demonstration of public approval for the reformist MP would be an unequivocal message to parliament that its powers would not be tolerated. William Hone was appointed to the committee that organised the celebrations. He and his colleagues realised that their priority was to keep the day peaceful. They needed to prove that crowds were not always violent; dissatisfaction was best expressed in joyous celebration, not with barricades and handfuls of stones. Violence would play into the government's hands; a rampaging mob would be used as evidence that the friends of free speech were dangerous revolutionaries, the destroyers of private property, a disordered mob of anarchists. Hone and his colleagues made the procession as grand as possible; they decorated a coach, had banners made, and published information about the route. They begged the crowds to remain peaceful on the day, even if they were provoked by the military. To that end, they appointed stewards to police the demonstration.

Seemingly all London came out to celebrate the release of their hero. From the Tower to Piccadilly they lined the streets and gathered in windows overlooking the route. Shops were decked in Burdett's trademark blue colours; people sported blue cockades; banners were displayed everywhere proclaiming 'Magna Charta' and 'Hold to the Laws'. The procession was to pass St Paul's Cathedral, go down Ludgate Hill, and along Fleet Street and the Strand. The connexion between Burdett's principled stand and the liberties of the press was explicit; by travelling in splendour along these streets he would pass the myriad print shops and publishers. The crowd was there to welcome their hero, who had stood up to the high-handed parliament; they were also there to affirm their support for a press free from parliamentary control.[40]

The people waited, but Burdett did not appear. As one of the organisers, Hone and his family waited with Lady Augusta Murray on Ludgate Hill for the procession. The MP was eagerly expected to come by in his triumphal coach at any minute. After a while, a rumour circulated that the Champion of the People had left the Tower in disguise, avoided his supporters, and slipped away by boat to his Wimbledon retreat. Hone was indignant at the ingratitude; his greatest day was in ruins. He and his guests pulled off their blue sashes and cockades; Lady Augusta gave hers to Hone's baby boy Alfred to play with.

Burdett later claimed that prison had made him ill, and he wanted to retire home in peace. But his thousands of supporters were disgusted that their reception had been spurned. The richly decorated carriage was pulled through the streets, but it was left empty. The crowds dispersed. 'Public expectation had never been so excited –' commented the *London*

Alfred '– public expectation was never so completely disappointed.'

Hone and his fellow committee members had organised the first peaceful and self-policed public demonstration. They had shown that public protests were not necessarily violent, that the London crowd could be moderate, peaceful and well ordered. Amazingly, given the bloody history of demonstrations in the capital, there was not a single instance of violence or criminal damage. If nothing else, the protest was vindication of grassroots political organisation and showed that the crowd could express dissatisfaction without descending into a destructive rampage. It was a crucial victory for the Westminster reformers – they were just as much the moderates, the defenders of public property as respectable conservatives. The government and its friends in the press had associated 'reform' with the anarchy of the French Revolution; the committee had in July 1810 proved that it could be a respectable and, to use a favourite nineteenth-century expression, a 'polite' cause.

In the same year, Hone's bookshop was closed, and he and John Bone were gazetted as bankrupts. This was a time of economic depression; harvests were ruined by bad weather, the mounting costs of the war added to the tax bill, and the blockade of European trade put the economy into depression. Bookselling was one of the first trades to suffer, and even Sir Richard Phillips, one of the most established bookseller–publishers in London, was forced out of business. Hone managed to get a job as a clerk to a book auctioneer, but his employer was declared bankrupt shortly after. The Hone family returned to Mrs Johnson's home in Lambeth, and William opened a bookshop in Bloomsbury. When this failed, he was appointed to a prestigious post – that of Trade Auctioneer of the London book industry. His auction house was at 45 Ludgate Hill, and he took an office a few hundred yards on the other side of St Paul's Cathedral in Ivy Lane. He moved his family to tiny lodgings in the Old Bailey, their home for the next eight years.

For the next four years Hone presided over the disposal of vast libraries of ancient books in sales that sometimes lasted as long as two weeks. The position of Trade Auctioneer allowed him to indulge his bibliomania and continue to mix with the literary world of London –

the writers, collectors and booksellers who frequented the auction house in search of rare books and manuscripts. He was still a poor man; in 1874 one of his acquaintances remembered that at this time Hone 'wrote for small periodicals, and starved a large family with the scanty proceeds'.[41] Although the family never actually went without food, Hone's income as auctioneer and occasional journalist was never large. By 1812, with a wife and six young children to feed, he could not afford to hazard his meagre savings on political adventures any more. Hone had outgrown the naïve optimism that had encouraged him to risk all on projects like Tranquillity; he was, in his early thirties, a more circumspect man.

3

Hard Truths

. . . the silence of the higher powers is perhaps a worse compliment now-a-days; and when the Attorney General withholds his condemnation, we may turn round and ask whether we have said anything slavish.
Leigh Hunt, 1812[1]

To libel, metaphorically speaking, is *to aim a blow*.
William Hone, *Critical Review*, December 1814

In the early 1810s journalism was increasingly becoming a career which bordered on the illegal. Whilst parliament lashed out against the opinions of Sir Francis Burdett and John Gale Jones, the government revived an active policy of censorship that was to last until the 1820s. In the first eight years of the nineteenth century there were just fourteen *ex officio* informations filed by the Attorney-General against publishers and journalists and just one during the fourteen months in which the Ministry of the Talents held office. Yet between 1809 and 1812 Spencer Perceval and his Attorney-General, Sir Vicary Gibbs, prosecuted forty-two publishers, editors and writers.

When Hone became a Fleet Street editor in 1814, the mode by which the government silenced critical voices was entrenched, and its efficacy proved. Between 1810 and 1814 the most prominent reformist journalists and politicians had suffered severe punishments for venting dissatisfaction with the government. In 1817 Hone was to suffer the same kind of prosecution that had so effectively dealt with William Cobbett, John and Leigh Hunt and Thomas, Lord Cochrane, amongst others. According to the Whig Henry Brougham, Vicary Gibbs punished many more publishers, journalists and hawkers without the need for a trial because 'he harassed his victims by anxiety and delay; he exhausted them by costs'.[2] Those that did come before the Court of the King's Bench had to contend with the most powerful weapon in the government's armoury, Lord Chief Justice Edward Law, first Baron Ellenborough.

At this time, London tobacconists renamed 'Blackguard', a particularly strong and peppery snuff, 'Ellenborough'.[3] The vast success that the government had in punishing its critics owed much to his presence on the judgment seat. He was, according to his biographer, John, Lord Campbell (a junior barrister in the Chief Justice's last years), 'a man of gigantic intellect; he had the advantage of the best education England could bestow'.[4] He was educated at the Charterhouse and then Peterhouse, where his father, the Bishop of Carlisle, was master. The Law family was distinguished for its intelligence; Ellenborough's father was a respected theologian, famous for his tolerance and Whiggism; one of his brothers was Bishop of Bath and Wells, and another Bishop of Elphin; amongst his nephews were an MP and a follower of George Washington. His son became Governor of India and 1st Viscount Southam and Earl of Ellenborough.

As a schoolboy, the judge was remembered as 'a bluff, burly boy, at once moody and good natured, ever ready to inflict a blow or perform an exercise for his schoolfellows'. This description was repeated by his biographers because he had not seemed to have changed much as a sixty-year-old judge. Campbell and his fellow advocates were terrified of the judge's 'prevalent vengeful enthusiasm' combined with a 'bad temper, an arrogance of nature, too great a desire to gain a reputation by dispatch, and an excessive leaning to severity of punishment'.[5]

If a defendant could be shouted down, treated with contempt or twisted into knots by legal sophistry, Ellenborough would not hesitate to exercise his caustic wit. He seemed genuinely delighted to live up to the stereotype of a testy, irascible, short-tempered judge; his performances in court were masterpieces of theatrical performance designed to inspire fear in the accused, and an aura of indisputable authority for a jury: 'He possessed a strong voice, an energetic manner, and all physical requisites for fixing attention and making an impression upon the minds of others.' As he reached the judgment seat before each trial he would begin to breathe heavily, puffing his cheeks in and out, like a boxer approaching the ring: 'You would suppose he was going to snort like a war-horse preparing for battle.'[6]

He was a notorious Regency personality, feared and admired by allies and opponents alike. His brilliant legal arguments were punctuated with withering sarcasm and fierce outbursts of impassioned rage. His 'broad and commanding forehead, his projecting eyebrows, dark and shaggy, his stern black eye', compounded a vituperative manner, hostile style and sharp tongue. Sir James Mackintosh said he spoke 'with the coarse violence of a demagogue' and Leigh Hunt described his face 'dilating with aristocratical enjoyment'. Actors who played stereotyped judges on the stage would latch on to his distinctive Cumbrian accent, aping his pronunciation of the days of the week as 'Sounda', 'Moonda', 'Toozeda', 'Wenzeda', with 'Lunnen' and 'Brummagen' for London and Birmingham. His presence was just as unwelcome in parliament as it was in court; his fellow Lords 'thought that he was not sufficiently refined and polished for their delicate ears'. In the memorable words of Leigh Hunt, Ellenborough's voice was 'meminiscent of mouthful and burly with luxury'.[7]

Ellenborough was compared to the vilest of all Chief Justices, the sadistic Judge Jeffreys. Whilst this may be grossly unfair, Ellenborough did share his predecessor's political bias and willingness to serve as the tool of powerful men. 'Ellenborough's Act' added ten new felonies that carried the death penalty at a time when the statute book was full of minor offences that could be punished by hanging. In court and the Lords he would defend his decisions to execute people who had stolen just five shillings. His partiality was never in doubt, for he held a post in the cabinet whilst judging journalists and politicians who criticised his colleagues. As an undergraduate at Peterhouse, Cambridge, in the late 1760s, he would undoubtedly have encountered William Pitt, a sickly adolescent studying on the other side of Trumpington Street at Pembroke Hall. Both men subsequently became members of Lincoln's Inn, and were called to the bar on the same day. Ellenborough came from a family that was firmly Whig; he, however, sided with the Tories, joining his political allies in fierce attacks on the aristocratic families who were at the heart of the old Whig party. In parliament, Ellenborough made no effort to conceal his hatred for reformists and hostility to free speech. Even the *Quarterly Review*, a Tory publication, censured Ellenborough's 'monstrous attempt to tinge the ermine of justice with the colour of party'.[8]

He was avowedly a political judge, and he was in close partnership with Henry Addington, first Viscount Sidmouth, a former Prime Minister and Home Secretary from 1812 to 1822. 'I am yours,' he wrote to the minister, 'and let the storm blow from what quarter of the hemisphere it may, you shall always find me at your side.'9

Ellenborough had been an active and successful Lord Chief Justice, but he comes into the story of Hone's life in 1810 when he tried William Cobbett for seditious libel. Cobbett was the editor of the *Political Register*, the most important of the reformist papers. It sold 6,000 copies a week – by the standards of the time a remarkably high figure.* He attracted the eye of the public prosecutor when he wrote an article criticising the government for allowing British militiamen to be flogged by Hessian mercenaries. Cobbett, a former soldier who had already exposed abuses in the British army, wrote: 'At the flogging of a man, I have frequently seen seven or eight men fall slap upon the ground, unable to endure the sight, and to hear the cries, without swooning away. These were as stout, hardy, and bold men as anywhere to be found.'

Cobbett argued that by employing foreign mercenaries to coerce British volunteers with a cat-o'-nine-tails, the government had degenerated into a Bonapartist absolutism. 'Well done Lord Castlereagh!' he wrote addressing the Secretary of War. '. . . *Five hundred lashes each*! Aye, that is right! Flog them! flog them! flog them! They deserve a flogging at every meal time.'10

The trial was held before the Chief Justice in June 1810, in the midst of the excitement over Burdett. The Crown Office packed a jury with men it knew had voted for ministerial candidates in the 1807 general election. Sir Vicary Gibbs charged the *Register* with 'imputing tyranny, cruelty, and injustice to the government'; Cobbett rashly decided to defend himself and built his case around parliamentary records which cited MPs' attacks on the ministry for its severity in dealing with the

* By selling 6,000 copies a week, Cobbett was almost certainly the most widely read journalist of the time; the *Morning Post* sold 1,250 daily, and *The Times* not many more. The *Examiner* made a handsome profit for its proprietors with a sale of between 2,000 and 3,000 copies a week. For patterns of distribution, see chapter 8.

militia. He wanted to show the jury that what he had argued was commonplace, reasonable and sanctioned by parliamentary example. Ellenborough ruled his evidence inadmissible. The defendant was unable to answer the firm decrees of the judge. The performance of the most famous journalist in England was a risible failure, and demonstrated the weakness of the press in standing up to the government. Francis Place, who attended Cobbett throughout the trial, wrote:

Cobbett made a long defence, a bad defence, and his delivery of it and his demeanour were even worse than his matter. He was not at all the master of himself, and in some parts where he meant to produce a great effect he produced laughter. So ludicrous was he in one part that the jury, the judge, and the audience all laughed at him. I was thoroughly ashamed of him, and ashamed of myself for being seen with him.[11]

Cobbett was laughed out of court, and Ellenborough dealt with him with the same ease as he would have swatted away a fly. In defending himself, the journalist said that he had written his article in 'haste and passion'; his words represented a personal rage, and, he said, were not intended to rouse people to dissatisfaction. His defence was lame, it struck an inappropriate apologetic note, and many saw it as cowardly. Leigh Hunt wrote in the *Examiner*:

... Mr Cobbett, I think, would have made a more politic, more confidant and more noble defence, had he frankly and fearlessly acknowledged that his object was to excite the public indignation against the present state of things, – not for the purpose of rebellion, – but that the country might grow more and more ardent in the great cause of Reform. A man in such a situation, especially with Mr Cobbett's powers, ought to have one glorious and absorbing consideration before him – the love of truth.[12]

In summing up, Ellenborough used well-calculated and emotive words:

I am bound to declare to you my opinion, which is, that the publication admitted by the Defendant to be sanctioned by him – nay, that he is the author of it – carries to my mind the certainty of conviction that it is a most seditious libel, tending to the most dangerous purposes, by disuniting the army, on which at this most awful crisis the safety of the country so much depends. Gentlemen, you will consider your verdict.[13]

And so they did – for two minutes. The jury reached a unanimous verdict of guilty. Cobbett was sentenced to two years in Newgate and fined £1,000. When he was released he would have to find bail of £3,000 and two sureties of £1,000 each for keeping the peace for seven years. His publishers John Budd and Richard Bragshaw went to gaol for two months, and his printer, T. C. Hansard, for three, with fines amounting to £800. Many more convictions against pressmen followed. Peter Finnerty was sent to Lincoln gaol for reporting that Lord Castlereagh had ordered the flogging of Irish peasants in 1798; it was in vain that the journalist defended himself on the grounds that what he had said was true. Gale Jones was imprisoned for his libel on parliamentary privilege, which had precipitated the Burdett affair. Daniel Lovell of the *Statesman* was found guilty of three counts of seditious libel, sent to prison for three and a half years and fined £1,000 for reporting the conduct of the Guards during the Burdett riots, criticising the treatment of French prisoners of war, and attacking the heavy-handed methods of tax officials. John Drakard followed Finnerty to Lincoln gaol as punishment for an article in the *Stamford News* on military flogging.

In 1809 Jeremy Bentham had written a treatise on the law of libel, which, ironically, he had to suppress from fear of the laws he criticised. In it he commented that the liberty of the press 'has all along maintained a rickety, and maintains a momentary half-existence'.[14] The truth of his assertion was apparent in the subsequent years.

In December 1812, Ellenborough faced a harder task when he tried the *Examiner* newspaper. The Tory *Morning Chronicle* had celebrated the Prince Regent's fiftieth birthday with glowing tributes: 'You are the *Glory of the People* – You are the *Protector of the Arts* – You are the *Maecenas of the Age* – Wherever you appear, you *conquer all hearts*, wipe away tears, excite *desire and love*, and win *beauty* towards you – You breath *eloquence* – You inspire the Graces – You are an *Adonis in Loveliness*.'

Leigh Hunt replied to the *Chronicle*'s extravagant praises in his Sunday newspaper, the *Examiner*:

What person, unacquainted with the true state of the case, would imagine, in reading these astounding eulogies, that the *Glory of the People* was the subject of millions of shrugs and reproaches! . . . That this *Conqueror of Hearts* was the disappointer of hopes! That this *Exciter of Desire* . . . this *Adonis in Loveliness*, was a corpulent gentleman of fifty! In short, that this *delightful, blissful, wise, pleasurable, honourable, virtuous, true,* and *immortal* Prince was a violator of his word, a libertine over head and ears in debt and disgrace, a despiser of domestic ties, the companion of gamblers and demireps, a man who has just closed half a century without one single claim on the gratitude of his country or the respect of posterity . . . These are hard truths; but are they *not* truths?[15]

Charles Lamb had contributed a poem to the *Examiner* the week before:

> Io! Paean! Io! Sing
> To the finny people's King.
> Not a mightier Whale than this
> In the vast Atlantic is;
> Not a fatter fish than he
> Flounders round the polar sea.
> See his blubber – at his gills
> What a world of drink he swills,
> From his trunk, as from a spout,
> Which next moment he pours out.
>
> . . .
>
> By his bulk, and by his size,
> By his oily qualities,
> This (or else my eyesight fails),
> This should be the PRINCE OF WHALES.

In February 1811, George, Prince of Wales, had been declared Regent when his father, George III, succumbed to blindness and senile decline. For the first year of his Regency, George was restricted by parliamentary limitations, and he was bound to retain the Tory ministry headed by Spencer Perceval. The Prince had been close to the Foxite opposition in his youth, and the Whigs saw the Regency as a chance to return to power. He kept his first cabinet waiting whilst he spent an hour before the bust of Charles James Fox, his political mentor. But when the restrictions were lifted, in February 1812, Prince George seemingly abandoned his old friends and confirmed the Tories in power. Leigh Hunt believed that the Tories and their hirelings in the press were flattering the Regent with extravagant praise in a bid to retain power; his article was an attack, not on Prince George, but on the people who misled the Crown with honeyed words.

The *Examiner* had been started in 1808 by the Hunt brothers, when Leigh, its editor and chief leader-writer, was twenty-four. The paper was at the centre of the intellectual network of the reform movement and English letters. Francis Burdett was, Leigh said, its hero. The Hunts were part of a milieu of writers that included Byron, William Hazlitt, Charles Lamb, Samuel Coleridge, William Wordsworth, Percy Shelley and John Keats. From 1813 Hazlitt wrote political essays and his 'Table Talk' for the *Examiner*, and in 1816 Leigh Hunt introduced Keats and Shelley to the reading public in an article called 'Young Poets'. From the outset, the paper was dedicated to arguing the cause of liberal reform: abolition of the slave trade, parliamentary reform, an end to political corruption, and the freedom of the press. The *Examiner* distinguished itself with a literary style that surpassed all other contemporary newspapers. 'As a journalist', Alexander Ireland wrote, 'no man did more than Leigh Hunt . . . to raise the tone of newspaper writing, and to introduce into its keenest controversies a spirit of fairness and tolerance.'[16]

John and Leigh Hunt marked themselves out as the most lucid and intelligent critics of the government; whereas many so-called 'radicals' were stigmatised as ill educated ruffians, the *Examiner* dignified the movement with learned, animated articles and the glamour of the London literati. From its foundation, the *Examiner* achieved sales greater than those of the established daily papers such as the *Times* or *Courier*, making it the foremost advocate of liberal opinion in Britain.* The government had tried unsuccessfully to punish the Hunts on several occasions since their paper first appeared. Their barrister, Henry Brougham, a Whig and future Lord Chancellor, had them acquitted on a charge of seditious libel for raising the flogging issue, despite

---

* Leigh Hunt wrote in November 1808: 'The paper gets on gloriously indeed: our regular sale is now two thousand two hundred, and by Christmas, or a few weeks after, I have little doubt we shall be three.'

Ellenborough's biased pronouncements from the judgment seat. But in 1812 the Attorney-General was confident enough to renew the attack on the press by filing charges against John and Leigh as proprietors of the *Examiner* for a libel on the Prince Regent.

On Sunday, 6 December, three days before the trial, Leigh Hunt wrote an open letter to Lord Ellenborough. It was an abuse of judicial authority, Leigh wrote, for Ellenborough to try the *Examiner*. As a Privy Councillor and avowed hater of reformists and the free press, Ellenborough would be biased in favour of the prosecution.[*] And added to his unconcealed partiality, the judge was 'proverbial for an overbearing temper'. He dominated the court with his fierce manner; barristers would be silenced and the jury bullied into giving a verdict favourable to the government. Leigh told him in the letter: 'you are in the habit of evincing that species of temper, which is familiarly termed passionate, and which is incompatible with the very nature of judgement.'[17]

The trial came to pass as Leigh had predicted. The Hunts were ably defended by Henry Brougham, who had recently and unsuccessfully contested the parliamentary seat at Liverpool against the Pittite former Foreign Secretary George Canning. But the trial was flawed from the outset; it was alleged that at least five jurors were government employees. And, as usual, Ellenborough acted as though he was leading the prosecution rather than administering impartial justice; he interrupted Brougham's speeches frequently and aggressively.

But however much Ellenborough frustrated Brougham's defence, the outcome of the trial turned on the judge's charge to the jury at the end of the day. When he came to do so, Ellenborough had worked himself up into a passionate fury. He aimed to use his powers of persuasion to obtain the verdict the government wanted. Throughout his speech, he referred to the Hunts as 'libellers' as if they had already been found guilty, and he repeated words like 'law' and 'libel' in a vague and general sense, without much legal argument, trusting that his authority as Lord Chief Justice would be enough to give the jury the impression that

---

[*] Lord Ellenborough was not in fact a Privy Councillor (although he had been a cabinet minister), and Leigh Hunt apologised for his mistake in the following week's *Examiner*; he did not recant his opinion that the judge was biased.

his personal interpretation was legally correct. It had the same effect as a judge in a murder trial would have if he referred to the accused as 'the murderer' throughout the case.

He told the jury that it was up to them to say '[w]hether we are to live under the dominion of libellers, or under the control and government of the law'. It was clear from his argument that the truth did not matter as regarded Leigh's article. Brougham offered proof that the Regent was indeed a 'corpulent man of fifty', an adulterer, a friend of 'gamblers and demireps'. But Ellenborough dismissed the defence as irrelevant: the Regent might well be all these things, but that was not the point. He told the jury that men in high office must have immunity from criticism, or else government would become impossible and rulers hated: 'the higher the character, the more calumnious and degrading the imputation'. The trial of the *Examiner* was of greater significance than the mere words Leigh had used; the jurors were charged with deciding an important precedent for the press in general. If journalists could ridicule and bring into contempt the great men of the state, the jurors would live to see the 'general wrack of the community' and a 'disordered state of the world'.

'Gentlemen,' Ellenborough told the jury, 'if you think society can stand with the allowance of the unlimited liberty of libel, say so by your verdict.' Ellenborough concluded his impassioned harangue, saying of Hunt's article: 'I feel it my duty to pronounce it, a foul, atrocious, and malignant libel.' The Ellenborough touch was effective, and the jury returned a verdict of guilty after the shortest possible discussion.[18]

On 29 January 1813 the painter Benjamin Robert Haydon dined with Leigh: 'We talked of his approaching imprisonment,' Haydon recorded. 'He said it would be a great pleasure to him to be sent to Newgate, because he should be in the midst of his friends – and then we both laughed heartily . . .' On 3 February the Hunts attended court to hear their sentence: two years in prison and a fine of £500 each, and sureties of £500 upon release. 'My brother and myself instinctively pressed each other's arm,' Leigh remembered. 'It was a heavy blow; but the pressure that acknowledged it, encouraged the resolution to bear it; and I do not believe either of us interchanged a word afterwards on the subject.' They were taken off in Hackney carriages, Leigh to Horsemonger Lane prison in Surrey and John to Coldbath Fields in Clerkenwell.

At the end of 1812 the liberty allowed the press had been decided in Ellenborough's court. It was criminal to express an opinion that flogging soldiers was cruel. The mere reporting of the Prince Regent's corpulence and political apostasy was an offence punishable by fine and imprisonment. The Hunts survived their imprisonment in some degree of luxury. Charles Lamb said that Leigh's cell surpassed any scene of a fairy tale. The ceiling was painted with blue sky and clouds, the walls covered with trellises of roses, and the windows furnished with Venetian blinds. Hunt was surrounded by his books, his busts, and even had a pianoforte. He met Byron and Hazlitt for the first time in Horsemonger Lane, and entertained a constant stream of writers and artists. His gaolers were in awe of their prisoner and his famous visitors. John Hunt charmed the governor of Coldbath Fields, and was allowed free access of his garden.

The *Examiner* continued to appear every Sunday. But if the Hunts were permitted privileges and weathered their incarceration with ease, other writers could not expect such lenient terms. Publishing and journalism were expensive and poorly rewarded trades. Cobbett's fines of £5,000 amounted to more than most journalists would earn in a career; £500 would be more than enough to ruin a small business. Leigh and John had enough money to rent handsome apartments in their gaols, an opportunity not open to most other writers and publishers. The Hunts were not representative of the wider press; their imprisonments and fines did not serve as vindictive punishments but provided a powerful deterrent to all other journalists. Charles Knight wrote in his memoirs that the cases of Cobbett, the Hunts, and others at this time demonstrated that 'the uncertainty of trial by jury in matters of political libel could give a public writer no great confidence that incautious words, without evil intentions, might not be visited with punishment such as is earned by atrocious crimes'.[19]

Few could pretend that the felonies committed by Burdett, Cobbett and the Hunts were high crimes that warranted punishment – theirs were opinions shared by many Britons. Yet it appeared that moderation, humour, personal belief and statements of fact could have no immunity from severe repression. Well might Jeremy Bentham say, 'By law there exists no more liberty of the press in England than in Morocco.'[20]

Hone was appointed editor of the *Critical Review, or the Annals of Literature* on 1 January 1814. Quite why a little known philanthropist, book dealer and sometime political publisher was considered an adequate editor of an international literary paper, which had once been edited by Tobias Smollett and which Dr Johnson commended to a young George III, will remain a mystery. That Hone was an avid reader, familiar with a vast range of literature from his fourteen-year career as a bookseller and trade auctioneer, is without a doubt true. But an intimacy with books does not qualify an indigent publisher and would-be journalist for a job of reviewer, let alone literary editor.

Yet his talent had been recognised by someone highly placed in the literary world, and he was given 'sole and entire management' of the paper at £75 a year.[21] Just before he took up the post, however, Hone instigated a fresh reform campaign:

I was in a Coffee Shop in Fleet Street, sitting next to Alderman Waithman, when James Bevans came in. We talked on the subject of mad-houses; I of the abuses and cruelty to the patients, and he (an architect) of the buildings.

. . . I proposed a committee to investigate, and wrote to Edward Wakefield in the country, who came to London. Subsequently, at a meeting held at Fry's in the Poultry, Basil Montague [*sic*] proposed that we should not bring matters to an issue until a sub-committee should have inspected the Lunatic Asylums, and named to that intent Edward Wakefield, William Hone, and James Bevans. Thus self-authorised, we knocked at the door of one Asylum after another.[22]

As in the period 1800–1806, the reformers were in eclipse, harried by the law and ignored by the public. Once again they sought new areas of activity. Hone and his friends planned to raise £100,000 to build a new lunatic asylum in London – another quixotic plan, but one that was to prove far more successful than Tranquillity. The foundation of the asylum reform movement shows the kind of circles within which Hone was now operating. Robert Waithman, the Ludgate draper, sat on the London Council; in 1823 he was to be a popular Lord Mayor.

Throughout his political career Waithman was a key figure amongst the reformists, a close connexion of Burdett, and one of the most famous politicians in London.

Edward Wakefield was also a notable figure. Originally a farmer from Romford, he had devoted his life to philanthropic projects. He busied himself with private education schemes, and in 1813 had published a study of conditions in Ireland, which attracted widespread praise. He was one of the most active of philanthropists at this time, and had con-siderable status with politicians and reformers.

Basil Montagu (not Montague as Hone would have had it) was an equally significant associate. Montagu, a barrister and essayist, was established in the *Examiner* circle; in this same year he included Lamb's famous essay 'Confessions of a Drunkard' in his book *Some enquiries into the effects of Fermented Liquors*. A well-known practical joker, he would naturally get on with Hone, who had a reputation as an ingenious impersonator of politicians in tavern debates. They would also have plenty to talk about: Montagu had dedicated his career to writing books about the iniquities of the laws treating bankrupts. Wakefield, Waithman and Montagu were important and famous figures in social and political reform, and close friends of Lamb, Hazlitt, Hunt, and others within the *Examiner* circle. To sit on a committee with them was an undoubted privilege and signalled a change in Hone's fortunes. He was given the responsibility of drafting a letter to Wakefield, sug-gesting their plans and soliciting his help; the letter was the impetus for an investigation which was to last for a year and a half.

Wakefield wrote back to Hone on 28 December 1813: '... the maxim of Locke that "he that will not stir till he infallibly knows the business he goes about will succeed, will have little else to do but to sit still and perish" is always apparent in my mind when excellent plans for amelio-rating the condition of mankind are afloat.' He immediately planned to give up his job as land agent in Bury St Edmunds and come to London to involve himself in the scheme, and recommended Hone as secretary because he was the man who 'would best discharge the duties of an important office. I am inclined to think that you are particularly adapt-ed for it.' Two days later he upgraded Hone to 'Steward' or 'Governor' of the proposed asylum. The committee was announced at a public meeting on 6 March 1814 at the City of London Tavern, comprising the leading London reformers at this time: Hone, Wakefield, Sir Richard Phillips, James Mill, Basil Montagu, William Allen (a chemist and prominent philanthropist) and Francis Place. Over the next year they would complete a thorough investigation into the conditions in mad-houses in their quest to found a new kind of asylum. Hone used his new position as editor of the *Critical Review* to publicise the campaign.[23]

The committee found London asylums to be in a disgraceful state of decay; there were no panes of glass in many of the windows, no ventila-tion, and no provision for outdoor exercise. Wakefield described their initial inspection: 'We first proceeded to the women's galleries: one of the side rooms contained about ten patients, each chained by one arm or leg to the wall; the chain allowing them merely to stand up by the bench fixed to the wall, or to sit down on it. The nakedness of each patient was covered by a blanket gown only . . .' One woman, a Mrs Fenwick, was educated and fluent in several languages and appeared harmless, but she had been left naked and chained to the wall for years. Wakefield could 'hardly imagine a human being in a more degraded and brutalising situation than that in which [we] found this female'.

Hone and Wakefield seized upon the example of one James Norris, an American who was chained by his arms and neck to a wall in the New Bethlem Hospital (Bedlam), but appeared to be quite harmless.[*] He was shackled in such a way that he could only lie down on his back or stand against the wall. These were the only positions he could be in; he could not even turn on to his side. Worse still, his 'keeper' – the asy-lum's attendant – could draw in his chains from the adjoining room whenever he felt like it, forcing Norris upright against the wall. The poor man had lived like this for twelve years, during which time he had become so emaciated that the handcuffs were too large for his wasted muscles:

This person [Wakefield reported], we were informed, was mostly lying down, and that as it was inconvenient to raise himself and stand upright, he very sel-dom did so; that he read a great deal of books of all kinds, history, lives, or any

---

[*] Norris's Christian name was variously given as James and William in the press and by the committee, a telling example of how personal identity was lost in the chaos of Bedlam Hospital.

thing that the keepers could get him; the newspapers every day, and conversed perfectly coherent on the passing topic and events of the war, in which he felt a particular interest. On each day that we saw him he discoursed coolly, and gave rational and deliberate answers to different questions put to him.

The committee visited him on several occasions, bringing MPs and other public men to observe this innocuous fellow, who was more inclined to read newspapers and books than lash out in deranged fury. Hone and Wakefield visited him for the first time on 25 April 1814. In May, the management ordered that Norris be released from his chains. The managers rather weakly claimed that they were going to release Norris anyway, but it was clear that the moment Bedlam was investigated properly for the first time abuses were covered up and conditions improved. At the same time Mrs Fenwick was released from her chains and given proper clothing. She was, Hone and Wakefield found, 'an entirely different creature since she had been treated like a human being'. People dumped their deranged relations in asylums and thought no more of them. Who would protect them? The committee took it upon themselves to defend the most neglected people in early nineteenth-century society. The Bedlam administration was thrown into a frenzy of self-justification and cover-up in response to Hone and Wakefield's campaign.

In the letter that he sent to Wakefield which set in motion the investigation, Hone said that the committee should be sensitive to different types of mental illness; rather than shackling all inmates, asylum attendants should take account of the various mental conditions of their patients. Whilst some dangerous lunatics might need to be shackled, many more, like the placid James Norris, should be treated in ways most suitable to their condition. As Hone wrote in the *Critical Review*, 'insanity' was 'a disease admitting of no definition, presenting symptoms and appearances as various almost as its numerous victims'; mankind, the reformers demanded, should find a more sympathetic way of treating the insane than merely deploying coercion and restraint indiscriminately.[24] The committee put together a report and presented it to a select committee of the House of Commons, recommending a new type of asylum, designed by Bevans, which would discriminate between different types of malady in the treatment of its patients and provide adequate sanitation, food and places of recreation for the inmates. The committee was chaired by the supporter of Tranquillity, George Rose, who knew at first hand the amateurish treatment of the mentally ill from the time he had spent with George III.

Meticulously researched, the report was devastating in its exposure of abuses and maladministration in asylums. In the words of Roy Porter, it was a 'momentous pivotal point' in the history of parliamentary inquiry, which 'brought to light and preserved for posterity a non-pareil moral and physical panorama of the Georgian madhouse world and its *misérables*'.[25] James Norris was referred to throughout the hearings as an example of the way in which even the most peaceful inmate was treated. Restraining anyone with the slightest inclination to mental instability had become orthodox practice, a fate meted out to George III during his periods of derangement. The committee made a strong case that this unthinking policy was both inhumane and medically unsound, and none knew this better than Rose, who had witnessed the King's humiliation at the incompetent hands of 'mad doctors'. The committee's devastating revelations were unanswerable, and forced the resignation of senior staff at Bedlam. Although full-scale reform would not come for another twenty years, it was an unprecedented achievement for a self-appointed committee, a vindication of public action.

By the time the report burst upon the political world, Hone had been jettisoned by Wakefield, who assumed full credit for the work. 'The evidence of Wakefield is correct, and was founded on our joint notes,' Hone said of the parliamentary select committee. 'I was unable to appear, myself, owing to a severe attack of quinsy and a prolonged illness which increased my pecuniary difficulties; and he never mentioned my name in connexion with the report.'[26] Notwithstanding the ingratitude he was shown, Hone would add fire to the campaign by publishing the picture of Norris shackled to the wall of his cell which had been displayed as evidence for MPs; it was an important addition to the committee's policy of rousing public indignation by shaming Bedlam as a place of inexcusable cruelty.

Hone could feel justifiably bitter about Wakefield's behaviour; he had produced much of the research that contributed to the unprecedented success of the report. In his evidence, Wakefield mentioned the many visits he had made to London asylums; but the only people he mentioned by name were MPs and officials; people like Hone had to put up with the appellation 'other gentlemen'. Yet Hone did not suffer by his rough treatment. He was now a leading figure amongst the most active non-parliamentary politicians in London. Making the government take account of reformist demands depended on a full control of facts, statistics and other empirical evidence. It was not enough to shout loudly about injustice or make sweeping statements in the press. The asylum committee was a success because it was better informed than MPs. Hone learnt his journalistic skills as one of Wakefield's lieutenants at this time; during the next few years he would become the most rigorous of investigative journalists, bringing the same techniques to Fleet Street and the press.

Hone managed to combine his full-time editorial job with the duties of the asylum committee. Perhaps unsurprising given his political ambitions, the *Critical Review*, under Hone's aegis, was transformed from a mildly Whiggish review into an avowedly political paper, an important mouthpiece for Burdett and Cochrane, and virtually an adjunct of the *Examiner*.

The *Review* was a monthly journal with a distribution throughout northern Europe and America.* Each number comprised some hundred pages of long book reviews and notices of forthcoming publications; its format left no room for editorial comment or non-literary content. Hone discharged his duties well, providing scholarly reviews for his readers, but in time the paper came to reflect his personal political opinions. He managed to get round the rules of impartiality by including long quotations from books in favour of reform, leaving few readers any doubt as to the editor's political opinions. Within a few months, regular readers were complaining that the *Review* had become a reformist paper. When it was sold to a new proprietors at the end of 1814 Hone was kept on as editor, but under strict conditions that he restrain his political views.

* The *Critical Review*'s main outlets were in London, Cambridge, Oxford, York, Edinburgh, Dublin, Paris, Hamburg, Amsterdam, Leipzig, Berlin, Riga and St Petersburg, but it could also be bought in bookshops throughout Europe and America.

'Criticism is the touchstone of Genius; and, impartially administered, gives a noble emulation to the pursuits of literature,' the new proprietors grandly announced. They were conscious that they were
custodians of a paper that had once been pre-eminent in literary circles,
but which had been in sorry decline for a number of years. Hone's editorial decisions were to be regulated by a manifesto, which was published in December 1814. He had to be strictly impartial 'for the
Proprietors are uninfluenced by party, on all subjects'. The editor had
to avoid politics and party bias, restricting the articles to those on literature and drama.[27]

But the directions were like a red rag to a bull; never one to accept
authority, Hone made the *Review* his paper entirely, showing his pen-
chant for all things connected to Westminster constituency politics and
Leigh Hunt. Vast portions of the journal were taken up with articles
that had originally been published in the *Examiner*, articles which did
little to meet the requirements of the *Critical Review*, and owed everything to the caprice of the editor. The satirical profile of leading politicians, 'Parliamentary Portraits', which had been serialised in the
Examiner, dominated the *Review* for two months.

During his editorship, the suppression of critical voices by biased
courts continued. At the beginning of the new regime at the paper,
Hone used the *Review* to further the attack on Ellenborough and
defend Lord Cochrane MP from an unjust prison sentence. In 1814,
Thomas Cochrane was arrested on a charge of abetting a stock-market
fraud. In February, Cochrane and his uncle, Andrew Cochrane-
Johnstone (also an MP), had made an enormous profit speculating on
government stock. On Monday, 21 February London had been awash
with rumours that Colonel Du Bourg, aide-de-camp to Lord Cathcart,
Britain's ambassador to the Tsar, had arrived in London bringing news
that Napoleon was dead and the war over. There was a flurry of speculation on the Exchange, and, with the promise of peace, government
stock soared in value. In the afternoon it became clear that the rumours
were unsubstantiated and the stock fell again. But, at that moment, a
coach carrying French officers wearing the white cockade of the
Bourbons came down Lombard Street and passed the Exchange. Here
was proof that Napoleon was dead or defeated and Louis XVIII

restored to the French throne. The market picked up, only to crash in the evening when the rumours were finally scotched. Cochrane-Johnstone and his associate Richard Butt had bought stock on credit at its lowest value, and sold it when the market reached its temporary market peak. They made a considerable fortune that day. It seemed that they knew that the surge in the price of stock was an aberration based on a lie, and had advance warning about the optimum time to sell their investments.[28]

On that day Cochrane had not been at the Exchange, but had visited a factory to inspect the manufacture of a new lamp. When he got home he received an acquaintance, Charles Random de Berenger, a soldier who was on day release from debtors' gaol. He told Cochrane that he wanted to visit Lord Yarmouth in order to obtain an army commission, but he did not want his gaolers to find out he was preparing to flee prison to serve abroad. Cochrane grudgingly lent him a civilian greatcoat and hat to conceal his green sharpshooter uniform. Later, it transpired that it was Berenger who had masqueraded as Colonel Du Bourg, beginning the rumours that had so affected the market. When he was arrested, he was found with banknotes issued by Cochrane-Johnstone, Butt and Lord Cochrane, obviously his pay for perpetrating the fraud. It was further alleged that Cochrane had lent him the hat and coat to conceal the fraudulent Du Bourg uniform so that he could make an easy escape.[29]

Ellenborough presided over the trial of the fraudsters. Although Butt and Cochrane-Johnstone were certainly involved, Lord Cochrane had a strong defence. His broker had been instructed to sell the stock when the market had risen by 1 per cent; this was a long-standing agreement. Had Cochrane known about the plot, he could have sold his investments when the market was it its peak and made a far larger profit. He also explained that his bank notes found in Berenger's possession had originally been given to Richard Butt in settlement of a private debt; Butt must then have paid Berenger for his part in the fraud with these notes. And he presented affidavits from many witnesses affirming that Berenger had come to his house dressed in his green sharpshooter uniform, not the red staff coat of the Du Bourg costume.[30]

It was a good case, but Cochrane foolishly decided to stand trial alongside his obviously guilty uncle; had he stood alone, he would have been able to dismiss the charges against him as trumped-up and malicious. As it was, Ellenborough used every effort to have one of the government's most damaging critics consigned to ignominy and ruin. Campbell wrote that Ellenborough's actions in the trial were 'palpably contrary to the first principles of justice':

The trial coming on before Lord Ellenborough, the noble and learned Judge, being himself persuaded of the guilt of all the defendants, used his best endeavours that they should all be convicted . . . The following day, in summing up, prompted no doubt by the conclusion of his own mind, he laid special emphasis on every circumstance which might raise a suspicion against Lord Cochrane, and elaborately explained away whatever at first sight appeared favourable to the gallant officer. In consequence the Jury found a verdict of GUILTY against all the defendants.[31]

Cochrane was sentenced to a year's imprisonment, a fine of £1,000, and a day in the pillory at the Royal Exchange.* But he never stood in the pillory because the government suddenly abolished that punishment for all crimes bar insubordination and perjury. They had to. Burdett promised to stand alongside his fellow MP. The London crowd would have come out to support their heroes; it would not have been a punishment, but a victory for the Westminster MPs.

Cochrane was confined to the King's Bench Prison and expelled from the House of Commons. His constituents, knowing injustice had been done, re-elected him, but their decision was declared void because the MP was serving a prison sentence. In December 1814, the Captain wrote a letter to Lord Ellenborough complaining of the judge's 'unnecessary interferences' and arguing the trial had been mismanaged, and most of the evidence for the defence suppressed. It was a one of the most systematic critiques of Ellenborough's flaws as a judge, and one of the few complaints against him that contained substantiated instances of deliberate suppression or misrepresentation of the defence's evi-

---

* Napoleon, no doubt bemused that one of his greatest enemies was being punished by the British, said of his sentence: 'Such a man should not be made to suffer so degrading a punishment.'

dence. The judge had prevented some of the defence witness's affidavits being heard, and he had refused to hold a retrial when new evidence was presented to him; Cochrane highlighted all instances when
Ellenborough exercised his considerable influence in securing a verdict
of guilty. This letter appeared in the pages of Hone's *Critical Review*, a
glaring dissent from the proprietors' promise of impartiality. Hone
introduced the letter, stating the reasons for exposing Ellenborough's
misconduct and giving Cochrane's interpretation of the trial: '. . . happy
should we be, if our good wishes, supported by the manifestation of his
Lordship's innocence, could restore him to that rank, in EVERY
Englishman's heart, which is the proved reward for gallant merit.'[32]

Hone continued to be one of Cochrane's greatest supporters and
publicists. A few months after the letter was published, the former MP
escaped from prison, and was apprehended as he entered the House of
Commons to take his seat as MP for Westminster. He was returned to
prison, and released on 3 July at the end of his year's imprisonment; he
went straight to parliament, where he was allowed to take his seat. It was
not until August 1816 that he was tried at the Surrey Assizes in
Guildford for escaping from prison. Present at the trial were Burdett,
the Westminster reformists, and Hone, who reported the case in a
book, *Lord Cochrane's Reasons for Escaping; The Trial of Lord
Cochrane*, for the MP's loyal constituents who had not been able to
travel out to Guildford. 'The Civil Court was crowded to excess at an
early hour', Hone wrote, 'with the nobility, gentry, and respectable
inhabitants of the county, in expectation of hearing his Lordship conduct his defence in person.' Cochrane explained that he escaped
because, as an MP freely chosen by the voters of Westminster, he had
immunity from imprisonment: 'I therefore effected my liberation with
the sole view of assuming my seat in Parliament, and of reminding that
Assembly, that *their* sentence of expulsion had been reversed by the
People . . .'[33]

Upon capture, he was confined in the strong room of the King's
Bench Prison for three weeks, during which time he became seriously
ill. This rough treatment, he told the jury, had been punishment
enough for the escape. The jury found him guilty of escaping, but
demanded that Cochrane be shown mercy. The MP shouted at them, 'I

want justice, not mercy!' The judge ignored the jury's request for leniency, and fined Cochrane £100.[34] He refused to pay, and it was left to Hone to raise the money by advertising a subscription from the people of Westminster. It was an act of generosity Cochrane would never forget.

The *Critical Review* continued to be a literary magazine, notwithstanding Hone's occasional bias towards the *Examiner* and the Burdettites; there were lengthy reviews of all the latest books. But Hone's political ambitions began to show. His stint as editor coincided with one of the most exciting times of recent years: the end of the war, and the exile of Napoleon to Elba. The restoration of Napoleon and the war that followed were yet to happen, and Hone was editor at the beginning of the first substantial period of peace for over ten years. He joined the reformists in demanding that the wartime system of finance be dismantled. During the conflict, the government had introduced income tax and customs duties. The circumstances of war had placed a high financial burden upon the people and augmented the power of the Crown with a large standing army and an unofficial army of tax assessors and collectors. The 'Inquisitorial nature' of war taxes, a reviewer in Hone's paper wrote, were 'utterly abhorrent to the genuine freedom which is emphatically the birth-right of ENGLISHMEN'.[35] The temporary end of hostilities in 1813 had brought little relief; the coercive mechanisms of the state were kept in place, taxes remained high to the benefit of none but the government's friends. Consequently the over-taxed people suffered poverty and bankruptcy.

The *Critical Review* talked of a 'frightful spectacle of national anticlimax' with the ending of war; calamities continued owing to the 'peculiar character of the late war – to unforeseen contingencies – or to the impolicy of our governmental councils'. It was 'justice to demand at the conclusion of the war, the immediate abolition of all taxes instituted for its support' and 'the dismission of a numerous body of governmental dependants' who were bleeding the country dry.

But the government stuck to its system of finance, dismissing neither its cadre of tax-gathering agents nor the large standing army. The duties on imported food kept food prices high, and once again the London crowd was angry. In March 1815 Hone happened to be in Old Burlington Street in Piccadilly when there just happened to be a crowd protesting against the artificially high food prices outside the home of Frederick Robinson, a ministerial MP. It is unlikely that Hone was just passing the protest; he was a journalist with an instinct for a story. As he watched, the protesters were suddenly shot at by soldiers secretly stationed in the MP's house. Two of them, a nineteen-year-old midshipman called Edward Vyse and Jane Watson, a twice-widowed twenty-six-year-old woman, were killed.

Hone gave evidence at the inquests into the deaths of Vyse and Watson. When he was called to the witness stand he was given a blank document to sign. 'I hesitated,' he later reported, 'and expressed a wish to know for what purpose a *blank* paper was given me to sign.'

'You will sign this,' the Coroner said, 'and we will put a Copy of your Deposition upon it afterwards.'

'I am very sorry, but I cannot sign a *blank* paper. It is impossible, and,' he continued, turning to the jury, 'to say the least of it, it is irregular.' The court acceded to his wishes, and made him stay in court so that he might read the transcript before putting his name to it.[36]

In his evidence, Hone told the court that he had come across a crowd of forty people in Old Burlington Street on the night in question. The so-called 'riot' comprised mainly young boys: 'They seemed to be what is vulgarly called "larking".' These excited youths had not made 'a general attack upon the house', although a few stones had been thrown at the windows. Hone later reported that there were many other witnesses in court who would have affirmed that the shooting was unprovoked. These people were not called to give evidence.[37]

The two inquests marked Hone's maturity as a journalist and reporter. He was rightly suspicious of the Coroner's treatment of the evidence; the official account of Ellenborough's summing up in the Cochrane trial had been altered to tone down his more outrageous utterances. It was common for courts to doctor the judicial record in politically sensitive trials; unwelcome testimonies could be made to look innocuous, instances of bias edited into moderate legal reasoning. When it was published in the newspapers, the public would read a version of events totally different from the case the jury actually heard.

Hone decided to stay in court with his notebook open on his lap: 'I exerted myself to report every syllable that was uttered in evidence, with scrupulous fidelity.'[38]

Hone published verbatim reports of the inquests within a few days of each hearing in two books: *Circumstantial Report on the Extraordinary Evidence and Proceedings before the Coroner's Inquest on the body of Edward Vyse* (an account of the riots, the shooting, and subsequent inquest, with a diagram of Vyse's head wounds) and *Report at large of the Coroner's Inquest on Jane Watson*. It was rare for a journalist to report a coroner's court; if such things were newsworthy, the papers would republish the official version with little comment. Hone had been involved at every stage of the story, present at the events, and a key witness at the inquests. He was the only journalist to spot the political importance of the trial as another example of the government's desire to stifle criticism, except that this time it had lashed out at protesters who were breaking no law, like Vyse, or Watson, an innocent bystander. It was an important moment in Hone's journalistic career, the first of his exposures of partial and tainted justice. Journalists, he believed, should not accept the findings of courts, even if it was a minor coroner's court, without testing the official account.

Unlike the attacks made by journalists such as Cobbett or the Hunts, Hone, at this stage of his career, aimed to demand reform by marshalling irrefutable evidence, exposing shortcomings and shameful abuses, and presenting an unanswerable case that could not be prosecuted for libel. The system was to be attacked and weakened, not with the niceties of constitutional debate, but by delving into the margins of society: the victims of the Poor Laws, lunatic asylums, coroners' courts, and instances of injustice in the daily lives of ordinary people. Even this seemingly irrelevant case, which few journalists were interested in reporting, had produced a jury which condemned the government in the strongest terms. Its verdict was an unequivocal statement of public opprobrium at heavy-handed measures: 'Wilful Murder'.

Hone had the audacity to review his book on the Vyse inquest in the *Critical Review*. The article was overtly political, and included the jury's recommendation to the coroner which had been rejected and expurgated from the official account of the trial: 'The verdict was accompanied by the following strong memorandum: "It is the opinion of the jury, that the military acted improperly, by entering the house of Mr Robinson without proper authority to do so. It is our opinion, from the evidence adduced that there was no necessity for firing with shot at the time Mr Edward Vyse met his death. It is our opinion that the firing was unconstitutional.'"[39]

Hone's conversion of the *Critical Review* into a mouthpiece for his own and his friends' political programmes was contentious in itself. The inclusion of the Vyse case signalled an end to any pretended neutrality. On the last page of the May 1815 edition, Hone, at the behest of the proprietors, wrote: 'Memorandum: The Editor has the honour to announce his retirement with the close of the present number, on account of THE POLITICAL CHARACTER lately assumed by this Review. He will be succeeded by superior talent.'[40]

Hone could afford to take a light-hearted view of his enforced resignation and turn it into a joke. He had been utterly contemptuous of his proprietors' editorial directions, and it is a wonder that he lasted so long in the job. The experience of editing an international review had set him up as a journalist. He had marked his arrival in Fleet Street with the success of the lunatic reform campaign; his books on the Vyse and Watson cases put him in the front rank of London journalists; the network of contacts he had made marked a new phase in his career. With a reputation as a pioneering reformer and, at last, some money in his pocket, Hone set up a bookshop and publishing business at 55, Fleet Street. From this tiny shop, which had a frontage just three feet across, he was to write and publish 130 books and pamphlets and edit two national newspapers within two and a half years.

4

An Elaborate Investigation
The Case of Eliza Fenning

...if human life be worth protection, or laws are to be considered as the equal right of the poor and the rich, it is one that sensibly touches the national interest and the national honour.

William Hone

I never was more convinced of anything in my life than of the girl's innocence.

Charles Dickens, 1867

'I was going down Newgate Street on some business of my own,' William Hone remembered of a day in July 1815:

I got into an immense crowd that carried me along with them against my will; at length I found myself under the gallows where Eliza Fenning was to be hanged. I had the greatest horror of witnessing an execution, and of this particular execution, a young girl of whose guilt I had grave doubts. But I could not help myself; I was closely wedged in; she was brought out. I saw nothing but I heard all. I heard her protesting her innocence – I heard the prayer – I could hear no more. I stopped my ears, and knew nothing else till I found myself in the dispersing crowd, and far from that dreadful spot.

The story of the terrible injustice Eliza Fenning suffered was one of Hone's greatest journalistic triumphs. The claim that his involvement was accidental was either self-deprecating modesty or a sign that it in later life he was deeply ashamed at having once sought out such scenes to make a story. There were over 50,000 people present at the execution; to be one of a few close enough to have heard her last words suggests some premeditation. Certainly, at the time, Hone was less reticent about his participation in great events. The barbarous execution and the rumours prevalent in London that the girl was innocent roused his two most pronounced instincts: compassion and revolt at injustice.

He visited a friend on the day of the execution: 'I made my way to the house of a bookseller with whom I was very intimate; I asked him for a glass of water; I sat down and told him where I had been, and that the people were saying the unhappy girl had "died with a lie in her mouth".'

'Friend Hone,' the bookseller said, 'she is with her Almighty Father; I have visited her in prison, so have many of my friends, and we are satisfied of her innocence.'

'Why, then, was she executed?' Hone asked.

'We made every possible exertion to save her life', replied his host, 'but we were not listened to'.

'The public must be roused about it.'

'You are the man to do it,' his friend said, 'and I will print what you write.'[1]

When Hone took up it up, the case was already preoccupying the London press. Eliza Fenning had been tried and executed for attempted murder, but many shared Hone's belief that she was innocent. He could not claim to have discovered the story, but he spent several months investigating the crime, Fenning's trial and the government's subsequent attempts to cover up any hint of injustice. Before his investigation was published in November 1815, the press was inundated with rumour, speculation and, in some cases, downright falsehoods about the case. Hone's *Elaborate Investigation into the Mysterious Case of Eliza Fenning* was a thorough analysis and examination of the evidence, the handling of the trial, and the scandalous interference on the part of ministers, judges and journalists to ensure Fenning's execution. The findings were sensational, and the questions Hone asked of the probity of English justice wholly unprecedented; there had never been a comparable exposé of injustice.

The case seemed to be a typical London criminal trial. In February 1815 Eliza Fenning had been engaged as a cook by Orlibar Turner, a Chancery Lane legal stationer, in a house he shared with his wife Margaret, son Robert and daughter-in-law Charlotte. Eliza was a twenty-year-old girl who had been in service elsewhere in London since she was fourteen years old. On 21 March she cooked two dinners, one for the Turners and another for the rest of the household, two seventeen-

year-old apprentices named Roger Gadsden and Thomas King, and
Sarah Peer, the maid. The Turners, except Margaret, who was in
Lambeth, sat down for dinner at three o'clock; the meal included six
yeast dumplings, which were flat and burnt. But that was not all that
was wrong with them. 'I found myself affected in a few minutes after I
had eaten,' Charlotte Turner said when she gave evidence at the Old
Bailey a few weeks later. 'I did not eat a quarter of a dumpling. I felt
myself very faint, and an excruciating pain; an extreme violent pain,
which increased every minute. It came so bad, I was obliged to leave the
table. I went upstairs.'

Robert was the next to leave the table. 'I followed him very shortly,'
Orlibar affirmed during the trial. 'I had gone into my parlour below. I
came into the passage at the foot of the stairs; he told me that he had
been very sick, and had brought up his dinner. I said I thought it very
extraordinary. I was taken ill myself in less than three minutes afterwards. The effect was so violent, I had hardly time to go into my back
yard before my dinner came up. I felt considerable heat across my
stomach and chest, and pain.'

Two local surgeons, John Marshall and Henry Olgilvy, attended the
family. The Turners and Roger Gadsden, the four people suffering terrible pain, eventually recovered. Marshall investigated the kitchen, and
in the dumpling pan found the residue of a white powder. This he identified as arsenic. The cook was taken into custody without further
thought.

'Eliza Fenning was indicted', read the Old Bailey Session Report,
'for that she, on the 21st day of March, feloniously and unlawfully did
administer to, and cause to be administered to Orlibar Turner, Robert
Gregson Turner, and Charlotte Turner his [i.e. Robert's] wife, certain
deadly poison (to wit arsenick), with intent that said persons to kill and
murder.'

The trial was held before the Recorder of London, Sir John ('Black
Jack') Silvester at the Old Bailey on 11 April. Charlotte Turner, called as
the first witness, described the immediate and painful symptoms that
the entire family had experienced upon eating the dumplings. She went
on to tell the court that a few weeks before the poisoning she caught
Fenning in the act of seducing the two apprentices: 'I observed her one

night go into the young men's room partly undressed.' The next morning she punished Eliza, and gave her notice. The maid, Sarah Peer, affirmed that the prisoner had vowed vengeance on Charlotte, who had dismissed her without references. The Turners and their servants confirmed that their cook had been noticeably sullen and querulous since she had been given notice.

For two weeks before the poisoning, Eliza had nagged Charlotte; she wanted to prepare yeast dumplings for dinner, but the Turners were not convinced that she was competent enough to make them properly. On 21 March, Fenning acted on her own initiative, and ordered some yeast and set about preparing dumplings. Charlotte and Sarah Peer testified that she had been alone in the kitchen all afternoon without leaving.

Orlibar Turner told the jury that his shop was plagued by rats and mice, so he kept a packet marked 'Arsenick, deadly poison' in a drawer in his office. Eliza, he said, opened this drawer every day to collect scraps of paper to kindle the household fires. The poison had gone missing on 7 March. The apprentice Roger Gadsden avowed that Eliza had warned him not to eat the dumplings on the twenty-first; he ignored her, only to find himself convulsed in the same agonising pain as his employers. While the Turners and Gadsden suffered the full effects of the arsenic, Eliza watched them, according to Charlotte giving 'not the smallest' assistance; Orlibar told the jury, 'she did not appear concerned at the situation'.

After hearing the evidence given by the Turners and their household, the court heard expert testimony from the surgeon, John Marshall. He told them that he had discovered a white powder in the dumpling pan. When he investigated the powder, he found that it corroded his knife and tarnished it black, signifying that it was arsenic. He added that the reason the dumplings had not risen when Eliza put them before the kitchen fire was that they had been contaminated by poison.

According to the official report of the trial, Eliza Fenning was proven to have a clear motive for the crime; she had premeditated it since 7 March, when the arsenic had gone missing; and she showed neither surprise nor concern when the dinner she had cooked produced its terrible effects. She had been alone in the kitchen all afternoon, so she was the only person who could have come into contact with the dumplings before they were placed on the table. The trial report contained Fenning's paltry defence; she had not called any witnesses, had no alibi, nor could she reasonably deny any of the charges against her. Eliza, when she came to speak, only managed a few garbled sentences. 'I am truly innocent of the whole charge,' she exclaimed. 'I am innocent; indeed I am! I liked my place. I was very comfortable.'

The evidence was overwhelming, the judge convinced by the prosecution, and the jury showed no hesitation in giving a guilty verdict. Eliza Fenning was sentenced to hang. The Sessions Report, the indubitable testimony of the cook's guilt, was sent to the Home Office, Lord Chief Justice Ellenborough, Lord Chancellor Eldon and the Prince Regent. There were no grounds for an appeal or commutation of the sentence in such a clear-cut case. On 26 July, Fenning was duly executed.

It was not until November 1815 that Hone published his 240 page book about the case, *The Important Results of an Elaborate Investigation into the Mysterious Case of Eliza Fenning*.* It was a masterpiece of investigative journalism. Hone levelled severe and substantiated criticisms at the legal system, revealing layers of conspiracy and calculated injustice. It was the most complete and damaging exposure of state-sanctioned malpractice hitherto written in Britain. It was, as he said, a case in which a 'remarkable instance of cruelty . . . chances to bring a train of grievances in view which the world at large never thought had any existence'.

The official version of the trial seemed so straightforward; Fenning's execution was justified by the weight of evidence produced against her by all independent witnesses. Hone began his book by giving a completely different account of the trial. The Old Bailey Sessions Report, he discovered, had been 'mutilated, garbled, and dispossessed of the

---

* The book was attributed to Dr John Watkins, a legal expert, but this was only a device to give it an air of authority. Watkins collaborated with Hone, advising him and providing some letters he had written to the Regent. In the Hone Papers in the British Library, there is a note in his own autograph stating bluntly, '*I wrote* the work entitled *An Elaborate Investigation into the Case of E.F.* – On the title page John Watkins LLD appears as the author – He had interested himself to save her, and lent me his name.' The *Examiner*, when it came to review it, was clear that it was 'a pamphlet written by Mr Hone'.

most material parts of the evidence *favourable to the prisoner*'. Hone spent the first part of his book reconstructing the report based on the notes taken down by Job Sibly, the official shorthand writer of the Corporation of London. Sibly's account was not perfect, so Hone found other documents and witnesses who could remember what had actually happened.

Eliza had been represented by an obviously deficient attorney, one of the hacks who made a living trawling Newgate for poor clients. He had failed to put up much of a defence for the girl, and had left the court before the end of the trial. And with further harm to the servant's case, the Sessions Report omitted whole sections of evidence. Charlotte had testified that Eliza had been alone in the kitchen all day. But she contradicted herself, saying that Eliza had taken a beef pie (the servants' dinner) to the baker's at one point during the afternoon. This crucial piece of evidence, which destroyed the assumption that no one else could have had access to the meal other than the cook, was deleted. Every other slip, equivocation and mitigating circumstance in favour of the prisoner uttered by the Turners and their servants during the trial were expurgated from the official account as if they had never been said.

The report went on to show that Eliza had not put up a defence to any of the charges. In fact, Hone proved that she had a defence and that it was cogent and substantial. The prosecution established a motive for premeditated murder when it told the jury that the defendant had a long-term grievance against the Turners because she was under notice. Her brooding dissatisfaction, affirmed by all the witnesses, strengthened the case. But Fenning had always denied that she had been given notice. Charlotte's assertion that she was punished for entering the servants' bedroom in a state of near-nakedness was also a fabrication. It was true that she had gone into the young men's room late one night, but she had been fully clothed, and had only gone to fetch a candle. Charlotte contradicted herself again, saying that she had forgiven Fenning when she discovered her real reason for going into the boys' bedroom. Margaret Turner had defended the cook on that occasion, and Eliza was not under notice. It also seemed that Sarah Peer had instigated a quarrel with the cook a few weeks before the crime, but the maid later claimed that it was Eliza who had taken against her.

The report left out Sarah Peer and the Turners' retractions, giving the impression that Eliza nursed a hatred of Charlotte and the other servants when it was really the other way round – Charlotte and her maid had for some reason developed a resentment of the cook a few weeks before the poisoning. This part of Eliza's case was left unreported, making her pleas ('I am innocent; indeed I am! I liked my place . . . ') seem irrelevant, unsupported and desultory. She also presented evidence from five witnesses, all of whom described her as a mild-mannered and amiable girl. The image of Eliza as a perpetually sullen member of the household was an invention concocted by Charlotte and Sarah Peer. Eliza produced an affidavit from an acquaintance, one John Smith, who had seen her two days before the alleged poisoning. Smith had never seen her so happy. 'I like my place very much,' he remembered her saying, 'I have never been more comfortable off since I have been in service.' Silvester would not allow her to present this to the jury, and the request and its refusal were not noted.

When the case came under review the senior legal officers, the Home Secretary and the Regent would have read the Sessions Report to assess Fenning's case. It was a crucial document, the veracity of which would decide whether the cook lived or died. Decisive pieces of evidence may have been suppressed, but the most glaring omissions were the Recorder's interventions on behalf of the prosecution. Eliza's main witness should have been Thomas King, one of the apprentices. She claimed that he would tell the court a very different version of events than those given by the Turners, Gadsden and Peer. He would tell the jury that Fenning always asked for scrap paper before she lit the fires, that she had never seen inside the drawer containing Orlibar's arsenic. King would tell the truth about the bedroom incident. Censored from the Report was Fenning's request to the Recorder that the apprentice be called:

Recorder: 'You should have had him before.'

Prisoner: 'My Lord, I desired him to be brought, and I wish him to be sent for now.'

Recorder: 'No it's too late now – I cannot hear you now.'

It was as if time was the only consideration deciding whether Eliza lived or died. None of this was mentioned in the trial report. 'Why was not Thomas King a witness?' Hone asked. 'Would his evidence have been *in favour of the prisoner?*' King was the decisive absence from Fenning's defence; as she said, he 'will not dare to deny the truth'. The Home Office and Lord Chancellor, when judging the strength of the verdict, should surely have been told that the jury had been prevented from hearing this evidence.

The judge, by calculation, and the defence barrister, by ineptitude, ensured that other witnesses were ignored. Only one of the two surgeons had been called – Marshall, a friend of the Turner family. His colleague, Henry Olgilvy, was not heard, although his evidence was crucial to the defence. He would have told the jury that Fenning had herself been poisoned. The statement that she looked on impassively as her employers writhed in agony was a malicious lie. The cook, who apparently had formed a sort of servants' league when she warned Gadsden not to eat the dumplings, had gone ahead and consumed something she knew to be contaminated with a slow-corroding, agony-inducing poison.

Marshall was also called as an expert witness, who affirmed that he had found traces of arsenic in the leftover dumplings. He based his assumption on the fact that the white residue had tarnished his knife and because the dumplings had failed to rise, both supposedly indicative of the presence of arsenic. But as Hone pointed out, arsenic does not stain metal black, and its presence in dough does not necessarily prevent yeast from rising. The supposedly 'expert' opinion was no more than idle speculation, as the testimony of another witness could have proved. And furthermore, the amount of arsenic found in the traces of dough in the dumpling pan would have been enough to kill outright an entire village. The Turners, Roger, and Eliza had consumed whole dumplings, and yet they had all recovered within a few days. Was there really arsenic at all, or was it simply a case of severe food poisoning? It was never proved, and Silvester was content to take one man's flawed opinion as irrefutable evidence. As Hone said, the proof given that arsenic accounted for the condition of the dumplings 'was nugatory and unsupported by fact or experience'.

The jury had heard all this, and yet they found her guilty. The unexpurgated report would have shown why they did so. The trial was

rushed through with exceptional speed, and none but the most perceptive jurors could possibly have noted all the inconsistencies in the
Turners' testimonies or the scientific flaws in the evidence. The trial
hinged on Silvester's charge at the end of the trial. None of it was tran-
scribed in the report, and if it had been, this part of trial alone would
have been enough to cast serious doubt on the verdict. The jury was
subjected to a violent, almost hysterical harangue from the Recorder.
Hone's book reported for the first time his words at the conclusion of
the trial. Silvester had gone through the evidence, omitting anything
favourable to Fenning, and then rounded on her with almost unbeliev-
able ferocity. Reminding the jury of the Turners' assertions that she had
been impassive to their pain he said, 'Gentlemen, if poison had been
given even to a dog, one would suppose that common humanity would
have prompted us to assist it in its agonies: here is the case of a master
and a mistress being both poisoned, and no assistance was offered.' As
Silvester well knew, this was a shameless lie. Yet it was the deciding
moment in establishing Fenning's character as a cold and malicious
murderess, one quite capable of premeditating a torturous death for her
household.

The vilest of Silvester's vile machinations, however, was when he
told the jury: 'Although we have nothing before us but circumstantial
evidence, yet it often happens that circumstances are more conclusive
than the most positive testimony.' The very fact that it was purely circumstantial evidence should have counted in Fenning's favour; instead
it was used against her in the most appalling manner. The prosecution's
interpretation of events, based entirely on what the Turners thought
had happened, was presented to the jury as nothing less than conclusive proof. The tirade could not be denied or qualified by the defendant, for her barrister had left the court.

With a biased judge presenting a pack of half-truths as fact, the jury
convicted Eliza, which was understandable, bearing in mind the way
Silvester railroaded them, twelve men ignorant of legal proceedings.
Hone's considerable achievement was in demonstrating how a serious
miscarriage of justice had occurred. The people who framed the report
had not merely papered over the unsatisfactory parts of the evidence
and Silvester's judgments, but actively connived in her execution.

Although Hone had demolished the Sessions Report, showing that the trial was flawed, the Recorder biased and the evidence purely circumstantial, he had not proved Eliza Fenning's innocence. The second part of the book revealed the most shocking aspect of the case: the extraordinary efforts that had been taken to secure the poor girl's execution after the trial itself.

The Eliza Fenning case played itself out on Hone's doorstep. The crime was committed in Chancery Lane, a few yards from his shop on Fleet Street. The trial was held in a courtroom across the road from Hone's lodgings in the Old Bailey, and the place of execution was round the corner from his home. It also drew in many of his friends from his days as a penniless philanthropist. Although Eliza stood alone during her trial, she soon attracted a band of followers determined to save her life. Basil Montagu, Hone's comrade from the lunatic asylum reform committee, tried to get the Home Office to review the case. So too did a number of other influential Londoners. A handful of middle-class Quaker reformers rallied around Fenning to seek justice before her execution.

One of these mysterious, forgotten men who had busied themselves in Eliza Fenning's cause, a chemical expert who chose to remain anonymous, decided to reconstruct the crime in his home. The prosecution had alleged, and the jury accepted, that the reason the dumplings had not risen properly in the oven on 21 March was because the traces of arsenic made this impossible. This chemist made a series of dumplings, introducing arsenic at every stage. At no time did its presence affect whether the dough rose or not. He then reconstructed an alternative, but equally plausible, scenario of what might have happened on the day the Turners' and their servants fell ill. He told his own cook to make him some dumplings for dinner. He crept into the kitchen, and was able to contaminate the dumplings without the cook noticing any traces of arsenic crystals or altered consistency in the dough.

Armed with these discoveries, he visited the Turners at home and explained his findings. What followed was the most intriguing incident in Hone's investigation. Orlibar was convinced by the chemist's explanation, and told him: 'If there is anything which I can do for her, I will go to the top of the ladder to do it.' The visitor said that all he need do was sign a petition of mercy, the one act that would save Eliza from the gallows. 'I will with pleasure,' Orlibar said, and Robert was prepared to do the same.

At that moment, by coincidence or because he had been told what was happening, Sir John Silvester entered the Turners' house. They all talked over the case, but the Recorder 'turned a deaf ear' to the new evidence. He then left Orlibar and the chemist, retiring for a private conversation with Robert. 'I am glad sir, that I have seen the Recorder,' Orlibar told his guest, 'for now I know that with *him* she [Fenning] stands no chance; he is quite inexorable.' He was about to sign the petition when his son came in.

'The Recorder says you must not sign any petition,' Robert told his father; '– if you do, it will throw suspicion on the rest of your family.' Orlibar turned to the chemist, who was still proffering the petition: 'I cannot, sir; you heard what the Recorder says.'

Fenning's fate was sealed at that moment. If victims expressed mercy, the death penalty would be commuted; Orlibar had this power, but he was too scared to use it. Why?

Somehow the Turners were under the absolute control of Sir John Silvester. In his detailed critique of the trial, Hone showed that the Turners, Roger Gadsden and Sarah Peer had colluded in their evidence. During the trial, Eliza's barrister had asked Charlotte and Sarah if coal had been delivered on the day of the poisoning. This was vital for Eliza's defence; one of her duties was to take receipt of the coal, and if she had done so on the day in question she would have been absent from the kitchen for a long period of time – long enough for someone else to enter and contaminate the dinner. Charlotte and her maid had denied that there had been a delivery that day. However, Hone discovered a bill sent by the coal merchant to Orlibar, clearly stating that a batch of coal had been delivered on 21 March. This vital piece of evidence was not found until August, but it showed that Charlotte and Sarah had told the same lie to strengthen the prosecution's case. Similarly, Gadsden had backed up Orlibar's statement that Fenning had access to the drawer containing the arsenic, a contention denied by the defendant and, it was suggested, by Thomas King. The entire household had apparently concocted a sequence of events that would incriminate the cook.

Basil Montagu thought he knew why the family were desperate to have their cook hanged. He had heard rumours that one of the Turner household had once threatened to kill the family. He investigated, and uncovered one Mr Gibson who worked at Corbyn and Co., Chemists and Druggists of 300 Holborn. 'Mr Turner, *junior* [i.e. Robert], called at our house appearing in a *wild* and deranged state,' Gibson was quoted by Hone:

'I invited him into the back room, or counting house . . . Mr Turner, junior, used most *violent and incoherent expressions* – such as, "*My dear Gibson, do, for God's sake, GET ME SECURED OR CONFINED, for if I am at liberty, I shall do some mischief; I SHALL DESTROY MYSELF and MY WIFE: I must and shall do it, unless all means of destruction are removed out of my way; therefore do, my good friend, have me put under restraint: something from above tells me I must do it, and unless I am prevented, I certainly shall do it."*'

Suddenly, the whole investigation made sense. The Turners had every reason to lie in court, where all their statements implied Fenning's guilt, and anything in her favour was conveniently forgotten. No wonder the family (especially Robert) were at pains to pass all guilt on to their vulnerable and friendless cook when the prophesied 'destruction' finally occurred. Knowing this, the Recorder had subjected them to intense pressure and sinister threats, preventing them from pleading for clemency when the verdict came under scrutiny.

Montagu wrote to Silvester, convinced that no jury would ever have convicted Fenning if such evidence had been presented in court. The Recorder wrote back saying 'that the Production of such evidence would be wholly useless'. Nonetheless, Fenning's new friends went as a deputation to confront Silvester. They did not get a chance to meet him to discuss their points. And they never would; their investigation had a catastrophic effect. Just twelve hours after reports that Robert Turner was 'deranged' and suicidal became known, Eliza hanged.

The time Hone spent researching the Fenning case almost ruined him. He remembered:

I took lodgings away from my family, for I could do nothing among them, and for three weeks I was wholly engrossed on the case of Eliza Fenning . . . On the fourth Saturday, in the dusk of evening, my wife came in. I said 'Sit down and be quiet, I am writing, I cannot speak to you at present'; there she sat in silence, and I wrote on. At last she said, 'Father, the children have no bread – there is no money for the papers tomorrow morning.' 'Go home,' said I, 'and I will bring you the money.' She went, but I had no idea where to get it; I had not sixpence. I went to the closet where I kept what I had to eat; I had been living chiefly on tea; there was nothing but a stale crust of bread. I ate my bread and drank my water . . .

Hone had only one option – to lay the blame on the bookseller who had commissioned the work.

'I went up to him, "You must lend me four pounds".'

'I shall do no such thing,' the astonished bookseller replied.

'*You must*,' insisted Hone.

'What should I do that for?'

'My children are starving – you have made me neglect my family.' The bookseller relented, and the Hones could afford to buy some food at last.

The romantic image of the writer, blinded to the realities of life by passionate zeal, starving himself and his family, was one that Hone tended to cultivate. He told the story against himself as a way of illustrating the intensity that drove him during the months investigating the Fenning case. It was not that he didn't love his wife, but she had to submit to his compulsive need to write. Little is known of Mrs Hone, but she always seems to have been there, a presence silent to posterity who loyally supported her husband, who helped to run the shop and prepare his books for the press. Hone only alludes to her as his 'dear wife' – he never went into details about home life in his writing – but there is no reason to doubt that this was a happy marriage. Sarah certainly had to suffer much from it, especially in 1817 when her husband faced a lengthy prison sentence, but she took it all in her stride, keeping the publishing business alive during William's absence. In a hurried pencil sketch by George Cruikshank she appears to have been a large, matronly-looking woman; her eyes half-closed with laughter – she is almost the mirror image of her husband. The Hone household, even if it sometimes lacked the basic requirements of life, was clearly a happy place.

'When attention has been once excited,' Hone wrote of the Fenning case, 'and the reality of great enormities has been sufficiently proved, an obligation is imposed on every member of society to pursue investigation with keenness, and call upon others for their assistance.' This duty was the driving force of Hone's life, from the abortive Tranquillity project, the lunatic-asylum reform campaign and the cases of Edmund Vyse and Jane Watson. His mind was always on the problems facing society, rarely on those within his own home. It was a serious flaw in his character, and one which he would repent in old age. He could always count on his wife and daughters to support him, but, as we shall see in another chapter, his sons resented their father's obsessions.

Hone always did things in his own way; from his childhood there was hardly a moment when he compromised his values. There was a high price for this stubbornness, and Sarah and the children paid it. But in this case, the achievement almost atones for the shameful neglect of his family. Hone's book was a pivotal moment in the history of investigative journalism, the first systematic exposé of the secret machinations of the administration of justice and the means by which corruption was hidden from public view. Hone showed how journalists could ignite public indignation by combining detailed research with powerful human emotions. The result was a pioneering piece of journalism, a lesson in how the press could exploit instances of cruelty to the greatest effect.

In July or August, when he was living on bread and water, he had already done the work of demolishing the official trial report and had established that Silvester had used undue influence to force the Turners to perjure themselves and, later, to desist from pleading mercy. In the months between August and the publication of *The Important Results* at the beginning of November, the investigation itself merged with the story of Eliza Fenning. The case became a matter of concern for the legal establishment. By investigating the case at all, Hone and his associates were exposing a weak flank of the English judicial system. Regardless of Fenning's guilt or innocence, the probity of the Old Bailey had to be defended from the prying eyes of journalists.

Silvester had not acted to defend a legal stationer's deranged son when he meddled with the case. His sole concern was to protect his own reputation. 'Black Jack' was a much-maligned magistrate; he was well known as a hanging judge, and was notorious for his prejudice against female defendants. There were rumours that he granted mercy in return for sexual favours. During the public controversy that followed the Fenning case, he said that the only reason people believed Eliza and not him was because she was 'a pretty woman'.[2] Silvester was under considerable pressure in 1815. He therefore made every effort to discredit the condemned girl and slander her defenders as the dupes of a seductive harlot. Silvester's mishandling of the trial and subsequent cover-up threatened the repute of English justice; his superiors were compelled to defend him.

The investigation was attacked at every turn. When the *Public Ledger* considered printing an article on the miscarriage of justice, its editor was threatened with an *ex officio* prosecution by the Attorney-General. Basil Montagu and the Quakers began to petition the Lord Chancellor, Home Secretary and Regent in June and July, and Hone published his initial finds in the paper he was then editing and publishing, the *Traveller*, and later in the *Examiner*. In response, a campaign began which rubbished the investigation as idle speculation. The *Observer* was prominent in dismissing the findings of Hone and his friends. It retailed unsubstantiated gossip that Eliza had a reputation as a lecherous and lewd servant. She was clearly capable of murder; the paper 'never saw a woman of more malevolent disposition'. John Marshall and Henry Olgilvy, the two surgeons, wrote letters to the *Observer* and *The Times* claiming that Fenning had refused all treatment when she was suffering the effects of the arsenic because she realised that her murderous plans had failed, and she would be found out. 'She had much rather die than live,' they reported her as saying, 'as life was no consequence to her.'[3]

Marshall had not mentioned this at the trial, and he began to pedal it only when the investigation censured him for failing to inform the jury that Eliza had suffered the same symptoms as her employers. He published his own book, *Five cases of recovery from the effects of arsenic . . . to which are annexed many corroborating facts, never before published, relative to the guilt of Eliza Fenning*. It was intended as a counterblast to the Hone inquiry, but it was a weak effort, adding little new and nothing substantial to the prosecution case. Marshall revealed his hand when he said that he and Henry Olgilvy were close friends of the Turners. His evidence in court and subsequent study of the case were thus hardly reliable testimonies, and it proved that all the prosecution witnesses, even the supposedly independent experts, were intimates or dependants of the Turners. At the same time, the turnkey of the condemned cell at Newgate prison signed and published an affidavit saying that Eliza had always admitted her guilt, but had protested her innocence only under pressure from her shamed father.

The conservative press launched a bitter attack on those who would defend Fenning. And the *Observer* admitted why they were taking such a close interest in this case. Magistrates, it said, should have immunity from the investigations of journalists. The controversy was not about the rights and wrongs of the trial. It was about the sanctity of the judiciary and the rights of the press. The pains that the *Observer* and other newspapers, John Marshall and Henry Olgilvy, and the turnkey took to attack Fenning served the purposes of the state in insulating the courts from public censure by validating the sentence decreed by Silvester. When the Regent and the Home Office ignored the new evidence, it was to protect the legal system from outside influence, even if the complaints were justified. When they refused to look at the true Sessions Report to see the flaws of the trial, they were consciously turning a blind eye to judicial corruption. Fenning was a small price to pay to maintain the reputation of the courts. Hone was right when he said that one instance of cruelty would expose a world of systemic corruption.

In defending Silvester, the government had raised a completely different issue to cover up the investigation. Hone argued that it had played upon the fears of people who kept domestic servants: 'Thus a sort of general cry was raised for the hanging of Eliza Fenning, as an example to all maidservants suspected, upon presumption of murderous intentions.' He said that there was a problem of trust; people were obsessed with a delusion that their servants could have nothing but murderous intentions: 'All the *masters and mistresses* of families, whose credulity or idleness rendered them proper subjects for *alarums*, were incessantly devoted to the vociferous execration of the wickedness of *servants*, who *poison* those who give them bread and work.'

Fenning was the sacrificial victim, and the courts ensured that the appropriate revenge was exacted. Hone saw the whole incident as an act of arbitrary justice, motivated by a conscious political imperative, regardless of the cost in innocent blood. She must die to teach other servants a lesson and thwart the meddling of troublesome journalists.

But if the higher powers could pick on Fenning for an instance of exemplary justice, Hone could rescue her voice from obscurity, and show the world a model of abused female purity contra the image of malevolence manufactured by the court and the conservative press. The government might have got its blood, but the public had a right to know the quality of that blood.

Half of Hone's book was detective work and destruction of the prosecution's case. The rest was an insight into the character of Fenning. This was the most important part of the investigation, for it gave the case a story of human suffering; it was a moving portrait of an innocent victim, and it sparked an enormous response in the public. The fascination with Fenning dominated newspapers and gossip for the rest of 1815. Only news about Napoleon and Waterloo could rival it.

In death Eliza became a saint in the public imagination; portraits of her were consumed as if they were religious icons; ballads were composed in celebration of her virtue and godliness. And all this suffocating hagiography and myth-making stemmed from Hone, who controlled a monopoly of all Fenning-related information. The chemist who had discovered how arsenic mixed with dumplings was a constant visitor of Fenning in the condemned cell at Newgate. He collected all her letters, and gave them to Hone, who published them in his book.

Throughout the autumn, Hone leaked some of the letters to the *Examiner*, and wrote a couple of articles for the Hunt brothers. He dribbled out his findings throughout the summer and autumn in the *Traveller*. A few days before publication, he allowed the *Examiner* to preview the investigation and quote in full the ten pages of the book that detailed Silvester's extraordinary appearance at Orlibar's house to prevent the family signing the petition of mercy, the most shocking of all Hone's many revelations about the conspiracy. The *Examiner* praised Hone's painstaking reconstruction of the trial report and his detailed research into the state's campaign against the inquiry, whilst the *Critical Review*, loyal to its former editor, said, 'This work cannot be too widely circulated.'[4] As a result, gossip was endemic. The public had been tantalised to such an extent that the book arrived amidst a blaze of publicity.

The main draw for the general reader was Hone's descriptions of the condemned cook, a girl the *Observer* had savaged as a malevolent whore, whom her defenders had eulogised as a paragon, and who had provoked such interest from the public. *The Important Results* was the only account that gave a complete portrait of Eliza Fenning by printing for the first time a complete collection of her letters and describing her behaviour in the condemned cell at Newgate. Hone needed to counter the charge that she had admitted her guilt in Newgate, but then suppressed it at the behest of her embarrassed father.

Although it is unlikely that Hone ever met Eliza, he reported that those who had visited her in gaol had 'found a lively, open, communicative girl, willing to answer every question put to her, and who rather courted than shunned an investigation into her case'. Her letters also showed that she was a forgiving Christian, the epitome of spotless virginity and female virtue. She wrote to Charlotte Turner offering 'prayers for you and your family'; another time 'she freely forgave all who had given evidence against her, but she could not forget the sense of what she considered the injury done her, as an innocent person'. At the same time 'it was a cruel thing to suffer for the guilty!' Just before her execution she would write,

I trust to a merciful God, that knows the most secret thoughts of all hearts, will grant me grace, and renew me with a new heart, that my past and present sufferings may prove an acceptable sacrifice for my past faults, and that they may be so imprinted in my breast, that they may prove a sufficient monitor, to deter me from violating the laws of God, should I be so happy as to be once more restored to society again.

But the best presentation of her brave and generous character comes from Hone's description of her execution. The account elevated the book from a mere account of an investigation to a moving tale of state-sanctioned brutality.

On *Tuesday* morning she took her last farewell of her Father, who exhorted her to meet death with fortitude; and by the firmness of his manner, under the dreadful circumstances of their separation, he exemplified the courage which he wished his child to sustain upon the scaffold. The parting scene with her mother was heart rending. They were separated from each other in a state of dreadful agony . . .

Hone's readers would not have forgotten a letter that Eliza Fenning wrote to Home Secretary Sidmouth, in which she begged him to spare her life, not least because, of her parents' ten children, she was the only survivor. Hone's narrative continues with the early hours of the morning of her execution,

A reprieve was very confidently expected for her, and the prisoners in their cells were restless in anticipation of its arrival. In the meantime *she slept until four o'clock* in the morning, when she rose and washed herself; and in particular, she washed her feet very carefully. She gave each of the women who attended her, a lock of her hair, 'to keep', she said, 'in remembrance of her' . . . About *seven*, she said, 'She was *bewildered*, and that it all appeared *like a dream to her*'.

At this point her friend and defender the chemist came to comfort her in the last hours of her life. He remained anonymous.

Mr – prayed fervently, and she clasped her hands, and looked upwards: not having done so before, he asked her to pray. 'I cannot *speak*, sir,' she said, 'but I pray from my *heart*.' Her countenance became tranquil and serene, and she observed, 'I wish to leave the world – it is all vanity and vexation of spirit. But it is a cruel thing to die *innocently*: yet I freely *forgive* every one, and die in charity with all the world, *but cannot forget my injured innocence*.'
      . . . As she departed, she lifted up the sash of the window, and looking through upon the prisoners, who remained locked in their cells, but who had mounted up to their different windows to see her go out to die, she kissed her hand to them, and said cheerfully, 'Good bye! Good bye! to all of you.' She leaned on Mr –'s arm, and *for a moment* he perceived that the weakness of human nature prevailed – she staggered but recovered instantly, and passed on to where criminals are *bound*.
      . . . *Elizabeth Fenning* walked to the spot steadily . . . The hangman approached her: he bound her arms, by the elbows, to her body, and tied her hands together in front – she stood erect and unmoved: he then tied a halter

Supplier: Dawson UK Ltd.   Reference:
Order date: 12/05/06   Order number: SM05003828
Quantity: 1   ISBN: 0571224709
Unit price: 16.98 GBP   Format: Hardback
Instructions: LAN

Author: Wilson, Ben, 1980-
Title: The laughter of triumph William Hone and the fight for the
               free press / Be
Publisher: Faber

Spine label: Main
Site: LAN
Budget: LANHIS/GEO
Stock Cat: 4 week
Quantity: 1

Dawson ref: 389722-011

round her waist. At this ceremony her fortitude was astonishing even to those who had been accustomed to witness these appalling preparations for the living for premature death. No fear started from her eye; her lip did not quiver for an instant; not a feature changed; not a muscle of her countenance moved.

Mr – *then*, in the hearing of all present, addressed her in these words: 'Elizabeth! I most solemnly adjure you, *in the name* of that GOD, before whose presence you are about to appear, if you know one thing of the crime for which you are about to suffer, make it known.' She replied in these words, distinctly and clearly, 'Before GOD, *then*, *I die* INNOCENT.'

The cavalcade then, preceded by the sheriffs and their officers, with Lord Yarmouth and other spectators moved slowly through the dark passage.

The crowd moved out of the gloomy prison into the light of a July morning. No longer solemn and private, Fenning was in front of a noisy crowd of some 50,000 people.

... She ascended the scaffold with firmness and even energy, and was the first of the three unfortunate convicts that appeared.

She seemed in earnest and solemn devotion as she passed on to the further end of the scaffold. Her step was rather quick, but not hurried – it was the pace of a person walking in abstracted thought, amidst a crowd. – She stood still – with her face towards Ludgate Hill ... the hangman standing behind her, took a white cotton night-cap from his pocket, and attempted to draw it over her face, but it was too small, as were two others, which he also tried ... He produced a pocket handkerchief which had evidently been used. She disliked this, and desired it might not be put on. She cried, 'Pray do not put it on – pray do not – pray do not let them put it on.'

... She expressed her firm assurance of happiness hereafter – denied that she was guilty – and resolutely persisted in her *innocence*. The platform fell: she raised her arms, and dropped them immediately. – Her *last words* were, 'I AM INNOCENT!' She died without a struggle.

Before she was cold, Eliza's father was presented with a bill for fourteen shillings to recover her body. He was forced to borrow the money. In a final humiliation, handbills were immediately published and distributed throughout London, informing people that Fenning's last protestations of innocence were forced upon her by her father in order to save his reputation; Eliza Fenning, the press said, had died with a lie on her lips.

Throughout Hone's book Eliza Fenning metamorphoses from the artless girl cowering in the dock of the Old Bailey, unable to form a coherent sentence, into an eloquent heroine. With such a powerful description of her courage on the day of execution, it is little wonder that the public were so obsessed by all the details of her life. Hone gave her a forum to exonerate herself, and address the public on equal terms.

But he also invented the Eliza Fenning of the popular imagination. She seems too good to be true. And so she was; the maid of Hone's book was carefully crafted to rouse public opinion and engrave the memory of the victim on the popular mind.

The men who surrounded Fenning in her last days, and Hone as her posthumous biographer, all had a vested interest in presenting her in the best possible light; her maligned reputation needed rehabilitation, the protectors wanted to be proved correct in their belief in her purity. The letters, the reported conversations, the account of the execution may be fiction, or embellishment. Most likely the accounts are based in truth: she was a pious young woman; she met her death with bravery. Yet this did not prevent Hone from gilding the story. He admitted to editing her letters, improving the grammar and spelling. Whether this was the full extent of his tampering will never be known.

Fenning, as she was represented by Hone, was pious, forgiving and naïve, an anonymous girl lost in the city, and subsequently the male-dominated legal system, where she is harried to death by a disgusting, chauvinistic judge, who avowedly hates women. She therefore appealed to the compassionate middle classes, and especially women. But there is also a peculiar charge of eroticism that pervades her portrait. She certainly fulfils certain male fantasies: meek and dutiful, pretty and virginal, whilst at the same time completely under the control of powerful men, be they judges or her band of devoted male protectors. Whilst she is wholly submissive, even fatalistic, she meets her death with admirable pluck.

Eliza Fenning was deliberately and subtly sexualised by Hone. When she died she chose to wear a dress intended for a future wedding. Her white muslin gown tied with a satin riband and pale-lilac laced boots symbolised not only the death of innocence, but a concept of unobtainable maidenhood, and the transition from virtue to bur-

The approved view of a wronged maid: in this engraving by
Robert Cruikshank for William Hone, Eliza Fenning is made to
look both voluptuous and pious.

geoning sexuality. The image of a young bride swinging on the gallows
is a powerful one, but also deeply disturbing. It gave Fenning a sexual
identity, a young girl yearning for the consummation of nuptial joy. But

before consummation can come, she is executed: innocence remains intact, and male power is reiterated.

The Eliza Fenning of myth was deliberately ambiguous; anyone could project whatever identity they wanted upon her, sexual or not. Just as celebrities are created with universal appeal in mind, so Hone posthumously refashioned Fenning. But Hone had a very serious intent, unlike manufacturing a celebrity for titillating a capricious public, when he beatified Eliza. The treatment of the maid at the hands of a cruel administration revealed a corrupt and vindictive judicial system. People had to be made aware of the canker at work in the courts of the country, and Eliza Fenning was the perfect example to illuminate the evil because she was young and powerless. Hone commented:

The extraordinary interest taken by the Public in the very peculiar and affecting Case which constitutes the subject of these sheets, is at least an honourable proof, that, however lax may be the practice of virtue, the principle still continues to be the National Character. A more striking evidence of this can hardly be adduced than the spontaneous movement occasioned by the prosecution, condemnation, and execution, of the unfortunate young woman, in whose lamentable fate all classes and descriptions of persons seemed to be animated by a common feeling of pity and indignation.

The execution had given rise to a 'sentimental tide'; this was quite common when vulnerable people were executed. It was Hone's job to ensure that the 'conversation . . . [which became] general and loud', should be sustained as more than just a passing fancy before 'something new arrives to engage the public attention'. Hone hoped his book would be 'more than the gratification of a momentary curiosity – that every individual in the community, from the highest to the lowest, will be impressed with a sense of the dangers to which he would be exposed, if suspicious circumstances alone are to be combined into a charge that shall affect his character or his life'.

By juxtaposing Eliza's impotence and pure character against the malice and cruelty of the state, Hone aimed to make it such a notorious case that people would be awakened from the somnolence of 'blind confidence' in the courts. If the public could be roused by this appalling incident – 'one of the most extraordinary cases that has ever happened in a civilised state', according to Hone – then they could be on guard against corrupt judges, and stop the law, which was 'designed for the use of the virtuous, and the protection of the helpless', being delivered 'into the hands of the crafty and vindictive'. In this way, the 'sufferings of the innocent, and the insolence of the oppressor, may be productive of good'.

Hone's investigation was designed to prove that the law had been 'converted into an engine of oppression, and an instrument of vengeance'; but, 'though the fate of the unfortunate girl has been decided, her History should not be forgotten. Every part of the Narrative rings an alarm to the present, no less than a warning to future generations, not to trust to presumptive evidence, and to put little confidence in the reasonings of fallible magistrates who have grown old in the ministration of death, or in the testimony of witnesses who are actuated by their prejudices.' It is the dream of all journalists that their news should not just be interesting when it is new, but remembered for ever. Hone's investigation lodged in the public mind for a century.

The case of Eliza Fenning has never been forgotten. Throughout the nineteenth century it was used by legal scholars as a warning of the dangers of relying on circumstantial evidence. In 1833 *The Times* revived the controversy when it reported that a man claiming to be Orilibar Turner's brother had died in an Ipswich workhouse confessing that he had administered the arsenic when Fenning was out of the kitchen. The unsubstantiated rumour was revived in 1852, when a contributor to *Notes and Queries* recalled 'the great excitement' Hone sparked in the public.[5] The House of Lords' committee on capital punishment in 1856 mentioned it, and, as the *Annual Register* reported, a year later the defence counsel in a Glasgow murder trial brought up her case, 'which, 42 years ago, was the subject of division of opinion of every household in the land'. In the succeeding years, newspapers continued to mull it over after a Baptist minister suddenly alleged that he had heard her confess her guilt in prison. *Blackwood's Magazine* repeated the story in full. And then, in 1867, Charles Dickens weighed in, telling a journalist who worked on his *All the Year Round*, 'I never was more convinced of anything in my life than of the girl's innocence,' and attacked the Baptist minister as 'muddle-headed' and his story as conceited distortion.[6]

Dickens was three years old when Hone's investigation was published; he could not have been aware of it at the time, but picked up on memories that were kept alive throughout the succeeding decades. That the details of the case were still fresh when he was in his fifties is evidence of the powerful effect that this piece of journalism had. A little later, in 1871, Charles Hindley wrote on Fenning's beauty and innocence, claiming that Robert Turner had set her up when she refused to sleep with him. Even as late as July 1909 the debate was still alive when a correspondent with *Notes and Queries* cited details from Hone's investigation. A week later, a legal scholar joined the discussion, saying that Fenning's evidence had never been proved; journalists like Hone had manipulated the case 'for political purposes'.[7] It was the same debate with the same political inferences as in 1815. The truth of the matter could never be resolved. But the style and investigative brilliance of *The Important Results* fuelled public controversy for almost a century.

By creating an Eliza Fenning emblematic of the law's inhumanity, and particularly of its treatment of poor women, he gave popular culture a viable personality to latch on to. Fenning entered the public imagination for a century. But if she did become an iconic figure, fodder for gossips, it did serve a specific political purpose. Her name was for ever twinned with the idea that governments could arbitrarily kill the weak to satisfy their need for blood to scare others into obedience. Hone tackled the government head on; if they could select people for exemplary punishment, he could in turn elevate them to the glare of the public eye, cleansing them of the taint of imagined crimes.

Hone's intention was clear: Eliza represented *all* victims who went unnoticed; Silvester, *all* callous magistrates. By providing an insight into her life, he created a typology of weakness and victimhood which could be utilised in creating the pathos necessary to mobilise public opinion. One could not imagine a young male clerk or a middle-aged matron having the same long-term effect on the popular consciousness. Hone built her up into a personality never to be forgotten. Silvester was right when he said that people like Hone were only interested in her because she was young and pretty. But it was not for the sexual motives he imagined; it was because they knew the public would only respond to someone like her.

The Important Results stands at the very beginning of a long tradition of criminal journalism which combined assiduous research with poignant melodrama, and it is still as fresh today as it was in 1815. Although Hone did not have access to modern scientific techniques, his investigation holds its own alongside most modern journalism. And, in its historical context, his investigation was revolutionary. No comparable text had been available to lay readers; the only works treating legal matters were written for and by scholars and lawyers. Crime and execution gave rise to a popular press of lurid details, bloodstained prose, and, depending on the victim, gushing sentimentality. Even innovative newspapers like the *Examiner* did not employ journalists to investigate stories and find alternative explanations to those presented in the courts; it was enough to republish trial reports as stories in themselves. So when Hone followed up every aspect of the Fenning case, he was pursuing a story in a way that had never been attempted before for the general reader. His methods had more in common with the fact-finding research of utilitarian social-reform campaigns than traditional journalism. But unlike the dry statistical analysis of the utilitarians, his book married sound research to the language and style of the popular press. It is in this way that Hone's work bears a greater resemblance to modern reportage than anything that existed before.

Every statement in Hone's book was backed up by documentary evidence; all his objections to Silvester's conduct were legally sound. Hone far surpassed the supposed experts in the legal profession, whose case before, during and after the trial was exposed as amateurish and unjustifiable. He rubbished their findings, and there was nothing they could do except answer his substantiated charges with baseless accusations against Fenning. The reader follows Hone through the twists and turns of the inquiry, and his conclusions are hard to dispute – the sheer weight of evidence makes it entirely convincing and overwhelms the arguments put forward by the prosecution. The publication of *The Important Results* was an important moment in the development of British journalism because, for the first time, the machinations and incompetence of the judicial system were laid bare for the public by the superior skill of a journalist.

The combination of sophisticated legal reasoning and intense human drama made it a commercial and political success. It changed forever the way that crime was reported. Hone raised the standards of Fleet Street journalism with *The Important Results*; imitators abounded after its publication. The barrister James Harmer (the inspiration for Dickens's humane attorney Jaggers in *Great Expectations*) started writing books for the general reader exposing partial justice and reclaiming traduced victims along the model Hone established. The two men were acquainted, and the barrister was taught a valuable lesson by Hone in the ways in which a legal debate could find a mass market. The role of the journalist was no longer merely that of commentator; the specialisation of investigative reporting became intrinsic to the role of newspapers, an aspect of journalism of which Hone was the pioneer.[8]

Within a few months of his arrival in Fleet Street, Hone's reputation as a talented and successful journalist was established. In the next couple of years his output was remarkably high. He published Leigh Hunt and Charles Philips, investigated other crimes, wrote satires and political pamphlets. He worked seven days a week, and often long into the night. And he needed to. Successful as he was, he could only afford to feed his family when he sold his books and pamphlets. Amongst the gems, he wrote and published eye-catching and titillating broadsides, trashy pamphlets, ephemeral and low-quality works that provided a meagre income. He was reduced to retailing tittle-tattle, such as a satirical broadside entitled, *Appearance of an Apparition to James Sympson, of Huddersfield, Commanding Him to do Strange Things in Pall Mall, and what he did,* or *Guy Mannering, the astrologer, or the prophecy of Meg Maerilies the Gipsey* (both 1816).

He was compelled to write a rather tawdry and sentimental pamphlet on the Fenning case to make some money, a tale based on 'The Thieving Magpie' in which a maid is blamed for the theft of jewels actually committed by a magpie. Hone saw the play in Lincoln's Inn Fields one evening when he was writing the Fenning book. 'I went home', he remembered, 'and said to my wife, "Give me a pair of candles and snuffers upstairs, and send for George Cruikshank." He came; I said, "Make me a cut of a Magpie hung by the neck to the gallows" – and I put my head on one side, and looked as much like a dying Magpie as I could.' Yet he claimed that this hurried piece sustained the public interest between the execution and the publication of the detailed investigation. Most importantly, the sale of a thousand copies of 'The Maid and the Magpie' provided his family with enough money to live on from July until November, when *The Important Results* was ready for sale.

Such was the nature of the early nineteenth-century publishing industry, a writer with a large family and a small business was dependant on a constant output of saleable prints, pamphlets and books; Hone can be forgiven if much of his work at this time did not meet the high standards of the Fenning case, the comedic brilliance of his later satires, or the intellectual range of the *Critical Review*. Yet the time would come when he was established enough to abandon the dregs of the publishing trade and produce journalism that complemented his talents and ambition.

In 1816 and 1817, Hone used the same methods of investigation twinned with emotional arguments, but it was to be transferred from isolated cases to the dramas of national politics. New victims and new abusers, this time with deeper, more tangible, implications. Hone was to be persecuted by the government within a couple of years for daring to do this. The same kind of exemplary punishment he had highlighted was to be meted out to him.

The lessons taught by the Eliza Fenning tragedy were to be prescient in Hone's next few years as a journalist. He concluded his book:

If the people are not moved into some indignation at the neglect of their *soi-disant* guardians, the healthful spirit of society is defunct, and the community is degenerating into a base rabble, similar to that which marked the declining Empire of Rome. On the other hand . . . if the people at large should be thus convinced [of corruption] it is barely possible that polite people may find the hanging of an innocent person now and then as something more than a bagatelle, and Nero cease to fiddle amidst burning Rome.

5

Cursing Made Easy

You taught me language; and my profit on't
Is, I know how to curse.
Shakespeare, *The Tempest*

The typical perception of William Hone at this stage of his career is, for modern historians, a ruffian journalist, a barely established and opportunistic Grub Street hack who catered to the tastes of a low market with salacious ephemera. He was, it is commonly maintained, a political outsider and marginal figure before his trials in 1817. Yet there is much to suggest that he was a prominent figure and respected writer long before circumstances thrust him before the public and guaranteed his place in posterity.

Hone prospered when the reformers' cause chimed with public dissatisfaction. In the years between 1812 and 1815 the last campaigns of the Napoleonic Wars, the first peace of 1814 and the conclusion of the wars at Waterloo dominated the news. Reform would gather momentum as a national movement, but in the final years of the conflict it was in eclipse. The battle continued to be fought by journalists such as William Cobbett and Leigh Hunt, or Burdett, Cochrane and their followers in parliament. Hone's three earliest pieces of journalism – the cases of Vyse, Watson and Fenning – helped to show that reform was not just a matter of elevated constitutional debate; a corrupt and insulated House of Commons, a militarised state and biased courts could make a victim of any law-abiding subject, as his *causes célèbres* ably demonstrated. At a time when reforming opinions were stifled by the state or ignored by an indifferent public, Hone was one of a few who were vocal and successful in keeping alive popular political dissent.

Life was never easy. Any publishing business was precariously balanced between subsistence and failure; Hone had to keep up a constant output of books and pamphlets to survive. But if he was often poor and rarely free from the fear of commercial failure, he was rich in friends and political connexions. At the age of thirty-five, and after fifteen years at the centre of reformist campaigns in London, Hone was a prominent Fleet Street personality. The alliance with Sir Francis Burdett, Lord Cochrane, Francis Place and the Westminster reformers was as old as his career. By the mid-1810s he was ensconced in a wider network of writers and pressmen. The lunatic-asylum reform campaign, editorship of the *Critical Review* and the Fenning case had brought him into contact with men such as Basil Montagu, Edward Wakefield and James Mill. Through them he moved into the orbit of the *Examiner* newspaper and the literati that surrounded it.

It is frustrating that much of Hone's social life was conducted over his shop counter or in London taverns. Little remains of the face-to-face world of Fleet Street in the 1810s. Charles Lamb, a member of the *Examiner* set and one of Hone's closest friends in the 1820s, wrote to Wordsworth extolling the pleasures of London life:

The lighted shops of the Strand and Fleet Street, the innumerable trades, tradesmen and customers, coaches, wagons, play houses, all the bustle and wickedness round about Covent Garden, the very women of the Town, the Watchmen, drunken scenes, rattles, – life awake, at all hours of the night, the impossibility of being dull in Fleet Street, the crowds, the very dirt & mud, the Sun shining upon houses and pavements, the print shops, the old book stalls, parsons cheap'ning books, coffee houses, steams of soup from kitchens, the pantomimes, London itself a pantomime and a masquerade, – all these things work themselves into my mind and feed me, without a power of satiating me.

Hone's little shop was part of this hectic whirl of city life, standing as it did in the middle of Fleet Street with a window display of prints to attract the crowd. William Makepeace Thackeray recalled walks as a schoolboy down the Fleet Street of the 1810s, when he would take in 'gratis' exhibitions of cartoons and satirical verses displayed in the windows of the print shops: 'Knight's, in Sweeting's Alley; Fairburn's, in a court off Ludgate Hill; Hone's, in Fleet Street – bright, enchanted palaces . . . There used to be a crowd round the window in those days of grinning, good-natured mechanics, who spelt out the songs, and spoke them for the benefit of the company, and who received the points of humour with a general sympathising roar.'[1] Hone's bookshop and publishing company would have become a meeting point for many writers and politicians as well; in 1817 he noted cabinet ministers and MPs amongst his customers.

His shop was a London landmark, his journalism acclaimed and his place within the milieu of reformist writers and politicians assured. At this time William Hone was becoming close to some of the greatest men of his age. He was on the fringe of the Romantic movement. And he found his place within the society of talented men because of his charm, wit and intelligence in private and his courage as a journalist.

'Mr Hone is a very good-natured man,' William Hazlitt wrote, '. . . he is mild and inoffensive in his manners . . . utterly void of guile, with a great deal of sincere piety, and . . . his greatest vice is that he is fond of a joke.' If much of the conviviality and friendships that Hone encountered in his daily life is lost, his relationship with William Hazlitt provides a rare insight.[2]

Much later in the century, George Patmore stated in his reminiscences: 'If I were required to name the person among all Hazlitt's intimates in whose society he seemed to take the most unmingled pleasure – or I should perhaps rather say, with whom he felt himself most at ease and "comfortable" – I should say it was the late William Hone . . .' He evidently found Hone a pleasant and easy-going fellow. By contrast, Hazlitt was an impossibly difficult man; no one entered into a friendship with him easily. Coleridge said that 'his manners are 99 in 100 singularly repulsive; brow-hanging, shoe-contemplative, strange'. And Thomas Carlyle was equally scathing: 'William Hazlitt takes his punch and oysters and rackets and whore at regular intervals; escaping from bailiffs as he best can, and writing when they grow unguidable by any other means . . . I never saw him, or wished to.'[3]

Even Charles Lamb, his most faithful and long-suffering friend, worried for his sanity, thinking him incapable of trusting even his closest companions. Hazlitt abused his friendship, using him to 'divert a spleen, or ventilate a fit of sullenness'. The anger of his prose bubbled up and spilled out into actual tantrums. Famously patient, Lamb would put up with his friend's abysmal behaviour: 'I never in thought swerved from him, I never betrayed him, I never slackened in my admiration of him; I was the same to him (neither better nor worse), though he could not see it, as in the days when he thought fit to trust me.' Hazlitt best describes himself, a man imbued with 'the spirit of martyrdom'.[4]

Hazlitt could seem impatient and rude to those he encountered, and few escaped his harsh words or brusque manner; John Clare recalled 'a silent picture of severity' when he first met him, and Patmore thought him a sinister character until he became better acquainted and realised that Hazlitt was merely shy. The fluency of the essays was not reflected in his conversation, and in company the writer would lose his poise, 'labouring to drag his thought to light from its deep lurking place'. Hazlitt had a 'timid distrust' of expressing himself in company, repeating himself as he sought the words or phrases that came so easily when he was alone at his desk with the pen in his hand. Yet in Hone's presence he seemed a different man: 'With almost everybody else Hazlitt seemed to feel some degree of restraint on some point or other.' His dark mood and natural reticence would lift whenever the Fleet Street journalist entered their favourite haunt, the Southampton Arms on Chancery Lane.[5]

Hone was one of few men who could lift him from what Patmore called 'intellectual dejection and despondency', and Hazlitt the 'scholar's melancholy', which haunted him.[6] The instinctive charm and easy, affable conversation of Hone was a tonic for the lonely, splenetic writer. Hazlitt dined most nights at the Southampton, and his unchanging habits were so well known that he attracted egregious hangers-on: tedious young men with literary ambitions; people who came hoping to be witnesses to one of the great writer's witticisms or intellectual discourses; visitors to London eager to spot the sullen critic; would-be tavern debaters, 'coffee-house politicians', as he called them. Hazlitt held court in the Southampton 'after a certain hour of the night (and till a very *un*certain hour in the morning)'. Stumbling over his sentences and hesitant in expressing his ideas, he 'made truth, rather than triumph the object of discussion. He enjoyed anecdotes illustrative of character, spoke pithily upon occasion, and, when in good spirits and good humour, was the most delightful gossip in the world!' Hazlitt occasionally treated his auditors to an outburst of petulant rage, or fled to the refuge of a theatre, seldom welcoming the unwanted interruption of indifferent conversation to his evening meal. John Clare described his 'sneer that cuts a bad pun and a young authors [*sic*] maiden table talk to atoms'.

He sat to the right of the fireplace, 'upright, motionless, and silent as an effigy, brooding over his own thoughts'; occasionally he would glance nervously at the door, 'partly in hope, partly in the fear, that the in-comer might be some one of his own particular intimates, who came there, as he knew, solely to seek him'. However, Hone's presence was always a delight, for he 'united the most perfect freedom, familiarity, and bonhomie, with that delicate deference and respect which the extraordinary intellectual powers of Hazlitt were calculated to excite in all who were capable of duly appreciating them. He also never failed to keep Hazlitt in that active and good-humour with himself which was so indispensable to his personal comfort, and to that of all who conversed with him.'[7]

Hone combined humorous conversation, punctuated with jokes and banter, with an intelligent discourse on politics. He never argued for argument's sake, unlike so many of the pretentious men who disturbed Hazlitt's evenings. 'There was something in the social and intellectual character of William Hone particularly suited to the simple, natural, and *humane* cast of Hazlitt's mind.' The essayist mocked coffee-house politicians, who 'do not seem to talk for the sake of expressing their opinions, but to maintain an opinion for the sake of talking'. He shared with Hone unaffected conversation and a straightforward manner, which was 'plain, amusing, convincing'. Neither had much time for fatuous discourse or pretension. Hazlitt admitted that he envied men who plunged into life with high spirits and a hearty laugh, who were not held in bonds by reticence or melancholy – men like Hone. Unlike most of the drinkers in the Southampton, he had 'a buoyancy and joyousness of spirit which, whenever Hazlitt met with it, acted upon his memory and imagination in a beautiful and affecting manner.'[8]

For his part, Hone thought his drinking companion one of the greatest writers in English, and certainly the greatest living writer. He was in awe of Hazlitt's talents, and considered it a great privilege to become his publisher in 1819. Yet, like many others in their circle, he found Hazlitt

hard to warm to. W. Carew Hazlitt closed the biography of his grandfather with Hone's assessment: Hone 'used to speak of him as one of the
most candid of men, and as wanting in that natural tenderness which
we are all apt to have for our deficiencies and frailties'.[9]

In the opinion of some scholars, the date of Hone and Hazlitt's first
meeting was 31 January 1819, at a dinner at John Hunt's house which
led to the publication of Hazlitt's *Political Essays* by Hone. Yet it is
unlikely that they met for the first time so late. Hone's professional and
personal connexion with the great prose writers of the early century
was apparent from 1815 when the Hunts' *Examiner* published his articles on the Eliza Fenning investigation and previewed the book a week
before publication. A letter survives from Charles Phillips, a famous
Irish lawyer and reformist writer, which establishes Hone's standing
within the *Examiner* circle. Phillips wrote to Hone from Dublin saying
that he had sent his book on the Irish statesman John Philpot Curran
'some time ago to Leigh Hunt, hoping that he might mention it in the
Examiner . . . I do not suppose that he thought it worth notice. Perhaps
he may pay *you* the compliments of which he has not deemed *me* worthy – I have to request you would exert your interest with him or his
brother for me . . . '[10]

But Hone was identified more firmly with William Hazlitt and the
Examiner circle over the fate of Europe in 1815. Whilst the majority of
the press and the public cheered on the final destruction of Napoleon,
they were struck with pessimism and disgust at the behaviour of their
country. At no point in his career as a publisher and public man was
Hone so estranged from the current of public opinion; he sacrificed the
commercial success of his business and risked the stigma of unpatriot-
ic Bonapartism in the dogged pursuit of his convictions. His refusal to
celebrate the triumph of British arms fixed him within a tiny group of
Romantic writers and poets.

Napoleon stood as a symbol of liberty against the *anciens régimes* of
Europe. Hazlitt revered him 'because he had put down the rabble of
Kings'. He was also inspired by 'a love of glory, when it did not interfere
with other things, and the wish to see personal merit prevail over external rank and circumstance. I felt pride (not envy) to think that there was

one reputation in modern times equal to the ancients, and at seeing one man greater than the throne he sat upon.' For all his faults, Napoleon, alone among all Europeans, represented the triumph of the common man and opposition to royal absolutism.

It was a view with which Hone wholeheartedly agreed. In the spring and summer of 1815 he could not keep silent during the final days of the Emperor. Napoleon's return from exile and restoration meant a new dawn for European liberty. He had returned to his throne with the support of the French people and promising to reform the government. 'The Genius of Europe', the *Critical Review* rhapsodised, 'has emerged from the darkness in which for centuries she has been imprisoned, and the Angel of Liberty, waving her white wings in the skies, and pointing to England and France, calls aloud to the oppressed of every region "GO YOU AND DO LIKEWISE".' But in the initial post-war settlement in 1814, when Napoleon was thought safely deposited on Elba, Britain had shamefully imposed the Bourbons upon the French throne, in direct opposition to the will of the people. And the same return to the *status quo ante* 1790 was replicated throughout Europe, undoing whatever good had been done for liberty and secularism. Byron never forgave Britain's Foreign Secretary Lord Castlereagh for lending his support to the old tyrannies that had been swept away at the revolution. The brief glimmer of popular rights and liberty in Europe had been trampled underfoot by the force of British arms.

Hone, the unswerving reformist, could do no less than welcome the return of Napoleon and the destruction of what he saw as Castlereagh's plans for enslaving the European peoples to their old tyrannies. Napoleon's return under constitutional limitations was, he argued, comparable to Britain's Glorious Revolution, and the second deposition of the Bourbons to that of James II: 'His establishment of a "limited monarchy" (like the King of England) on a throne from which the Bourbons are a *second* time solemnly barred, must, we think, have produced an amazing and salutary shock through the whole intellectual surface of the continent.'[11] There was a glimmer of hope that what harm Castlereagh had wrought on Britain's behalf would be undone and democratic principles once more restored to Europe.

But the debate about the future of the continent was lost amidst an

outbreak of patriotic enthusiasm focused on the popular notion of
'Little Boney', the Corsican dictator. Far worse than satire or mindless
patriotism, however, were the hysterical *Times* leaders which masqueraded as learned comment. When Napoleon was restored as emperor of
the French in 1815 after his brief exile to Elba, *The Times* was prominent in the calls for another war to rid Europe of the revolutionary
menace. Its editor, Dr John Stoddart, and Edward Sterling, the chief
leader-writer, began a daily tirade of abuse against Napoleon, attacking
him with fervid and exaggerated language. They aimed to direct public
opinion into support for the war by rousing popular anger at the person
of Napoleon. An example of their style of political writing comes from
April 1815:

The law of nature denigrates him a perjurer, a robber, and a murderer; the law
of nations stigmatises him as a breaker of treaties, a disturber of public peace,
an incendiary; the law of his own country denounces him as a traitor and a
rebel . . . Not to apply to this disgrace of the age we live in those epithets
which he merits, is to be a coward and a betrayer of the great cause of truth
and justice . . . [12]

Hone and the *Examiner* writers were disgusted by this kind of writing. Those that wanted another war against Bonaparte should answer
their critics with a reasoned justification. A true debate on the rights of
the people and the freedom of Europe was being avoided because the
Tory press had degenerated into Billingsgate. As Hone wrote, Stoddart
'mistook passionate heat for the enthusiasm of genius, a habit of loud
talking for talent, a ranting way of writing for reasoning, and pertinaci-
ty of manner for firmness of character'. [13]

Hone sought a way to express his anger at Britain's policies, and
retain the favour of the public, avoiding the stigma of Francophilia. The
most appropriate way to draw attention to Stoddart's jingoistic rants
was with humour. He set out to mock *The Times*' crudely animated and
unthinking leader articles. The subsequent campaign led to an intriguing Fleet Street war, which was to culminate in a surprising but important political victory. It also brought him closer within the circle of
Romantic writers. In the early summer of 1815 Hone wrote and published his first, and one of his finest satires, *Buonaparte-phobia, or*

Cursing Made Easy to the Meanest Capacity, an imitation of the front page of *The Times*. It was a faithful copy of the newspaper, broadsheet-sized and written under its hallmark royal crest.

The layout was in the style of *The Times*, but Hone parodied the language and setting of his favourite novel, Laurence Sterne's *Tristram Shandy*. In the novel Dr Slop, an ugly and vituperative 'man midwife', arrives at the Shandy household to deliver Tristram. Sterne described the midwife: 'Imagine to yourself a little squat, uncourtly figure of a Dr Slop, of about four feet and a half perpendicular height, with a breadth of back and a sesquipedality of belly . . .' When Obadiah, the servant, enrages Slop by tying the strings of the medical bag with heavy knots, Mr Shandy hands him the 'Great Curse of Ernulphus', a list of epithets and curses 'suitable to every occasion'. This is read by the midwife as a ceremony of anathematisation on the troublesome Obadiah. The meaningless words salve Slop's irritable humours, the act of swearing fulfilling a ritualistic punishment. In his satire, Hone parodied Sterne, inventing an interview between Uncle Toby and Dr Stoddart, rechris-tened 'Dr Slop'. Like the 'Great Curse' in Sterne's novel, it was a 'Vocabulary of Easy Epithets, and Choice Curses against Buonaparte – from his leaving Elba . . . Exhibiting the elegant phraseology of the Eminent leader of public opinion', Dr John Stoddart.

In *Buonaparte-phobia* Stoddart's anti-Napoleonic language is re-edited into the crazed invective of a paranoid. Every sentence ends in an exclamation mark, and words such as 'Monster', 'Corsican', 'Viper', 'Hypocrite' are repeated over and again, with new adjectives. Hone stripped away Stoddart's verbiage, revealing the nonsense of Tory jour-nalism, which had been whipping the public into a frenzy of patriotism. This was an interesting way of attacking opponents, and particularly suited to Hone's campaign. It appealed to a pro-war, anti-Napoleon audience because it satirised sloppy journalism without celebrating the country's enemy. The caricature of the editor of *The Times* was delight-fully scurrilous. By the end of the satire Slop/Stoddart becomes a rav-ing lunatic, much to the consternation of Toby:

That execrable *Villain*! that *hypocritical* Villain! that *bare-faced* villain! that *daring* Villain! that perjured Villain! that *Disgrace of the Human Species*! the

Second Edition, Corrected---Price One Shilling.

With the *PORTRAIT OF NAPOLEON AS HE NOW IS;* from the fine original Picture painted by the celebrated DAVID.

BUONAPARTE-PHOBIA, or
Cursing made Easy

TO THE MEANEST CAPACITY:---*A DIALOGUE*
Between the EDITOR of " **The Times**,"---DOCTOR SLOP, MY UNCLE TOBY, & MY FATHER;
EMBRACING

The  **Times**

VOCABULARY of Easy EPITHETS, and choice CURSES, against BUONAPARTE--from his leaving Elba; *shewing HOW TO NICKNAME AND CURSE NAPOLEON, to the best advantage, upon all occasions; being the approved terms regularly served up for some time past, in many respectable Families, with the Breakfast apparatus:* (*Designed FOR THE USE OF MEN, WOMEN, & CHILDREN, of "all Ranks & Conditions,"* throughout his Majesty's Dominions of England & Wales, & the Town of Berwick upon Tweed.)

By the Editor of " The Times:"

EXHIBITING THE ELEGANT PHRASEOLOGY OF THAT EMINENT LEADER OF PUBLIC OPINION.

SCENE, a Room at DOCTOR SLOP'S in Doctors' Commons.---Present, DOCTOR SLOP, MY FATHER, and MY UNCLE TOBY.

DAVID'S PORTRAIT OF **Napoleon**, AS HE NOW APPEARS.

Corsican! the *low-minded* Corsican! the *wily* Corsican! the *vile* Corsican! the *once-insolent* Corsican! the *beaten, disgraced and perjured* Corsican! the *faithless, perjured, craft-loving* Corsican! – a *Fugitive!* – an *Adventurer!* a *blustering Charlatan!* such a *Fellow!* – *a scoundrel,* with a degraded character! – an *Impostor!* a *despicable* Impostor! a *notorious* Impostor! an *hypocritical* Impostor! – a *Wretch!* a *desperate* Wretch! *such* a Wretch! – a *robber!* a mere Brigand! an *atrocious* brigand!

And so it went on. Whenever Toby questions Slop's assertions, the journalist responds with another string of curses, as if that settles the matter. Hone had a caricature of Stoddart immediately recognisable from *Tristram Shandy*. The characters were Sterne's, but the words themselves all came from *The Times'* recent leading articles. 'If the reader will take the trouble to examine "The Times" and "The Courier" since Buonaparte left Elba,' Hone wrote, 'he will find there, amongst others, every EPITHET AND CURSE used by Dr S– in this Dialogue with my Uncle Toby and my father.'

Hone's inspiration for the Dr Slop satire came from a long-running duel in print. Stoddart was Hazlitt's brother-in-law, and they had once shared a high regard for French Revolutionary principles. In the 1790s, Stoddart had been a virulent republican; the violence of his arguments had shocked even the most radical of his friends. But when conversion to Toryism came, it was total. Stoddart retained his hectoring style and extraordinary language, but the epithets were now reserved for his former friends. Hazlitt believed he had been seduced from his principles, bribed by the government to be 'the intellectual pimp of power' with a lucrative sinecure. He and Sterling were hired pens, employed to work themselves up into paroxysms of rage and fury against Napoleon, never wavering in their desire to see him crushed.

Hazlitt criticised them in a series of articles for, first, the *Morning Chronicle*, and then the *Examiner* between 1813 and 1814. Leaving aside the question whether Napoleon was a rapacious tyrant or not, his principal issue was with Stoddart and Sterling's belief that a common man with no royal blood was unfit to rule an empire. The two *Times* journalists venerated 'legitimate' sovereigns, who ruled by lineal succession and denied that the people had any right to make or unmake a ruler. Hazlitt's political writing was dedicated to exploding 'the Lie of Legitimacy' or 'that old bawd, Legitimacy', for him a decayed doctrine propped up by the force of armies against the democratic spirit of the European peoples.

Hazlitt argued that Stoddart's articles worked on the passions of the reader, encouraging people to hate Napoleon with a blind fury, considering neither the implications for liberty nor the inevitable restoration of the *anciens régimes*. Stigmatising Napoleon with a vocabulary of 'republican', 'monster', 'tyrant', 'Corsican' taught people to hate a caricature and blinded them to the real intentions of the allies: the restoration of the detested Bourbons with unqualified powers.

'Why then pertinaciously affix these obnoxious epithets?' Hazlitt asked. 'They are bad ornaments of style – they are worse interpreters of truth.' He believed that Stoddart's epithets would only serve to push Britain back into war to save Europe from parvenus like Napoleon who threatened the ancient doctrine of divine right. If they had put the case of English liberty against Bonapartist absolutism, they would have had a reasonable argument; as it was, they were consumed with vengeance: 'The cold blooded fury and mercenary malice of these panders to mischief, can only be appeased by the prospect of lasting desolation. They rave, foam at the mouth, and make frantic gestures at the name of peace. These high priests of Moloch daily offer up their grim idol of the same nauseous banquet of abuse and lies . . . '[14]

When Hone wrote *Buonaparte-phobia* the *Examiner* essays had implanted the caricature of Stoddart in his mind; Hazlitt's vision of the editor raving and foaming provided the basis for Slop. But he did something that Hazlitt could never do in an *Examiner* leading article. Hazlitt said of Stoddart's style, 'It is thus that our author always defeats himself. He is fond of abstruse reasoning and deep investigation in exact proportion to his incapacity for them – as eunuchs are amorous through impotence!'[15] Hone illustrated this in the most efficient and explicit way possible, simply by making an insane Dr Slop repeat Stoddart's vocabulary. In *Tristram Shandy*, 'Dr Slop was stamping and cursing and damning . . . at a most dreadful rate, – it would have done your heart good, and cured you, Sir, for ever of the vile sin of swearing, to have heard him'; and so the satire was intended as an antidote to Sterling and Stoddart's unmannerly style of journalism. Hone evoked Sterne's idea that listening to the deranged Slop was an argument in itself against cursing to illustrate Hazlitt's contention that 'instead of contradicting [Stoddart] it is better to let him contradict himself; no one else can do it effectively'.[16]

In June 1815 Benjamin Haydon recorded his friend's reaction to

Waterloo: 'As for Hazlitt, it is not to be believed how the destruction of Napoleon affected him; he seemed prostrated in mind and body: he walked about unwashed, unshaved, hardly sober by day, and always intoxicated by night, literally, without exaggeration, for weeks.' Others said that he took Napoleon's defeat by Britain and subsequent exile personally, as if it had been done to spite him.[17]

In 1816 Hazlitt began another series of essays in the *Examiner* redoubling his attack on *The Times*: 'This paper is a nuisance which ought to be abated.' Napoleon had been exiled beyond recall to St Helena, but Stoddart continued to savage him in the same old style. He held up the defeated emperor as an example of the fate that awaited usurpers, arguing that Waterloo was a victory for the principle of legitimate monarchy. He implied that revolutionary ideals were associated solely with Napoleon, that his destruction put an end to the spirit of liberty. Hazlitt was incensed, his democratic instincts offended. Napoleon's failure should not mean the failure of liberalism, nor give *carte blanche* to repression and despotism. These were the wrong lessons to be learnt from twenty years of war; the people should still demand their natural rights from tyrants. And so another campaign got under way against *The Times*.

In 1815 Hazlitt had been Hone's inspiration. A year later it was the other way round. Hazlitt adopted Hone's satirical language: Stoddart becomes 'Dr Slop' – 'the little pert pragmatical plebeian editor' – in his essays. Although Hazlitt admired Sterne's writing, it had not occurred to him to apply the character of Slop to his old enemy until after the appearance of Hone's satire, when 'Dr Slop' had become the universal nickname of the editor of *The Times*. The image of Hone's comic creation infused his prose at this time; for Stoddart/Slop, 'The thought that all men (himself among the rest) are not born the property of kings, inspires him to a canine rage amounting to hydrophobia.'[18] The image of the rabid editor in *Buonaparte-phobia* was transposed to the new *Examiner* essays.

Hazlitt referred directly to Hone's satire by adopting the idea of 'Dr Slop's curse'; the litany of 'compound epithets' and 'accumulated impotent hate' was derived from *Buonaparte-phobia*, almost amounting to parody. In one essay he put a string of curses into Stoddart's mouth, imitating Hone; one sentence uttered by Hazlitt's caricature of Stoddart runs to almost three pages in the *Collected Works* without a full stop, the sheer length mirroring the editor's hysteria. By imaging Stoddart 'gnashing his teeth, rolling his eyes, and dashing his head against the wall', he captured the spirit of Hone's satire.[19]

The renewed attack on Stoddart was a joyous denunciation of the man himself, full of scathing personal comments. *Buonaparte-phobia* had mocked Stoddart as a former Jacobin:

'I thought,' answered my Uncle Toby, 'that there was a time when *you* Dr S–, used *very* different language concerning revolutionary *principles* and revolutionary men? –'

'I? – I? – I? – When? Where? Pho! – Pish! – Psha!' – cried Doctor Slop, 'What if I *did*! *What* if I did – What then? But no matter for that, – No matter for that, Sir I say! – no matter Sir! What is *that* to the readers of "*The Times*"? What is it to any body? Buonaparte's a *Wretch! a Villain! an imperial Robber! an infamous, bloody, execrable, audacious, atrocious, ferocious –*'

This charge of inconsistency was a central part of Hazlitt's attack on the editor: '*Once a Jacobin and always a Jacobin* is a maxim ... *Once an Apostate always an Apostate*, we hold to be equally true.' The same was true of a host of older Romantic poets who had apparently betrayed the cause of liberty: Wordsworth, Coleridge, Southey. Hazlitt was disillusioned with them all; the attractions of power had enticed them from the ideals of liberty. When Uncle Toby challenges Dr Slop or questions his motives in *Buonaparte-phobia*, the editor tries to mask an empty case with another string of worthless curses. On Stoddart's rejection of Jacobin ideals Hazlitt wrote in 1816, 'It is because he cannot resume them again in good earnest, that he endeavours to make up for his want of sincerity by violence, either by canting till he makes your soul sicken ... or by raving like a Bedlamite, as does the editor of *The Times*. Why does he abuse Bonaparte and call him an upstart? Because he is himself, if he is anything at all, an upstart ...'[20]

Hazlitt's words on Stoddart could be applied to the 'court poets'. 'And is it possible that the Writer in the *Times* can be sincere in all this?' Hazlitt continued. 'O yes; as sincere as any man who is an apostate from principle, a sophist by profession, a courtier by accident, and a very head-strong man with very little understanding and no imagination, who believes whatever absurdity he pleases, and works himself up into a passion by calling names, can be.' Stoddart had been hired by the government, and he used all his training as a lawyer to weave complex but essentially hollow arguments:

Such a person (and no one else) would be fit to write the leading article in *The Times*. It is this union of rare accomplishments . . . that enables that non descript person to blend the violence of the bravo with the subtlety of a pettifogging attorney – to interlard his furious appeals to the lowest passions of the middle and upper classes, with nice points of law.[21]

Hone had also highlighted Stoddart's background in the law as the origin of his sophistry by (mis-)quoting *The Tempest*: 'They taught me *language*; and *my* profit on't / Is, – I know HOW TO CURSE!'

Petty as it might seem, Hone and Hazlitt's campaigns of vilification had a major political impact. *Buonaparte-phobia* was a runaway success; it went to several editions, and was republished by popular demand well into the 1820s. The nickname 'Dr Slop' became better known than Dr Stoddart. Thousands of people who had never picked up a copy of *The Times* knew of the hypocritical, canting, crazy Dr Slop, who apparently broke down in 'canine rage'. Even today, whilst Stoddart is long forgotten, the nickname is remembered. The entries for 'Slop, Dr' in *Brewer's Dictionary of Phrase and Fable* and *The Oxford Companion to English Literature* refer to Hone's nickname for John Stoddart, showing just how deeply the epithet penetrated popular culture.

Dr Slop became a household name, a byword for shoddy journalism. That was what Hone and Hazlitt intended. They wanted to completely discredit one of the government's most influential writers. The success of their campaign was apparent by the end of 1816, when Stoddart was dismissed from *The Times*. The paper stated:

He [Stoddart] knows full well that his articles were rejected from our columns, on account of the virulence and indiscretion with which they were written; and that, for more than the twelve months proceeding, whatever articles attracted notice by their merit, were exclusively the productions of other gentlemen.

The last words must have been a particular joy to Hone and Hazlitt:

There are, in the Office, sacks full of his rejected writings; which, if they were published, would exhibit an accurate criterion of his puffed up abilities: the sale of our Journal increased the more, the less he wrote.[22]

The owner of *The Times*, John Walter II, had supported his editor's political decisions. It was not until November that he found 'the Doctor's outrageous Bourbon zeal . . . disagreeable' to the reputation of the paper.[23] Stoddart could no longer be taken seriously, and Walter was forced to exert his influence and moderate the language of the leader articles. Hone and Hazlitt together had destroyed his reputation, exposing his 'puffed up abilities'.

It was a significant political victory. From 1817, under the editorship of Thomas Barnes, a friend of Hazlitt, Hone and Hunt and a former *Examiner* journalist, *The Times* became a leading voice in the reform movement and began its ascendancy to the highest-selling newspaper in the country and self-styled representative of public opinion. The consequences of satire had proved its worth as a weapon for journalists like Hone. In 1818 Hazlitt was to write on the political effect of nicknames, perhaps with this example in mind:

Give a dog a bad name and hang him, is a proverb. 'A nickname is the heaviest stone that the devil can throw at a man.' It is a bugbear to the imagination, and, though we do not believe it, it still haunts our apprehensions . . . it connects the person's name and idea with an ugly association, you think of them with pain together, or it requires an effort of indignation or magnanimity on your part to disconnect them . . . [24]

And that was what the appellation 'Dr Slop' did to the editor of *The Times*. Hone made Stoddart a laughing stock. *Buonaparte-phobia* would have been pasted on his shop window; the crowds that flowed along Fleet Street at all times of the day and night saw it, and laughed. Stoddart was mocked out of his job. The nickname endured for the rest of Stoddart's life; few took him seriously hereafter, and the *New Times*, the paper he founded in 1817, was notorious as a less-than-subtle mouthpiece of the government. In its obituary of Hone, *The Times* commented that the nickname he gave to its former editor 'effectively demolished that very frothy and pompous person'.[25] Hone was delighted with the way 'Dr Slop' caught the public imagination, and styled

himself 'the Doctor's political godfather'. The slight was neither forgotten nor forgiven by Stoddart.

Buonaparte-phobia was popular despite the favour it showed to
Napoleon because Stoddart's style of journalism was universally derid-
ed as tawdry, offensive and intellectually redundant. He was as hated on
the street as he was ridiculed in high literary circles. Hone's satire was
not seen as Bonapartist propaganda, but a much needed rebuff to *The
Times*, which was degenerating into a ranting and badly written rag.

Hone's next foray into satire was not received with such universal
approval. He published a number of prints designed by George
Cruikshank illustrative of a series of leader articles written by Leigh
Hunt that appeared in the *Examiner* between September and
December 1815. Hunt looked with horror at post-war France. He was
no supporter of Napoleon, but Britain had disgraced herself by first
subsidising Louis XVIII, and then imposing him upon the French with
unconditional powers after Waterloo. The 'White Terror' followed,
when Jacobins and even Protestant communities were persecuted.
Britain had connived in the establishment of a tyranny. In Hone's hand-
somely embellished satirical print, *Louis XVIII Climbing the Mât de
Cocagne*, the French King clambers the greasy pole, supported by
Wellington's sword, and grabs at a crown, shouting '*Support* me or I
shall *fall*'. John Bull looks on with approval saying 'Come take my
Money'. This cartoon was followed by *Fast Colours*: Louis, dressed as a
washerwoman, tries to bleach a tricolour (white was the colour of the
Bourbons). In the next cartoon in the series, *Afterpiece to the Tragedy at
Waterloo*, Hone acknowledges that his is an unpopular view: John Bull
is concerned only with military glory.

But his satire found a ready market. Although Waterloo was met with an
outburst of celebration, there were many who took the *Examiner* line. A
minority of liberal opinion was prepared to take a sanguine view of
Waterloo and criticise the worst consequences of British policy: men and
women who were as indignant at the cruelties inflicted upon the peoples of
Europe in the name of victory as the treatment of lunatics in London mad-
houses. There were enough customers to make such work a commercial
success, even if Hone was swimming against the tide of popular patriotism.

Amazingly, given the near-universal rejoicing and self-congratulation, the prints made a profit. Hone's main rival in London publishing, a Strand print-seller named Sidebotham, asked if he might purchase the impressions of the anti-Bourbon prints and offered payment below cost price. Naturally enough, Hone refused, so Sidebotham copied the drawings, and then had the gall to send a messenger with six copies of the pirated editions to Hone with the request that he exchange them for six originals. Hone replied by tearing up the imitations, sending the boy back with the scraps. Sidebotham retaliated by prosecuting Hone for damages at the Court of Requests, Guildhall. This sorry Fleet Street feud ended satisfactorily for the defendant: 'The Court conceiving that Mr Hone had received great provocation, as well as sustained serious injury by the plaintiff's piracy, dismissed the summons.'

The Bonapartist, anti-Holy Alliance satires affirmed the Hone publishing firm's place at the heart of the *Examiner* circle. It is to be supposed that many of his customers read the *Examiner* each week and were familiar with Leigh Hunt and William Hazlitt's essays. They also mark the beginning of Hone's long collaboration and close friendship with George Cruikshank, the engraver of those cartoons. The first time their relationship can be dated is from a cartoon of 1811 which shows Hone deep in conversation with George and his older brother Isaac Robert, also a highly talented caricaturist. Their father, Isaac, had been one of the few great political cartoonists of the 1790s and 1800s, a rival of the great James Gillray. Isaac died in 1811 after a particularly hard-fought drinking competition. His two young sons inherited his joyous and irresponsible conviviality, but also his artistic skill; as George said later, he was 'cradled in caricature'.[26] When Hone began to employ them, the Cruikshank brothers, both in their early twenties, were the most artistically gifted, technically complete and prolific freelance cartoonists and illustrators in London.

They were also notoriously dissolute. Robert and George enjoyed the lifestyle of young bucks, making assaults on London's nightspots, never discriminating between low taverns in the slums of St Giles's (Covent Garden) or fashionable routs in St James's. Quarrels with nightwatchmen were not uncommon. As a result of this boisterous existence, their political commitment was slight. George did draw very perceptive cartoons in the 1810s, but presumably through the fug of some gin-induced hangover, the subject matter dictated by political publishers. He only used his artistic talents so that he could afford the next adventure in London's pleasure palaces. A contributor to *Blackwood's Magazine* noted that Cruikshank 'seems to have no plan – almost no ambition – and, I apprehend, not much industry'. In his late teens and early twenties, he was free-wheeling, happy-go-lucky and politically ambivalent: 'a clever, sharp caricaturist, and nothing more – a free handed comical young fellow, who will do anything he is paid for'.[27]

It was in every faction's interests to secure his talents because his cartoons were so devastating in knocking down rival political theories. Therefore, taken as a whole, Cruikshank's cartoons of the 1810s have no consistency. On one day he could depict the Prince Regent as a disgusting debauchee, the shocking effects of Britain's war, or John Bull emaciated and abused by his rulers. On another, he would attack the people who advanced those ideas as gin-swilling gaolbirds and dangerous anarchists bent on destroying Britain, if he was paid enough by publishers loyal to the government. George, it was well known, would draw anything so that he could afford beer in the evening. In the 1810s, George Cruikshank was a long way from the man who was to provide Charles Dickens with the brilliantly emotive drawings for *Sketches by Boz* and *Oliver Twist*, or the teetotaller who illustrated that great piece of Victorian melodrama *The Bottle* for the Temperance Society.

Hone employed the brothers whenever he could for satirical prints and book illustrations. George engraved a portrait of James Norris and the anti-Bourbon prints; Robert produced Hone's portrait of Eliza Fenning. It was intermittent work, and Hone was by no means a major source of income for them. It was not until 1819 that he became George's most significant patron, and they collaborated on a series of important and wildly popular satirical pamphlets. Although Cruikshank retained his freelance status, drawing anti-radical cartoons for conservative publishers, his emerging social conscience is commonly dated to the period after 1819, when he embraced a reformist world view under the influence of William Hone. It has been suggested that Cruikshank posed the same question as Gillray did in his cartoons: whose side is he on? For both caricaturists, everyone is deserving of their anger, and even those they appear at first glance to take the side of are spared none of the vitriol. The audience is dogged by a sense of unease at the ambivalence of the artist; Gillray and Cruikshank seem to have no principles: all they can see is the depraved and vicious in public figures, as if all politicians are reduced to the same abhorrent immorality whatever their beliefs or

Robert Cruikshank (l), William Hone,
George Cruikshank (r). From *The Scourge*, 1811.

behaviour. Robert said that the words always on his brother's lips were 'Damn all things'. But George differed from Gillray in one important respect. When he attacked the reformists as crazed revolutionaries tearing down the edifice of church and state, he sometimes depicted himself in the company of Hone. Even when George mocks Hone, he is at his friend's side, and they are both spared the worst that caricature can inflict. Cruikshank's work is not entirely without a moral core; it is expressed in loyalty to his best friend.*

Throughout the 1810s they developed a close friendship, perhaps the longest and most intimate of William's life. Hone often took the part of the older man, attempting to school George in the ways of political reform and domesticity. The Hone household, when it moved to a spacious and well-furnished building on Ludgate Hill, became a refuge for

* See, p. 314 and p. 331.

Cruikshank when his fast-living existence became too much. Sarah, Hone's eldest daughter, recalled: 'Both our mother and father sought to draw him from the loose companionship he indulged in, by keeping him at home in the evenings, and often to sleep – he was the only one our mother ever had a bed made up for.'[28]

Yet Hone was not as puritanical and stern as Sarah's description might suggest. He was not averse to joining Cruikshank's drunken evenings on the town, and they did much of their work over pints of ale or glasses of wine in the Southampton Arms.[29] They both respected the other's talents, and George particularly appreciated his patron's easy-going attitude to life and business. They differed in that Hone was a family man, with eight children in 1816, and the owner of a small business, whilst Cruikshank guarded his feckless life with jealousy. The most eloquent description of George's attitude to the Hones comes in a couple of hurried pencil sketches dashed off absent-mindedly on a piece of scrap paper in the late 1810s. One is of Sarah Hone, a plump, jolly woman, her faced creased in laughter at some forgotten joke. Cruikshank emphasises the dimples in her cheeks, which have become prominent as she laughs. He also enlarges her breasts and backside to a spectacular degree. But is not an erotic drawing: it is a buxom matron he wishes to depict. The other is a full-length profile of William, capturing a mischievous twinkle in his eye. Here he is, at his prime, a bulky man with bullish neck and thick lips, which seem to be barely repressing some witticism, or on the brink of a bellowing laugh. These two caricatures, quick sketches obviously completed in a few seconds, preserve the warmth of a long friendship.

The exchange of ideas between Hone and his friends is the key to locating Hone within his social and political milieu. He was not merely a gutter journalist cheapening the political debate with his reflexive outpourings of anger or trivialising important stories with mockery. Hazlitt's use of the 'Dr Slop' epithet dignifies *Buonaparte-phobia* and recognises the political power of Hone's nickname. The inclusion of a satire by Leigh Hunt in Hone's book *An Historic Character of Napoleon* also legitimates humour as a valid adjunct of political journalism. Whereas Hunt and Hazlitt expressed the reformist case in general in their carefully crafted essays, Hone found real instances of oppression and misgovernment in his investigations into legal abuses, or shot out poisoned darts at his enemies. His journalism was intended for immediate effect, to infest the public's imagination with nicknames, catchphrases or Cruikshank's cartoons. In the Southampton Arms the joyousness of Hone's spirit and his knowing, confident, plain-speaking manner contrasted with the brooding introspection of William Hazlitt. Hone's publications display the same kind of wit and passion that made him such a popular companion in private.

Hone began his association with this group when they were in an unpopular minority, when they were not embarrassed to express their disgust at Britain's heavy-handed policies abroad. Hone would return to the subject of Napoleon, a man who fascinated and repelled him in equal measure. In April 1816, he played a controversial role in another public scandal, which he exploited to revive the memories of 1815. On 18 March 1816, Lord Byron wrote his poem *Fare Thee Well*. It was addressed to his wife, with whom he had signed a preliminary separation agreement the day before. On 8 April he privately published fifty copies of his poem; on the fourteenth it appeared unauthorised with *A Sketch from Private Life* in the *Champion* newspaper, and on the twenty-first in the *Examiner*. Although separations were not uncommon in aristocratic society, Byron was a literary celebrity; knowledge of his various affairs and rumours of his incest made the poems compelling reading. At the same time, these poems and several others were republished by Hone in a book, *Poems On His Domestic Circumstances*. He was not the first to pirate them, but his book brought the poems to a large audience; by the end of the year, the volume was in its twenty-fourth edition. Such a work was lapped up by a gossip-hungry public, eager to read about Byron's private affairs. Hone used the opportunity to reaffirm Byron's association with Napoleon and the cause of European freedom. Included in the domestic poems were verses on Napoleon, Waterloo and France. His 'Ode From the French' concluded:

> But the heart and the mind,
> And the voice of mankind,
> Shall arise in communion –
> And who shall resist that proud union?

> The time is past when swords subdued –
> Many may die – the soul's renewed:
> Even in this low world of care,
> Freedom ne'er shall want an heir;
> Millions breathe, but to inherit
> Her unconquerable spirit –
> When once more her hosts assemble,
> Let the tyrants only tremble, –
> Smile they at this idle threat?
> Crimson tears will flow yet.[30]

These were Byron's words on Waterloo. Hone pirated them because he wanted to associate the poet with his cause; he appropriated the name and the verse to give dignity to his lonely fight to fix the public's attention on the consequences of the war. He exploited a moment of public interest in a high-life scandal for political ends.

Napoleon and Byron were Hone's great heroes. But his admiration was betrayed in April 1816. When he pirated Byron's poems, he also published his own satirical verses in another book. His motive was 'to plead . . . the cause of truth and virtue against the haughty and combined efforts of rank and talent'. Byron's infidelities were 'so fashionable a vice', and his position as the leading man of letters made them 'more than usually dangerous to public morals'. In the same volume he attacked Napoleon, who had also been callous to women. In Hone's mind, these two men were linked. Both had set the world alight; both had abused their position – power in Napoleon's case, genius in Byron's. Influence and leadership were squandered by vanity and weakness; there was a melancholy inevitability in their fall. Hone was willing to enlist them in the reformist cause, but he also recognised the wasted potential and the danger they represented. There was little, it seemed, to distinguish his would-be champions from the old elites; power corrupted everything it touched. As he wrote,

> The weak *may* fall, the ignorant offend,
> And Pity's tear lament their hapless end;
> But when the strong are vile, the great are base,
> Derision and contempt their steps shall chase.[31]

Hone also mourned the world's ignorance at the end of the war. Mankind had learnt little after a quarter of a century of revolutionary conflict. He had written about Napoleon and Europe, but he had been ignored; the public should understand that the end of wars would eventually have an impact on domestic politics. The triumph of the old order, the repression of dissidents and the victory of 'legitimacy' rang a warning to the British. Conservatives blamed the French Revolution on the infidelities and violence of the people, but as Hone argued, the 'growing abuses of centuries produced a dissolution of the ancient authorities in one of the most powerful monarchies in the world; and society, reduced to its elements, effervesces with extraordinary heat and malignity'. Revolutions had 'barbarous consequences'; but it was not the fault of the people ('who are naturally indisposed to political change'); they had been goaded into rebellion. Throughout the wars, the British government had stigmatised the reformists as followers of 'French principles'. But in peace, it could not have that luxury; having fought a war in liberty's name, it would have to account for liberty at home. Recent history taught that misgovernment and corruption led to revolution; the regimes in Britain and Europe should be aware that 'unless government's are *free* and *prospective*, the same circumstances must sooner or later effect changes in them all. What have been called FRENCH PRINCIPLES ... are EFFECTS *not* CAUSES – the heated absurdities of men in a state of high excitation; and, good or bad, were produced by the Revolution, and not the Revolution by them.'[32]

Hone's predictions were to be proved correct; the next years would be characterised by protest and repression, the extent of which had not been seen since the 1790s when Hone was a teenager.

PART II

'The wantoness of impunity'

6

Necessary Slaves

They sigh for a PLOT. Oh, how they sigh! They are working and slaving and fretting and stewing; they are sweating all over; they are absolutely pining and dying for a plot!

William Cobbett, *Political Register*, 14 December 1816

One can never feel that the King is secure upon his throne till he has dared to spill traitors' blood.

Lord Liverpool[1]

... when complaints are freely heard, deeply consider'd, and speedily reform'd, then it is the utmost bound of civil liberty attain'd, that wise men look for.

John Milton, *Areopagitica*

On 24 February 1817 the Home Secretary, Lord Sidmouth, told the Lords that 'a malignant spirit' haunted the country. The people had been seduced from quiescent obedience to the government by a flood of dangerous pamphlets and newspapers, emanating from London publishers. 'These seditions', Sidmouth told the House, 'have been spread over the country with a profusion scarcely credible, and with an industry without example . . . every town is overflowed by them; in every village they are almost innumerable, and scarcely a cottage has escaped the perseverance of the agents of mischief; hawkers of all kinds have been employed, and the public mind has, in a manner, been saturated with odious poison.'[2]

The Home Secretary was preparing parliament for the introduction of legislation that would censor the press. The country, he told the assembled peers, was on the brink of revolution, and reformist journalists were to blame. The worst offenders were William Cobbett, Thomas Jonathon Wooler and William Hone, the polluters of the public mind; it was their seditious literature that had forced Sidmouth to act.

Hone had launched his *Weekly Commentary* in January 1817. In the last week of the month it was renamed the *Reformists' Register*, a weekly news pamphlet costing twopence. It was timed to coincide with the opening of the 1817 session of parliament, one which Hone and the reformists believed would be the most significant in British history. The reform movement had become a national one, and the new parliament was deluged with petitions from a million men and women demanding fair representation and the purging of corruption from government. Hone's paper would chart the campaign for reform, and parliament's response to it, week by week as the pressure mounted on Lord Liverpool's government.

In his speech at the beginning of the session, the Regent informed the two Houses that a great task awaited their attention. Those who hoped that he would order a systematic investigation into the state of the country were to be disappointed. The key part of the Prince's speech referred to the dangers of armed insurrection:

I am too well convinced of the loyalty and good sense of the great body of his Majesty's subjects to believe them capable of being perverted by the arts which are employed to seduce them; but I am determined to omit no precautions for preserving the public peace, and for counteracting the designs of the disaffected: and I rely with utmost confidence on your cordial support and co-operation in upholding a system of law and government from which we have derived inestimable advantages . . . [3]

The London crowd was seething. The real problems of the country were to be ignored whilst the state suppressed the voices of discontent. Hone described what happened after the Prince had delivered his speech:

On the Regent's return, the most offensive epithets were applied to him as he passed along in the State Carriage, guarded on both sides by a strong escort of Guards and Constables. The crowd, clamour, and insults increased, but cries of 'God save the King', and huzzas were mixed with vociferations personally offensive to the Regent – and it had proceeded half way down the Mall, the window was shattered . . .

No shot was heard above the noise of the protesters, but suddenly two small holes were smashed in the window of the carriage. A few seconds later the pane was destroyed by a stone. The Regent's equerry, Lord James

Murray, thrust his master onto the floor of the coach and bravely held his hat up to the window to block out further attack. The coach picked up speed and the Prince was rushed from his would-be assassins.[4]

The House of Lords was informed immediately. Lord James Murray was brought to the bar of the House and questioned. Asked what had caused the two small holes in the window, he replied: 'I have not the slightest doubt that they were produced by bullets.' In his opinion, a gunman hidden in one of the trees had taken aim at the Regent, and narrowly missed. His version of events was generally accepted. It was held up as the culmination of the reformists' campaign, and the peers had no doubts that the press was to blame. Lord Valletort told the Commons that reformists who 'preached the most dangerous innovations' aimed to 'withdraw altogether the confidence of the people from the disposition and wisdom of parliament'. The press and demagogues had, according to Lord Wellesley, been successful in their attempt 'to stir the minds of the people to sedition'.[5]

A few weeks later Committees of Secrecy appointed by both houses delivered to parliament their investigations into another insurrectionary plot. In December, some 50,000 men and women had gathered at Spa Fields in Clerkenwell to sign a petition requesting the Prince Regent to force the government to relieve their poverty with tax cuts and retrenchment. A demagogue named Watson had brandished a French tricolour and shouted to the crowd, 'If they will not give us what we want, shall we not take it? Are you willing to take it? Will you not go and take it? If I jump down amongst you, will you come and take it?'

The crowd roared its assent, and followed Watson down St John Street to Smithfield, where they looted a gunsmith's shop. With their stolen weapons, the mob marauded around London, intending to burn down the Bank, seize the Tower and release prisoners in the City's gaols. According to the committee, as anarchy descended, the radicals would depose the King, redistribute land, and proclaim a republic.

This first indication of revolutionary action had been put down by constables backed by the army. But the Committee of Secrecy discovered that the thwarted uprising was evidence of a much wider plot. Throughout the country, villagers were joining Hampden Clubs – subversive societies named after John Hampden, the MP who had defied Charles I's illegal taxes in the 1630s, led parliament in an attack on royal misgovernment between 1640 and 1642, and died fighting the Royalists in the Civil War. The name of the club had a particular resonance for reformists; Hampden was a respectable hero, synonymous with the struggle for constitutional liberties against absolutism. For conservatives, however, the name conjured up the dark days of popular discontent, bloodshed and regicide. Hundreds of thousands, the committee said, were arming themselves for a concerted rebellion that would destroy the constitution and abolish private property. The prayers that were ordered to be said in churches throughout the country in thanksgiving to divine providence for the preservation of the Regent's life implored the Almighty to spare the flawless constitution from 'the madness of the people'.

From the first day of the session, Burdett and Cochrane introduced petitions to the House of Commons signed by 30,050 people from Manchester, 24,000 Londoners, 15,700 from Bristol, and many more from smaller towns and villages, demanding universal suffrage, annual parliaments and the abolition of wasteful sinecures. On every occasion, the two MPs were shouted down by their fellow members when they began to read from them, or the ministers would refuse to hear them on the grounds that they libelled parliament. 'It was impossible', Lord Castlereagh said on one occasion, 'for the House to receive petitions containing such gross insults to its authority.' George Canning expressed genuine pity for 'innocent, but misguided persons, whom their distress expose to be the dupes and tools of every leader that addresses himself to their wants, their prejudices, and their passions'. But most revealing about the attitude towards public opinion was the assertion that the thousands of signatories could not have understood the content of the petitions. The common people were simply incapable of not being duped by the men who drew up the demands; ignorant of the issues and confused by fiery polemic, they blindly signed whatever was put to them. Indeed, Burdett and Cochrane were guilty of 'gross impropriety' for bringing the voice of the people to such an august forum at all. The demand for universal suffrage and abolition of sinecures was considered by parliament to be the language of treason. 'But now, it seems,' Burdett sarcastically told his critics, 'the House is not to hear anything like the truth; nothing but an adulatory sort of language is to be addressed to it.'[6]

The petitions were considered as great an act of treason as the riots. MPs were more concerned to legislate to forestall a revolution than to answer the people. They had evidence that the country was inflamed to the point of insurrection, and the overriding priority was to silence the voices of sedition. But how much did ministers and MPs know of the state of the country? How reliable was their evidence?

In the aftermath of Spa Fields, Hone published two broadsides explaining what had actually happened. The report of the Committee of Secrecy sounded convincing. However, its description of events differed from the impression of most people who were in the City on the day. Rather than a massive uprising aimed at seizing the state and redistributing property, it was a peaceful meeting which called for limited reform. Unfortunately, some 200 people out of 50,000 broke away in a spontaneous riot. Hone said that, for the huge crowds at Spa Fields, the rioters were a 'scoffed-at rabble', and when news of their blundering violence became known to Londoners, the reaction 'was like that of an electric shock'. Most of the violent group were recently demobbed sailors, who had been discharged without pay. They targeted food shops and victuallers, not the buildings of the state. Yet what Hone called the 'venal hireling press' described the whole meeting as a thwarted uprising. 'But', said Hone, 'the quiet good sense of the people of the metropolis had foiled the machinations of their foes . . .' Indeed the peaceful nature of public protest was to be welcomed, and the people should be praised for 'their patience beneath their undeserved afflictions, under a load of calumny, during the strongest incitements to disorder from all quarters'. He attacked the 'mischievous ingenuity' of the Tory press for using an isolated food riot to libel the whole people as dangerous revolutionaries.[7]

One of the sailors was executed in March. John Cashman had left the navy owed several years' back pay. When he arrived in London he was hungry and penniless. He and his friends had managed to get drunk, before stumbling upon Spa Fields, unaware that it was a political meeting. 'I have done nothing against my King and country but fought for them!' he said at his trial. As he was taken to his execution in Skinner Street, he shouted at the cheering crowd, 'Hurrah, my hearties in the cause! success! cheer up!' When the noose was put around his neck and the executioner prepared to let him drop, Cashman shouted, 'Now, you buggers, give me three cheers when I trip.'* He cheered as the board fell from beneath his feet, before the noose tightened around his neck. The crowd cried 'Murder!' and 'Shame!' Cashman's patriotism and defiance made him a martyr for people who felt the government had disparaged them as disloyal mal-contents; his were not the words of a regicidal Jacobin or an inarticu-late dupe of reformists. Lord Liverpool, the Prime Minister, expressed the government's dispassionate attitude to exemplary jus-tice: 'One can never feel that the King is secure upon his throne till he has dared to spill traitors' blood.'[8]

The government was equally casual in its assessment of the assassi-nation attempt on the Regent. When the windows of the Prince's coach had two holes smashed in them, it was immediately accepted that they were bullet holes. The expression of love and loyalty from Tory papers was overwhelming. However, in many quarters the comment was a lit-tle more circumspect. Indeed, the government and press hysteria was looked on with some contempt. The idea that someone had taken a shot at the Prince was based on the testimony of one witness. Lord James Murray, the equerry who was riding in the coach with the Regent, propagated the idea that there was an armed assassin who had shot at the Regent. No one in the crowd had seen or heard anything. And what had happened to the bullets that had apparently whizzed in front of the Prince's nose?

The *Examiner* pointed out that 'two small perforations were made in the window by some missiles or other, which did *not* perfo-rate the opposite one, and were *not* found in the coach' – odd con-sidering the force and speed of the bullets. Strange too that Murray had then defended himself and the Prince against further shots with nothing more resilient than his hat. 'Well done Lord Murray!' wrote

---

* 'The term Cashman is said to have used', Hone explained when he expurgated some phrases from the sailor's last words, 'is of disgusting import to polished ears, but is the usual phrase of salutation amongst sailors, and as applied by them in common conversa-tion, is of the same meaning as "comrade", or "good fellow!".'

Hone in his *Register*. 'Nobody who reads his Lordship's evidence, and considers the material composing the bullets, will think of looking for them beyond his Lordship's *head*.' The *Examiner* asked why papers such as the *Courier* were so concerned about the prince; surely poor people huddled under bridges should arouse more sympathy than 'a single high-living prince who had his coach window cracked'.[9]

There was no assassination attempt on the Regent that day; the window had been smashed by two small stones. People in the crowd had been pelting the coach with apples and stones at the time the windows were broken. In such a *mêlée* it was more likely that the window had been broken by a piece of rubble than by bullets, especially when no shot was heard by any of the witnesses and the bullets were never recovered. Hone published a satire, *The Bullet Te Deum; with the Canticle of The Stone*, which mocked Tory newspapers, particularly the *Courier*, for being so zealous in promulgating the bullet story. It also parodied the Church's prayer for the preservation of the Regent's life, which had called upon God's help to spare the state from its people. The holes in the coach window were to be blessed because it gave the government the excuse it needed to censor the press. The suppositious bullet legitimised repression, justified the idea of journalists as dangerous incendiaries, and allowed the state to extend its powers with impunity:

> Day by day: the Courier doth magnify thee;
> And it worships thy name: every night without end.
> Vouchsafe, O Bullet: to keep this year without Reform.
> O Bullet have mercy upon us: have mercy upon us.
> O Bullet keep Reform afar from us: as our trust is in thee.
> O Bullet, in thee have we trusted:
> Let the Reformists forever be confounded.

At the end of their Te Deum, the worshippers of the divine bullet hand over freedom to three judges: 'Now to the Right Honourable LORD ELLENBOROUGH, SIR JOHN SILVESTER, and Mr JUSTICE HICKS, be committed the entire disposal of the Liberties of the People of England at this time and forever hereafter. Amen.'

The government was poised to act against the reformist press in February 1817, and it was obvious that some form of censorship would be put in place early in the parliamentary session. It was the weekly periodical press that would be the target of the new measures. William Cobbett's *Political Register* was once again incurring the wrath of the Home Office. In the latter half of 1816, the paper's circulation had leapt to some 60,000. In his memoirs, the bookseller and publisher Thomas Dolby wrote of this time: 'We all went politically mad ... Our domestic politics I had never looked into,' he explained; 'but finding a hubbub gathering about me concerning parliamentary reform, and a great call for all manner of books in that subject I was obliged to throw down my apron and sleeves and fetch Cobbett's Register. The more I fetched the more people wanted ... I had to fetch up and sold 5,000 Registers in one week!' Dolby's bookshop was based in Wardour Street, Soho, and the number of copies of Cobbett's paper that he sold from this outlet alone was greater than the national daily sales of newspapers such as *The Times* or *Courier*. [10]

Early in 1817, when the market for political literature was at an historic peak, Hone started his *Reformists' Register*. The reform campaign had gathered momentum; meetings were held throughout the country from the end of 1816; petitions were signed by hundreds of thousands. For the first time, reform had become a popular cause. To compete with Cobbett was a daunting task; he had been a rare spokesman for parliamentary reform since the 1800s, when men such as Place and Hone had turned their attention to other projects, such as the Poor Laws, lunatic asylums and tainted justice; and so his paper was the first that people turned to when they were awakened to political action. But the *Reformists' Register* had an advantage over Cobbett. Hone's paper would connect the newly emerged national voice with the Westminster Committee and its parliamentary leaders, Burdett and Cochrane. It was started with the help of Francis Place, Hone's old political ally from the days when he had his first experience of reformist politics as the joint owner of the bookshop at 331, The Strand.

William Cobbett spoke for rural England, based as he was at his farm in Botley, Hampshire. Hone would give a different focus to the reform campaign from his position at the centre of Westminster agitation and in close personal contact with politicians such as Place, Burdett and Cochrane, and other key figures: the Hunts, Hazlitt, Bentham and James Mill. Even though Cobbett made all the running in the early part of the year, Hone was able to secure a share of the market. Francis Place wrote an extra-ordinary mid-week edition of the *Reformists' Register* attacking the Whig MP Henry Brougham, who had backed away from the reformists, fearful that association with the Spa Field rioters and the petitioners would tarnish his party as the abetters of Jacobins and revolutionaries. Place wrote that Hone's 'profits were considerable' from the sales of the *Register*.

The third reformist writer to attract the attention of the government was Thomas Wooler. If Hone did not know him before, they certainly became firm friends at this time. They dominated reformist journalism in 1817; both were to be the victims of show trials legitimising government censorship: of the eighteen press prosecutions conducted by the Attorney-General in London, seventeen were against journalism and satires published by them. Wooler was born in Yorkshire in 1786, and had served as an apprentice in the printing industry in Sheffield before migrating to London to become a journalist. Who his parents were, and what sort of education he had, the journalist chose to keep to himself. He was described in his obituary in the *Gentleman's Magazine* of 1853 as 'tall and inelegant, with a countenance of plain and unmarked features, which showed no indication of the master mind that dwelt within'. Wooler was certainly conspicuously tall, but his obituarist was inaccurate in describing his physical characteristics; a portrait from 1817, when he was thirty-one, shows a formidable and brooding man: a dark complexion with deep-set, surly eyes flashing aggression at the viewer. Yet clever he certainly was. Upon arrival in London, as a precocious twenty-two-year-old stranger, he started the *Stage*, a journal which reviewed the latest plays. From 1810 he attracted attention as a leading member of the 'Socratic Union', a debating club where 'various subjects were discussed, exclusive of any on religion or politics'. During the debates, Wooler 'displayed considerable talent, not only as a speaker on all subjects that were proposed, but as possessing a great fund of general information, particularly in history and general polite literature'. Like Hone and many other writers of his generation, his

learning came from patient self-education. As the crises of the 1810s
unfolded, Wooler turned his considerable mind to politics, joining a
debating society which met at the Mermaid Tavern in Hackney. After a
day in the print room of his paper's office, setting the week's edition to
type, he would hurry to the debate without any notes, and deliver an
extempore speech two and a half hours long 'with a facility, power, and
eloquence which would have put any of our M.P.'s [sic] to the blush'.

As a political debater, Wooler quickly became renowned for his
spontaneous and insightful speeches. He 'displayed a conspicuousness
of language and elegance of diction, as well as infinite knowledge of his
subjects always equal, and often superior to his political adversary'.
Wooler took it upon himself to publish the debates in a journal called
the *Reasoner*. The venture was a commercial failure. But the talents of
the fiery young Yorkshireman had become famous in the networks of
London publishing and opposition politics. He went on to succeed
Cobbett as editor of the *Statesman*; but he was to preside over its
demise as a political paper, and as editor he issued its last number. Prior
to 1817 Wooler was an unsuccessful critic and political campaigner,
renown only for his oratory; but in that year, the veteran reform campaigner Major Cartwright sponsored his latest venture, the *Black
Dwarf*, which would make Wooler one of the most famous journalists
of his generation. His political writing lost none of the impassioned
rhetoric of his tavern debates. The *Dwarf* would be one of the most
daring and vitriolic of the reformist papers.[11]

'Nothing puzzles an Englishman so much as the constitution of his
country,' Wooler wrote in the first number of his *Black Dwarf*. 'It is
harder than the enigma put to Edipus [sic]. So many things opposite in
them selves, have been constitutional in their turn, that the constitution
is every thing and nothing – a blessing, and a curse – the offspring of
inaccurate wisdom – the produce of weaker intellect.'[12] Wooler set out
to investigate the perplexing constitution and unravel its mysteries for
his readers. For this purpose he invented the fictional 'Black Dwarf', an
invisible demon who journeyed to Britain to scrutinise the state of the
country; with the eye of a stranger, it would point out the ludicrous
nature of British politics. The Dwarf represented the bulk of the disenfranchised people, who were indeed strangers in their own country,

estranged from their constitution and forbidden share of power. And it was also an emblem of the press itself; incorruptible, inquisitive, ubiquitous, it would undertake myriad roles 'in listening for evil at the portals of the temple, under the canopy of the throne, and in the gallery of the lower house; in weighing the patriotism of our patriots; in comparing the disinterested independence of our journalists; besides the stranger occupation of seeking for honesty in the mazes of the law, and humility on the bench of bishops . . . '[13] Although Hone did not use such colourful imagery, his *Register* was imbued with the same spirit of independence and inquisition. But unlike Wooler's idea of the people as strangers to the workings of government, Hone would make them central to political life, placing the transcripts of debates held at public meetings alongside deliberations in parliament, dignifying a public who were as articulate, rational and important as their *soi-disant* rulers at Westminster.

The political excitement that gave Cobbett, Wooler and Hone a market for their papers arose out of the depression that accompanied peace. 'Instead of that happiness, which we were so respectfully promised,' Hone wrote of the post-war crisis, 'we find ourselves plunged into misery unspeakable; and while distress, bankruptcy, and ruin, are sweeping before them the middle class of society, the labouring classes are actually perishing under the various and indescribable sufferings of a state bordering on absolute starvation.'[14]

Britain had dominated world trade for the decades that Europe was tied up in war. Whilst hostilities lasted, the British navy had blockaded the continent, pinning French merchant ships in their home ports. Artificially protected, domestic industry and agriculture flourished. But when the blockade was lifted, British merchants and farmers were forced to compete with cheap foreign imports, both at home and in the lucrative American markets. Many farmers who had purchased land at high prices and made a handsome living feeding the country during the war found that peace brought bankruptcy. The war had cost £1,039 million, and the massive national debt had to be paid off by taxing staples such as soap, candles and paper. The labouring poor, artisans and the middle classes – who had benefited from the distorted wartime economy – suffered the most. Hundreds of thousands were living at starvation level, and the numbers of distressed were swollen by demobbed soldiers and sailors (such as John Cashman) who returned home to find mass unemployment and high food prices.

To add to the woes of the nation, food was scarce because bad weather had ruined the harvest of 1816. The *Examiner* described the sorry state of Britain: 'The people wait; – but in the mean time the rains come down, the distresses increase, bankruptcy crowds upon bankruptcy, – the poor are compelled to retrench, some of them almost to starve, – the fields and roads are swarming with beggars, – debts, excuses, mortifications, grinding humiliations of all sorts, sadden the houses of the middle classes.'[15]

Explaining the decayed state of post-war Britain, Thomas Wooler wrote: 'Her sons have lost the high distinction of *freemen*, which raised them pre-eminent over all the nations of the earth. Liberty is banished from our shores . . . We are *ruined* because we have suffered *ministers* to be *prodigal*. We are *bankrupts* and *insolvent* because we have been careless and foolish.' The merchant had found that 'the markets in which he formerly traded without a rival, crowded with competitors . . . who undersell and outstrip in all, because he has to pay taxes more than the prime cost of all the materials and the price of labour combined'; in the midst of the economic disaster, the tradesman 'finds that all his industry tends to impoverish himself, and to render his shop a high road to the workhouse'; and the artisan and mechanic saw that the political system and taxes had 'robbed them of the hopes of obtaining a bare subsistence in their native country, and degraded them to the commission of crimes, or compelled them to abandon their connexions, to seek a refuge in the wastes of America.'[16]

The miseries of the post-war depression gave Hone the chance to elaborate on the themes that he had been developing in his journalism for a decade. The corruption of politics and the abuses of those in power had become a matter of interest for everyone in the country. If people had been prepared to tolerate such things hitherto, the decrepit condition of Britain pointed to a stale and decayed parliamentary system that produced MPs who neither knew nor cared about the state of the population they claimed to represent. 'For the laws . . . to be just and suitable,' Hone wrote, 'Parliament, which is the fountain of law, must be itself pure and well informed; its Members must be well acquainted with the wants and wishes of the People, and its proceedings be independent of the dictates of all undue influence; particularly of all dictation by Ministers.'[17]

But the ideal of disinterested MPs defending their constituents from arbitrary executive government and stringent taxation was a fantasy. They were ill-informed and subject to unfair influence; and this was, according to the reformists, because they were not accountable to their constituents. The problems facing the country were of little concern to MPs who had no voters to court. Apart from cities like London or Liverpool, most constituencies had only a handful of voters: rich men who selected MPs to protect their interests at Westminster. In Edinburgh County, for example, only thirty-four people were qualified to vote out of a total population of 122,954.

It was a familiar story, but Hone included facts and statistics about the state of representation in Britain for people who were coming to the debate for the first time. He wanted to inform and educate the public, and rouse them from passive acceptance of the corrupt old system. He revealed that eighty-seven peers between them controlled the election of 218 MPs, whilst ninety wealthy commoners returned 137. The government and the Crown also controlled the selection of a significant sum. So in total 487 MPs were nominated by the prevailing interest, leaving just 137 independent of direct control. Parliamentary seats were seen as private property, which the owner could dispose of at will. Peers and magnates 'controlled' the election because, as landlords and employers, they directed their tenants to vote for their choice of candidates. Voting was done in public and anyone who dissented from his landlord's decision could expect rough treatment.

Hone reported Lord Cochrane's exposé of a scandal in the borough of Ilchester, where a hundred houses had been demolished and the families sent to the workhouse when the tenants defied their landlord's command in an election. Another illustrative example of the way in which 'borough-mongers' had an absolute control over elections was Gatton, in Kent, a two-member constituency. Sir Mark Wood had purchased the seat in 1801 for £90,000. The numbers of voters in his seat fluctuated; in one year it peaked at seven. When one resident voted against Wood's two candidates, the constable, an employee of Wood, disqualified him as an elector. Wood made a useful return on his investment, charging 10,000 guineas for nomination to the second seat. Hone wrote an imaginary conversation between Sir Mark Wood and the Prince Regent. Although the conversation never happened, the details were all correct.

Q: You are the proprietor of this borough Sir Mark?
A: I am, may it please your Royal Highness.
Q: How many Members does it send to Parliament?
A: TWO, sir.
Q: Who are they?
A: Myself and my son.
Q: You are much beloved in the borough, Sir MARK?
A: There are not many who tell me otherwise, your Royal Highness.
Q: Were there any opposition candidates?
A: None, sir.
Q: What is the qualification as an elector?
A: Being an inhabitant, paying scot and lot.
Q: Only six electors, then! For I see you have only six houses in the place?
A: Only ONE elector.
Q: What, one elector, and return two members! How is that? But what becomes of the other householders?
A: By buying the borough, I am the freeholder of the six houses; I let five by the week, pay the taxes myself, live in the other, and thus, being the only elector return myself and my son as Members, at the election!

The qualification in this constituency to vote was as a payer of 'scot and lot', or a proportioned share in municipal corporation tax; others who could vote would be magistrates, churchwardens, overseers of the Poor Laws, vestrymen, surveyors of the highways and the collectors of taxes. Sir Mark held all these jobs, and he paid the entire scot and lot contribution, so by 1817 he was the only voter. (It was at least better than the seat of Old Sarum, which was uninhabited.) Between 1809 and 1815 Wood had spent £50,000 returning fifteen pro-government candidates in a number of seats.[18]

Gatton may have been an extreme case, but it was indicative of hundreds of seats where the dominant interest nominated the representative in the House of Commons. The size of constituencies was not standard throughout the country. Although many thousands could vote, they were concentrated in a handful of constituencies like Westminster or Middlesex. The popular voice was diluted by the majority of seats that contained only a few voters. Modern cities like Manchester or Birmingham were not represented, whilst Dunwich on the Suffolk coast, which long before had been one of the largest ports in the country but had been falling into the North Sea since the Middle Ages and was a remote hamlet by 1817, returned two MPs. Looked at another way, the two members nominated on the whim of Tory Sir Mark Wood cancelled the parliamentary votes of Sir Francis Burdett and Lord Cochrane, who represented 12,000 Londoners.

'*Why*, in the 19th century do these practises still continue?' Hone asked, 'simply because THE PEOPLE *have not done themselves justice*. They have left the ordering of the state to the *wisdom* of their rulers, who take care to keep them in ignorance, the better to abuse them.' Whilst explaining the state of parliamentary representation to his readers, Hone shot out darts at the government and his countrymen. They share the blame for the mess; venality and misgovernment have taken root because the public have been passively tolerant or wilfully indolent. His prose style expresses the anger that has been simmering within him throughout a long and frustrating career on the margins of the political debate. At last, in 1817, he has found an audience who have awoken to the shameful state of modern Britain. He relishes the chance to unleash his vitriol; the words and epithets rain down like blows. The liberal sprinkling of italics and capitalisation in the text was deployed to give his writing the quality of an extempore speech, where he can unburden his rage.

The ignorance of MPs without constituents and ministers without opposition has reduced British government to a confused mess; there is no coherence in policy, no direction in legislation, and the result is an impoverished and degraded nation of sickly infants:

We have been dandled, and nursed, and lapped, and regulated, till we are rickety. We want our bonds and restraints gradually loosened, and the free use of our limbs and bodies, to enable us to go alone. We have been over-legislated to. Acts amending and altering, declaring and explaining, prohibiting and encouraging, enacting and repealing, heap our Statute book with provisions creating the evils it would remedy. Every fresh *meddling* increases our help-lessness, and we pray *to be let alone*.

The people are helpless victims, Hone repeats week after week; lib-erty consists in free choice and with public opinion correcting the flaws of misgovernment and over-government by informing ministers and MPs of their useless or wrong-headed policies. Reform of parliament, universal suffrage and annual parliamentary elections would cure this malaise and re-establish some of the traditional traits of the British spir-it. The venality and selfishness of the country's decadent rulers will be kept in check by the inherent common sense and frugality of John Bull when reform sweeps away corruption and his voice is heard. The promise of a more democratic future gives Hone the chance to flatter the national character – honesty, economy, openness, toleration – which he believes has made Britain the greatest country in the world. Reform the constitution, and 'honest dealing and uprightness in every possible way would *then* be countenanced, where they are *despised*'.[19]

The free-flowing prose, shouted without restraint or elaborate sentence construction, complements his clarion call for personal liberty. It is designed to contrast with the sophistry and pedantry with which minis-ters and their hired pens rebuff opposition. Neither Hone's nor Wooler's writing aims to confuse or trick. The wild and vigorous style is supposed to represent the country's passions; it seeks to come straight from the heart, to be genuine and unencumbered by flashy words or artistic flour-ishes. It is intended to resemble good old-fashioned conversation or tavern debate, mocking and railing at the foolishness of executive government.

Hone gives the reader a sense that they are participating in his cam-paign for reform. He self-consciously aims to make his prose sound like his voice. If one were to meet him in a public house or on Fleet Street, he seems to say, this is what he would sound like when provoked to anger at the thought of corrupt and self-interested politicians. He would not grasp for words or aim to make his harangue a polished piece of rhetoric; and the same voice and strength of personality rings loud in the *Reformists' Register*.

It is not just in the words and simple language he uses, but the way he writes. Frequently the text is interrupted when he hears news of a fresh development in parliament; he reports, and then continues. Sometimes he is at the printer's, correcting a proof of the week's edition just before it goes to press, when he hears something and inserts it. The way the paper is composed adds an important quality to the spontaneity and reflexive anger of the prose; the reader is drawn into the performance and he or she feels Hone's rage or is with him when he suddenly hears a story for the first time. There is a sense of immediacy with Hone, and the rough edge of the style makes him seem honest and open rather than self-conscious and polished.

Wooler did something similar, but more daring. He did not write down his articles with pen and ink, but stood next to his printing press, picking up the metal blocks of letter-type and putting them directly on to the press. His hands reached for the blocks of letters as quickly as he could pronounce sonorous and stylish phrases aloud to an imaginary audience. He dispensed with the penned draft, scorning amendments and revisions, so that his ideas flowed onto the printing press 'as they were formed in his mind'. The reader could be sure that every mistake would be reproduced; Wooler would never retract an opinion or re-write for better effect. The finished page is unchanged from the original performance. The result is journalism at its rawest.[20]

Spontaneity was key to the reformist argument. Hone and Wooler's style aims to arouse the reader with vivid imagery, striking words and their flights of fantasy. Often the political situation is fictionalised or given comic treatment. The styles of the two editors were very similar, and reveal much of what reformist journalists were trying to do in 1817. Every week in his paper, Wooler included a letter from his impish creation the Black Dwarf to his colleague 'The Yellow Bonze of Japan'. Both were experts in oriental despotism and well-seasoned connoisseurs of slavery. The Black Dwarf had journeyed to London to observe the state of liberty in Britain. It had been led to believe from its history books that Britain was a country where freedoms flourished and the population was independent and intolerant of absolutist pretensions. When it got there, it found Britain identical to every other despotism it had visited. This was Wooler's device to lacerate his readers for their political passivity and cringing acceptance of the government's unbounded power. The Black Dwarf was amazed by the contrast between the much-trumpeted ideals of liberty and the sorry reality: 'These islanders will certainly kill me. I am at one period convulsed with laughter at their folly, and at another stifled with sighs at the misery they exhibit.' What was so sad was the British tendency to refuse to admit that they were thus debased. 'The only difference between an European and a Japanese slave', the Dwarf wrote to the Yellow Bonze, 'is that the fetters of the one are forced upon him, and the other *asserts* that he wears them of his own *free-will* . . . There are *Englishmen*, even Englishmen, who are *proud of being slaves*; – and who crouch to the tyranny that condescends to use them as servile tools.'[21]

The pages of Hone's and Wooler's papers lift the lid on a seedy world of nepotism and jobbery with the same verve and bravura style. The venality of politicians is made to seem putrid and disgusting. Whilst many starved, the politicians and their connexions profited from the political system they controlled. The voice of the people was lost at Westminster when politics became nothing more than a scramble for patronage.

Mocking them with a vocabulary more appropriate for the victims of the economic depression, Hone divided the ruling class into two groups:

1st, those who have the actual sweets of office, viz. money wrung from the people; power over the nation, which enables them to indulge their ambitious propensities; and what are called honours, to flatter self-love, pride and ignorance. 2nd, Their dependants gasping for jobs, and contracts, and emoluments, – for themselves and their hungry, proud, beggarly relations.[22]

The kinds of jobs that MPs and their friends gasped for were numerous and very attractive. A good career with a generous income could be got fairly easily, if one had the right connexions. For some, it was a state benefit system existing for the aristocracy. Most jobs were relics of a medieval court, with no use in the modern world. Lady Arabella Heneage had inherited the nebulous but salaried job of Chief Usher in the Court of Exchequer, and the Duke of St Albans got £1,372 a year as

Master of the Hawks. In the eighteenth century, Lord Chancellor Hardwicke said that sinecures were 'a kind of obligation on the Crown for the support of ancient noble families, whose peerages happen to continue after their estates have worn out', and it was still partly true in Hone's time. Hazlitt, Wooler, and other reformists, called them 'Noble Paupers' or 'State Paupers', the beneficiaries of a wildly generous kind of private poor law.[23]

But most sinecures were doled out to men who had worked their way into political life. Lord Eldon, a career politician rather than an underemployed aristocrat, racked up the fortune of £42,600 a year. Only £18,000 came from his jobs as Speaker of the House of Lords and Lord Chancellor; the rest was made up from many appointments which required no work, such as Visitor of Catherine and Pembroke Halls in Cambridge, as a governor of the Charter House or as a lord of trade and plantations. Eldon made his brother an admiralty judge with a salary of £6,704, and an annual pension of £4,000.[24] Even the most humble MPs were able to secure sinecures for themselves and give jobs in the civil service, tax collecting, the army and local government away to their connexions, dependants and families. And to add to the treasure chest of political preferment, there was a host of courtiers, bishops, clergymen, diplomats, colonial governors, lawyers and the like who had access to sinecures, places and pensions – rewards out of all proportion to the work they actually did. To be born into a class of office holders, or to buy influence in the Commons, meant a life of easy luxury.

And it was the impoverished taxpayer who filled the reservoir of state bounty. In a brilliant piece of invention, Wooler took on a voice of faux naïvety to create an image of parasitic sinecurists. Poor starving John Bull, suffering during the worst depression of modern times, leaves his valuable meat unattended for a moment:

Look at that fine piece of beef. See how beautiful, how tempting it is. Yes very fine; but what have we here. A fine parcel of maggots, truly! How fat and lively they are! and merry as possible. Why yes, in sooth, they may well be merry. Why they will never get through all that sirloin! There is an abundance to eat, and the sun shines upon them all very pleasantly. There, there is a fine large fat fellow. See, he is going to begin upon a part untouched . . . How the poor man that expects his dinner of it will swear when he finds them out!²⁵

At another time, Wooler reminded his readers that every act of their slavish existence profited the sinecurist: 'The hand of taxation is so very long, that a child cannot purchase a rattle, or a farthing's worth of gingerbread, without giving one half of the purchase-money towards the maintenance of the monarch, the lords spiritual and temporal, the ministers, and half the members of the house of commons.'[26]

'The enormous amounts of taxation and debt', said Lord Cochrane in the Commons, and reported in the *Reformists' Register*, 'were the real cause of the nation's misery, and, combined with the objects of placemen, pensioners and sinecurists, the enormous civil list, the military establishment of 150,000 men in profound peace, were a gross insult to the understanding'.[27] But why would MPs vote to relieve the distress of the country by cutting taxes if it meant the reduction of their incomes? Would they ever retrench state expenditure, if to do so would be to abolish the jobs they craved and a system of finance that paid rich dividends? In 1817 it was clear that they would not. Public opinion, expressed at meetings, in petitions and in the press was ignored in parliament with self-confident and proud defiance.

A constitution that provided vast incomes would never be reformed at the instigation of men who benefited from it, the reformists argued. But even worse than the unseemly and wasteful competition for the spoils of political life was the *political* cost of the sinecure system. The plenitude of high-paying jobs was in the gift of ministers. The useless positions and generous pensions, they alleged, had been created so that the government could buy support in the House of Commons, judiciary and press. It was the prop for a tyrannical administration, which could do as it pleased secure in the knowledge that opposition would be muted. Charles James Fox memorably called MPs who were paid by the Crown to support the ministerial party 'marketable flotsam'.

The journalists represented the ministry as a 'cabal' comprising Home Secretary Lord Sidmouth, who wanted to be remembered as 'the country gentleman's secretary of state', rather than represent the country; the Foreign Secretary Lord Castlereagh, the infamous flogger of Irish peasants and British soldiers and supporter of the Holy Alliance; and George Canning, the most polished speaker on behalf of the anti-reformers. Other ministers featured seldom in the attack, and the Prime Minster, Lord Liverpool, not at all. It was this trio of despots (to use the reformist vocabulary) that exercised their iron grip upon their followers, providing pay-offs for MPs, journalists, bishops, electors, businessmen and anyone else who might be useful to them. Wooler talked of 'gradations of *necessary slaves*' permeating society who would vote for the government on any occasion as long as their livelihoods were guaranteed. Even if they disagree with the government, dissent is impossible because 'slaves they are to the "existing system": but they live upon the system: and very few could obtain a living by other means'. It did not matter which ministers were in charge of the country, for there was, as the *Examiner* said, only one qualification for high office: 'any set of noodles that can feed the borough-mongers are enabled to carry on the administration'.[28]

Irreverent journalism and satirical invective were in huge demand as the country slid further into depression, and the government refused to reform. The language of insult and mockery was a way of venting anger and inflicting punishment upon detested ministers. Hone knew that the public wanted revenge, and satire satisfied their seething anger. His sense of humour and comedic invention was entirely appropriate for the post-war crisis. Sitting on the pinnacle of the monstrous mountain of licensed banditry was the Regent, the sinecurist supreme. He consumed money to pay for a lavish lifestyle and an addiction to gambling, feasts, drink and mistresses. His extravagance provoked huge anger, which Hone capitalised on. The Portuguese had presented the Regent with a captured French cannon, mounted on a plinth, as thanks for Britain's help during the Napoleonic Wars; it was unveiled on 12 August 1816, the Prince's birthday. In slang, cannon was called 'bomb', and bomb was pronounced 'bum'. Hone latched on to the scatological pun with alacrity, celebrating the unveiling of the 'Regent's Bomb' in satirical verse in 1816. The names of the fawning ministers were thinly disguised.

> Oh what a Bomb! Oh heaven defend us
> The thought of Bombs is quite tremendous!
> What crowds will come from every shore
> To gaze on its amazing bore!

What swarms of statesmen, warm and loyal
To worship a Bomb so truly Royal!
And first approach three secret hags,
Then him the R[egen]t calls 'Old Bags' [Lord Chancellor Eldon]
 Methinks I see V[ansittart] come
And humbly kiss the Royal Bomb
While T[ylney] W[ellesley] (loyal soul)
Will take its measure with a Pole;
And C[astlereagh] will low beseech
To kiss a corner of the breech;
And next will come old Georgie R[ose]
And in the touch hole shove his nose.

Saluting the R–t's Bomb was accompanied by a cartoon drawn by
George Cruikshank showing ministers kissing the Regent's impressive-
ly large backside. In a government dominated by sinecures, the Regent
was the biggest sinecure holder of all. He received hundreds of thousands of pounds from the civil list, and appointed people to jobs and
pensions. If ministers had plenty of people flattering them for money
and favour, they still had to kiss the Regent's behind to secure their own
privileges. Such satire is timeless; the image of obsequious politicians
kissing arses for preferment can never be misunderstood. The opportunity to invoke it at this time was not to be missed, and Hone could
indulge his love for coarse jokes for the benefit of like-minded laughers.
In his *Register*, Hone invented another way to describe the sinecurists'
and ministers' condition of shameful dependence upon the Crown's
bounty: 'As to the King, their love for him is like the dram-drinkers' love
for the gin-shop keepers.'[29]

Addressing their readers, Hone and Wooler wanted to identify a public
which was part neither of the refractory mob nor of the corrupt elite.
Corruption had a protean quality; it spread through society like an epi-
demic, soiling the most noble of British institutions and characteristics,
drawing people into the honey-trap of patronage to become the 'necessary
slaves' of Castlereagh, Sidmouth, Canning and their tribe. Hone and
Wooler warned their readers that such temptations were powerful, but
degrading. Bribed MPs and journalists suffered the same kind of addic-

Eldon is on the far left; then 'three hags', George's mistresses; Nicholas Vansittart is lovingly kissing the breech; Tylney Wellesley handles the pole; George Rose, a man made rich by the sinecure system, sticks his nose into the touch-hole of the 'bomb'; Lord Castlereagh, on the right, awaits his turn to kiss the royal birthday-boy. The mortar, mounted on its elaborate plinth, can still be seen on Horse Guards Parade.

tion as the lowest gin-addled beggar. Wooler argued: 'men of moderate incomes . . . stand in the gap between anarchy and despotism'. They represented the temperance and common sense of the country because they avoided the abuses of the elite and the impulsive passions of the mob. 'The *rabble* in high life, and the *rabble* in low life differ only in dress,' he wrote. 'Their intellects are quite on par, and they are equally mischievous when they take the lead. The *people* are distinct from both; that title should unite the thinking and honest portions of all classes; and they form a body too numerous to be deceived. In this body should be all the middling classes, as in their natural sphere.'[30]

Hone's and Wooler's language was so exaggerated and energetic because they wanted to shock the quiescent and respectable middle classes out of complacent acceptance of the *status quo*. Words like 'slaves', 'tyranny', 'fetters', 'dependence', or the images of an enervated, supine country were fired off with little embarrassment about degenerating into hyperbole. In case anyone thought that the middle classes enjoyed a special status, or entered the considerations of ministers, Wooler bluntly told them:

It is difficult to adopt any mode of address to the *unrepresented* part of the British public . . . The *unrepresented* are mere expletives in the political creation; and if they were not called upon to *obey* laws in the enactment of which they have no share, they might be abandoned to the apparent insignificance to which they are told the constitution has consigned them . . . Well then, gentlemen, although you are not mocked with the title of '*worthy and independent freemen!*' – although your suffrages are not counted, and *nobility*, and *wealth*, and *respectability* disdain to take you by the hand once in seven years, yet you are *something* while you have *anything*. The minister is not above taking your *money*, although he is not in need of your advice.[31]

The vast majority of the country shared a status of 'insignificance'. The restricted franchise and the sinecure system had destroyed all other divisions in the country; as one commentator said, 'Now we have two classes existing in this country – the many and the few.'[32] Or put another way, the tax-payer and the tax-receiver, the non-voter and the voter. In an editorial Wooler told all those who considered themselves to be middle class that such a synthetic distinction was irrelevant: they had worked hard all their lives and tolerated the political system, only to be 'told they have *no stake* in the country', just like everyone else.[33]

Hone and Wooler spoke directly to those the government had insulted by labelling the entire reformist movement seditious and republican when it considered restrictive legislation after Spa Fields and the assassination attempt. Southey wrote: 'It is the people at this time who stand in need of reformation, not the government.'[34] Hone printed a list of some of the terms that MPs, ministers and peers had used in the 1817 parliament to describe the people they were supposed to serve: '*wild – visionary – disgusting – malicious – disloyal – seditious – rebellious – rash experimentalists – mad enthusiasts – demagogues – malcontents – liars – enemies of social order – incendiaries, mediating civil war and bloodshed.*' And the petitions that hundreds of thousands of men and women had signed and sent to their representatives in parliament had been described as '*a farrago – vague – dangerous – impractical – pernicious – mischievous – blundering – intended to produce incalculable mischief – inciting people to revolt and rebellion*'.[35]

If parliament stereotyped all reformers in this way, it allowed Hone to compete for the sympathies of the respectable members of the community. MPs, he said, believed that 'there was no "*Public*" – nothing but a horde of wretches, miserable slaves, too few and too contemptible to claim the notice of the mighty persons who wrangled and abused one another'.[36] Reformists were not republicans and Jacobins, but included among their number some of the most industrious, 'upright', loyal and patriotic groups in the country. Where else did sane public opinion reside if not with these people? Hone wrote of the growth of the reform movement in 1817: 'An extent of talent and political knowledge has been displayed from one end of the island to the other, which no man could have anticipated.'[37]

In the first number of his *Register*, Hone said that there was 'a blaze of intellect' being displayed throughout the country; it was evident in the public meetings throughout the country and the petitions sent to parliament. 'But', he asked, 'in which class is it that we witness this knowledge – this improvement in understanding?' In answering his question, he described the kind of people he was trying to reach: 'It is to the MIDDLE CLASSES *now*, as at *other* times, in this country, the salvation of all that ought to be dear to Englishmen must be confided: it is amongst *this* class that the great improvement has been going on; it is from this class, informed as no class in any country, at any time, ever were informed, that whatever of good may obtained will proceed.' And as he investigated the groundswell of public opinion throughout Britain, he found that his initial assumptions were correct. Reporting a reform meeting in Yorkshire in March, he wrote that it was the 'independent gentlemen' who were giving a lead to the community by framing petitions and organising public conventions. These educated and propertied gentlemen were the natural 'leaders of the People'; they were 'heart and hand with the People, and men who, if supported by the People' would rouse the country in a unanimous call for reform.[38]

These were the kinds of people with whom Hone identified: the polite and respectable. Their articulate and rational voice would force the government to reform. 'The war against mind is to ensure defeat. A man cannot be made to unlearn that which he knows; nor can any laws prevent him from communicating his knowledge; and sooner, or later, 'statesmen will be taught what they alone seem ignorant of – that "KNOWLEDGE IS POWER".'[39]

On 28 February, Sir William Garrow, the Attorney-General, was called upon to advise parliament. He was not surprised 'that gentlemen should view with abhorrence and disgust the publications which for some weeks past have been industriously circulated in every part of the country, and which are unquestionably of a tendency that must prove most destructive to the best interests of the country'. The ever-loyal Tory *Courier* agreed: 'Having all a common interest in the welfare of the state, we must all intuitively feel that the common good will be promoted by the EXTINCTION of these writings which aim only to unsettle all our notions in religion, morals and politics.'[40]

Lord Sidmouth promised 'vigorous measures for protecting the public peace and safety'. At the end of February, *habeas corpus*, the obligation of the law to show justifiable cause of arrest, was suspended by Act of Parliament until July. Many saw this basic freedom as one of the few things distinguishing Britain from other European countries. The *Examiner* described it as

the right of walking about your home without molestation, of sleeping in your own bed, of going where you please, of having your reputation in your own keeping; it is the right of not being, in any political respect, at the mercy of others, of not being condemned before you are heard, of not being taken up on suspicion, and thrown into a dungeon, perhaps a solitary one; – it is the right, in short, and the whole real description, of being a free man.[41]

The suspension of *habeas corpus* seemed to prove all that Hone had been arguing throughout the previous two months. It showed how a parliament dominated by sinecurists and placemen operated. The Committee of Secrecy's report on the Spa Fields riots had sparked the fear that reformists were preparing a revolution and it paved the way for repressive legislation. He printed a table showing how much each member of the committee earned from his state pensions, sinecures and other rewards. In all, they received £53,351 a year: 'Thus the freedom and birthright of Britons are basely bartered for gain!'[42]

In the first week of March Sidmouth indicated the people he wanted to be arrested first under his emergency powers when he sent a circular letter to all the Lords Lieutenant in the country empowering them to arrest publishers and hawkers they believed guilty of disseminating sedition. Hone identified the key issue: 'Arbitrary and unfeeling, they reject *all* legislative measures for abolishing either sinecures or *useless* places. In the insolence of their power, they oppress us with severe statutes – in the wantonness of impunity, they answer our supplications for relief, by taking away the only security of our persons from imprisonment, when they choose to throw us into dungeons.'[43]

It was no longer mere rhetoric. Cobbett, Wooler and Hone had been identified as the main threats to the country's peace and security. Every hard word, contemptuous epithet or criticism of ministers was now a step towards the prison cell. The government promised the harshest repression of the press since the prosecutions brought against members of the London Corresponding Society over two decades before. The press prosecutions of 1810–13 had been piecemeal and sporadic; Sidmouth was intending a much more sustained campaign than any of his predecessors at the Home Office. The three editors were living under the constant threat of arrest, and every new edition of their papers brought the danger closer. 'Fellow countrymen,' Hone wrote, the confidence of his journalism soured with pessimism, 'every one of us who feels he has a country now feels his mind distressed, his heart heavy, his courage fail him.'[44]

Fully aware that he was a marked man, Hone went to visit William Cobbett at his London address in Catherine Street, just off the Strand, on 15 March. Both men knew that imprisonment was not just a threat, but by now inevitable; their continued freedom was contingent upon the tender mercy of Sidmouth. 'Our salutation was mutual jocular congratulations upon our liberty, after the suspension of the Habeas Corpus Act,' Hone wrote with sarcasm a couple of weeks later. The good-natured banter about the punishment awaiting them only lasted as long as the meeting. On 5 April Hone conceded the grim reality of their situation: 'I seem to have the sound of his voice in my ear. I see his very attitude, as he sat in his chair when I left him by his fireside in Catherine-street. I cannot get these little incidents out of my head. We attach importance to such trifles when they are connected with recollections of those whom we esteem and admire, and whom we shall perhaps see no more.'

Cobbett voluntarily suspended the *Political Register* and fled to America. It was a considerable victory for Sidmouth that the mere threat of censorship could close newspapers even before he had the chance to exercise his new powers. Cobbett realised that he was facing another long spell in prison and perhaps a more stringent fine than he had received in 1810; he contended that it was no man's duty to sacrifice himself to the unbounded power of the state.

Before he left, Cobbett went to the Old Bailey to advise Hone to accompany him into exile, suggesting that money was available to subsidise his passage abroad, and enough for his large family to follow later. Hone turned to his wife: 'What shall we do, my dear?' 'Stay where you are,' Sarah told him.

'You don't know my husband,' she continued to William Cobbett, 'if you imagine he is the coward to desert a cause he believes to be right; but if he determines that he ought to go, whenever it may be, Mr Cobbett, we all go together; there will be no following.'[45]

7

Phantom of the Imagination
The Government and the Press

They hate the press, and they confess their hatred. It is the spectre that haunts them incessantly . . . While they rule truth must be proscribed, for truth is to them, their dread and their poison. A free press would dismiss them all to tend sheep; or to drive hogs, instead of insulting men, and rendering a nation ridiculous. The prop must therefore be destroyed . . .
Thomas Wooler, *Black Dwarf*

We have laws also against poisoning the minds of the people to prevent the exposure of unwholesome meat in our markets, and the mixture of deleterious drugs in beer. We have laws also against the poisoning the minds of the people, by exciting discontent and disaffection . . .
Robert Southey

The desertion of William Cobbett immediately made William Hone and Thomas Wooler the foremost reformist journalists, and consequently most in danger of prosecution. Both continued to publish in defiance of censorship.

When he advised parliament on the legal means by which seditious and blasphemous writings could be suppressed, Attorney-General Garrow alluded to only one journalist. William Hone, he told the Lords, was the author of the most 'infamous' and 'immoral' pieces that flooded the country. In February 1817, when the government was marshalling all the powers at its disposal to silence its critics, Hone made the most significant decision of his life. He wrote and published a series of parodies on the liturgy of the Church of England which he must have known from the start would be subject to prosecution for criminal libel.

Hone's target was not the Church or religion, but MPs and ministers. The government had the awesome power to exercise its will with impunity because it had at its gift pensions, sinecures and other emoluments to buy parliamentary votes and subdue criticism. What better way to satirise the ministers than as divine beings, and MPs as worship-pers at the font of patronage? Hone's three parodies – the *Political Creed*, *Political Liturgy* and *Catechism of a Ministerial Member* – did just that. In Hone's imagination, an aspiring MP is catechised so that he understands his supine loyalty to the cabinet as a religious obligation:

Question: What is thy duty towards the Minister?

Answer: My duty to the Minister is, to trust him as much as I can; to fear him; to honour him with all my words, with all my bows, with all my scrapes, and all my cringes; to flatter him; to give him thanks; to give up my whole soul to him; to idolize his name, and obey his word; and to serve him blindly all the days of his political life.

Q: What is thy duty towards thyself?

A: My duty towards myself is to love nobody but myself, and to do unto most men what I would not that they should do unto me . . . to learn to get the Pensions of myself and my colleagues out of the People's labour, and to do my duty in that department of public plunder unto which it shall please the Minister to call me.

It has a timeless quality; whereas much of Hone's satire is meaningless without the context that gave rise to it, this one could be put into the mouths of modern backbenchers who sacrifice their principles on the altar of their ambition. Despite the passing of almost two centuries, its humour is still alive. Hone's version of the Lord's Prayer captures this perfectly:

Our Lord who art in Treasury, whatsoever be Thy name. Thy power will be prolonged. Thy will be done throughout the Empire as it is in each session. Give us our usual sops and forgive us our occasional absence from divisions; as we promise not to forgive them that divide against us. Turn us not from our places; but keep us in the House of Commons, the land of Pensions and Plenty; and deliver us from the People. Amen.

Hone's vision of ministers as demigods demanding and receiving unthinking devotion from a congregation of hypnotised MPs captured the popular imagination. It was a delicious conception of parliament as a promised land, where only the truly devout were rewarded with the milk and honey of pensions. His Fleet Street shop was inundated with customers of all social classes. Even ministers, members of parliament and magistrates, the men whom he caricatured as spineless, were eager to buy copies. Hone withdrew them from sale within a week, claiming that he did so at the behest of his pious father.

Yet the short print run made them famous; scarcity entailed cult status. The 3,000 copies that were released circulated briskly throughout the country, sold and resold by provincial booksellers and hawkers. For many they were vibrant symbols of discontent – the most penetrating and vicious attack on the inflated power of ministers and the purblind obedience of their corrupted followers. Wealthy Londoners offered Hone bribes far exceeding the cover price for copies of the suppressed editions. Rival publishers released pirated editions or invented their own parodies of a catechism, the Liturgy or Creed. Within a month, publishers in Bristol, Newcastle, Manchester, Southampton and Birmingham had pirated the satires and issued them under their own names. The Home Office received reports from around the country that they were being hawked in remote districts, and read aloud in taverns everywhere. Their ubiquity was such that the MP Colonel Thomas Wood found one in his children's nursery; his verdict was that they were 'very good; but very shocking'.[2]

The Attorney-General brought copies of the liturgical parodies to the House of Commons to show MPs evidence of the most disgusting reformist writing. Obviously relishing his performance, he produced the satires but refused to read from them lest he offend the tender sensibilities of the assembled gentlemen and shock their ears with Hone's depraved humour. Instead, he secured them with the seals of his office and placed them on the table of the House, so that no MP could be exposed unwittingly to such filth; any member brave enough to break the seals and read of them could do so. Their author, Garrow promised, would be 'severely punished'.[3]

Such works, Sidmouth told the Lords, represented the most glaring evil of a free press, 'tending not only to overturn the existing form of government and order of society, but to root out those principles upon which alone any government or any society can be supported'. The Poet Laureate and fierce pro-government writer Robert Southey, in common with many Tories, believed that loyalty to the constitution was learnt with the Creed and the Catechism; that to fear God was to hon-our the King. The people were led away from Christian obedience to the state when doubt was provoked by the mocking words of malicious London journalists such as Hone. Lord Sidmouth articulated most clearly the view that contempt for religion was the first step to danger-ous radicalism in politics: 'When the people of this country are deprived of all the consolations of religion, they will be the better pre-pared to throw off their allegiance, and lose their accustomed respect for the laws and the constitution.'[4]

The uproar that the parodies caused in parliament could hardly have surprised Hone. And he knew that risking a charge of blasphemy played into the government's hands. The public was hostile to profane publications, and juries rarely acquitted blasphemers, for as Lord Erskine told the Lords, 'libels of that description required no legal knowledge to ascertain their pernicious effects'. Why then did he risk his freedom and the fortunes of his family by choosing to extend the attack on the government with parodies of *The Book of Common Prayer*? The most obvious answer was that the catechism offered a rich vocabulary of submissive phrases to put into the mouths of cringing backbenchers. Yet the temptation for the atheist Hone to use these texts to imagine MPs worshipping their political masters did not justify the risk.

In spring 1817 Hone did not give a ready answer. He claimed not to have been aware of the offence they would cause to good Christians such as his father or Sidmouth, so withdrew them in deference to pub-lic opinion as soon as possible. But this is hardly a convincing explana-tion; even a publisher with the most basic knowledge of the laws would have known the dangers such a step involved. Hone was no novice when it came to the law, and he was only feigning naïvety. His decision to publish 3,000 copies must count as a deliberate act of provocation, daring a response from the government. This must have seemed like madness or suicidal recklessness at a time when Sidmouth was primed to unleash a war on the press, with blasphemers at the top of his list of offenders. It would only be in December, when Hone was on trial, that the country became aware that the decision to publish these parodies was a calculated act with an intent that went beyond its obvious function as a piece of irreverent satire. As ever, Hone's first thought was the fight for the freedom of the press.

The offence of blasphemous or seditious libel did not consist in the words or arguments a writer used. Lord Liverpool said that certain parts of *The Decline and Fall of the Roman Empire* were blasphemous, but it would never be subject to government prosecution because it was read only by educated men who were wise enough to resist being seduced from their religion by Gibbon's arguments.[5]

A publication became culpable under law when it was distributed among the uneducated and heedless mob, people who could neither resist artful rhetoric nor understand the difference between political debate and a call to revolutionary action. Hone's old enemy, Dr John Stoddart, described the typical reader of reformist literature as the labourer whose 'understanding barely enables him to distinguish between a cabbage and a potato'.[6] In the *Quarterly Review*, Robert Southey depicted an horrific account of what was happening in the country when the common people had their fill of Cobbett, Wooler or Hone: 'It is the weekly paper which finds its way to the pot-house in towns, and the ale-house in the country, inflaming the turbulent temper of the manufacturer and disturbing the quiet attachment of the peasant to those institutions under which he and his fathers have dwelt in peace. He receives no account of public affairs . . . but what comes through these polluted sources.'[7]

Sidmouth said that no government in British history had ever encountered a press that could reach every corner of the kingdom. The danger he wished to contain in 1817 was so serious because it was so new. 'Never was there a period when blasphemy was so completely enlisted in the service of sedition,' he told the Lords, explaining why censorship had become imperative. 'A greater number of persons can read now, than at any former period; they are better informed; they are collected more in large bodies, especially in manufacturing towns; there are also, I am sorry to say, more ale-houses. Besides, these publications are very cheap, almost gratuitous . . . '[8]

Sidmouth and Southey believed that the industrial revolution and the explosion of the popular press were twinned. Lost in the new metropolises, uprooted from their villages and small market towns, they became strangers to the Church and oblivious to habits of deference; the soulless factory and dank slum bred disloyalty and fitted them to be the credulous victims of malicious journalists. In a word frequently used by ministers, London publishers had turned the circulation of their loathsome works into an 'industry'. The reach of reformist journalism was so perplexing to the government because it used recently pioneered techniques, relying upon an informal network of individuals stretching throughout the country. Broadsheet newspapers were easy to regulate, and their distribution quantifiable. They were subject to tax; the prices were therefore high enough to be affordable only by a wealthy readership, and their circulation was recorded by the Stamp Office. But papers like the *Reformists' Register* and the *Black Dwarf* evaded formal control because they were published as pamphlets, and therefore not taxable. The Home Office was ignorant of how many copies were sold, or who read them. Ministers had to rely on anecdotal evidence, the reports of magistrates and informers, or their own crude suppositions. But they were in no doubt that reformist literature had penetrated society and was read by the whole country.

The desertion of William Cobbett had an impact on Hone's life other than making him the government's most hated journalist. The ways in which Hone and Wooler got their newspapers from central London to towns and villages they had never visited, nor had any contacts in, had been developed by the veteran journalist. At the end of 1816 he requested that his readers act as agents for him in their home towns. He would sell his *Political Register* wholesale to booksellers, shopkeepers or private individuals, and he cited one agent who made seventy-five shillings a week profit selling 1,000 copies. If people would take it upon themselves to sell just 100 copies, they would make enough money to feed their families for a week. He also advised the wealthier agents to employ hawkers to extend the distribution out of major towns to the remoter villages and hamlets in their region.[9]

In 1817 one of Sidmouth's informers wrote to the Home Office from Hull, reporting that a grocer was the 'principal agent for Cobbett' in that town. He ordered about 1,500 copies of the *Register* a week, and, according to the informer, he 'employs *underagents* in Hull, Sculcoats and Holderness' to sell the paper in the wider district. In February Robert Southey encountered a sailor in Rydal who had been given a stock of reformist papers to sell as he travelled to his ship at Whitehaven. And such networks were established throughout the country; copies of the *Political Register* would emanate from Catherine Street in London to obscure parts of the country via a chain of amateur agents, booksellers, grocers, stationers, their underagents, and itinerant salesmen; each link in the process profited from the continued sale and resale. Even innkeepers and publicans, the most important customers, would benefit, for an alehouse's stock of weekly papers was considered a major attraction. [10]

The agencies were essential to the distribution process. Any publisher who developed connexions and struck deals with these strangers would have the possibility of capturing a national market. In late 1816 and early 1817 Cobbett controlled a monopoly of the distribution process through well-developed relationships with the men and women on the ground. When he suspended the paper in March, Hone moved in on his territory, and inherited many of the provincial agents as wholesale customers for the *Reformists' Register*. When Hone recorded his final meeting with Cobbett, he made it clear that they were close friends and political allies; he said that they exchanged books and ideas, and their politics were identical. To Cobbett's abandoned readers, he said, 'I claim your support for this publication.' Hone's paper would continue Cobbett's work, and preserve his ideals, whilst the great man was abroad. The *Political Register* was defunct, and Hone's *Reformists' Register* was its natural successor.[11]

But it was not individual readers he was trying to convince in the first instance, but the all-important local agents, who would determine the success of his paper. Perhaps Cobbett passed on his list of contacts to Hone and recommended him to his agents, for a week after Hone recorded their last meeting, he advertised that 'Applications for the Reformists' Register should be made to the different persons who sold Mr Cobbett's Weekly Political Pamphlet'. Indeed, he wished to spread his *Register* to villages and towns Cobbett had never reached, and requested that his readers establish their own agencies to sell the paper to their neighbours. People were asked to write to Hone at the Old

Bailey stating on which coach they wanted their copies to be sent. Bundles of the *Register* would then be wrapped in 'conveyance parcels' and put on one of the public coaches which serviced the more important towns. The principal agents would collect their parcels from the coach, and divide the copies into smaller bundles to be sent to book-sellers and general stores in their locale, which were not on the coach routes. These tradesmen re-divided their parcels, and sold batches to hawkers, who would make the final journey in the process, taking the *Register* to shopless hamlets.[12]

Wooler developed a similar network for the *Black Dwarf*. In April, a man named Deakin was arrested in the Staffordshire town of Hanley for selling the paper in the market without a hawker's licence. Giving evidence, the hawker said that he had been employed by one Fletcher to sell the *Black Dwarf*, who in turn had received his copies from a schoolmaster named Parkinson. How Parkinson got *his* copies is not recorded, but the story is an example of how a reformist paper travelled from an office on the Strand to the market of a Black Country town, places no London editor could visit, or develop personal contacts. And the method of distributing information out from London worked in reverse. Hone published letters from readers, reports of reform meetings and extracts from local newspapers from parts of the country as diverse as Warrington, Exeter, Yorkshire, Plymouth, Norwich and Edinburgh, showing something of the range of his paper.[13]

Because the papers were circulated from amateur to amateur in an anonymous chain, there are no readership figures for reformist journalism. To use the language of parliament, it was a complex machine, operated by thousands of invisible cogs. The editors themselves were deliberately vague about the numbers of readers. They wanted to perpetuate the illusion of universality that the government had persuaded itself existed. In the 19 April number of the *Reformists' Register* Hone wrote: '[the *Register*] is now higher in circulation than any daily, or weekly publication whatever – it is higher that the highest of them in sale, by MANY THOUSAND COPIES, and increases each week . . . '[14]

But estimates of readership or claims to high sales were meaningless. As Wooler wrote, 'A thousand and ten thousand unconnected links will not form a chain; and mere readers are only atoms in a rope of sand . . .

To be important, men must meet each other, unite their knowledge, compare their sentiments, weigh together the force of opposite statements.'[15] The editors knew that their readership was far larger than the numbers of individual copies sold. The typical practice for reading a newspaper was in groups, whether in taverns or coffee houses, reading societies, reformist meetings and work places. The republican journalist Richard Carlile wrote that when he was working in the tin mines in 1817 his copy of Wooler's paper 'got illegibly black' after it had passed through the grubby hands of all his fellow workers.[16] In the later 1820s the *Westminster Review* said that for every single copy of a newspaper there were an average thirty readers. Once the papers left London in their conveyance parcels, there was no way of knowing who, or how many, would read them. Robert Southey, exercising the Laureate's pen in support of censorship, conjured up the nightmarish scene of illiterate workers intoxicated by a cocktail of strong drink and reformist poison. 'Where one who can read is to be found, all who have ears can hear,' he informed the readers of the *Quarterly Review*. 'The weekly epistles of the apostles of sedition are read aloud in tap-rooms and pot-houses to believing auditors, listening greedily when they are told that their rulers fatten upon the gains extracted from their blood and sinews; that they are cheated, oppressed and plundered.'[17]

That politicians really believed the journalists had captured the popular mentality with their vitriolic publications was reflected in the words of the minister William Huskisson: 'The public mind had been poisoned on the subject of sinecures.' The government believed that the press had a protean quality; something that eluded all control, saturated the country, and monopolised the public imagination with impunity. Its circulation was seen as a mysterious process, and summed up best in Wooler's description of the press's ghostly emblem 'The Black Dwarf', who was 'dangerous from his power of division (for like the polypus, he can divide and redivide, and each division remain a perfect animal)'. This sense of ubiquity and invisible, almost organic, diffusion played on the deepest fears of ministers, who were frightened by something which defied their control. As Wooler said, it was an incubus, the 'phantom of the imagination'. [18]

Lord Sidmouth claimed to know the effect that Hone's *Reformists'*
Register or his profane satires and Wooler's *Black Dwarf* had on law-
abiding subjects; it was comparable to taking mind-altering drugs:

I have myself seen the effects of these pernicious doctrines on some misguided
men; and had heard from some of them . . . that it was the influence of this poison that has taken them away from their regular duties . . . they had been industrious and well-affected members of society; but that these and hundreds of
their unfortunate neighbours, have been corrupted by the insidious principles
disseminated by these itinerant hawkers of seditions and blasphemy.[19]

The laws of libel allowed ministers to prosecute journalists they
believed to be threatening the safety of the country. In his circular letter
to the Lord Lieutenants Sidmouth empowered them to arrest hawkers
and publishers they believed guilty of distributing 'seditious' or 'blasphemous' libels. It allowed magistrates and judges wide latitude in
defining these terms. The laws of seditious and blasphemous libel permitted political writing which was held to be within the bounds of 'fair
and temperate discussion'. But as Dr Johnson said of drinking, he knew
what indulgence was, he knew what abstinence was, but temperance
was impossible to understand. According to Ellenborough, any publication was culpable under the libel laws 'which tends to excite the discontent of the people or, either by calumny or design, to bring the
established Authorities of the Government into disesteem'.[20]

The definition of the law was deliberately vague. Judges and juries
were required to assess the effect that an alleged libel would have on the
public mind, or, in the words of the law, its tendency to provoke people
to criminal acts. If the readership consisted of educated gentlemen, a
violent polemic would not be libellous, because they could discriminate between truth and falsehood, and would be unlikely to commit
criminal acts as a result of their reading. But if, as the ministers and their
propagandists maintained, the readership consisted of gullible inebri-
ates who were inflamed to rebellion by reading about sinecures and
other corrupt practices, reformist journalists were guilty of criminal
libel.

The laws of libel also existed to protect men in high office from the
contempt of the crowd. In a judgement in 1804, Lord Ellenborough

ruled that the right of journalists to criticise great men was restricted by
the laws: 'It has been observed, that it is the right of the British subject
to exhibit the folly or imbecility of the members of the government. But,
gentlemen, we must confine ourselves within limits. If, in so doing,
individual feelings are violated, there the line of interdiction begins,
and the offence becomes the subject of penal visitation.'[21]

The 'line of interdiction' was so subjectively defined that any criticism could count as libellous if it hurt the feelings of ministers or
brought them into contempt. Leigh Hunt's words on the Regent, for
instance, were libellous because they suggested that the Prince was fat
and unloved. Although it was true that he was corpulent and unpopular, the article rendered the Regent ridiculous and cast odium on the
monarchy; it was therefore criminal. The law also defended the state
from derision. It was a criminal libel to bring the constitution or laws
into disesteem and, in terms of Hone's alleged offence, the law followed
Lord Chief Justice Matthew Hale's judgment in the seventeenth century that 'the Christian Religion is parcel of the Common Law of
England'. *The Book of Common Prayer* was defended by Statute Law; to
'revile' it, or make it 'contemptuous', was criminal. The words and
phrases used to describe the offence of libel were kept vague, for it gave
the state wide latitude in deciding which journalists to punish.

Under the law, the offence of libel rested on the tendency that writing
had to encourage others to commit a crime or render men in public life
ridiculous in the minds of the people. The only way of determining the
libellous nature of a piece of journalism was an assessment of the intelligence of the public. The intention of the writer was not taken into
account, and nor could a defendant defend himself on the grounds that
what he had written was true. As one MP said, the libel laws existed to
defend men in high office from being 'exposed to the blind resentment
of a misguided mob' – and a statement of fact could inflame them as
much as a malicious falsehood.[22] Henry Brougham introduced a Bill
for Securing the Liberty of the Press to the Commons in May 1816, in
which he wanted to change the law so that only writing that was deliberately misleading and manifestly false could count as libellous. Samuel
Shepherd, the Solicitor-General, was shocked that Brougham could
suggest such a reform of the law. Without a hint of irony he said that if

journalists merely had to prove that what they wrote was based in truth
the government could be criticised with impunity. If verifiable facts
defended the press from government regulation, a journalist would 'day
after day, or year after year, repeat the publication of the libel, and when
called to account, get off by proving the truth of it. Would not such a
case show the impolicy, the injustice, of such an alteration in the law?'
Brougham could get no support for his bill; MPs agreed with Shepherd
that political journalism should not be allowed to hide behind the
truth, or that personal opinion should be immune from prosecution.[23]

Sidmouth believed that writers such as Hone and Wooler were
guilty of malicious intent when they debated reform, because they
knew that such a discussion would wean their semi-literate readers
from loyalty and obedience. Publishing facts about sinecures and voting practices was just as dangerous as spreading lies. He believed that
such men had 'parliamentary reform in their mouths, but rebellion and
revolution in their hearts'.[24]

The *Guardian* commented on the definitions of libel: '*Blasphemy*
and *treason* are any thing which persons in office do not *like*.' And ministers' prejudices dictated how the law worked in its operation. Once
they decided that a journalist was guilty of seditious or blasphemous
libel, the Attorney-General had *ex officio* power to file what was called
'informations' and arrest them without notice. The government could
not try every journalist that offended them, but it could threaten arbitrary punishment on selected individuals. As an Austrian observer
noted, English censorship was not comprehensive, but directed like a
'thunderbolt' on specific targets. Lord Liverpool said that although
'libel' was an indefinite offence, such a flexible system gave the government the ability to police the press on a pragmatic basis: 'On that
description founded the justification of the discretionary power
entrusted to judges.' It was designed to make examples of a few writers,
scaring the rest with the example of severe punishments. George
Canning praised the discretionary exercise of law as its greatest benefit:
'The law is, of necessity, general in its terms, but must, of right, be partial in its application.'[25]

No writer was free from the whim of the government when it could
file informations *ex officio* against journalists without restraint. There

was no need to apply to a Grand Jury to determine whether the indictment was justified. It was at the moment of arrest that censorship was
most efficient. As Lord Stanhope told parliament in 1808, a writer
'could be imprisoned for a misdemeanour before he was found guilty of
the slightest offence, and . . . kept in prison till the trial, which his prosecutor might delay as long as he pleased . . . A man not guilty of any
crime might be imprisoned for more months than the Judge might punish another person who was found guilty.'[26]

Holding men for political crimes without trial might have been contrary to the first principles of British justice, but Sidmouth said that the
state had to reserve powers to defend the state from imminent threats:
the swift operation of the law was absolutely essential given the dangerous powers of the press and the serious nature of the crime; libellers
had to be arrested immediately, or otherwise 'they could go on in their
shameful trade, adding offence to offence, and with increased momentum propagate the mischief up to the very moment of trial; and then
perhaps abscond into another quarter'. 'And what could be more just
and necessary?' Ellenborough asked the House of Lords, agreeing with
his master. 'My Lords, suppose for a moment, that you should stand
upon so miserable and decrepit state, that publications of a most
inflammatory nature are scattered over every part of the country, and
you have no power to call the mischievous authors to immediate
account . . .' The threat of a long spell in prison was a powerful deterrent for journalists and publishers; the calculation was that they would
be impoverished by a lengthy spell on remand when removed from
their small businesses. Economic misfortune would do the work of censorship more effectively than any trial.[27]

But if the criminal informations filed against a journalist ever came to
court, the government had another weighty advantage. Libel trials were
held in front of a Special Jury, twelve men qualified by their wealth and
standing in the community. They were chosen by the Crown Office
from the so-called 'better sort': merchants in cities and squires in
provincial towns. It was considered by some an anomaly that such
juries should be used to regulate the press, when treason, the highest
crime in the land, was tried by a common jury. As Sir Samuel Shepherd
told the Commons in 1816, 'libellous' publications should rather 'be

judged by a jury of enlightened men, than by one composed of the lower and more ignorant members of society'.[28] The government could rely on Special Jurors to share the view of the reformist press as a pestilence. They were required to validate the Attorney-General's definition of such vague terms as 'bring into contempt', 'render ridiculous', 'revile' or 'bring into disesteem' as they applied to alleged libels. They were not obliged to hear evidence of the effect the piece of journalism had already had on the public, but to say what they *believed* would be the likely effect. If they read Southey's articles or Lord Sidmouth's speeches they would be more likely to assume that the reading public was credulous and prone to unthinking anger. It was a short leap of logic to declare reformist writing libellous on the grounds that the tendency it had on its readers was dangerous to the state. Wooler wrote that this made justice a joke: 'You appear before LAW, you are tried by LAW; because the LAW OF LIBEL is just *what the judges say, when the jury will believe them.*'[29]

Jeremy Bentham said that the one-sided law made the Lord Chief Justice 'the master manufacturer of *libel law* – and in effect the absolute master of the *press*'.[30] Any journalist marked out for exemplary justice knew that he would be enmeshed in a protracted, complicated and partial legal process that exacted punishment with or without a jury. The trial itself would only be one of many rigours, and mild compared to the economic ruin that a spell in prison would inflict on the victim. William Cobbett knew from experience what awaited him and his fellow writers. Explaining why he fled to America, he wrote:

I did not retire from a combat with the Attorney-General, but from a combat with a dungeon, deprived of pen, ink and paper. A combat with the Attorney-General is quite unequal enough. That, however, I would have encountered. I know too well what a trial by Special Jury is. Yet that, or any sort of trial, I would have stayed to face. So that I could have been sure of a trial, of whatever sort, I would have run the risk. But against the absolute power of imprisonment without even a hearing, for a time unlimited, in any jail in the kingdom, without the use of pen, ink and paper, and without any communication with any soul but the keepers, – against such a power it would be madness to attempt to strive.[31]

There were a few who were mad enough to continue publishing at the risk of instant imprisonment. Hone and Wooler remained at large throughout March and April, even though they had written many articles which counted as seditious and blasphemous under the government's interpretation of the libel laws. Sidmouth and the Attorney-General promised parliament that they would be dealt with, but the two editors continued to publish. A worried Robert Southey wrote to Lord Liverpool wondering whether the laws were 'not altogether nugatory' when the *Examiner* and the *Reformists' Register* 'are daily and weekly issued, fresh and fresh' and read aloud in every tavern throughout the country.[32]

However the Laureate need not have worried. The government delayed because it was preparing public opinion for a spate of prosecutions. Worryingly for Hone, the ministers made the issue of blasphemy their greatest priority. Sidmouth and Southey were pious churchmen, and were genuinely offended by Hone's satires. Yet raising up Hone's parodies as the worst kind of reformist journalism served a useful purpose. It gave their policies a veneer of moral respectability, allowing them to appeal to respectable public opinion and persuade potential Special Jurymen that they were not merely acting on political prejudices but from Christian duty. The religious cry was to be the stalking horse for the war against the press in 1817, and Hone had made himself an easy target.

The Annual Register for 1817 said that the overwhelming majority in the Commons that supported the suspension of *habeas corpus* 'sufficiently indicated the affright which was spread through the most opulent, and the most timorous class of the nation . . . '[33] Hone's prose was wild and impulsive, never sparing a harsh epithet or metaphorical blow. The government's problem was that it confused hard words with physical force, as if violent language was the same as violent action. Robert Southey was guilty of this. He read attacks on him in the reformist press and was terrified of what reformist writers would do to him if there was a successful revolution and they took power. The thought of Hone, Hazlitt and Leigh Hunt ruling the country as a revolutionary triumvirate when the government was deposed was ridiculous because

Southey took a hugely inflated view of their actual power over the public and because he mistook their political moderation for crypto-Jacobinism. But it was this kind of suspicion and ignorance of the aims and intentions of journalists such as Hone that put them in danger.

The ministers would not engage with public opinion, and their refusal to do so only made the situation seem worse. Their ignorance and prejudice prevented them from taking a realistic view of the press. Had they actually investigated the effect of Hone and Wooler's words on readers they might have found that it was possible for the majority of people to read political debate without being inspired to rebellion. There was no way in which they could discriminate between Hone and Wooler's moderate demands and a call to arms by genuine revolutionaries. The entire opposition press was crudely stereotyped as malicious and destabilising. If anybody was incapable of differentiating potatoes and cabbages, it appears to have been the ministers. Wooler mocked their complete ignorance of the peaceful state of public opinion and the tendency to see Jacobins in every mild expression of grievances: 'Get a smile *painted* up on every face,' he advised his readers,

– and while his hand is in, let the painter give you all plump, ruddy complexions ... Some of you do look mighty cadaverous and lean: therefore you had better get into flesh or semblance of flesh; and for the latter purpose you will find that *red ochre* is cheaper than *roast beef*; but get into seemly and contented looks I beseech you, lest you appear disaffected, when in point of fact, you may be as loyal and good meaning sort of folks as hunger and the gripes will let you.[34]

Leigh Hunt said that journalists in 1817 had been 're-despoted, browbeaten, judged before-hand, told how to write, overhauled like so many bankrupt's books, called up and corrected ... [to] have the rod shaken at us like trembling boys with their exercises before a peda-gogue, by a – Censorship! ... But the people will be vigilantly on their guard, after any man in this country has dared even to hint such a scandalous degradation of us.'[35]

But just who was going to step forward to defend the rights of free speech was left unclear. Cobbett had been laughed out of court when he had tried to defend his personal convictions, and even a barrister of

Henry Brougham's skill had not managed to defeat Lord Ellenborough. As Wooler said, writers had for too long

bent before the driving blast of persecution, in the idle hope of evading, or palliating, its fury; instead of resisting like the oak, and preferring rather to be torn up by the roots, and scattered in fragments over the desolated waste. Public writers have deserted their opinions, or what has been of more injury to their cause, shrunk from the personal avowal and defence of them, when called before the public eye.[36]

8

Ellenborough College

Bad men are only strong when the virtuous are timid and irresolute.
William Hone

He knew how to make his way among the great and over the small.
Leigh Hunt on Lord Ellenborough

When the powers that be encroach so much and so daily by new precedents against us it is worth trying, surely, to make them go back a little and create a precedent *for* us.
William Hone, letter to John Hunt, May 1817

On Saturday, 3 May 1817 William Hone and Thomas Wooler were arrested on the orders of Lord Chief Justice Ellenborough and the Attorney-General, Sir William Garrow. 'I wrote my last *Register* at home in the midst of my family,' Hone wrote a few days later. 'Since then the reign of terror has commenced, and I now write from prison.' The war against the press had begun; and as Hone said, 'I am the first object selected . . . as a victim and an example.'

Hone was walking back to his home at the Old Bailey when he was arrested; he had left for a quick and rare break from his press room. Characteristically, he was deeply ensconced in a book as he drifted up to the corner of Fleet Street and the Old Bailey. As he read a sentence in an essay by Dr Johnson – 'Shall a poor pickpocket or a highwayman be hanged for a little loose money, and these wholesale thieves, who strip a nation of their lives, liberties, and estates, and all they have, not be looked after?' – he was rushed, and seized by two men. 'You are my prisoner,' said one of his assailants. 'I have a judge's warrant against you.' Hone calmly closed his pamphlet, and marked his place in the text with his finger. As they were a few yards from his house, Hone asked if he might be allowed to go inside for a moment.

'No, I shall not suffer you to go home,' replied the arresting officer.

'We are going past the door. You will surely step in with me, and let me speak to my wife?' Hone repeated.

'No, you must go with me.'

The officer said that Hone's bail was set so high that he could not delay in taking him to a lock-up house. 'What has my the bail got to do with my going home or not going home?' Hone asked. 'Go along with me; I shall not detain you, or run away from you.' After further fruitless argument outside the front door, Hone conceded to the officer: 'Very well. Do as you please. I am in your power. Where are you taking me to?'

'Here is the judge's warrant – Lord Ellenborough's warrant,' the officious agent continued. 'Read it.'

'No, not here. I will read it at the place you take me to.'

'No,' ordered the man, 'read it at once – here it is.'

'There is no necessity for it now, in the street.'

'Yes – you had better read it here.'

Hone leant against a post, casually read the warrant, and handed it back to the officer. It was an order for the immediate arrest of William Hone signed by Ellenborough on 28 April. No reasons for the apprehension were stated in the warrant. The law had waited five days to make a supposedly emergency *ex officio* arrest. He read it and was put into a coach; as it went through the Old Bailey, he saw Sarah outside the front door of their house, and was able to lean out of the window and tell what had happened. The officer informed Hone that he might be bailed if he made an application to Ellenborough before eight o'clock that evening. The coach went to the Sergeant's Inn coffee house to find Mr Gibbons, the head tipstaff of the King's Bench Court, to arrange bail. The officer went to the door, and 'said in a most important tone of voice, "Tell him I have got Hone"'.

But Gibbons was not at the inn, and no one knew where he was. As the clock ticked towards eight, Hone asked the officer to hurry; he wanted to be bailed before the deadline passed. He also asked why, given that the warrant had been out for five days, there was such a last-minute dash to make the deadline for bail. He was given no satisfactory answer. When they got to the lock-up house, he was informed that prisoners had to give a minimum notice of forty-eight hours for bail. He was due to appear before Ellenborough on Monday morning to hear the charges against him and enter a plea, so there had never been the smallest chance that he could have been bailed in the first place. Ellenborough had waited until the last moment to seize Hone, ensuring that he would be sped to court ignorant of the charges against him and deprived of the chance to seek legal advice.

In the meantime he was kept in close confinement. When Hone arrived at the lock-up house on Saturday afternoon, his cellmate recoiled in horror. Only a dangerous criminal could be kept as securely and with such close attention as this new prisoner. Hone had to convince the man that he was no murderer, merely an editor.[1]

Wooler was arrested under a similar warrant on the same day. He was not forthcoming about the circumstances, and he kept up the fiction that it was the Black Dwarf who had been locked up. The creature wrote to the Yellow Bonze in Japan saying that it had attempted to blend into British life by aping the national character, but in living up to the ideal it had given itself away and was gaoled; how, it asked the Bonze, had it come to be arrested in this famous land of liberty when it had previously survived the 'heathen world'? – 'It is my urbanity that has betrayed me.'[2]

The arrest of the two editors enlivened their writing. They were now to be the principal actors in British politics in 1817, not merely commentators watching events. Hone was now the subject of his political journalism. The arrests proved what they had been arguing for the previous months. Their experiences were vivid examples of what happened in a state cowering under the threat of arbitrary government; when *habeas corpus* was in suspension any law-abiding subject could be pounced upon whilst he or she was reading in the street and dragged away from their families without an explanation. Hone's arresting officer was a parody of the agents of the state: humourless, unremittingly punctilious, and obsessed with the minor concerns of his insignificant job. Urbane Britons were at the mercy of such petty despots – heavy-handed state-employed bullies. The experience of arrest was, at first, their chance to set up humorous contrasts between mild-mannered writers and their arrogant persecutors.

First thing on Monday morning, still ignorant of why he had been arrested, Hone was taken to the Court of the King's Bench. Here he joined Wooler to hear the charges against them for the first time and to plead guilty or not guilty in front of a tribunal of senior judges, headed by Ellenborough. 'I was hurried off so quickly,' Hone reported a few days later in the *Register*, 'that to despatch a messenger to my wife, or any friend, to acquaint them of this sudden proceeding was impossible: being put into a coach, I was rapidly driven down to Westminster, placed on the floor of the Court, and after some routine business, called to plead immediately to *three Criminal Informations*, which I had never before heard of'.

The Attorney-General read out the charges against them. Hone was accused of publishing a libel called *The Political Catechism*. Garrow apologised for offending pious ears before he read from the disgusting and sacrilegious parody, but he had to do so to establish the sordid and reprehensible nature of Hone's libel. For Garrow, the most repellent part of the libel was the bastardised Ten Commandments, the solemn obligations Hone imagined that a minister required from MPs:

1. Thou shalt have no other Patron but me.

2. Thou shalt not support any measure but mine . . .

3. Thou shalt not take the Pension of the Lord thy Minister in vain.

4. Remember that thou attend the Minister's Levee day, on other days thou shalt speak for him in the House, and fetch and carry, and do all he commandeth thee to do . . .

5. Honour the Regent and the helmets of the Life Guards, that thy stay long in the Place, which the Lord thy Minister giveth thee.

6. Thou shalt not call starving to death murder.

7. Thou shalt not call Royal gallivanting adultery.

8. Thou shalt not say that to rob the Public is to steal.

9. Thou shalt bear false witness against the people.

10. Thou shalt not covet the People's applause, thou shalt not covet the People's praise, nor their good name, nor their esteem, nor their reverence, nor any reward that is theirs.

He was accused of ridiculing the Catechism 'with intent to scandal-
ize and bring into contempt *The Book of Common Prayer*, and Church
of England, as by law established'. He also faced two other identical
charges of criminal libel for his *Political Litany* and *Sinecurists' Creed*.
He had committed three identical crimes, but they were to be tried separately. Garrow showed how closely heaven protected the Church of
England and cabinet ministers when he asserted that Hone had published his satires 'to the great displeasure of Almighty God'.

Wooler was charged with two seditious libels. The first was for an
article in the *Black Dwarf* in which he claimed that ministers, in particular George Canning and Lord Castlereagh, were guilty of treason and
criminal subversion of the constitution by doling out sinecures and
abolishing the legal right of *habeas corpus*. In making this attack,
Wooler had libelled the constitution and brought government ministers
into contempt, intending to undermine the people's loyalty to their
rulers. The lesser offence was a piece that cited King John's signing
Magna Carta, the trial of Charles I, and the Glorious Revolution of
1688–9 that deposed James II and brought in William III, as precedents
for popular resistance to tyrannical government. Wooler wryly
observed that he had merely written historical essays, so the charge was
tantamount to saying that he had libelled four dead kings, and the law
was seeking retribution on their behalf. Commenting on his friend's
case, Hone said that although history had condemned King John, in
1817 he had suddenly become a 'poor, dear, dead, and now, it appears,
never-enough-to-be-beloved King'.[3] Wooler pleaded not guilty to both
charges, and was put on remand.

But Hone refused to plead. Throughout the prosecution he insisted
that at every stage the government treat him fairly and follow the letter
of the law. As he told Ellenborough, 'It is impossible for me to answer
on the sudden, when I am unprepared.' He could not enter a plea of
guilty or not guilty without studying the alleged libels in detail. Garrow
had read the three parodies just once, and Hone said he needed time to
consider his legal position before answering the charge. He claimed
that the hurried and confused nature of his arrest made it hard to come
to a reasoned judgement of how he should plead. However many times
Garrow read the libels was immaterial; he would only comply with the

court when it allowed him to plead in a fair and legal manner: 'I do therefore implore and I *demand* of this Court ... copies of the informations, or whether I sink on the floor of this Court, through weakness, whilst hearing them read, I still persist in my demand, because I think it founded in justice.'

The court would only provide the texts if Hone paid for them to be copied. The defendant maintained that it was preventing him entering a plea by withholding vital information; he would plead as soon as he was given the chance to re-read the parodies. However, in a vindictive move, Ellenborough decided that Hone would have to wait until the first day of the next legal term, a fortnight later, before he could come before the court again. Hone saw this as a gratuitous and cruel way of punishing him; he was being prevented from answering the charges and held in prison as a reward for his reasonable complaints. Ellenborough denied that this was the case: Hone might go home to his family as soon as he paid bail. So Hone gave notice for bail, only to be told that, given the serious nature of his crime, it amounted to £1,000.

Hone had no chance of paying such a huge sum of money. He renewed his complaint that he was being deprived of a fair hearing, earning one of Ellenborough's sharp asides: 'The time of the Court must not be occupied in vain discussion.' The judge ordered the tipstaff to take the prisoner to the King's Bench Prison to await another hearing. Hone was not convinced that justice had been done; he was being imprisoned without the charges being fully explained. Ellenborough silenced him: 'Let the Defendant be committed till the first day of the next term.' Hone, in his account of the trial, said that he 'bowed to him, looked him in the face, and inquired, aloud, "My Lord, for what am I committed?" Lord Ellenborough looked at me, reclined backwards, and made me no answer; nor did the other Judges make answer; and I knew not *why* I was committed ... I therefore *repeated my desire to know* this, till the tipstaff took me by the arms and forced me off the floor of the court.' [4]

Hone and Wooler had at first treated their arrest as an excuse for a joke, but the opportunities for comedy and satirical fancy were not always so easy. Hone was in considerable pain when he was brought to court that morning. His gaolers had not allowed him to perform an act of nature over the weekend, and he was therefore in no state to defend himself properly on Monday. When he asked Ellenborough if he might sit during the hearing, the judge shouted 'No' so loudly that it echoed through the back of the courtroom. A cartoon shows Hone asking to S*it, bewigged and ruddy-faced Ellenborough bellowing 'Noooooo . . .!' and a shocked Garrow, ear-trumpet in hand, saying, 'Not S–t!'* With a scatological humour typical of the time, the cartoonist encapsulated the gratuitous brutality of the judge, the senility of the Attorney-General, and Hone's helplessness in the teeth of a hostile legal system, which controlled everything – even his right to perform the most basic of human functions. The cartoon was called 'Law *versus* Humanity or a Parody on British Liberty'.

Other journalists who had been arrested for alleged libels had co-operated with the courts; like Wooler, they had pleaded immediately to hasten a trial in front of a jury. But Hone believed that the mechanism of censorship should be resisted from the very outset. He wanted to prove that the way in which writers were arrested and forced to plead to vague charges was contrary to the principles of British justice. Journalists who compromised with their prosecutors by complying with every order made by the court were acknowledging the unfair advantage of the state in censorship trials. It was his duty, he believed, to make a stand against legal harassment, on behalf of all persecuted journalists. If he co-operated with Ellenborough's rushed justice, he would be acknowledging the right of the state to arrest on spec and commit people to prison without showing due cause. He knew full well the contents of his parodies, and he did not need copies of the informations. But that was not the point; the court must be forced to follow the letter of the law; otherwise it could bully and harass journalists with impunity. They should not become willing dupes to the dictates of biased judges.

Hone's brave stand was an example of the kind of peaceful resistance to arbitrary laws that he had advocated his readers to follow. The courts deliberately threw up confusing and arcane practices to trap the

---

* Garrow is confused with his successor, Shepherd, whose poor hearing compelled him to use an ear trumpet and prevented him from becoming a judge.

LAW versus HUMANITY or a *Parody on British Liberty*.

unwary; they were balanced in the government's favour; and no one should be forced to acquiesce in illegal proceedings or help the government in their own condemnation:

As every man living must see the rapidity with which we are hurrying towards *absolute despotism* [Hone wrote], so every man who is persecuted should resist despotic power with all his might. Tyrants are only cruel whilst they possess force ... they often cower before men who oppose right to might. Besides, nothing is gained by submission to base oppressors; they flatter, and fawn, and coax, like crocodiles, for no other purpose, but to allure their victims to more certain destruction.[5]

A few days after arriving in prison, Hone wrote to John Hunt, who had just paid Sarah a visit at the Old Bailey to offer his help. His letter describes the situation which faced him:

King's Bench Prison
8 May 1817

Dear Sir,

Your kind conversation with my wife on Monday sensibly affects me – I
am often backward in expressing acknowledgement of services but I am
never insensible of them. On the present occasion, however, many unto-
ward accidents have combined to prevent me from dropping you a line
until now – I was ill when I came here, seriously ill. My application to the
Court for leave to sit until the Second information was read proceeded
from real Indisposition. I was ready to fall and I believe had the Court
declined it in civil terms I should have fallen. – But Lord Ellenborough's
No! – (you might have heard it in the Entrance door of Westminster Hall
from Palace Yard) – was as good as Thieves' Vinegar*; it startled and
recovered me till I was out of court.

I have met with very little accommodation too at this place – so that,
though I am in general pretty adaptable to circumstances, no great comfort
has been my portion. The prison is very full and a decent room not to be
had at an enormous price. I think I shall have one tomorrow which though
dark and not very airy will be better than wandering in the area or idling in
the Coffee room† . . . Like the Seer of old I shall get a table and chair and a
stool (and a few books withal) and make myself as happy as I can.

. . . I have received so many kindnesses from you and I owe you so
much of service on the Fenning account that nothing I can say on paper or
verbally will put you in possession of my feelings . . .

. . . I want your opinion on the stand I should take to obtain Copies of
the Informations before pleading – this you see is refused on the grounds
of custom-precedent – which I say would be more honoured in the breach
than in the observance. When the powers that be encroach so much and
so daily by new precedents against us it is worth trying, surely, to make
them go back a little and create a precedent *for* us –

I am Sir, with great respect,
Your faithful servant
W. Hone

Throughout the next few months, Hone and Wooler would be searching
for just that – a precedent in the courts that would mark out the liberties of
the press. [6]

* Thieves Vinegar – a mixture of herbs and vinegar taken to ward off plague.
† Prisoners were required to rent rooms.

Censorship was at first a dismal failure in the sense that the confines of a prison cell imposed no limitations on Hone and Wooler, and there was nothing legal that the government could do about it. Both journalists continued to write their papers in the King's Bench Prison, sending out manuscripts to be published. The *Black Dwarf* came out as usual on the Wednesday two days after the first hearing, and the *Register* on the Saturday. They even had powerful defenders arguing their case, the most important being Lord Grey, the *de facto* leader of the Whigs, who told the House of Lords that the government was guilty of crass hypocrisy for accusing Hone of blasphemy, when its real intent was to censor his political views. As soon as it was noticed that prison held no stigma, and was not a deterrent, the Home Office decided to go beyond the boundaries of the law in its campaign against the press. It decided on a tactic that would, if it worked, silence the two editors for good.*

Hone was never the most robust of men, and the King's Bench Prison had a detrimental effect upon his fragile health; when he was brought to gaol after the hearing he collapsed, and was found 'senseless in his room there, not having performed an office of nature for several days'. One day, as he lay recovering on the bed in his cell, a man unknown to him entered the room. This person was smooth and charming in conversation, and immediately made clear his support and sympathy for Hone, promising to help his campaign. Hone, he said, was the perfect leader for the poor and distressed in the country. Britain was in 'a bad state, the people greatly distressed, the whole population of some districts ripe for anything'. He continued that with good leadership the people 'would inevitably overwhelm the Government'. The natural leaders had to act immediately; it was an 'opportunity not to be missed'. The man asked Hone to list his political contacts in Birmingham, Leeds, Liverpool and other manufacturing towns because he was about to make a journey to the north and wanted to meet like-minded men. He offered to act for Hone throughout the country in a campaign to 'crush' the government. Hone politely turned

---

* Robert Southey wrote to Lord Liverpool at this time in reference to the prosecutions of Hone and Wooler: '. . . I beseech you do not hesitate at issuing that vigour beyond the law which the exigence requires, and which your own personal safety requires as much as the vital interests of the country . . .'

down the offer. He told his mysterious guest that he believed in reform by 'constitutional means only' and 'deprecated all attempts to further incite or goad the people to acts which would endanger the public safety'.

The man, Hone informed his readers, 'attempted with much ingenuity and suavity to reason down what he called my scruples, and want of confidence, which he said prevented public men from uniting to obtain a complete victory over the government'. The stranger spent a long time in the cell, trying to provoke Hone to reveal his real thoughts concerning revolution. 'He continued to prolong the conversation a considerable time,' Hone reported, 'very dexterously feeling his way, and returning to his points, interlarding his remarks with praise and flattery.' Hone again refused, and the visitor went over to the adjoining staircase to have a word with Wooler, for whom he offered to pay bail so that the famous orator could tour the country encouraging insurrectionary movements. The editor of the *Black Dwarf* refused as well.

It was not the first time that Hone had been courted by 'revolutionaries'. In March he had received prospective clients, giving him 'bushels of manuscript of very dangerous tendency' they wished published, which he immediately destroyed. One commission came in a handwritten note requesting Hone to publish several thousand posters that co-ordinated a popular uprising. The poster would have had a woodcut emblem of weapons, and written instructions for the people of England to arm themselves and meet at their local churchyard on 7 April to threaten the government with a show of militancy. Hone was to have them printed, and then use his network of agents and shopkeepers throughout the country to distribute them. It says something for the efficacy of the distribution system that the unnamed agitator assumed that Hone could get the posters from Fleet Street to his customers in every part of the kingdom within a day.

Hone suspected from the start that his visitors and correspondents were not real Jacobins at all, but emissaries of the state. He took the manuscript poster to the Under Secretary of the Treasury at once so that he would not be accused of abetting a revolutionary plot. At the same time Hay and Turner, a London printing firm, had been given orders for similar posters. Expense bills were to be charged to an attorney named Nicholls. Messrs Hay and Turner told Hone that they took the poster to the Home Department to appraise the authorities of an imminent threat. They were shown to an antechamber to await an interview with Sidmouth. Ten minutes later they were joined by a stranger; this man was 'presently familiarly beckoned' into Sidmouth's study. After a further hour, Hay and Turner had to leave for another appointment. Subsequently the printers discovered that their honoured companion in the Home Secretary's antechamber had been the same Mr Nicholls who was supposed to pay the bills for the insurrectionary posters. Upon further inquiry, it was found that this friend of Lord Sidmouth had commissioned identical printing jobs from at least two other London publishers.

So when Hone was approached in his cell in May or June he knew that there was a 'deliberate plan to ensnare persons connected with the press' in a plot manufactured by the Home Office. He was suspicious of his charming visitor because he and many of his colleagues knew that formal censorship was accompanied by an unofficial campaign to libel pressmen with charges of high treason. If journalists were not actually sponsoring armed revolution they had to be bribed into criminal acts.

There was nothing but circumstantial evidence connecting the administration with the commissions, so the conspiracy went unreported. But in a number of trials for high treason in 1817, the key witnesses for the prosecution were professional informers who had inveigled people into seditious conversation and encouraged political demonstrations. From the transcripts of these trials, it became clear that the government was indeed engaged in a policy of entrapment. It had employed *agents provocateurs* – the most prolific being John Castle and one Oliver (pseudonym of W. J. Richards), who had toured the country enticing impoverished labourers into treasonable conversation.

In June, the *Leeds Mercury* reported that Oliver had turned up in the town and used his charm to beguile people into idle speculation against the government. He also organised poor workers into revolutionary societies, goading them into direct action. According to the *Mercury*, the Yorkshire magistracy wrote to the Home Office to ask how they should proceed against this dangerous rabble-rouser. Sidmouth replied saying that the stranger should be left alone because he was a government agent. Castle had given evidence in the trial of John

Watson, the Spa Fields agitator. The spy had wormed his way into a friendship with Watson, and at the trial repeated various private conversations they had shared, and which were used as a way of condemning the defendant. In return, Castle was given legal protection for his crimes: harbouring a bawd and committing perjury. Watson was acquitted, but in 1817 Sidmouth's creatures had accomplished their tasks with aplomb. Many had got off, but in 1817, Oliver, Castle and others had betrayed many other unwitting men to the state.[7]

When the story broke, Hone and Wooler compared notes, and discovered that their friendly visitor was Oliver. It was unlikely that either journalist would have acquiesced in his violent plots, committed as they were to constitutional reform. But if they had humoured his suave arguments, however innocently, they would no longer have been facing prison, but a charge of high treason, and, with it, the possibility of execution. Any belief that the government might be prepared to vindicate its campaign against the press in a fair way according to the principles of justice was utterly dispelled. Hone was incensed at the underhand way in which spies were being employed to cajole him into unmeaning and ill-considered conversation which would be construed as treason. Mere imprisonment of a critical writer was not punishment enough for the enemies of the press – they would have his life. Hone made a direct comparison between the government's entrapment and the Eliza Fenning case; the state seemed determined to mete out exemplary punishment by bribing people with 'blood money'.

'Is it possible that the employment of spies and informers, now unblushingly avowed, has subjected us to such dreadful machinations as these?' he fumed in the *Register*:

I firmly believe it has. Having escaped the insidious and horrible attacks of concealed incendiaries, surely in prison, and under three Government prosecutions, men might suppose themselves secure from further persecution, and yet Oliver's attempt to entrap Mr Wooler, and the like attempt made on me, I believe by the same man, show the unrelenting earnestness with which these wretches prosecute their cruel purposes. Surely, surely, we have a right to supplicate vengeance on these who thirst after innocent blood.[8]

A few days after Hone's arrest, Sir Richard Phillips wrote to Francis Place saying that the prisoner's strategy should be 'not to act as a defendant – not to plead or parley – but to consider his assailants as the true culprits'.[9] Hone and Wooler continued with their joint campaign to expose the censorship as illegal, and, if carefully undermined by obstinacy, unworkable. Hone wrote to the marshal of the prison, complaining that his arrest and committal were illegal, and he should be released on the grounds that he was being held without charge. The marshal replied that he had no jurisdiction, and Hone would have to apply to the court. On 15 May the prisoner filed an affidavit to Ellenborough, Sir Samuel Shepherd (the new Attorney-General, Garrow having ended his tenure on the day of Hone's first hearing) and the Solicitors to the Treasury, asserting that his arrest and subsequent imprisonment were untenable.

Two days later, Hone was in court to present his affidavit. In it, he claimed that he should be released because Ellenborough's court was deliberately obstructing justice by withholding essential information relating to the case, such as the warrant and the copies of the libels. Ellenborough neatly side-stepped the complaint by claiming that Hone had made a couple of minor mistakes in the affidavit, and had failed to follow the rules and forms the court required in presenting the document. Hone replied, saying that he was no lawyer, and could not be expected to understand the arcane practices of the Court of the King's Bench. He asked for the judge's help in making the proceedings intelligible and framing his complaints in the correct manner. But true to form, Ellenborough said that he was not required to hold every common criminal by the hand and guide him or her through the intricacies of the law. The complaint was thrown out.[10]

Hone continued to assert the unfair bias of the state in censorship trials. It had ensured that he was under an unfair disadvantage in the courts, and in the country it had raised a hue and cry against him, intending to prejudice potential jurors. Lord Sidmouth had created hysteria amongst the governing classes, repeatedly invoking the spectre of blasphemy, and saying that irreligious pamphlets were ubiquitous in the country, so that his 'saps' 'bandy it about without end'. As Hone said, his name had been blackened in that 'his Lordship, in the House of Lords, repeats *blasphemy* with all stage effect, until, during a whole debate, it is on the mouth of every speaker, on both sides of the House; and then, by the mere sound of the word, by ringing the changes upon it, *blasphemy* is "the common cry of curs", from one end of the country to the other'. Sidmouth, he said, was like Judy in the puppet show, crying 'murder' upon any pretext. And his scare-mongering meant that Hone's parodies were associated in the public mind with utter depravity and social danger. 'I, in prison, before either of my trials, before even I have pleaded, am, in fact, tried, condemned, and sentenced by a common jury of fools, knaves, bigots and hypocrites, especially empanelled, throughout the whole kingdom.'[11]

Whilst Hone engaged in a systematic campaign against every aspect of the censorship, Thomas Wooler was eager to face a jury. He lacked the patience of Hone, who seemed prepared to stay in prison indefinitely, or at least until Ellenborough backed down. He hated the sheer boredom of the King's Bench Prison (which he dubbed 'Ellenborough College' when giving the correspondence address for the *Black Dwarf*) and wished for a trial as quickly as possible. He told his readers, 'My confinement . . . now begins to be insufferably tedious. I have seen all my fellow prisoners. I have counted how many faces are within the circumference of the walls by which I am enclosed. I am familiar with every remarkable face, in the motley group that the policy of this wise country locks up to do nothing while they are here, and to learn nothing when they get out. Every stone on the pavement has been pressed by my feet, as I have wandered in silent cognition, abstracted from the moving automata who now and then jostle me into the recollection that they were near me.' With the prospect of a trial, he began to consider the consequences: 'I am not much afraid of a prison; but may hereafter despair of being able to do any good.'[12]

Wooler entered a plea at his first hearing, and the trial was held on 5 June in front of Lord Justice Abbott and a Special Jury of London merchants. Sir Charles Abbott distinguished himself in a long career for his humanity, dignity and quiet manners. The son of a hairdresser, he raised himself from humble origins to become a senior judge on the King's Bench. As a boy he befriended Lord Thurlow's illegitimate son at the Free School in Canterbury; Pitt's Lord Chancellor recognised a promising talent, and Charles Abbott secured a place at Oxford, where he excelled his early potential, and published his prize-winning essay, which was, ironically enough, on the subject of satire. He was elected a fellow of Corpus Christi, before becoming a barrister. But he was a hopeless mediocrity in court; he had not the power of eloquence to win over a jury, and it was said that he had never won a case in his life. Yet he had a capacious mind, and, for all his failings as an advocate, he was an unrivalled authority on the law, and the author of legal texts. His talents were recognised by Ellenborough, and Sir Charles was appointed a judge of the Court of Common Pleas in 1816. A year later, he was transferred to the King's Bench as Ellenborough's deputy; in 1818 he became Lord Chief Justice. He was the polar opposite of Lord Ellenborough, unable as he was to influence a jury with force of personality and powerful rhetoric. In the 1817 libel trials, his job was to overwhelm journalists with the weight of law, and make the government's case unanswerable with the store of legal knowledge at his disposal.

The new Attorney-General, Sir Samuel Shepherd, began proceedings claiming that a free press was absolutely essential to a happy society, but 'it must not be subject to abuse. It is impossible for any man who contemplates the welfare of society, not to feel, if he be an honest man, and have a correct understanding, that without metes and bounds the liberty of the press would become licentiousness, and anarchy would be destructive of every blessing man can enjoy in this or any other government.'[13]

Wooler had gone far beyond these 'metes and bounds' by suggesting that ministers were despots bent on destroying the liberties of England. By calling ministers a 'junto of rough-riders and political jockeys' and vultures preying 'on the life blood of the empire', Wooler was, in the opinion of the Attorney-General, 'stirring up the spirit of insurrection and rebellion in the people of this country, for the purpose of destroying the venerable constitution as settled and established by law'. The language with which parliament had lambasted the press in general throughout the 1817 session was now applied to Wooler in particular.

The Attorney-General told the jury how significant the trial was for

the future of the state. They should acquit Wooler only if they wanted
to see the victory of anarchy:

If we are indeed arrived at that state of society in which all this is to be done
with impunity; – when a writer shall be at liberty to destroy all the peace of
men's minds, and to attack, without fear or restraint, characters the most exalted in the state, then you may pronounce that it is not libel, and all we have to
do is to say they have so pronounced it in judgement, and we shall be reduced
to that dreadful situation of having no preservations for our constitution and
laws – no protection for the private character – no guards against insult for
those entrusted with the direction of the state.[14]

Wooler at first seemed to be intending to scrutinise his article in
detail, proving that what he said was true and not libellous. He even
subpoenaed Canning and Castlereagh as witnesses. To have cross-
examined them would have been something of a coup, allowing Wooler
the only opportunity open to him to directly engage his political opponents in debate. But he declined to call them, and the ministers were left
waiting all morning in the judge's antechamber – so, at the very least,
Wooler had been allowed the delicious experience of giving orders to
his rulers.

Instead, his tactic was to implore the jury to guard the right of free
expression, and he joined the Attorney-General in claiming his case as
an important show trial. The main point in his defence was that it was
the inalienable right of an Englishman to express his opinions without
punishment, and without being accused of making a revolution. The
trial lasted only one morning, and was taken up with Wooler's well-pol-
ished speeches about the principles of free speech rather than disputes
on points of law. He argued that the point he made in the article about
the increasingly despotic nature of ministers had been proved by the
way he had been treated:

They have commenced the system of destruction; they have aimed a fatal blow
at one of the most invaluable privileges of Englishmen: we are no longer free –
we can no longer boast our liberties compared with the rest of enslaved
Europe. Every man now is subject – not to the king – not to the laws – not to
the constitution, but – to the warrant of the Secretary of State. The moment
any man quits the gates of this court, before he can take leave of his family and

friends – without charge or suspicion, he may be arrested and immured in a dungeon, under the warrant of one of these Ministers who complain of libel because they have subverted the constitution. If at last the unhappy man is discharged, it is only at the grace and favour of the Secretary of State, and for this dismissal he is expected to feel grateful! I assert that all this is true to the letter, and that I had a full right to assert it openly and fearlessly, and I have asserted it only in the exercise of a legitimate right as a public writer.[15]

The Attorney-General had asserted as much when he praised the liberty of the press. Wooler took issue with the way he thought the limits of that liberty should be decided. 'If the liberty of the press is to have its metes and bounds,' he asked the jury, 'will you suffer that they should be chalked out by the Attorney General? . . . [H]e is the very last man to be trusted.' Setting the boundaries of freedom of expression should not be a political decision, left in the hands of the state; public opinion should be the sole judge of what was, and what was not, acceptable for a society. And it was the jury that should represent the people's decision, not the warrant of Lord Ellenborough or the Secretary of State.[16]

'I am not here to answer for my principles,' he told the jury, 'but to avow and defend them: whatever these principles may be, however mistaken they may be, they are my own.' The jury was the guarantor of the rights of all journalists, and the outcome of this trial would set an important precedent; they should not be motivated by their personal political opinions, but look at the wider significance of the case. He did not defend his words, nor did he spend much time discussing whether they were libellous; instead, he asserted his right as an Englishman to say what he wanted. The trial was not just about Wooler's right to publish; as Shepherd intimated, it would have wide-reaching consequences as to what was permitted in society: 'The effect of this prosecution I am perfectly convinced is not so much directed against me as against the general privileges of public writers.' He told the jurors, 'It is your privilege, and a most important one, to stand between the oppressor and the oppressed – the accuser and the accused – it is for a British jury to interpose its aegis for the protection of British liberty: it is to say where tyranny begins, as well as where liberty begins; it is to say both to the one and the other, – "Thus far shalt thou go, and no further".'[17]

Shepherd and Abbott summed up by informing the jury that the law condemned Wooler; they should not be misled by the journalist's emotive arguments. When Shepherd told the court that a libel was to be assessed on its tendency to corrupt people and provoke them to violence, one of the jurors spoke out: 'Are we to understand that if we find what is stated here [in the *Black Dwarf*] to be true, it is still a libel?' Shepherd answered in the affirmative: any piece of writing that was likely to endanger the public safety was libellous. The juror interrupted: 'That is, that facts are libels?' The man had identified the inherent flaw in the libel laws: truth or falsehood was irrelevant; the verdict rested solely on a subjective interpretation of its effect upon the public mind. As the saying went at the time, the law could rule that black was white. The jury retired to consider their verdict.[18]

The weighty precedent required by both the government and the reformists was confounded by the behaviour of the jury. Although they all agreed that Wooler was guilty in theory, three jurors did not want to return an unqualified verdict. After two hours the foreman returned to the court, and pronounced that Wooler was guilty as charged. Abbott accepted his verdict, and the jury left the court. However, there was some doubt as to the veracity of their decision. The foreman had grown frustrated with the protracted discussion, re-entered the courtroom with three sympathetic colleagues and pronounced a verdict that had not been finally decided by all twelve jurors. 'This cannot be justice, My Lord!' Wooler exclaimed. Abbott decided it was.[19]

Wooler complained, but was summarily dismissed by Abbott, who turned to the clerk of the court and said, 'The sooner this discussion is closed the better: proceed to some other business.'[20] And the next business was the second charge against Wooler for seditious libel. The journalist was forced to defend himself again that same afternoon, without any notice or time for rest after the rigours of the morning. This time, Shepherd argued that the defendant was guilty of libel by innuendo when he wrote about the people's right of petitioning in history; by citing precedents of popular action he was goading people to revolutionary action. It was a piece of harmless satire, and Wooler hoped that he would not be sent to a dungeon 'because I have excited a laugh against the Ministers by a little effusion of harmless ridicule'.[21] It was a weak charge, and it should never have been brought to court in the first place. Wooler was able to convince the jury that writing about King John or the Glorious Revolution did not constitute a call to arms, and they returned a unanimous verdict of not guilty.

The next day, Wooler was back in court to file an affidavit about the circumstances of the first trial, and he was granted a retrial. On 19 June he came in front of Ellenborough and Abbott, this time to argue that a new trial would be illegal because the first had been widely reported and hence all potential jurors would be prejudiced by the gossip and reportage surrounding his controversial defence. 'I cannot . . . be in justice subjected to a new trial. I defended myself against the principles of oppression and persecution acted upon by my prosecutors, against the splenetic malevolence of the Attorney General . . .'

'This is not to be endured,' Ellenborough interrupted; 'speak more respectfully, or you shall be sent back to where you came, to form your argument with an amended sense of decency.'

Wooler toned down his vituperative language, and concluded that he should not be made to suffer injustice because of a mistake made by another.

'Have you done?' asked Ellenborough.

'At present.'

'For ever,' retorted the judge; 'let the prisoner be remanded.'[22]

Wooler went back to his cell in the King's Bench. He believed that his imprisonment was illegal; he had not been convicted by either jury. Sir Francis Burdett petitioned the House of Commons, asking why Wooler was kept in gaol under such circumstances. The Attorney-General answered Burdett, disingenuously claiming that Wooler was in prison by his own volition. In fact, no orders had been given for release, so Wooler served an extra week of imprisonment owing to the inefficiency, or vindictiveness, of the Crown lawyers.

Although he was free, his victory proved little. He had put on a magnificent performance, and proved that ignorant laymen could compete on equal terms with a court of law. Wooler had not won outright; the case against him had collapsed, and both the government and the press were cheated of their precedent. Wooler was released on the understanding that he could face a retrial whenever the Crown Office felt ready to proceed. Hone said that his friend had vindicated the right of free speech, and 'argued and defended those principles, with an ardent zeal for liberty, an irresistible force of reasoning, and a burning eloquence, alike fatal to the sophistry of the Attorney-General (Shepherd), and the bad law of the Judge (Abbott)'.[23] But he was only half right; the law still stood, even if the government's show-trial had ended in an embarrassing farce, and the reformists had been handed an important propaganda victory.

Hone did not hurry to his trials with the vigour and self-assured confidence of Wooler. His plan was to destroy the premises of the libel laws and undermine some of the state's unfair advantages. He wanted to fight his trials, when they came, on his own terms. In the week that Wooler fought his two trials, Hone was brought before Ellenborough and told to enter a plea. Once again he refused, saying that he would not comply with the 'unconstitutional and unjust' proceedings of the court.

The testy old judge was at the limits of his patience. 'You must plead one way or the other. Our time cannot be thus wasted,' he spat at the defendant. Hone refused again, only to be told that he was in contempt of court, and he could be sentenced without a trial. He had no other option but to enter a plea, and three separate charges of publishing the *Catechism*, the *Liturgy* and *Creed* were read out. To each of the three charges he answered, 'Not guilty. I protest against these proceedings, as arbitrary and unjust.' Once more he complained that the court's actions were unconstitutional, to which Ellenborough snapped, 'Well, then, protest, or do what you please, but go about your business.' Hone went straight back to his cell.[24]

Hone's resistance had postponed his trials for almost two months, far longer than the government had anticipated. His campaign against the way that journalists were arrested might have come to a halt when he was threatened with punishment, but there was another aspect of the censorship to undermine. In the next few months he and Wooler were to launch a systematic attack upon Special Juries, and it was to be one of their greatest contributions to the weakening of censorship.

The ability to select a Special Jury was one of the greatest weapons in the government's armoury in its struggle against the press, and the main reason why libel trials contained only a small element of risk. Wooler wrote a book at this time called *An Appeal to the Citizens of London Against the Alleged Packing of Special Juries*, which drew upon his trial and Hone's subsequent experiences. 'Our *immediate safety*', the book started, 'is the question for consideration. The enemy has prostrated before his despotic views all the barriers of our liberty but the Trial by Jury, and that is now menaced with destruction; or with a corruption more injurious than its annihilation could prove. The Citizens of London are no longer the judges of themselves.'[25]

When Wooler and Hone arrived to see their juries selected 'everything *seemed* so fair' at first. The Master of the Crown Office picked the forty-eight names at random from a book containing five hundred men of the 'better sort' of society qualified to sit on a Special Jury. Of the forty-eight chosen from the list, the defendant and the Crown could strike out twelve names each; on the day of trial, the final twelve jurors would be selected from the remaining twenty-four nominees. Wooler thought he had better investigate the book, and what he found challenged the supposed impartiality of the legal system.[26]

Of the 500 on the list, he estimated that 226 were dead or disqualified by non-residence. A hundred recent cases had been drawn from a college of jurors numbering just 274. Amongst these, there was a group of forty men who were regularly called to sit on a jury. This was a prepared list of jurors whom the Crown office considered likely to follow the direction of the judge. They were mini-sinecures; each juryman earned a guinea a trial, making them professional jurors in the pay of the government. As Bentham wrote, the selection of Special Jurors made trials for libel 'a melancholy farce': 'What are jurors, in all such cases, but mere *puppets*? *Jury Trial*, but a solemn indeed but disastrous *puppetshow*? The Judge, but *showman* . . . who moves the wires . . .' Richard Carlile said of this system: 'It produces, in effect, a mock trial before a mock jury of twelve men selected to bow to the nod of the judge.'[27]

Of these jurors Wooler commented, 'While they *behaved well*, they retained their places, but if they ventured to differ from the veterans in office, and refused to obey orders they were either *dismissed*, or remembered not to be called *upon duty*.' If a juror were stubborn enough to dissent from the government's wishes, he would 'lose a *profitable trade*

for indulging in honest opinion'. It was the situation in the House of
Commons replicating itself in the daily experience of Londoners. And
for Hone, it meant that the Master of the Crown Office had the discretionary power to pick a jury on political grounds from a list of friends of
the government. [28]

Lord Ellenborough claimed that although the power existed to
hand-pick a friendly jury, the Master in practice observed strict
impartiality. Wooler rejected this out of hand: 'It is no answer to say
that he will never exercise it. It is unsafe that he should possess it. It
may chance to fall into the hands of a villain, who could easily find
forty-eight assistants in London to aid him in any iniquitous enterprise.' The power was unsafe in theory – the Master was 'contending
for a power which it would be unsafe to place in the hands of an
angel' – and in Wooler's own experience the discretionary power *was*
being used, and a government employee had 'an absolute power over
every verdict'.[29]

Wooler publicised the abuse of the Special Jury system, but it was left
to Hone to weaken it beyond repair. When the supposedly random
choice of jurymen was made, Hone investigated each candidate, and
confirmed Wooler's suspicion that they were personal appointments
made by the Master of the Crown Office for political purposes. Indeed,
one supposedly impartial selection was an MP, whose authority would
surely be enough to sway the verdict of his fellow jurors. On 26 June
Hone, witnessed by Wooler, signed an official complaint and sent it to
the Master, stating that the Special Juries selected for his trials were
'imperfectly and illegally constructed; I, the above named Defendant,
do hereby protest against the Juries so nominated, and against all proceedings to try the said issues before the said Juries'.[30]

In a move that most commentators saw as unprecedented, the
Master of the Crown Office was forced to cancel the jury lists on the
grounds that they had been illegally 'nominated from an improper
source', and postpone the trials whilst he reformed the system. He
admitted that the law was partial when it came to trying journalists.
Hone and Wooler's campaign was an amazing success; Hone wrote in
triumph: 'The Crown itself has been unable to support *Special Juries*

nominated from such a source; hence it abandons them, and hence I am liberated.'[31]

Hone had to be released from prison once the Crown admitted that it was using nefarious and criminal means to convict him. His bail was reduced to three bonds of recognisance of £100 each. He wrote a moving piece on his sudden release after so long a struggle to prove that he was persecuted and unfairly punished:

This morning [5 July 1817], therefore, at nine o'clock . . . I was informed the prison gates were open to me. I ran up to my room, which was at the top of the prison, to take a last look from the window, at some objects whereupon my eyes had frequently rested, and my mind mused. Above the walls, in the distance, were the Surrey hills, clad in their verdure, whereupon, in the days of my health and youth, I had rambled alone . . . On those hills I had sat, with my face towards London, bending my mind's eye on the ceaseless turmoil and perplexity of man in crowded cities. I now looked towards the spot, where I fancied I had so seated myself, and so reflected, from a place how different – the depository of aches and cares; and sorrows, and jealousies; and vice and misfortune. The thousand ills and mishaps of social life were condensed within its walls . . . I turned the key in my door, to go down stairs and take leave of the few gentlemen, from whom I had received attention and kindness, and in whose society I had spent many happy hours. When I passed the gates, I seemed as a bird that had escaped from the fowler.[32]

His long and personally hazardous campaign to thwart the government and condemn its actions as biased had been entirely vindicated. No other journalist had been able to unravel the mechanisms of censorship before. He proved that the once the government was held to account, the illegal and one-sided nature of press prosecutions would be revealed for what they were: cruel and untenable. Those who had cringed before Ellenborough had done their fellow journalists a great disservice: 'Bad men are only strong when the virtuous are timid and irresolute. The present Administration – certainly the most contemptible that were ever laughed at – may become as cruel as Nero, if we do not resolutely oppose them as we thoroughly despise them.'[33]

9

The Three Trials

The State shall be my governors, but not my critics.
John Milton, *Areopagitica*, 1644

As if from a rubbish cart a continually increasing and ever shapeless mass of Law is from time to time shot down upon the heads of the people; and out of this rubbish, and at his peril, is each man left to pick out what belongs to him. Thus in pouring forth Law, does the Government, as it is written, *rain down snares*.
Jeremy Bentham

Who have been libelled? The good, the great, or the wise? No such thing.
Thomas Wooler, *Black Dwarf*

'It is now two and a half years since I commenced to publish; in the course of which I have issued upwards of one hundred and thirty pieces, chiefly of my own productions. Not a week has elapsed in that period without my having compiled or written something.' So Hone wrote in the *Register*. Between 1814 and 1817 he had become a prolific London journalist, a noted crime reporter, political commentator and, according to the Crown lawyers at least, a dangerously penetrating satirist.

He was an experienced journalist and connoisseur of arbitrary justice, but, as he sarcastically put it, he had 'inexpertness in certain trading requisites'. On 25 October he signed off as editor of the *Reformist Register* and announced the closure of his newspaper; it failed because of the 'distractions and cares of a little business, and a large family'. His incarceration at the decree of Ellenborough's court, the ever-present threat of government spies penetrating his circle of friends, combat with the morass of the libel laws, and the full-time job of writing and editing a weekly newspaper had shattered his health. And above these cares, the flaws in the system of informal distribution were exposed.

Most of the county agents took their batches of the *Register*, and never remitted Hone; throughout the summer of 1817 he was distributing copies of the paper gratis, in the vain hope of future payment. In any case, he was not able to keep accounts whilst in prison. As he said, the pressures of defending himself and writing 'prevented me from taking such steps as a keen tradesmen might have done to enforce payment'. And so, in the last number, he admitted defeat: 'This is the death-throe of the *Register*, and with it I bid my readers *farewell!*'[2]

With the collapse of Hone's paper, Sidmouth could at least be reassured that one of the premises of censorship was still intact. The more a publisher resisted the courts, the longer he spent on remand, the greater the likelihood that personal financial disaster would do the work of censorship. This was a piece of logic with which even Hone could not contend.

Whilst he had hindered the government's censorship, he had only given pause to the prosecutions. He might have thought for a time that the case had been dropped, or that he had weakened the government's legal machinery so completely that a trial was by now impossible. But in the last week of November a short hand-written note arrived from the Attorney-General calling him to trial. Hone replied, pleading that he be spared the trials given that he had forced the court to admit its unfair and illegal plots against him. One of his sons was sent with the note to Sir Samuel Shepherd's house, and he was shown into the dressing room, where Hone's chief prosecutor was shaving. 'Tell your father, my boy,' the Attorney-General said between razor strokes, 'that I am very sorry for him, but the action must go on.'[3]

The Master of the Crown Office had reformed the lists of Special Jurors, and the new book of qualified men now contained some 8,000 names. Hone went to see his juries chosen. The Master was supposed to put his pen between the pages of a closed book, make random marks, and then open the book and see which names had been touched by the ink; it was as random a system of choosing jurymen as could be devised (it was called 'pricking' a jury rather than 'packing' one with vetted nominees). This was done in front of Hone, and 144 pricks were made in the book: three short-lists of forty-eight jurors for each trial. But when the Master came to open the book to see where fate had directed his pen, he and two Treasury solicitors pored over the book, without letting anyone else witness their deliberations. Hone noticed that they skipped through it casually, sometimes turning over eight, ten or a dozen pages at a time without looking for the marks. Occasionally they would find four ink marks on one page, or the Master would scrutinise the names before reading out the supposedly random choices. It was clear to Hone that it was the same old system; the Master had a list of pre-selected jurors who would secure a conviction, and he was merely pretending that his nominees had been selected by chance. The defendant filed another affidavit, and once again the court had to admit that 'jury lists had been illegally, improperly and partially prepared'. The process was repeated, and, as far as could be seen, three Special Juries were selected in a fair manner, even if the jurymen were still drawn from the mercantile community, not Hone's peers. After almost six months' dispute about the legality of the censorship, the trials could now go ahead. Hone spent the few weeks before the trial rehearsing his speeches in George Cruikshank's studio.[4]

Hone's prospects could not be regarded with much optimism. The reformist press was never so pessimistic as in the weeks before the trials. Wooler put a black border around his paper, mourning the death of trial by jury. He gloomily mused that English common law was being turned on its head and used against the people, so that 'trial by jury may become as fatal to the liberties of England as the wooden horse was to the hapless Trojans'. The *Examiner* believed that the state had successfully turned back the clock to the days of absolutism: 'leaping with indecent, insolent (they will find one day or other) stupid haste into the open possession of their old pretensions, exactions and bigotries . . .' The dispute would be 'settled by mere physical force – the bayonet'.

The government already had a precedent. James Williams, a bookseller from Portsmouth, had been tried on two separate charges of selling cheap reproductions of Hone's satires, found guilty, gaoled for twelve months, and required to pay a total of £700 in fines and sureties. If a bookshop owner could be given such a severe punishment for merely passing on the parodies, it would not have been hard to imagine the fate awaiting the writer and publisher of the offending pieces. Hone had met Williams, a pro-government printer, whom Hone described as 'a loyal man; that is to say a thick and thin man; who, if a person in authority were to say go, he goeth; come and he cometh'. In this case someone in authority had commanded that he 'goeth' to prison. During their conversation, it transpired that once Hone was convicted, Williams would be released. *The Times* called the printer a government spy, who allowed himself to be used as a precedent to ensure a verdict of guilty for Hone.

Already, the Tory press was delighted, happily advocating the arrest of journalists *before* they had a chance to publish anti-government articles and arguing that jury trials should be abolished and replaced with a tribunal of judges. In its editorial on 26 November *The Times* warned: 'Hints are scattered from various quarters that Ministers have it in contemplation to propose some new restrictions on the liberty of the press ... We wait with some anxiety ... till we see the complexion of the proposed measures.' *The Times* was cryptic, but in higher political circles it was believed that Hone would be found guilty and sent to gaol, a new parliamentary session would commence a few weeks later, when the government would introduce a bill to take away the right of trial by jury for seditious and blasphemous libellers.[5]

The motives of the writer: first day

On Thursday, 17 December Hone left his lodgings in the Old Bailey to take the short walk to the Guildhall for his first trial. 'I rushed from my wife and children in bitter agony,' Hone recalled with a certain amount of hyperbole, 'leaving them sorrowing and hopeless of seeing me repass the threshold of their home – a home no more to them, if I could not defeat the powers then gathering themselves in Guildhall for my destruction.' Yet his dramatic prose should not detract from the serious task he faced that day. A verdict of guilty would have lasting significance for the press, but for the Hone family it would be an irreversible disaster. A prison sentence would wreck Hone's frail health and destroy his already beleaguered publishing business. The Hones were already impoverished, and if William was gaoled, there would be no income.[6]

A crowd had been queuing outside the Guildhall since eight, and the doors of the court opened at nine. Twenty minutes later the defendant

arrived with parcels of dusty old books and prints, which he placed on
the table of the court; the officers of the court were much surprised that
the table did not contain the usual array of legal text books. Hone,
described by Charles Knight as 'a middle-aged man, a bland and smiling man, with a half sad half merry twinkle in his eye – a seedy man, to
use an expressive word, whose black coat is wondrous brown and
threadbare', took his place at the table and sat patiently and alone until
the judge arrived.[7] At the other end of the table there was a huddle of
Crown lawyers; around the judgment seat sat the clerks of the court;
and surrounding the court, sheriffs and officers. Even William Jones,
the marshal of the King's Bench Prison, attended with some of Hone's
former guards – an intimidating presence for the defendant. And to
remind the jury that they had a duty to protect religion against the
machinations of atheists, there was at least one bishop prominent in
court during the three trials.

The Guildhall, a huge medieval building at the centre of the city,
symbolises the majesty and grandeur of the state; it is a cavernous hall
adorned with statues of the nation's heroes – a kind of secular cathedral
with all the trappings and emblems of feudal power: stained-glass windows, coats of arms, banners, minstrels' galleries. The emblems of the
Guildhall were a constant reminder that this trial stood within a long
history of important state trials: no one could forget that this was the
place where Lady Jane Grey and Thomas Cranmer were convicted of
high treason. When governments wanted to give their transactions and
ceremonies the highest publicity, they chose the Guildhall. It was here
that the five members of parliament excluded by Charles I in 1641 fled
to rally Londoners against the King. In 1688, the peers had established
themselves at Guildhall to restore order amidst the anarchy that
emerged during the interregnum of the Glorious Revolution. In 1814, it
had been the natural location for the banquet honouring the Tsar and
the King of Prussia after the first defeat of Bonaparte. And for
Londoners, it was the hub of the city, where all aspects of local administration were conducted; anyone who carried out a trade or sought justice was drawn within the orbit of Guildhall. It was at the centre of daily
life for thousands of Londoners, the most accessible and public forum
in the capital. Its choice as the court to try Hone was a statement of the

government's confidence that this was the occasion when its powers over the press would be demonstrated in front of the whole nation. The King's Bench sat at Guildhall out of term, but the trials of Cobbett, the Hunts, Cochrane and Wooler had taken place in Westminster Hall, an equally imposing building but nowhere near as large as the Guildhall. That this was a show trial is clear from the words of Sir Samuel Shepherd: 'Of all men Mr Hone seems the fittest object for prosecution . . .' He was the most dangerous of journalists, and his punishment would serve to show his fellow writers what happened when the state was provoked.

In defending himself, Hone would be dwarfed beneath the high ceiling, a miniscule and lonely figure in the great hall. And he would have to make his extemporary speeches and legal disputes in front of a thousand men and women. The significance of the trials for the future of the press was recognised by Londoners; they knew the importance the government placed on this prosecution, and the contest between Hone, an unlikely and somewhat obscure advocate for free speech, was to be the defining moment in the censorship campaign, whatever the outcome. Throughout the three trials, the crowd was to play an important role in Hone's defence.

Lord Justice Abbott, the trial judge, arrived at half past nine and a Special Jury was sworn in. Sir Samuel Shepherd's son, one of the prosecution lawyers, stood up and told the court that Hone was accused of publishing a libel 'with intent to excite impiety and irreligion in the minds of his Majesty's liege subjects, to ridicule and scandalise the Christian religion, and to bring into contempt the Catechism'. Sir Samuel then stated the law. *The Book of Common Prayer* was established by Act of Parliament; it was part of the statute law of the land; hence any attempt to vilify it was a criminal act. Hone had done just this in his burlesque of the Catechism, the Liturgy and the Ten Commandments. Shepherd said that the Catechism was used to form the minds of the young, building 'that proper foundation for religious belief which is to influence their future conduct'. It contained the Lord's Prayer and the Decalogue. 'If these works be not what ought to be held sacred from ridicule,' he said, 'what is there that can be called so in the mind of a Christian?'

'I take it to be proposition of the law', Shepherd told the jury, 'that he who attempts to parody these three sacred parts of Christian belief, and presents them to the mind in a ridiculous shape, does that which is calculated to bring them into contempt, and is therefore, by the law of the land, guilty of a libel.' He asked the jurors whether they would allow their children to be corrupted by such irreligion, and if not, would they put the publication in the hands of

the lower classes of society, which are not fit to cope with the sort of topics which are artfully raised for them? I ask you, if it be possible, that after such publications are thus cheaply thrown among this class of people, they can, with the same degree of reverence that becomes the subject, look at the Sacred Book of our belief? Nay, even in better cultivated minds, the firmness of moral rectitude is shaken, and it often becomes necessary to make great mental exertion to shake off the influence of these productions, and recall the mind to a true feeling towards sacred truths. They are inevitably calculated to weaken the reverence felt for the Christian faith.

Sir Samuel believed the satire so obviously blasphemous and illegal that he did feel it worth his while to spend too long establishing its evil intent; the language condemned it without further elucidation.

Shepherd quoted from the parody: 'I, the Minister, am the Lord thy liege, who brought thee out of want and beggary into the House of Commons.' When he wrote the parodies, Hone could not have conceived a better actor to intone his solemn words. The sound of the government's legal representative reciting Hone's phrases of ministerial omnipotence was too much for the crowd, and it broke into spontaneous laughter. Abbott halted proceedings, telling the audience that noisy laughter was an interruption to men 'who are of a graver disposition, and in the discharge of an important duty'. The Attorney-General concurred with the judge, and matched his humourless pomposity: 'My Lord, if there be any persons here who can raise a smile at the reading of the Defendant's publication, it is the fullest proof of the baneful effect it has had, and with which I charge it. It is for this very reason I charge it as a libel on the Law of England. I am not sorry for the faint smile just uttered in Court. It establishes the baneful tendency of the work.'

The entire parody was read aloud to the court. Hone then rose to his defence. 'If I feel any embarrassment on this occasion, and I feel a great deal,' he began, 'it is because I am not in the habit of addressing an assembly like this: I have never, indeed, addressed any assembly whatever; and therefore I hope that you and the court will show your indulgence to me standing here as I do, unassisted by counsel, to make my own defence.'* He began with a description of the punishments and rough justice that he had suffered since his arrest in May, paying particular attention to the time when he was found 'senseless' on the floor of his cell after the abuses he was subjected to during the first few days of arrest: 'That arose out of the inhumanity of Lord Ellenborough.'

Hone spent the first hour or so of his defence telling the jury that he had been traduced and vilified by the Court of the King's Bench, the Secretary of State, parliament and the Tory press. They had charged him with 'being an impious and wickedly disposed person'. A great prejudice had been raised against him throughout the country, he claimed, and this was done with the intent of biasing potential jurymen against him. That was why it was so important for him to recount his miserable experiences at the hands of Ellenborough. The campaign against his good name had begun at the moment of his arrest: the court had treated him like the worst of criminals to convince people that his crimes were of such high magnitude that it would be dangerous to allow him even the smallest moment of liberty. Since then 'a war-whoop and yell was set forth against me throughout the country'. He was unable to answer the weight of prejudice and invective:

It is impossible for a man so humble in life as myself to wage war with opinions broached by the Secretary of State; but when I heard Lord Sidmouth, in the House of Lords, rising every night and calling these little publications blasphemous, I have felt disposed to interrupt him. The odds are terribly against me in a prosecution of this kind, for I have to contend with the Secretary of State – a man whose opinions are adopted by a great number of persons of the first rank and consideration . . .

* The shorthand copyists employed by the daily newspapers to transcribe the trials put most of Hone's words in reported speech (except for a few sentences in which he was quoted directly). Here, the words of the participants have, where necessary, been converted into the present tense and the first person to give a more accurate (and less confusing) sense of what Hone, Shepherd, Abbott and Ellenborough said in December 1817.

Throughout 1817 Hone had learnt the painful lesson that 'however honourable a man's intentions might be, they might be construed into guilt, and the whole nation raised against him'. But, he said, he could be saved by a 'few cool, dispassionate, and sober persons' who comprised a British jury, men who could be trusted to ignore the bigoted opinions of the state and calmly 'determine the motives of the writer'. This was in direct opposition to Shepherd's case. The Attorney-General had claimed that libellers should be judged by the tendency their work had to incite irreligion in the public, and the laughter in court proved that Hone's words had caused them to scoff at the scriptures. 'I deny that,' Hone told the jury. 'The smile might arise from something wholly different from the feeling of the person who wrote that publication.' If the jury thought he had tried to incite irreligion, they should convict him; however, he should be acquitted if they thought his motives were something very different.

'I have told you it is the intention of which you are to judge,' he told the jurors; 'and I will sit down immediately, if the Attorney General can lay his hands on any publication in which, in any one passage or sentence, he could point out any thing tending to degrade or vilify the Christian religion.' He claimed to have a high respect for the Church and scripture, yet he had been 'held up as a man unfit to live, as a blasphemer, a monster, a wretch who has kept body and soul together by the sale of blasphemous publications'. He had withdrawn the parodies from sale after only one week on the advice of his friends: 'Had I been one who wished to ridicule religion, I should have taken a different course. I should have continued the publication and made money by it, as there was a great demand for it. In that case, I could have afforded to employ Counsel, and would not have been reduced to the necessity of standing in my present situation before the Court and Jury.' A very poor blasphemer he, who chose to suppress his parodies when he discovered they offended tender sensibilities. Hone assumed that he was a sufficiently famous journalist for the jury to be familiar with his writing and publishing. He asked them whether they could remember any occasion when the William Hone publishing firm had mentioned religion, let alone vilified it. As everyone in the country knew, he was a political campaigner, not a proselytiser of atheism.

Hone quickly moved on to the key part of his case. 'As to parodies,' he said, 'they are as old, at least, as the invention of printing; and I never heard of a prosecution for a parody, either religious or any other.' The evidence he used in his defence was the entire canon of English litera- ture, and the dusty old volumes he had piled in front of the judge were his witnesses: 'I have my books about me, and it is from them that I must draw my defence.' He produced a parody of the first psalm writ- ten in 1518 'by a man whom every individual in this court would esteem – a man to whom we are indebted for liberty of conscience': Martin Luther. 'Would any man say that Martin Luther was a blasphemer? and he is a parodist with William Hone.'

He went through a long list of religious parodies written by church- men throughout the ages, citing the Protestant martyr Bishop Latimer, John Milton and the Royalists of the Civil War, to name but a few of the exalted people who had written parodies. Abbott interrupted him on a point of law: Hone could not excuse his own blasphemy by saying that others had done similarly, 'defending one offence by another'. But Hone would not be deterred; he wanted to show that parodic literature had been used throughout history for instruction, and not to mock the works parodied. 'This sort of writing is familiar to me from my reading,' he said: in 1600 Dr John Boys (later Dean of Canterbury) had preached an attack on the Catholic rite of transubstantiation, which included the parody, 'Our Pope, which art in Rome, hellish be thy name, give us this day our cup in the Lord's supper . . .'

Abbott interrupted once more to deny that Hone's evidence was admissible as a way of defending his blasphemy: 'I think it better that the defendant should not read any more of this parody; it can only shock the ears of well-disposed and religious persons; and I must again repeat, that the law does not allow one offence to be vindicated by another. I wish the defendant would not read such things.'

'My Lord,' Hone replied, 'your Lordship's observation is in the very spirit of what Pope Leo X said to Martin Luther – "For God's sake don't say a word about the indulgences and the monasteries, and I'll give you a living," thus precluding him from mentioning the very thing in dispute. I must go on with these parodies, or I cannot go on with my defence.'

He continued to read parody after parody from his library; some were written by divines, whilst others came from English political history. Abbott tolerated this strange form of defence for a while, but eventually tried to silence Hone for good, saying once more, 'one instance of profaneness cannot excuse another'. Hone agreed with the judge's sound legal reasoning; but he was not trying to excuse his parody by citing others: it was a literary device, which did not necessarily mock the original text. Hundreds of pious Anglicans had adopted this technique: he insisted, in the context of hundreds of years of parodic literature written 'by dignitaries of the church, and by men high in the State', his contribution was surely a mere 'trifle'.

Parody was also a common way of conveying information in a way in which people could recognise it. If the jury could understand the ways in which parody was traditionally used, they would see that both his *Catechism of a Ministerial Member* and Ten Commandments had used the words and phrases of *The Book of Common Prayer* and the Bible to mock something other than religion. He claimed that parodies were a recognisable feature of daily life 'which the common people had been accustomed to for centuries'. These people knew what a parody was, and they could laugh at the satire without ridiculing the original text. To prove his point, Hone entertained the court by singing a parodied version of the carol 'God Rest You, Merry Gentlemen', a song which elucidated the Christmas story and was recited on the streets every Christmas. Parodies conveyed ideas to people, and they did so without making the thing parodied ludicrous. To say that the common people would be seduced and corrupted by a parody of the Catechism was risible, given that they encountered parodies everywhere in their culture.

In modern Britain religious parodies were ubiquitous. As part of the British propaganda against Napoleon, religious parodies had been translated into the European languages.* John Reeves, who in the 1790s had founded a loyalist society to spread anti-revolutionary propaganda, had published a parody of a Catechism. And how had this blasphe-

---

* For example:

Oh Emperor of France! we curse thee.	To thee all nations cry aloud,
We acknowledge thee to be a Tyrant.	BONEY, BONEY, BONEY!
Thou murdering Infidel! all the world detest thee.	Thou art universally execrated.

mous libeller been rewarded? He had become the official printer of *The Book of Common Prayer*. He did not say that these parodists were not blasphemers, but he wanted to make it clear that the law was biased:

It is essential to me that the jury should also understand, that had I been a publisher of Ministerial parodies, I should not now be defending myself on the floor of this Court. – It is essential to the friends of Justice, that all men should stand equal, when they were brought before the tribunal of the laws. But I deny that I am placed in this situation of equality, when I am singled out by the Attorney General to be tried for an offence, which, if it had been committed in favour of the Ministerial Party, would not have been noticed.

Hone then displayed a print engraved by the political cartoonist James Gillray which showed the Whigs Richard Sheridan as Judas and Charles James Fox as Beelzebub. Some of his other cartoons depicted ministers as Biblical heroes; in one, William Pitt was Elijah throwing down his mantle to the politicians who made up the present government. And because Gillray was an important tool for the Pittites, he had been given a pension of £200 a year, despite the fact that he had committed a crime identical to the one now on trial. Abbott stopped Hone, saying, 'You must not make these assertions.'

'I can prove it,' Hone said.

'But', rejoined the judge, 'if you can prove that he, being pensioned, published those things, will that form a defence for you?'

'My Lord, I have no pension.'

Hone went on to describe another Gillray cartoon, the *Apotheosis of Hoche*, a cartoon that parodied Michelangelo's painting on the ceiling of the Sistine Chapel, showing the French General Hoche as a Jacobin angel ascending to a revolutionary heaven strumming a harp made from a guillotine; in the background the cartoonist had, like Hone, parodied the Ten Commandments ('Thou shalt commit murder' etc.). Abbott stopped him again, saying that the fact that the state had sponsored such blasphemy made no difference to this case.

'It was on the right side – that made all the difference,' Hone maintained.

'I know nothing of a right or wrong side, in those cases.'

'It was very well,' Hone came back, 'as it was written for the

Administration. Mr Gillray, who published these things to serve the purposes of the Administration, had a pension for his parodies.'

But the government had done more than just pay or reward blasphemers. One of its members had actually written religious parodies. Lord Grey had reminded Hone that in the 1790s George Canning wrote an attack on the English Whigs, mocking them for venerating the French Revolutionary Lepaux as if he were a god; it was identical to Hone's parody in intent and style. As Hone said,

I was dragged before the Court, from behind my counter – and for doing what? For doing that which a Cabinet Minister has been suffered to do with impunity. I will assert that the Attorney General will act wrong – that he will proceed partially and unfairly – if he does not bring Mr Canning forward. If I am convicted, he ought to follow me to my cell – if my family is ruined, his family ought to be made to feel a little – if I am injured by this indecent, this unjust prosecution, he ought to be made to feel a little.

Hone had shown the jury many examples of how parody related to the original texts. A well-known literary work could be used because it was familiar, but not be attacked directly. His most important piece of evidence was Canning's parody, 'which is the same as my own: it is political; and it proves that the ridicule which the authors of the parodies attempt to excite, is not always intended to fix on the production parodied'. Hone read from his satire, inviting the jury to find anything which related to religion. He quoted from the catechism of a supine MP by his ministerial master:

Question: *What is your name?* – Answer: *Lick Spittle.*

Q: *Who gave you that name?* – A: *My sureties to the Ministry, in my Political Change, wherein I was made a Member of the Majority, the Child of Corruption, and a Locust to devour the good things of this Kingdom.*

The corruption he had mentioned, Hone said, 'was as notorious as the sun at noon day'; the majority of the Commons were 'always at the beck of the Minister'. He defied anyone to deny that either he or Canning were anything but political satirists. If the government wanted to prosecute him, he seemed to be saying, they should have brought a charge of *seditious* libel. Sidmouth had seized upon religious parodies as the greatest danger to the security of the state. The folly of this crusade was now being exposed. The question of why Hone had provoked the government and willingly courted arrest by using religious texts was at last answered. The government had ignored his political journalism, assuming instead that the satires were easy targets, things which no Special Juryman could consider anything but profane. By raising hysteria about the connexion between radicalism and irreligion, the ministers had fallen into a trap. The truth was that Hone's parody was *too* subversive: what at first sight appeared to be cut and dried blasphemy was, when scrutinised in the context of parodic literature, nothing but a political satire.

After speaking for six hours, Hone came to the close of his defence. He had avoided legal argument, instead attacking the government as hypocritical and vindictive in signalling him out for punishment. He undermined the libel laws not by saying that they were unjust, but that they were simply unworkable: 'There are . . . very few men who understand the law of libel. It is, in fact, a shadow – it is undefinable.' Had the prosecution managed to prove that parody constituted a criminal libel? He could not be found guilty unless the whole of parodic literature was equally culpable. The intention of a parodist was impossible to define as casually as the prosecution had done: 'It is an important feature of my defence, to show that parodies might be written, in order to excite certain ideas, without any desire to turn the original production into ridicule.' Luther and Milton were not blasphemous libellers. Neither James Gillray nor George Canning had mocked the Ten Commandments or Scripture, but attacked Jacobins by using words and stories familiar to their audience. If the jury were aware of the ways in which parody was used in literature and politics, they would see that he had not mocked the Prayer Book. He had used language recognisable to everyone in order to attack the government. The only victims of his attack were politicians; the religious issue was irrelevant. Any one could see that his *Catechism* satirised ministers, not the Church; by using the parodic form he had deliberately put *The Book of Common Prayer* outside the scope of his humour. As he said: 'It would be a most cruel hardship if I, who, from the long continuance of the system had been induced to adopt it, should be punished for that which my predecessors and contemporaries did with impunity. In my opinion the existence of such publications for so long a time, prove that they are not libellous . . .'

Hone had adopted a highly original defence. By avoiding legal issues he had grounded his case in common sense and plain language, appealing to the jurors' sense of decency. His parody must be judged within the context of hundreds of years of similar publications written by the most respected men in history. This mode of defence was unanswerable. When Abbott came to sum up, he was forced into the ridiculous position of asserting that he would prosecute Luther or Milton if they were still alive. Hone's argument was much more subtle than the government's ill-considered contention that parodies were intrinsically offensive to the original text. Hone proved that he was the expert on English literature; the prosecution were completely ignorant of how parodies related to the works they burlesqued – they were obviously out of their depth when they came to define what parody was and how it was used by writers.

Hone's defence was the vindication of the autodidact: he had built a cogent defence and a theory of parody from reading thousands of books that he had collected or sold over his lifetime. The case he made on the first day indicated years of research and deep thought; the court could not rival his expertise in English literature. He destroyed the government's belief that he was an unthinking atheist who had made use of the Bible casually and thoughtlessly. On the contrary, as a writer and student of literature and history, he had deployed a satirical form that was grounded in tradition and recognisable from an ancient political discourse. He made the prosecution and the judge seem amateurish, their judgements badly thought through. Most importantly, he established that they were hypocritical, partial and malicious.

It was the kind of defence that only a writer could make; a barrister would flounder and tie himself up in knots of legal procedure. Hone spoke to the jury in an informal way, proving that he was a reasonable and knowing man, hardly the kind of wild blasphemer who would deserve punishment. In contrast, Abbott and Shepherd sounded obscurantist and pedantic. Although they knew the law better than anyone, they could not engage with the jury in the way that Hone did.

Their condemnation of laughter was pompous and unrealistic. Hone did not defend himself on points of law, but widened the case into a general discussion about the use of literature. Had he intended to make people laugh at scripture? or had he rather put the reformist case in a novel and droll form? Whom had he mocked – God or the Regent? He left it to the jury to answer this simple question. After such a reasonable justification by the defendant, Sir Samuel must have sounded slightly hysterical when he told the jury that the parody was 'so injurious in its tendency, and so disgusting in its form, that any man, on the first reading, would start . . . with horror from it; it was like an infectious pestilence'.

The crowd coughed and jeered whilst Shepherd summed up. He clung on to his assertion that *all* parodies were offensive to the texts they drew upon. It must have seemed ill-considered and somewhat ignorant after Hone's scholarly lectures on literary theory. The jury retired after Abbott told them that an acquittal would be a victory for atheism and the justification of a high offence. He told them not to regard Hone's defence: previous examples of religious parody could not excuse a modern one. But this was dusty legal sophistry; even if Hone's evidence was, legally speaking, inadmissible, the jury had heard a compelling argument grounded in common sense. He had proved beyond dispute that this was a political trial; that the issue of blasphemy was a stalking horse for censorship. He exposed the law's obvious bias, and he dared Shepherd to bring Canning to trial if he wanted to refute it. There could be no denying the justice of Hone's case, and only a biased jury would dare to follow the direction of the judge. But the danger that this *was* a biased jury was very real.

Less than a quarter of an hour later the jury were back. The foreman stood forward, and announced a unanimous verdict of not guilty. 'The loudest acclamations of applause were instantly heard from all parts of the Court; *Long live an honest Jury*, and *an honest Jury forever*, were exclaimed by many voices: the waving of hats, handkerchiefs, and applause continued for several minutes.' Abbott ordered the crowd to leave, 'and as they proceeded along the streets, the language of joy was most loudly and unequivocally expressed; every one with whom they met, and to whom they communicated the event, being forward to swell the peal'.

In the Guildhall, meanwhile, Abbott made a mockery of the victory by ordering Hone to appear at nine thirty the next morning for his second trial.

Is a laugh treason? Second day

Abbott went straight to Lord Ellenborough after his defeat. 'Well! and the verdict?' demanded the Chief Justice.

'An acquittal!' replied an embarrassed Sir Charles Abbott.

'An acquittal!' Ellenborough shouted. 'Why! how did you charge?'

'How did I charge? Constitutionally, my Lord!'

'I'll go to him myself tomorrow,' Ellenborough snarled.

The Chief Justice had not presided over the first trial because he was ill; but Abbott's failure in so straightforward a case roused him to go to the Guildhall and make full use of his undoubted personal influence. It was a blow for Hone, for he would have to deal with a judge less forgiving than gentle Charles Abbott. According to Henry Brougham, Ellenborough did not like 'refinements or subtleties' in legal arguments brought before him; like Hone, he aimed to convince a jury with 'plain, sound, common-sense views'. Hone would be aware that the doughty old judge was more adept at silencing contrary views than Abbott. The force of Ellenborough's will and 'the thunder of his fierce declaration' meant that defendants, and even experienced barristers, were 'not suffered to bring forward all they had to state with that fullness and freedom, which alone can prevent misdecision, and ensure the due administration of justice'.

The confrontation between Hone and Ellenborough was a delicious prospect for the London crowd. It was to be a battle between two redoubtable characters, a test of will and nerve. Hone had shown that he was adept at capturing the ear of the court and presenting evidence that a judge had ruled inadmissible. If he was to do so again, he would have to best Ellenborough, of whom Brougham commented: 'Of sarcasm he was an eminent professor, but of a kind which hacks and tears, and flays its victims, rather than destroys by cutting keenly.' There would be no niceties or compromise in court that day between judge and defendant. Yet one thing counted in Hone's favour. Ellenborough had a grudging respect for men who refused to be cowed and bullied, who stood up to a browbeating: 'his courage was high, leaving him more scorn than compassion for nerves less firm than his own'. There was perhaps more in common between the two men than either would have been prepared to admit.[8]

That morning a freezing fog enveloped the Guildhall. But thousands of Londoners began to queue from the early hours of the morning, and even at this time the roads and lanes surrounding the court were blocked. When the doors opened at nine, a thousand managed to cram into the great hall, leaving twenty thousand outside to await news of the day's proceeding. Hone was alone in thinking that the government would drop the remaining two prosecutions after he had been acquitted on the first day. He was convinced that, having successfully defended himself against the charge, the government would acquit him of the two further libels by default; he hurried into court with his bundle of books just in time. It was an unwelcome surprise to see Ellenborough take the judgment seat. The Chief Justice was determined to convict Hone at all costs, and he believed that he was the only judge with the authority and experience to secure a verdict of guilty. As he made clear to Abbott, he would not scruple to use unfair means to get his way. The unscheduled appearance of Ellenborough threw all Hone's calculations; he would have to pursue a different course in his defence. In their previous meetings, the judge had undoubtedly come off the victor.

Lord Campbell, in his biographies of the Lord Chief Justices of England, wrote that Hone looked up at the judgment seat and said, 'I am glad to see you my Lord Ellenborough. I know what you are come for; I know what you want.'

'I am come to do justice,' Ellenborough growled.

'Is it not rather, my Lord, to send a poor bookseller to rot in a dungeon?'[9]

Although Hone's caustic welcome to the Lord Chief Justice was not recorded in the verbatim trial reports that appeared in the daily papers, the words are in the spirit of the defence, but might owe more to a memory of Hone's contempt for the judge than to reality. In any case, Ellenborough ignored the rebuke and announced his priority: to stop the crowd laughing and cheering as it had done during the first trial. His first act was to send for sheriffs, so that he could enforce his will upon the vociferous audience. Hone was then accused of blasphemy for publishing a parody of the Litany. Shepherd began his prosecution, repeating his assertion that mocking the Prayer Book was contrary to statute law and a serious libel. Once again he read from the offending publication. Hone had ridiculed the sacred words of the service book: 'Son of God, we beseech thee to hear us! O Lamb of God, that takest away the sins of the world, have mercy upon us!' He had taken this solemn prayer and rendered it ridiculous: 'Son of George, we beseech thee to hear us. O House of Lords that takest away so many thousands of pounds in pensions, have mercy upon us.' The parody continued:

O Prince, ruler of the people, have mercy upon us, thy miserable subjects.

O House of Lords, hereditary legislators, have a mercy upon us, pension-paying subjects.

O House of Commons, proceeding from corrupt borough-mongers, have mercy upon us, your should-be constituents.

Once again, the crowd found the Attorney-General incanting these mock-solemn words uncontrollably funny.

'Where are the sheriffs?' Ellenborough angrily demanded when laughter interrupted proceedings. 'I desired their attendance, and they shall attend.'

'My Lord, I have sent for them,' the under-sheriff replied; 'but they live a great distance from this, and they have not yet arrived.'

'Very well.'

The Attorney-General turned to the jury, and held up the laughter as proof of Hone's success in perverting the minds of the people. 'If the social bonds of society are to be burst asunder by the indecent conduct of a rabble, the Court may as well discontinue its proceedings.' He went on to contrast the intelligence and good sense of the jurors with the base passions of the mob. 'If there be any among you,' he told the jury, 'which is doubtless the case, who is the father of children, and the master of a household, I will ask him, if he would suffer that publication to be perused by his servants, who are not so well educated as himself?'

On the second day, the prosecution based its appeal to the Special Jury on the shared responsibility of all propertied gentlemen to defend the institutions of the country from the unthinking zeal of the common people. The second trial was to be much more bitter and rancorous than the first. Ellenborough wanted blood.

The Attorney-General was about to call a witness proving that Hone had published and sold the libel, when Hone readily admitted he had done both. Shepherd than produced The Book of Common Prayer. 'Do you admit that this is the Common-Prayer Book?' he asked.

I admit that this is the Common Prayer,' Hone replied.

'You admit that it is the Common Prayer of the Church of England?' Ellenborough inquired.

'Certainly, my Lord.'

Just before Hone began his defence, the sheriffs arrived, and the judge directed them to watch the crowd and prevent the people from laughing. The defendant began with the same arguments as he had on the first day, telling this new jury about his experiences in prison. He was just about to start to go through his collection of parodies by Luther, Boys, Reeves, Gillray and others, when he was interrupted.

'It is my decided purpose', Ellenborough told the jury, 'not to receive this in evidence . . . which I declare, judicially, to be inadmissible.'

Hone leapt to his feet. 'I would ask your Lordship, if you really intend to send me to prison without a fair trial?' The judge repeated that he would not listen to Hone's evidence at all. The defendant remained silent for a minute, then was on his feet:

'I really do not understand your Lordship; I state it seriously, that I am not aware of the exact meaning of your Lordship's intimation.'

'I think what I have stated is intelligible enough to every other person in court,' sneered Ellenborough.

'It certainly is not intelligible enough to my humble apprehension.'

'I can't help it.'

The trial had, it seemed, reached an impasse. The judge knew that Hone relied upon parodies ancient and modern to justify his own; deprived of this means of defence, his case would be in ruins, and he would have nothing to say to the jury. Hone took an equally uncompromising stand. If Ellenborough would not explain why the evidence was inadmissible, 'then, I have no defence ... and I am ready to go with your Lordship's tipstaff wherever your Lordship may think proper to send me'.

However, Hone had anticipated Ellenborough's intransigence. The Lord Chief Justice was attempting to deny him a fair hearing by throwing up complicated legal jargon about rules of evidence; Hone worked it to his advantage. In fact he proved that Ellenborough was mistaken in his interpretation of the law. He told the court that in 1792 Charles James Fox had passed a bill in the Commons which gave juries the sole right to decide what was libel and what was not. Up until then, the court defined libel; juries were only required to judge whether the accused had actually published the libel. Therefore, in this case, Hone had to inform the jury what legal precedents there were appertaining to parodies and satire. To do this, he had to produce as evidence parodies from all ages that showed that it was possible to satirise religious language without committing blasphemy.

By engaging Ellenborough directly on legal minutiae, he goaded the old judge into making a fatal mistake, paving the way for an unprecedented onslaught on the government's policies. Hone told the jurors that their decision regarding libel was, under statute law, the final one. Ellenborough interjected, as usual, saying that Hone's satire was 'in law and in fact a libel'.

With these words, the judge made explicit that he had decided Hone was guilty before the trial had begun. Even worse, he was wilfully ignoring Fox's bill, illegally taking responsibility for judging libel away from the jury. He was clearly partial and biased; the jury was being carried along by the judge's hostile interpretation before Hone could give his evidence. This is what had happened in most of Ellenborough's other prosecutions against journalists; but on this occasion the defendant had set a trap for the judge. 'His Lordship ... has declared his opinion,' said Hone in a triumphant tone; 'but let me say that, after all, it is the opinion of *one* man, it is but *his Lordship's* opinion.'

The crowd began to cheer and shout its approval. Ellenborough glowered, and Hone reassured him that he did not mean any offence. 'So I understand,' the judge replied; 'but it might be as well if a little decency were preserved at the bottom of the Court. If the officers take any person into custody who makes a disturbance, let him be brought up to me, and I will reward such conduct.'

The sheriff leapt to attention: 'The first man I see laugh after such a severe notice, shall be brought up,' he hopefully told a thousand laughing men and women.

Having won over the crowd by goading the judge to a petulant rage, Hone turned to the jury. He told them that, however much Ellenborough beseeched them and preached his own interpretation of the law, his direction 'is not to be final'. The jury should retain its independence without submitting to the Chief Justice's browbeating: 'His Lordship presides in this court, but not to try me. You are my judges; you are to try me; and to you I willingly submit my case.' It was they who must decide whether he intended to destroy established religion. He began to argue that he had been illegally arrested, and that the trial itself was unjust, when Ellenborough interrupted to say that he was imagining 'some Utopia' and not describing the law as it stood.

'My Lord, I am making my defence as well as I can under a thousand disadvantages,' Hone said. He continued to tell the jury about the circumstances of his arrest and imprisonment; Ellenborough interrupted him constantly. When he was discussing the fate of people arrested during the suspension of *habeas corpus*, the judge made another fatal mistake. 'This is only wasting time,' he said; 'proceed to the business of your defence. I will hear very anxiously what relates to your defence, but I will not let you be wasting time.'

'Wasting time, my Lord!' Hone shouted. 'I feel the grievance of which I complain; I am to be tried, not you! When I shall have been consigned to a dungeon, your Lordship will sit as coolly on that seat as ever; you will not feel the punishment: I feel the grievance and I remonstrate against it. I am the injured man. *I* am upon my trial *by these gentleman*, my jury.'

The discussion about the judge's partiality naturally moved on to a criticism of Sidmouth and the Tory press. Hone held up a copy of the *Day* newspaper, which had called him profane and criminal. Given their past dealings, it is of little surprise that John Stoddart (Dr Slop himself) was the editor and leader-writer of that newspaper. The paper had come out at six that morning, early enough for the jurors to read the

Tory view of the first trial. Ellenborough stopped the defendant: 'Really, you are getting so far out of the case: what have I to do with the libels published against you? We are not trying that newspaper.' Hone replied that the jury had to realise the way in which he had been traduced by his enemies in the government so that they '[would] be unprejudiced by everything they may have heard or seen out of court'. Ellenborough again dismissed it as irrelevant. 'My Lord! My Lord!' shouted Hone, 'it is *I* who am upon trial, *not your Lordship*. I have to defend myself, not your Lordship . . .'

He was drowned out by more cheering and shouting in the court. 'It is impossible that the officers can be doing their duty,' Ellenborough shouted at his sheriffs; 'let them bring any man before me, and I will put an end to this.'

The sheriffs could not pick out one laughing person among a thousand, so the officer of the court had to report that no one had been caught. Ellenborough biliously retorted, 'Open your eyes, and see; and stretch out your hands and seize. – You must have observed somebody. Mark where the noise comes from, and note the man.' The crowd were turning this trial into a farce, and the judge was losing his grip. He wanted to censor humour in the press, and suppress even the slightest giggle in his court. His failure was apparent to the jury.

The passions of the court only heightened when Ellenborough told Hone that he was free to bring a charge of libel against the *Day* and Dr Stoddart if he wished. 'God forbid that I should force the bitterest enemy I have into the Crown Office!' Hone exclaimed. 'I have suffered too much there already myself. No, my Lord, I would suffer the foulest imputations before I would take that step even against the man who has most deeply injured me.'

The early part of the trial was taken up with these spats between the judge and the defendant. In the end, it was Hone's cockney accent that prevailed over Ellenborough's brusque Cumbrian. Hone sought these confrontations and manipulated them. It might seem an obvious strategy, but no other defendant had been able to do it successfully against the Chief Justice. The spats were crucial to Hone's idiosyncratic defence, and the shabby writer was able to prolong them. The more Ellenborough was forced to interfere, the more Hone could make of the judge's bias. He was working on the pride of the jurymen, inviting them to chose between two alternatives: slavish obedience to Ellenborough or stolid independence. He cast Ellenborough as the villain – a would-be puppet master – making all his pronouncements seem like ways of bullying the jury and subverting the trial. He compared the government's mode of *ex officio* prosecution to the arbitrary doctrines of the sixteenth and seventeenth centuries; this trial was analogous to the Star Chamber, 'where a person accused, if he uttered a word offensive to the Judges, was not only subjected to a fine and corporal punishment, but even endured the torture of having a wedge driven with a mallet into his mouth to stop his utterances. The gag will be quite as effectual, if his Lordship upon this occasion lays his solemn injunction upon me not to proceed in the line of defence I have adopted.'

The judge had always relied on being the voice of authority and common sense for Special Juries. Hone robbed him of that dignity, throwing every word back in his face. The laughter of the crowd helped. As the trial slipped into farce, the basis of the prosecution itself began to seem ever more ridiculous. It was theatre, and Hone was stage-managing it for the benefit of the jury. The crowd loved every minute of it, and every time the defendant goaded Ellenborough they roared their approval.

When the noise abated, Hone moved on to his defence, the history of parody. Yet Hone's task was not made any easier; the judge kept up his interference, trying to prevent some of the religious parodies being read out. He believed, or feigned to believe for the jury's benefit, that Hone was trying to mitigate his offence by citing other unpunished parodies. This could not be used as evidence unless the defendant established his innocence of the charge against him. 'I do not know whether these were or were not read out yesterday,' he said, 'but they ought not to be our fare every day.'

'They were produced yesterday,' Hone informed the judge.

'I am sorry for it; that it is all.'

Although Ellenborough would not accept them as evidence, he would allow Hone to cite ancient parodies in an address to the jury, as long as they were not offensive. With great difficulty Hone went through his literary theory, attempting to persuade the jurymen that parodies were not always aimed at the texts they adopted.

At last Hone forced the judge into another carefully laid trap. Ellenborough professed bemusement that Hone should be citing a list of dead authors to aid the defence. At one point he said of a religious satire: 'It would deserve severe punishment if it were a modern publication.'

In that case, Hone said, he could provide a list of modern blasphemers whom the Lord Chief Justice might be interested in prosecuting: clergymen, cabinet ministers and Tory journalists. Ellenborough had unwittingly provided the perfect introduction to Hone's case that the government was duplicitous and partial in its attitude towards blasphemy. 'Let then this prosecution, which aims at so valuable a privilege as the liberty of the press, be put on its true ground, and be stripped of its hypocritical pretext,' he said: 'Is it fair that Ministers, to excite a prejudice against a man who has only been in the habit of doing what they themselves have done, should charge me with blasphemy – a crime they know I have never committed . . . If, therefore, they are to punish me, and do not punish Mr Canning, great injustice will be done. Justice to me must be justice to Mr Canning, and so the people of England will determine.' Hone said he had become 'an exception to the general rule', and if he was found guilty it would have a serious implication for politicians, newspapers editors, and writers such as Robert Southey and Walter Scott, who had written similar pieces.

He admitted that he had intended to incite ridicule in his readers' minds; yet it clearly was not religion he aimed at. Having told the jury how parody had been used in literary history, Hone elaborated on his motives and the likely effect it would have on the public. He went through his Litany line by line, showing whom he intended to laugh at. If laughter had been incited by the satire, Hone would show what had caused it. He had prayed for deliverance from 'an unnatural debt', 'unmerited pensions'; from sinecures; an 'extravagant civil list'; from 'utter starvation'; and from the 'imbecility of ministers'. And so he proved that each prayer was justifiable. The country had a large debt; that was, without a doubt, true. The distribution of pensions and positions was also unfair; there were 'those who derive fortunes from the public purse without any public service whatsoever; and how many such men are to be found in England!'

The need to be saved from utter starvation was obvious for anyone 'acquainted with London or any of the other great towns'; Hone himself had seen 'two human beings who had actually expired in the streets from absolute want' and he did not doubt that the jurors were familiar with such sights. And this at a time when men such as Canning were drawing small fortunes from the Treasury for doing no work. He justified the prayer to be 'delivered from all the deadly sins attendant upon a corrupt method of election' by saying sardonically: 'Such corruption is indeed as notorious as the sun at noon-day; and therefore this prayer can not be condemned, unless upon the grounds that truth is libel.' But even these serious abuses were not the targets of the satire. If Sidmouth and Ellenborough really wanted him to explain the butts of his joke in such an august forum, and in front of the national press, he would satisfy their curiosity. Hone claimed his real intention was to mock the feebleness of the ministers. He had prayed to be saved from their mistakes, and 'who could doubt the imbecility of Ministers? I for one, confess that I can't.' They were a bunch of inherently ridiculous pretenders who were mocked by the whole country: 'What then was to be expected from such a combination of integrity without talent, and talent without integrity? Nothing surely but imbecility.'

But as he did not attack them personally, it was no libel:

A man might be very amiable towards his family and friends, and exemplary in the performance of all the moral duties, while his mind is not large enough to conceive the obligations which attach to the character of a statesman. The mind of a good private man might indeed be quite incompetent to embrace a statesman's views, or to understand his duties. A very good man might, therefore, from such an incapacity, grope as the present ministers do, like a mole in the dark.

Hone relished the opportunity to treat the ministers as misguided and stupid and this gave way to blistering attacks on their motives. Satire was the only appropriate medium to comment on the laughable policies of the government. He was on trial only because grave ministers could not take a joke, because they feared laughter:

Their measures are those of little men with little minds; their measures are the objects of my pity . . . [the parody] is true and not libellous – that if there is ridicule, those who rendered themselves ridiculous, however high their station, have no right to cry out because they are ridiculed. I *intended* to laugh at them. They are my vindictive prosecutors, and my hypocritical persecutors; and laugh at them I will, till they cease to be the objects of my laughter by ceasing to be Ministers.

The administration should *thank* him for pointing out their mistakes: 'Why should the government be afraid of truth or falsehood in any case? Nothing but weakness can produce such fear, and that weakness must be pitiable.' He would have been thanked were not the ministers 'imbecile, self conceited and supine'.

In a final plea to the jury, he reminded them: 'The liberty of the press is attacked through me. The prosecution is nothing but a political groundwork.' One short but powerful speech must have stuck in their minds as the defining issue: 'I never intended by these parodies to excite ridicule against the Christian religion, and none but the weakest can honestly suppose so, and even they do it without consideration. My intention was merely political. It was done to excite a laugh. Is a laugh treason? Surely not.'

Hone was coming to the end of a defence that had started at quarter to ten; it was now five in the evening. There was, however, a final sting in the tail. Just as he was about to sit down, he reminded the court of some of the phrases Shepherd had used during Wooler's trial: 'God defend my understanding'; 'God knows'; 'God forbid'; and so on. In Hone's trial, the Attorney-General had said that the main part of the prosecutions case was that 'Thou shalt not take the name of the Lord thy God in vain'; but now it 'appeared that the learned gentleman himself has broken this commandment'. Yet Hone was prepared to absolve his enemy, for the Attorney-General surely never intended to blaspheme by his choice of words. He hoped such mercy would be reciprocated.

When Ellenborough summed up, he gave strict orders to the jury. He was required to direct them to convict Hone by the Act of Parliament that guarded *The Book of Common Prayer*; they were obliged to follow his direction out of Christian duty. Yet he was notably subdued, hardly the confident and supercilious judge who had arrived at Guildhall that morning. His voice could scarcely be heard by the jury.

The jury retired at quarter to six. Ellenborough's authority counted much higher than Abbott's: the jury conferred together until eight o'clock, a worryingly long time for Hone. The court remained packed, and the crowds filled the courtyard and the surrounding streets. The minority who were lucky enough to get inside Guildhall had watched a magnificent performance by the defendant, who had trumped Ellenborough at every turn. His concluding speeches, which mocked the imbecility of ministers, were genuinely entertaining because Hone had turned the sanctified environment of a court into a pillory for Sidmouth and other public men; it was the most public stage that any journalist could aspire to. The authority of the court had been turned on its head, exposed as the cradle of corruption and bias; the crowd relished every jibe and flourish. The credibility of the government, its foremost legal expert and the Lord Chief Justice himself lay in tatters. A fair jury would undoubtedly acquit him after such a defence. But no one could quite trust a Special Jury, nor could the personal influence of Ellenborough be underestimated. The tension mounted as the hours passed and no juror reappeared.

When the foreman gave his verdict, 'loud and reiterated shouts and applause ensued'. Once again it was not guilty. Ellenborough ordered the crowd to be silenced, but no one could contain the enthusiasm. The shouts spread from the great hall, into the corridors, and out to the courtyard. Hone tried to slip out of the court, but he was pounced upon by his jubilant supporters. He was exhausted, close to collapse, but he was obliged to acknowledge hundreds of his admirers and shake their hands. Eventually he escaped into the Baptist's Head Coffee House with Wooler, Waithman and other friends for some 'light refreshment'.

A little later he escaped, and no one recognised him as he walked home 'to his anxious family'. When he got there he was in a state of utter exhaustion. He collapsed into bed, plagued with the knowledge that he would have to go through the same ordeal again when he awoke. However drained and shattered he was, he must begin afresh the next morning; a new day meant a new jury, and the need to repeat all his arguments from scratch, not to mention the onus of seeing off the Ellenborough threat. Hone knew that the jubilation of his supporters was premature, merely the hasty passions of an audience which had been thoroughly entertained by the humiliation of a judge, a few incisive speeches, the unravelling of censorship, and the tension of a delayed verdict. For the defendant, it was back to square one, as if the first two days had never happened. The words Wooler had written back in the summer described Hone's living nightmare on the evening of 18 December: 'We almost doubt whether we exist in a world of reality, or whether we are entranced in some horrid dream.'[10]

Laughing stocks: third day

The next day, an even greater crowd was assembled at Guildhall, and the sheriffs and officers had been reinforced for the culmination of Hone's ordeal. On this, his third day of gruelling self-defence, Hone seemed to be a different man, hardly able to contain his bitter anger that he was being subjected to a third trial when he had been acquitted twice. He would have to rehearse the same arguments and go through the same spats with Ellenborough; everyone knew the essence of the case except for the new jury, which might be more pro-government than the last. The defendant was notably ill. The Attorney-General noted his frailty, and offered a postponement; Hone refused.

The prosecution went through its accustomed procedure, accusing Hone of blasphemy for the third and last time, on this occasion for parodying the Creed. The defendant had published a parody that declared belief in a Holy Trinity comprising 'Old Bags' (Lord Chancellor Eldon, so called because he came from a coal-mining family), 'Derry Down Triangle' (Lord Castlereagh's nickname derived from the instrument of torture he was supposed to have used in Ireland – a large tripod from which dissidents were suspended), and 'The Doctor' (Lord Sidmouth, whose father was a madhouse proprietor). His satire was a libel on the service of the Church which expressed belief in the Resurrection and the Holy Trinity: 'Glory be to old Bags, and to Derry Down Triangle, and to the Doctor. As it was in the Beginning, is now, and ever shall be, if such *things* be, without end. Amen.'

Hone's disgust was evident from the very start when he stood up to his defence:

'My Lord and Gentlemen of the Jury,' he said, turning from the jury box to the judge. With his eyes on Ellenborough he 'exclaimed with earnest vehemence': 'My Lord, I am very glad to see *your Lordship* here today', and then with an even more bitter tone, 'I say, my Lord, I am very glad to see your Lordship here today, because I feel I sustained an injury from your Lordship yesterday – an injury which I did not expect to sustain.'

He began his third defence by reading a legal opinion on the correct procedures for a judge in libel trials, rules which Ellenborough had ignored on Friday: 'the Judge *may* give his opinion to the jury respecting the matter in issue'; he emphasised that it said 'may' and not 'shall'. Ellenborough interrupted, to deny Hone's opinion.

'My Lord,' Hone said earnestly and slowly, 'I think it necessary to make a stand here. I cannot say what your Lordship may consider to be a necessary interruption, but your Lordship interrupted me a great many times yesterday, and then said you would interrupt me no more; and yet your Lordship did interrupt me afterwards ten times as much as you had done before you said you would interrupt me no more.'

'I feel it proper to make an observation upon this interruption,' Hone continued, turning to the jury box. 'Gentlemen, it is you who are trying me today. His Lordship is no judge of *me*. You are *my* judges, and *you are* my only judges. His Lordship sits there to receive your verdict. He does not even sit there to regulate the trial – for *the law* has already regulated it. He sits there only as the administrator of that law – to take care that nothing in the regulation of the law prejudices the Prosecutor or the Defendant.'

But Ellenborough *was* prejudiced and Hone had to inform the jury that the law forbade him from giving his own opinion as a way of biasing the verdict: 'His Lordship seems to think otherwise . . . I trust his Lordship today will give his opinion *coolly* and *dispassionately*, without using either expression or gesture which can be construed as conveying an entreaty to the jury to think as he does. I hope the Jury will not be *beseeched* into a verdict of guilty.'

Remarkably, Ellenborough made few interjections or remarks dur-

ing the rest of Hone's eight-hour address to the jury. At one point Hone
said that if he had employed a barrister he would have had to ask
prospective candidates a couple of simple questions: 'Will he be able to
stand up to my Lord Ellenborough? Will he withstand the browbeating
of my Lord Ellenborough?' The Attorney-General made an objection
to this attack on the authority of the court. But Ellenborough had been,
for once in his career, tamed by a defendant: 'I think the best course will
be to let the *thing* blow over us!'

The morning's edition of *The Times* had confidently predicted that the
third trial would be cancelled. The defendant had proved to two juries
that parodies of religious texts did not constitute blasphemy; surely the
government could not risk another humiliation; surely it could not try
him a third time after he had been acquitted twice on identical charges.
The Times, and all liberal opinion, was wrong. Hone thought he knew
why the prosecution was kept up:

It is hoped, I have no doubt, by certain grave members of the cabinet (my Lord
Sidmouth and my Lord Liverpool), that William Hone can not stand the third
day – that I will sink under my fatigues and want of physical power. 'He can't
stand the third trial,' said these humane and Christian Ministers; 'We shall
have him now; he must be crushed.' [*Great shouts of applause.**] Oh no! no! I
must *not* be crushed, you *cannot* crush me. I have a spark of liberty in my mind
that will glow and burn brighter, and blaze more fiercely, as my mortal remains
are passing to decay. There is nothing can crush me, but my own sense of
doing wrong; the moment I feel it I fall down in self abasement before my
accusers: but when I have done no wrong, when I know I am right, I am as an
armed man; and in this spirit I wage war with the Attorney General, taking a tilt
with him here on the floor of this court. The consciousness of my innocence
gives me life, spirits and strength, to go through this third ordeal of persecution
and oppression.

Hone rejected the good-natured defence of the previous trials. His
tactic was to lacerate the government for its cruelty and hypocrisy, to set

---

* It would be interesting to know whether Hone imitated Sidmouth or Liverpool's accent
at this point. We know that he was an accomplished vocal impressionist, and, as we shall
see later, he was adept at mimicking facial expressions. The audience's reaction to his parody of a generic minister's vindictiveness suggests that there was something in his delivery,
other than a mere statement of opinion, that made it worth applauding.

up a contrast between the persecutors and the persecuted. He said that he was physically and mentally worn out by the trials. Since the previous morning he had taken no food or drink except for a single glass of wine. He had been so weak the night before that he had been carried to bed. Were it not for medical treatment, he would not have been able to stand before the court on the third day. Yet he managed to turn his enfeebled state into comic effect; if he had been unable to stand, he said, he should have been carried to court in a bed, to make his defence lying on the table. The good-natured asides did not continue. He wanted to show that his infirmities had been caused by a persecution conducted by 'a ministry remarkable alike for its bigotry of spirit and hostility to freedom'.

The ministers had tried to bias the trial from parliament. The Tory press had been equally keen to destroy the defendant. Hone turned to Dr Stoddart, who had called him a seller of obscene books and bruited James Williams's trial as an important precedent. Hone revealed Williams's secret deal with the government, and then attacked Stoddart's falsehoods. He said that a man who attempted to bias the trial was '*a villain to the backbone*. And such I would proclaim Dr Slop to his face, whenever and wherever I should meet him.'

'Do not use such expressions,' a tamed Ellenborough said. 'You say you have got through life free from private and acrimonious bickering; do not say that now which may hereafter provoke it. I say this merely for your own preservation, and not with a view to interrupt you.'

'I assure your Lordship that I sincerely acknowledge the propriety of your interference, though it is difficult for me to restrain my feelings,' Hone replied:

It is nevertheless true that I cherish no hatred against this individual: he is indeed an object of contempt, and not of hatred, and is regarded by me in no other light than as a lost, unfortunate and abandoned man . . . although Dr Slop has attempted to do me this injury in the moment of peril, if the miserable man were in distress tomorrow, and it was in my power to relieve him, I would not hesitate to hold him out a helping hand [*murmurs of applause*].

He would also have forgiven the government if it had made a 'twelfth hour repentance' and withdrawn the unjust charges. 'See the odds

against me,' Hone exclaimed in a fervid tone; 'it is one farthing against
a million of gold. My prosecutors have made a wager with public opinion; but they will lose to their irretrievable shame . . . I am here on trial
for my life. If you, the Jury, do not protect me, my life must fall a sacrifice to the confinement that must follow a verdict of guilty. My
Prosecutors, my Persecutors, are unrelenting.' But the desire to wear
him out was a failure; Hone felt a sudden surge of energy when he
brought to mind the cruelties inflicted on him: 'I feel now as vigorous as
I was in the middle of my defence on Thursday last . . .'

He questioned the veracity of the proverb that experience made
fools wise: 'It made men of understanding wise, but not fools. If there is
any truth in the proverb, I should not be a third time in this court, after
being acquitted upon similar charges.' The deference of the previous
days was over. When Shepherd said the laughter of the crowd proved
the parodies had brought scripture into contempt, Hone was much
more blunt than hitherto, saying it was in fact 'the effect of the ridiculous allusions to his Majesty's ridiculous Ministers, without the least
reference or thought for an instant respecting the Athanasian Creed'.
Hone knew that he could not lose, and the court was now *his*, a forum
to punish his persecutors. 'All the authority is upon my side,' he said. 'It
is contained in the books that lie upon the table.'

Hone went through his familiar list of parodies, this time without suffering many interruptions. 'Parody is a ready engine to produce a certain
impression on the mind, without at all ridiculing the sentiments contained
in the original work.' He read and made comparisons for some hours,
making the same points he had done on the first two days. When he came
to the issue of ministerial parodies his anger resurfaced. Bitterness
inspired the best short speech he uttered in those three days; it summed
up his whole case. Referring to his *Sinecurist's Creed*, he said:

It was not written for religious but a political purpose – to produce a laugh
against the Ministers. I avow that was my object; nay, to laugh his Majesty's
Ministers to scorn; I have laughed at them and ha! ha! ha! I laugh at them now
and I will laugh at them, for as long as they are laughing stocks! Were there any
poor witless men less ridiculous than these Ministers, my persecutors; one of
whom is himself a parodist sitting now in Cabinet, winking at, instigating, aid-
ing and abetting this prosecution?

'George Canning is a parodist with William Hone and Martin Luther,' he vehemently declared to the wild applause of a, by now, thoroughly excited audience. 'George Canning come into court! George Canning come into court,' he shouted down into the hall, to clear a space for the arrival of the 'blasphemous' minister, 'make way for him if you please.'

He must have paused for a minute to increase the suspense, before continuing: 'No Gentleman of the Jury, you will not see Mr Canning here today; but had I him now in the box, I would twist him inside out ... Before, I have spoken of this Right Honourable with forbearance; but now I must speak with contempt of the man who could act thus towards the poor miserable, and supposed to be defenceless bookseller of the little shop in Fleet Street ... Mr Canning ought to have been a willing witness for me on the present occasion; he ought to come into the witness box, to confess his own sins, and plead the Defendant's cause.'

Indeed, the government should have stopped the proceedings if only for selfish reasons, to save Canning from execration; for humanity's sake, they should have had mercy on Hone.

There is Lord Sidmouth, a grave, a good, a religious, and surely a charitable man; there is Lord Ellenborough, a very grave man [even the judge managed to smile at this]; why did they not step forward to help a poor oppressed man. O no! he could not stand three days; their united force would crush the insect! No I defy their power. They can only immortalize me. I will at least go down to posterity with George Canning ... They would perhaps have spared me this third trial, if I have implored their mercy. But no; I anathematise their mercy. They are below the contempt of William Hone, the humble bookseller of No. 67, in the Old Bailey.

Drawing to a close, he said that he had no more intention to ridicule the Creed than he did to murder his wife and children when he went home that evening ('for I am sure the Jury will send me home to my family'). In any case, as a footnote to the trial, he said that the authenticity of the Creed was much doubted by theologians and historians. Archbishop John Tillotson (d. 1694), Bishop William Warburton (d. 1777) and Edward Gibbon denied that it was inspired by St Athanasius (the traditional authority for the Creed) at all, but was of a much later invention. Some said that the so-called Athanasian Creed was itself a parody. Hone was about to cite the late Bishop of Carlisle, Ellenborough's father, in his defence when he was suddenly interrupted.

'For common delicacy forbear!' implored the judge.

'O, my Lord,' Hone said in a subdued and excessively respectful voice, 'I shall most certainly!'

Hone finished his pugnacious and delightfully bitter tirade against the government. Of the three days, this was the most audacious and impassioned defence, one that earned him national celebrity; few had ever made such an outspoken critique on the government in a court of law. His rhetoric was often wild and jagged, quite clearly the words of a man shattered by his experiences; as he later admitted: 'That third day, I spoke like a man in a dream. I spoke and felt carried out of myself by the subject but I knew not what I said.' At times it showed. But certainly, none had managed to capture Ellenborough's court, and turn it into a forum in which to embarrass cabinet ministers. The defendant, whom the government had hoped would be exhausted by three days of legal argument, was still fighting as he sank to his chair after eight hours: 'The liberty of the press is attacked through me. The prosecution is nothing but a political groundwork. Two juries of cool, honest men have already acquitted me. I have no doubts that you, too, will send me home to dine on Sunday with my family.'

He sat down to the sound of cheers and applause from the floor of the Guildhall. Shepherd and Ellenborough summed up in one last desperate attempt to convince the court that Hone was, according to the law, a blasphemous libeller. And then the jury retired.

Twenty minutes they were back to do the inevitable. For some minutes the noise that came from within and outside the Guildhall prevented any other business. The applause and shouts of congratulation and celebration of over twenty thousand people were overwhelming. The London crowd had a new hero, and everyone wanted to see the victor, 'William the Conqueror', as he was dubbed. Those that had been inside the hall had witnessed the most brilliant attack on the government and its detested censorship; for the next few weeks people throughout the country would read every word he uttered and all the invective he had thrown at the government.

Hone put up what must rank with the best performances in an English court. Where others had failed, he had defeated the seemingly impregnable Ellenborough and made a farce of the government's attempt to define what fell under the jurisdiction of censorship. By avoiding dry legal argument and concentrating on the common sense of his case, he had won the sympathy of the jury. Legal opinion, even if it came from such undoubted authorities as the Lord Justices Abbott and Ellenborough, counted for nothing in the face of Hone's dignified and reasoned defence. Hone did not get off because he won on points of law; instead he established that the trial was biased and his prosecutors hypocrites. He relied upon the juries to sympathise with his status as victim and realise the political aspect of the prosecution. It was emotive, and it was devastating to lawyers used to the minutiae of legal debate. He took the jury into his confidence, and spoke to them as if they were engaged in pleasant conversation, something no barrister could do:

. . . I talk to you as familiarly as if you were sitting in my own room; but then, Gentlemen of the Jury, I have not twelve chairs in my house; but I have the pride of being independent. None is supposed to be independent without property. I have never had any property. Within the last twelve months my children had no beds. At this moment there is not furniture sufficient for the enjoyment of life. For the last two years and a half I have not had a complete hour of happiness, because my family have been in such misery that it is impossible for a man of my temperament to know any thing of happiness. I have been asked, why I have not employed counsel? – I could not *fee* counsel . . . Gentlemen you do not see me in that dress which my respect for you, and for myself, would make me anxious to appear in. I did resolve to get a suit of clothes for these trials, but the money I had provided for that purpose I was obliged to give for copies of the information against me. These things I mention to show you what difficulties I had to encounter in order to appear to possess independence of mind, and to let men know how cautious they should be of judging of men.

Hone was able to charm and flatter the jury, entrusting them with the responsibility to protect his life and independence, and his family's fortunes. His instinct for performance turned moments of the trials into theatre. This skill made Hone famous and attracted and won over huge crowds on the last two days. The background noise of agreement, cheers, laughter and applause was manipulated by Hone to aid his defence. The audience had responded to the wild and daring speeches, punctuated with satirical exaggeration. Their mirth had helped to show that the government's case *was* risible. It allowed Hone to dominate Ellenborough's court. Was laughter criminal? Could a joke be atomised, explained, and its effect defined in a court of law? Could humour be punished? None but the most portentous prig or corrupt hireling would possibly disagree with the essence of Hone's case. As Henry Crabb Robinson recorded in his diary, Ellenborough had been 'reduced to very silence, like an imbecile child'.[11]

Hone had acquitted himself with skill and an admirable verve on those three days. Yet the battle had begun months before with much less public attention. Hone's destruction of the corrupt selection of jurors meant that he met the prosecution with something approaching equality. He was the first journalist to wrest this privilege from the law. Had the Crown had its way, Hone would have made his defence to juries packed with friends of the government, including an MP. Even so, Special Juries, whether packed or pricked, were never free from the taint of corruption and partiality, or from the suspicion that they might be bribed; any one of the three appointed to try Hone could have sided with the state on political grounds. But it was the independence of the three juries that ensured victory. They resisted the sophistry of Abbott and the bluster of Ellenborough. Much later, George Elwall, an 'eminent London merchant' who had sat as a Special Juror on the third day, summed up the stubborn independence of the jurors when he declared the he was 'prepared to die, if need be, rather than pronounce a man "guilty" who was manifestly prosecuted, not for blasphemy or sedition, but for exposing abuses which were eating into the very heart of the nation'.[12]

The crowd in Guildhall and the surrounding avenues bayed for Hone when the verdict was known. The people who had awaited the verdict outside wanted to see the victor. A group of Hone's friends made an exit, and they were mobbed by people believing that their new hero was amongst them. The defendant 'afterwards passed out through the immense multitude, alone and unnoticed'.

PART III

'The pen and the sword'

Forced into Greatness

Of Mr Hone's merits I may say with truth (although I blush to say it), that he absolutely defeated, by dint of ability and manly exertion, the Judges and the Crown Lawyers. For oppression and undue advantage against a meritorious but defenceless man, this prosecution on the part of his Majesty's Ministers is without parallel.

Sir Francis Burdett

Hone the publisher's trial you must find very amusing; and as Englishmen very encouraging . . . Lord Ellenborough has been paid in his own coin – Wooler and Hone have done us an essential service.

John Keats

'What an insult, what a degradation of Courts of Law!' *The Times* stated in its editorial. It was shocked that the ministers had been forced 'to introduce their authority on an occasion like the present, only to be baffled and defeated!'

'However we must explain this matter,' the paper continued: 'we do not mean that the law has been defeated, but that law, free law, has been established, contrary to the opinions and rulings of those who in such cases have hitherto had most weight; that free law has been established by an unlearned man against the learned; by a brave man who made those whom the world thought so, crouch and tremble . . . Mr HONE is one of those whom pressure (we intentionally use a gentle term) has forced into consequence – may we not say greatness?'[1]

News of the victory was not confined to those who had been in the capital, when the outcome of the last trial was trumpeted through the streets. The morning after each trial *The Times* printed full transcripts of Hone's defence, which took up most of the pages of the paper; other newspapers and journals did likewise in the coming days and weeks. The whole country could read of Hone's brave defence, and the defeat of the government. People of all shades of opinion were enthralled by the story of an underdog who had risen above himself, and won a trial against all the odds. At Charles Lamb's house, Samuel Coleridge put aside his political prejudices and 'eloquently expatiated on the necessity of saving Hone in order to save English law'.[2]

Henry Crabb Robinson, the former *Times* foreign correspondent, recorded in his diary that Hone's trials were 'without a parallel in the history of the country ... I cannot but think the victory gained over the Government and Lord Ellenborough a subject of alarm, though at the same time a matter of triumph. Lord Ellenborough is justly punished for his inhumanity to Hone on a former occasion.' As a barrister, Robinson, like many of his colleagues, had never been able to perform to the best of his abilities in front of the Chief Justice; Hone's victory put the legal profession to shame: '... this illiterate man has avenged all our injuries. Lord Ellenborough reigned over submissive subjects like a despot. Now he feels, and even the Bar may learn, that the fault is in them ... Lord Ellenborough had sustained the severest shock he ever endured ... '[3]

The Lord Chief Justice's first act on reaching his home in St James's Square on the evening of the last trial was to write to his master, Lord Sidmouth. The letter 'cost him a deeper pang than drawing his last breath':

The disgraceful events which have occurred at Guildhall within the last three or four days have led, both on account of the public and myself, to consider very seriously my own sufficiency, particularly in point of bodily health and strength, to discharge the official duties of my station in the manner in which, at the present critical moment, it is particularly necessary they should be discharged ... I wish to carry my mediated purpose of resignation into effect as soon as the convenience of Government, in regard to the due selection and appointment of my successor, may allow.[4]

The ferocious bully, the indomitable spectre that haunted British justice and the House of Lords, had been destroyed by William Hone and the vociferous displays of public opinion in court. If nothing else resulted from the victory, the resignation of the Lord Chief Justice was an achievement in itself.

Campbell said that Ellenborough 'certainly never held up his head in public after'. He died on Sunday, 13 December 1818, less than a year after his defeat at the Guildhall. In the opinion of the people, he had been killed by the shame of defeat by a Fleet Street journalist.[5]

The Reformists were jubilant. Leigh Hunt congratulated his colleague. 'The public', he wrote in the *Examiner*, 'have now a remarkable proof, if they wanted one, what feeble as well as corrupt Rulers they have, and how much may be done towards regaining their constitutional rights, by those individuals of natural spirit and intellect, with which they abound.' Hone had taught the government that their policies would not be tolerated: 'It is impossible for the rulers of the present state of things to see the glorious results of our English Trials, at the very moment when Suspension Acts are in existence and hirelings are busy in threatening our remaining liberties, without feeling that arbitrary measures are not to be forced upon the world now-a-days.'[6]

In the *Black Dwarf*, Thomas Wooler saw the outcome as the final shock to the government, the clearest indication that a censorship based on the rickety libel laws was unworkable. But had it taken the stubborn resistance of one man to prove this to the world: 'We look back on the transactions of the past year with infinite delight. It will form an epoch in the history of our liberties: liberties so often assailed, and so often triumphant; but never before attacked by such a ruthless band of mercenaries – never before defended with more spirit and success. The sound of the clarion has been heard, and the spirits of our departed heroes have seen with pleasure that the race of MAN is not extinct in Britain.' In the middle of January 1818, Wooler reported that, as a result of Hone's victories, 'Lord Sidmouth felt it prudent to affect a little shame at the detention of men, whom he dare not put upon their trial'. Throughout the country, people who had been detained in 1817 on similar charges to Hone's were freed from their gaols, the government suddenly aware of the weakness of its system of policing reformist opinion.[7]

In a piece of satire called 'The Disconcerted Hypocrites', a valet comes to shave Lord Sidmouth, only to be dismissed by the Home Secretary: 'I am *shaved* enough.' The valet replies, 'This razor, please you is Your Lordship's own, / Just whetted too upon an *English* Hone.'[8] In 1818 a number of weekly pamphlets were started, probably in response to the freedom of the press heralded at the Guildhall. After the failure of government repression in 1817, Dolby started his *Parliamentary Register*, John Hunt the *Yellow Dwarf*, and Richard Carlisle the *Republican*. Many other London and provincial publishers began their own *Registers*: the *Gorgon, Medusa, The Democratic Reformer, The Cap of Liberty, The White Hat, Wardle's Manchester Observer, Edmond's Weekly Register* (Birmingham), *Lewis's Coventry Recorder, Patriot* (Dudley), *Spirit of the Union* (Glasgow). William Cobbett felt safe to return from the United States in 1819. Hone's victories gave many journalists the confidence to start their own papers and assert their right to criticise the powers in the state. In 1817 there were forty-two prosecutions for criminal libel; until the winter of 1819 there was just one.

However, the man who had fought for the freedom of the press alone, on the behalf of the country, had suffered a personal defeat. The government would not pay damages for the prosecution; Hone was impoverished. His enemies had exacted their pound of flesh.

Sir Francis Burdett, Lord Cochrane, Alderman Waithman and Thomas Wooler would not let their friend be ruined as a result of his resistance to egregious laws. They convened a meeting to announce a public subscription to relieve Hone's poverty at the City of London Tavern on 29 December 1817. Amidst loud celebration and boisterous conviviality, the grandees of the reform movement queued up to praise the saviour of the British press. Sir Francis told those assembled that they were there 'to support an honest countryman, struggling in opposition to the oppressions exercised against him, on scandalous hypocritical pretences –' At this point in his eulogy Burdett was silenced by applause. He continued: '– Those who made use of the pretences, seemingly intended only to crush an humble individual; but they meant, in reality, through his person, to destroy the free press of the country.'

Few men in the country [Burdett continued] could have fought their way with such manly intrepidity, and at the same time with such elasticity of moral and intellectual vigour. I believe the country is quite alive on the subject to which I now call their attention – and if they are so, to whom is it owing? Certainly to Mr Hone – who, at the peril of his life – at the expense of the destruction of his fortune – and, finally, when the annihilation of all his future views was threatened – stood forward, undismayed, and dauntlessly dared the worse his adversaries could do. [*Applause.*] For this we are deeply indebted to him.

Lord Cochrane, the greatest hero living in Britain, stood up to loud cheers. He had suffered a wounding humiliation and unfair punishment from Ellenborough; revenge had come at the hands of his friend Hone. Cochrane recalled the £100 fine that had been imposed upon him in 1816; but 'sooner than have paid that fine I would have rotted in prison'. Hone had helped raise the money to free the MP back then, and Cochrane remembered the generosity: 'That money I wish now to return; and with feelings of heartfelt thanks to Mr Hone for his manly and able exertions in defence of the liberties of the people, I will now lay down the one hundred pounds which I now hold in my hand . . .' The devourer of French frigates, the Sea Wolf, added: 'I never in my life did any act with more satisfaction than this. I wish I had the means of doing more.'

Thomas Wooler, Hone's companion in the King's Bench Prison, concluded saying that, thanks to 'Mr Hone's admirable defence', there were now 'two high barriers erected for the preservation of British freedom – one, the Trial by Jury – the other the Liberty of the Press'.

The City of London of Tavern was one of the largest public buildings in London. It was packed beyond capacity, and hundreds were turned away at the door. And no doubt the celebration was fuelled by alcohol; as the hours of laudatory speeches continued, the language became ever more exaggerated and the cries of the crowd louder. Clause after clause was added to the resolutions of the meeting, culminating in the drunkenly gratuitous, 'That the Thanks of this Meeting be given to Lord Cochrane, for his zealous endeavours on the present occasion.' When the men and women bayed for Hone, Waithman had to tell them that, although Hone was courageous, 'he would rather meet a host of adversaries in the field, than the friends assembled here today'. Deprived of their new hero, 'The crowd followed Sir Francis Burdett, at the conclusion of the meeting, with the loudest cheers, to his house at St James's-place,' in scenes reminiscent of the 1810 riots, but this time a peaceable and joyous celebration of a victory.[9]

The London meeting was publicised throughout the country. People in their thousands contributed to Hone's subscription fund. In addition to the two notes for £100 donated by Cochrane and Burdett, the Duke of Bedford, and the Earls of Darlington and Sefton all gave sums of £105, the Marquis of Tavistock £50, and an anonymous peer ('an enemy to persecution, and especially to religious persecution, employed for political purposes'*), £100. John and Leigh Hunt managed £5: 'not what they would, but what they could'. Their friend, the then little-known Percy Shelley, appears on the list, generously giving £5. Keats wrote to his brothers: 'Hone the publisher's trial you must find very amusing; and as Englishmen very encouraging . . . Lord Ellenborough has been paid in his own coin – Wooler and Hone have done us an essential service.'[10]

Contributions ranging from 10 shillings to £50 poured in from every corner of the country. Most people supplied their names, but some remained anonymous, preferring to sign as 'An Abhorrer of Tyranny and Oppression', or 'A Friend of Liberty'. Someone who gave £2 2s wrote simply, 'My name wou'd ruin me.' The government was troubled by the public support for Hone, and particularly the glittering names that adorned the subscription list. It was prepared to exact revenge on people who dared to show such support for an enemy. Lord Sefton attracted particular opprobrium when the letter he wrote accompanying his donation was published in *The Times*. He expressed his 'contempt for the spiteful imbecility' of the government and 'admiration of the intrepidity and ability of the individual who so triumphantly defeated the greatest and most dangerous conspiracy of the year 1817'. The Regent broke off his friendship with the earl, horrified that one of his intimates could support a public enemy. Their quarrel became a sub-

* The anonymous peer was most likely either the Earl Grey or Charles James Fox's nephew, Baron Holland, both of whom had used similar language in parliament regarding the charge of blasphemy against Hone. Grey told the peers that, had he been on one of the juries, he would have acquitted Hone. In December 1819 they were to cite Hone's subscription fund as evidence of the public's anger at press prosecutions (see chapters 11 and 14).

ject of gossip for thirteen years; in 1829 Charles Greville wrote in his diary: 'They have been at daggers drawn ever since, and Sefton has revenged himself by a thousand jokes at the King's expense, of which his Majesty is well aware.'[11] The Irish peer was only reconciled to the royal family with the accession of William IV. The treatment of the Whig lords was indicative of the shock the government and royal family felt at Hone's acquittal and the display of public opinion. Revenge was not spared in signalling disapproval: the Duke of Bedford's candidature for the Lord Lieutenancy of Bedfordshire was blocked as a reward for his generosity.

Conspicuous by his absence on the list of subscribers is William Hazlitt. He was probably too debt-laden to part with any money. Instead, he immortalised his drinking companion in an essay: Hone 'rose from the attack by the force of good nature, and by that noble spirit of freedom and honesty, in which to be unjustly accused is to be superior to all fear, and to speak truth is to be eloquent – but that he did not suffer himself to be crushed to atoms, and made a willing sacrifice to the prejudices, talent, and authority arrayed against him, is a resistance to the opinions of the world and the insolence of power, that can never be overlooked or forgiven' by his enemies.[12]

Hazlitt rounded off his praise of Hone with a quotation from Pope's *Essay on Man*:

A wit's a feather, and a chief's a rod:
An honest man's the noblest work of God.*

Hone's trials made him rich. If the government thought that they could ruin journalists by harassing them with months of legal entanglements, it was undermined by the generosity of the people of Britain. In all, the subscription fund brought in the small fortune of £3,000. Unfortunately, £900 was wasted on advertising the campaign and £1,000 was embezzled by the secretary of the fund. But the remaining £1,000 or so was enough for the Hones to move from their drab lodgings at the Old Bailey to a large building just around the corner at number 45, Ludgate Hill. The new premises were substantial: a former

---

* Hazlitt had used this quotation in 1807 to describe Charles James Fox.

auction house, they had enough room for a 'Great Hall' to hold exhibitions of books and prints, and rooms to accommodate Hone's large family, his prodigious library and a printing press. The London reformists and some of the Whig lords used it as an informal salon, and for a few years he was 'living and faring sumptuously every day'.[13] From this address Hone re-established his publishing career, becoming one of the most successful journalists of his generation. As Charles Knight wrote, after his trials, Hone 'was now a public character. Whatever little stinging pamphlets he issued were sure to find their way over the land.'[14]

Although much of the story hitherto has been dominated by the furious resistance of Londoners to political control of the press, it was now clear that the whole country was involved in the struggle. Money came from large industrial cities, middling market towns, and rural parishes; from clergymen, gentry, booksellers, journalists, tradesmen, schoolboys, bankers and many more. Hone's income from the subscription was augmented when he published verbatim reports of each trial, which he sold separately for a shilling each. They were national bestsellers, keeping the Hone press in business for the whole of 1818. The first trial ran to a total of twenty editions, the second fifteen, and the third sixteen. *The Three Trials of William Hone* came out later, and went to a further twenty editions. To subscribe to the Hone appeal, or buy one of the books, was an act of involvement in the fight for a free press, depriving the government of the pleasure of watching an acquitted journalist sink into crippling debt. Those that had not or could not put their names to the subscription list could contribute to the fortunes of the bookseller in other ways. Francis Place told Hone: 'Lord Erskine cannot publicly subscribe but will pay 20 guineas for a copy of your trials.'[15]

The books spread the knowledge of Hone's defence further than ever. There was a national fever to discover more about the blow that had been struck against the censorship. The *Scotsman* reported 'in answer to numerous inquirers': 'a second supply of the *Three Trials* was shipped last week on board a London smack and is hourly expected' in Edinburgh. Hone was by now an iconic figure, celebrated in cartoons, ballads, poems, newspaper articles and books. The Fetter Lane publisher Joseph Head sold a print to be displayed on people's walls as a totemic artefact to remind them of Hone's triumphs: 'This Print is intended to Hand down to posterity the Three Honest Juries who so honourably acquitted Mr Hone.'

Hone achieved national celebrity, which he retained for most of his life. Many of his contemporaries could not divorce his name from the principles of a free press. And with fame came the inevitable odium that accompanies it. Wordsworth said that Hone's acquittal was enough to make one fall out of love with a British jury, and many people joined him in seeing Hone as the enemy who had opened the Pandora's box of a free press. Most of the loyalist newspapers were content to denigrate him, saying that his guilt was obvious; the only reason he had escaped punishment was simply that the three juries had been mistaken. Lord Dudley wrote that the Tories were 'sadly grieved that his ears were not cropped, as they would have been by the Star Chamber'.

At one point in 1818 Hone was travelling in a coach, and began to talk to his fellow passengers. Inevitably, the conversation turned to Hone's trials, one of the dominant issues of the year. One uttered sharp remarks against 'that fellow Hone'; whilst another venomously spat out: 'I expect you would not be surprised to meet him furnished with hoofs and a tail.' Hone muttered something like, 'Well, I do not think I should,' before entertaining his companions with amusing conversation. So pleased with the meeting were the two men that they wished to 'improve an acquaintance' with their mysterious traveller. 'Perhaps', replied Hone mischievously, 'you may be less desirous when you know the dangerous company you are in.' But he had charmed them; Hone won the men over despite his public image, and they became lasting friends. The story was one of Hone's favourites; the greatest compliment was infamy.[16]

The reformists and the press were naturally inclined to welcome Hone's victories as a landmark of constitutional freedom, but what, if anything, had been won? The first discussion of the implications of what might result from the defeat of Ellenborough was held at Westminster on the anniversary of the attack on Prince George's coach. The Whig opposition used the outcome of the trials as the central part of their attack on the government during the debates on the Regent's

Cock a doodle doo !!!

WILLIAM the CONQUEROR. or The Game Cock of Guildhall

© British Museum

The vanquished Lord Ellenborough is on the left and
Sir Samuel Shepherd on the right.

speech which opened the 1818 session of parliament. For a number of
MPs, Hone's experiences in 1817 had revealed the excessive punishments that were inflicted upon journalists who were only *accused* of
criminal libel. The government had taken a sledgehammer to crack a
nut, and its brutal repression and overreaction to mild humour would
turn the country against any form of regulation for the press. When it
decided to renew the prosecution after the first trial it had set one jury
against another, suggesting that the public was not to be trusted with
trials dealing with such an important subject as the freedom of the
press. Many MPs believed that if one of the juries had convicted Hone,
the government would have had a justification for saying that jury trials
were unsuitable for dealing with the press. The Fleet Street publisher
gave pause to that plot. Lord Althorp stood up in the Commons to ask,

But why was the prosecution continued after a Jury had pronounced a verdict
of acquittal? – [*Hear, hear!*] – a Jury is the only competent tribunal to say what
is or what is not a Libel. The Judge had given his own opinion, in opposition
to the Jury, the only competent authority – [*Hear, hear!*] – The opinion of the

Judge was not desired on such a question. The evil of prosecutions of this sort is great indeed; but it is not to be compared with the evil of destroying the confidence in the Country in the Trial by Jury [*Hear, hear!*].

The MP told the House that he disapproved of Hone's irreligious pamphlets, calling them 'highly culpable publications': 'yet in common with the bulk of the nation, I rejoice that an unsupported individual has triumphed over the extraordinary and uncalled-for severity of his assailants'.

The three acquittals had shown the 'indiscretion' of the government in making press prosecutions a matter of party interest. By exposing the monstrous way he had been treated, and the political bias of the judiciary, Hone had, according to Althorp, forced the country to question the 'policy or propriety of the motives of the attorney-general in bringing the publisher before the public by three several prosecutions *ex officio*'. The defendant might even have been found guilty if the government had at least presented a show of equality between the accused and the prosecution. But the way it had proceeded against Hone convinced three juries that the Attorney-General had acted from 'vindictive motives', and that the defendant was the victim of partial and exemplary justice. 'This mode of proceeding cannot be considered candid or liberal,' Althorp said. 'An unfair advantage appears to have been taken of the accused, by subjecting him to reiterated trials, and reiterated painful exertions.'[17]

Censorship was threatened by its brutal efficiency, swift operation and very success. Sidmouth responded to the criticism, limply saying that he had acted 'leniently, but firmly'.[18] It was clear to the country that he had been neither merciful nor fair during the preceding twelve months. He had certainly been firm; the thousands of people who read Hone's trial reports could see the barely legal way in which the government treated its critics. Hone's achievement was in showing that the great advantages at the state's disposal – *ex officio* arrest, exorbitant bail, the Special Jury system, spies, bellicose judges and the discretionary right to define what constituted a libel – could actually work in favour of a defendant. Would a jury convict writers who were already reduced to poverty and had spent time in gaol, even if they believed them guilty?

Might they instead feel that punishment had been exacted by vindictive and illegitimate means before the trial even began?

The Whigs argued that the government had brought its mode of dealing with the press into contempt; juries would become disinclined to support ministers' personal prejudices against journalists, even if they agreed that 'seditious' or 'blasphemous' libel were evils. *The Times* believed that the public was offended by Hone's parodies and would have been satisfied if the author had faced appropriate penalties, but the government's 'determination to crush him, produced a sympathy for his impending fate, which few would have felt for his cause'. The bias of the Crown and its unfair advantage offended the British people's love of justice and faith in the impartiality of courts. Lord Holland told the upper House: 'When it is so evident to all the world, that the prosecutions brought against Mr Hone had been instituted for political reasons only, it is impossible for the country not to despise the hypocritical pretences under which they were brought forward.'[19]

The most significant result of the trials, in the short term, was the impact upon public opinion. Hone's instinct for self-publicity meant that his trials were the *cause célèbre* of the winter of 1817–18. The speeches printed in *The Three Trials* provided a history of his treatment at the hands of Sidmouth and Ellenborough, from arrest to eventual acquittal. The corrupt, partial and arbitrary methods of punishing journalists were revealed to the country in the story of Hone's hasty arrest and treatment in court, his experience of spies and informers, the battle against the selection of Special Juries, and the rigours of a three-day defence. As William Smith, MP told the House, in the public mind, Hone's 'case presented the strongest illustration of the intolerable injustice of the practise which prevailed at the crown office'.[20] And it was an instance of oppression that would not linger in obscurity, but become a lesson and precedent for ever. A martyr might have been forgotten – the memory of Cobbett's conviction in 1810 was one few recalled with relish – but the underdog who triumphed over Lord Ellenborough would always be a national hero.

If the government had lost the confidence of the public with a hypocritical prosecution and easy defeat, its ability to enforce its censorship in court would be destroyed. Lord Folkestone told the Commons that if Hone had been found guilty it would have served to 'bear out the assertion made during the last session, that the country teemed with blasphemous publications'. Ministers had staked a lot on having Hone convicted; they had cited the reformist press, and especially blasphemous publications, as the greatest threat facing the country, only to have the hypocrisy thrown back in their faces by three juries composed of eminent merchants, the professed representatives of moderate and loyal opinion. Sir Samuel Romilly said that 'by assistance of the religious cry' they had attempted 'to lay restraints upon the press'; their failure to carry the country with them in a crusade against critical writing when they prosecuted Hone was a signal that they were out of touch with the views of the country.[21]

Although Sidmouth and his colleagues asserted that the people would be seduced into revolution by atheistic journalists, all they could find to punish was the gentle William Hone, a man who out-reasoned their lawyers in court, and rendered them laughing stocks. When Smith told MPs that Hone had displayed a character 'nothing unbecoming the manners of a gentleman' he chose his words carefully.[22] Ministers had portrayed the Fleet Street publisher as an immoral wretch and incendiary, but it had become clear to the country that he was an intelligent, peaceful and brave man. His behaviour justified Wooler's promise to the country, in answer to the charge that the reformist press wanted nothing but violence and revolution: 'Wit, humour, and argument, are the weapons we would use.'[23]

When he read *The Three Trials*, Folkestone concluded that 'either the government were influenced by that spirit of persecution . . . or else that they were quite incapable of carrying proceedings of that nature'. Holland agreed, telling the Lords that Hone's successful and eloquent defence of the rights of the press proved that the laws 'could not stand the test of real inquiry'.[24] The trials inspired a motion in the Commons calling for an investigation into the legality of *ex officio* arrests. MPs were still confident that the laws were fair and workable however, and it was defeated by seventy-three votes to seventeen. In the Lords, Erskine's bill to subject the Attorney-General's power of arrest to the decision of a grand jury was supported by just thirteen peers. Hone's victories did not force the government to change the law, and other writers and publishers would be arrested on *ex officio* informations in the future. Yet after December 1817 it was apparent that the government could never be certain that juries would support its laws with wonted obedience. Public opinion had turned against censorship when press prosecutions were exposed so decisively as corrupt and actuated by political prejudice, and when Sidmouth's rhetoric about the dangers of an unbounded press was ridiculed as alarmist hysteria. The government's confidence had been shattered, and its initial response was to retreat from the policies of 1817. *The Times* said that the reaction to Hone's trials gave 'a just criterion of the existing state of the public mind in this country': 'The truth unquestionably is, that the people of England have seen and heard so much of imprisonment, without trial, that they, or any portion of them, are extremely cautious of consigning their fellow-subjects to prison by trial. That is the plain statement of the case . . . '[25]

During the debate about the trials that engrossed parliament, the press and much of the country, seemingly the only person who remained silent on the matter was William Hone. He evaded the celebrating crowds at the Guildhall and at the meeting held in his honour a week later. Rose Hone, William and Sarah's seventh surviving child, was born exactly nine months after the last trial. If he was eager to get home and avoid his supporters, we can at least exonerate him from the charge of po-faced puritanism. His private celebrations were obviously far more pressing than the attractions of ephemeral fame.

In the years following the trials, Hone began to research what he believed was to be the great work of his life, *A History of Parody*. It was intended, in part, to be a justification of his defence at the Guildhall. But it was also to be a rigorous academic work, Hone's contribution to scholarship, a way of showing the world that he was more than a Grub Street hack and sensationalist. Hazlitt supported the endeavour, agreeing to write the Prospectus, and in 1820 William Godwin and Dr Birkbeck recommended Hone to the directors of the British Museum as a worthy candidate for a pass to the Reading Room. The research for the book was to occupy him for the best part of a decade; in the meantime, he became the pre-eminent expert in parodic literature. [26]

But the events of 1817, from arrest to acquittal, had exhausted Hone. For a year he hardly published a thing. A letter to a friend describes the effects of having to battle to save his life:

I have been, and am, ill – dying, but not dead. Blood at the head, apoplectic affection – cupping – bleeding – blistering – lowering – a fortnight at Bath, &c. – vexation at home and habitual melancholy which increases upon me; all these are indications of that sure and certain event which happeneth unto all, and which may happen to me in an instant. I am in fact in a very bad way – the Trials have given me a physical shake which has compelled me to abandon what I entered upon with alacrity and spirit . . . I have, therefore, now to begin the world afresh nearly.[27]

But if 1818 was a fallow year of gradual recovery from the draining experience of imprisonment and the rigours of trial, the years after were a period of intense activity. In 1819 a refreshed and recovered Hone did begin the world afresh. Early in the year he and William Hazlitt were guests at a dinner party held by John Hunt. In August, Hazlitt's *Political Essays* was published by Hone, the volume beginning with a dedication 'To John Hunt, Esq. The tried, steady, zealous, and conscientious advocate of the liberty of his country, and the rights of mankind . . .' It is thanks to Hone that the essays were collated and reissued to a wider audience in book form. He asked Hazlitt to collect his political writings, and invested much of his savings in the project. He paid Hazlitt an advance of £100, and lost a lot of money when the 400-page book proved a commercial failure. The *Essays* was Hone's private passion; he wrote: 'No man has lashed political apostasy with more severity, nor given harder blows to tyranny and tyrants of all kinds, than Mr Hazlitt. His literary excellencies are unsurpassed by any living writer; especially in the just conception and masterly delineation of character. His volume is a Political Jewel House.' But his admiration for Hazlitt's political writing was not shared by the public. However, the essays attracted admirers in succeeding generations, and many of them have appeared consistently in selected writings by Hazlitt.

Hone and Hazlitt had been acquainted for years through their Fleet Street connexions, and Hone was the natural choice as publisher of the essays, many of which had appeared in the *Examiner*, a newspaper which played a crucial role in both men's careers. Hazlitt's political writings had attacked the government's war against free thought and its suppression of knowledge; Hone's victories at Guildhall were a vindication of the intellectual powers and indomitable spirit of the common man. The connexion between publisher and writer was made explicit in the essays that satirised John Stoddart with Hone's epithet 'Dr Slop'. The essays are of course very different from Hone's populist journalism; but they have common ground in a satirical language that is indicative of the reformist idiom deployed against the Liverpool regime throughout the 1810s and 20s. The publication of the *Essays* acknowledged a reformist milieu that had emerged from 1813 and coalesced around the intellectual lead of the *Examiner*. At that time John Hunt was suffering a prison sentence imposed upon him and Leigh by Lord Ellenborough. By 1819 it seemed that the powers that had condemned the Hunts and regulated the press had been mortally wounded by a subordinate member of that group. Hazlitt's book bore testament to the history of this Fleet Street circle and his close friendship with the publisher.

Hone could use his celebrity to promote books by his friends in the higher echelon of literature. He could also highlight abuses in the genre in which he was the acknowledged master: parody. In January 1819 Hone gave George Cruikshank a job that the cartoonist was to describe as the 'great event of his artistic life'. The 'great event' was a parody of the pound note. In 1797 the Bank of England and the government suspended cash payments and introduced paper money to fund the national debt. Paper money was hated because it caused inflation, but it also had a terrible impact on the poorest members of society. Pound notes were printed on cheap paper and had a crude design. They were easy to copy, and there were huge numbers of barely detectable forgeries in circulation. The law had to act, and the people most commonly caught and executed were the destitute people the forgers tempted to launder the forgeries. The huge number of victims of these forgers who were executed between 1797 and 1819 was a national scandal. Cruikshank wrote much later that he saw many poor women hanging outside Newgate prison, a short distance from Hone's new house. 'I felt sure', he wrote later in the century, 'that in very many cases the rascals who forged the notes induced these poor ignorant women to go into the gin-shops to "get something to drink", and thus *pass* the notes and hand them the change.'

In January 1819 Hone and Cruikshank designed and published a 'forged' banknote. At first sight (for who looks *closely* at something as familiar and transient as paper money) it resembled a real note; it was the same size, type of paper and a copy of the original design. Look closer though, and the £ sign is a curled noose; the Governor of the Bank of England's signature that of Jack Ketch, the notorious Newgate executioner; and Britannia a hag devouring her children. The serial number is replaced by a row of hanged paupers, and the corner design is a shackling iron.

The banknote caused a sensation. The close parody was an ironic commentary on the ease with which banknotes could be copied; the message was that either execution for forgery should be abolished entirely, or, more realistically, banknotes made harder to copy. Its resemblance to the original subverted the emblems of the pound note, turning them into representations of avarice and vindictiveness. Its very simplicity emphasised the casual manner in which people were killed, and the infanticide of Britannia savaged the sin of prizing money over human life. The parodic form had other benefits; it exploited the

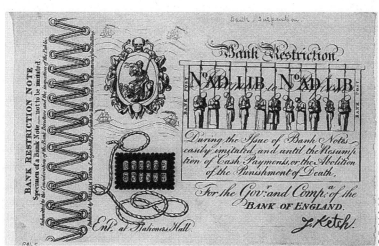

unthinking and casual ease of monetary exchange. Hone hoped that his satire would replicate the ubiquity of money itself: he wrote to a friend, 'I must get my note throughout the kingdom. I have set my heart on its going into every nook and corner where a *bank* note goes.'[28]

Hone and Cruikshank had hit upon a popular mode of criticism. Their design was well received; the *Examiner* wrote: 'This banknote is by Mr Hone, and ought to make the hearts of the Bank Directors (if they have hearts) ache at the sight.' 'When it appeared in the shop windows,' Cruikshank recalled, 'it created a great sensation, and the people gathered around his [Hone's] house in such numbers that the Lord Mayor had to send the City police . . . to disperse the crowd.' It became a national best-seller; Hone wrote in a letter some weeks after publication that the note was 'going like wildfire'. Within a few weeks Hone and Cruikshank had made £700.

In 1875 Cruikshank was on a mission to establish his name as one of the greatest men of the nineteenth century. He wrote an article grandly entitled 'How I put a stop to Hanging', claiming that as soon as the banknote came out, 'The Bank Directors held a meeting immediately upon the subject, and after that they issued no more one pound notes, and so there was no more hanging for passing forged one pound notes; not only that, but ultimately no hanging, even for forgery.' He was correct; paper money was phased out, cash payments were restored later in 1819. In the mid-1820s Robert Peel reformed the penal code, abolishing capital punishment for many minor crimes, including laundering small sums of forged money. But Cruikshank was wrong in crediting his banknote as the direct inspiration for the reforms. Cash payments were re-instituted for sound economic reasons; the national debt was much reduced, and the Treasury could return to the old system. Peel's legislative changes were driven by his evangelical convictions and sense of good government, not by a piece of satire. [29]

But Hone and Cruikshank had achieved something very important with the banknote. Although the points they made about the cruelty of hanging gin-addled old women for being the cat's-paws of professional forgers were commonplace and part of a long-running debate, the success of the satire was a powerful indication of public opinion. It was aimed at the sensibilities of Hone's accustomed clientele, the 'respectable' and 'polite' members of society – the disenfranchised mid-dling sort. The satirical banknote became almost as ubiquitous as the £1 note, passed from hand to hand and displayed in taverns and coffee-houses, like most other visual prints. Such high-selling productions were an indication to the government, perhaps the only indication, of how disengaged they were from middle class opinion.

Satire caught the public's attention in other ways in 1819. In the sum-mer, an advertisement in *The Times* bluntly stated: 'In a few days, DON JUAN.' The impact of this promise of another work by Lord Byron was immediate. 'The curiosity of the town was raised to the highest pitch to know the meaning of the enigmatical line,' Hone wrote sardonically in his book, *Don Juan Unmasked* of the tantilising words in the advertise-ment. 'The ladies, as was natural, supposed them to be used as a signal for happiness, previously concerted between some fond pair, whom time and space had separated.'[30]

Don Juan duly came out to the joy of fashionable ladies and men of taste. The edition was unusually expensive, and the publisher curious-ly withheld his name from the latest work by England's premier poet. Byron's publisher, as all the world knew, was John Murray. Why was he so reticent? Hone's book set out to unravel the mystery.

Hone did not stint his praise for Byron's poetry: 'It abounds in sub-lime thought and low humour, in dignified feeling and malignant pas-sion, in elegant wit and absolute conceit.' He particularly relished the contrast between refined elegance and the 'depraved and disgusting'; between the polished courtier, and the 'brawny bully of a brothel, full of strange oaths and brutal obscenity'. *Don Juan* resonated with Hone's coarse humour and love of scurrilous laughter: 'It turns decorum into jest, and bids defiance to the established decencies of life. It wars with virtue, as resolutely as with vice.'

Indeed, he appreciated it so much that he decided to pirate his favourite examples of 'low humour' in a cheap book, affordable to a larg-er market than Murray's expensive edition. Three days after *Don Juan* appeared on sale, Hone republished his favourite stanzas – those which described illicit passion, female lust, religious scepticism and other dar-ing opinions. And in pirating these outrageous pieces, Hone answered his question about John Murray's modesty: 'Not the least extraordinary circumstance connected with the history of this singular poem, is, that the Publisher to the Board of Longitude, and of the Quarterly Review – the Bookseller to the Admiralty, and a strenuous supporter of orthodoxy and the Bible Society, is the publisher of Don Juan.'

If anything 'Don John' Murray had shown an '*excess* of loyalty' to the government and the Church. Yet here he was surreptitiously publishing a work that could be prosecuted for indecency or blasphemous libel. Rather than dare the Attorney-General by taking responsibility for the poem, however, 'Don John' had put other booksellers 'in the front of the battle'; it was the unsuspecting tradesman who would be prosecuted for disseminating libellous books if the government chose to act. Hone thought it his duty to bring the state's attention to stanzas 205 and 206 of the first canto, which even Byron admitted were somewhat daring in 'these canting days':

> Thou shalt believe in Milton, Dryden, Pope;
> Thou shalt not set up Wordsworth, Coleridge, Southey;
> Because the first is crazed beyond all hope,
> The second drunk, the third so quaint and mouthey:
> With Crabbe it may be difficult to cope,
> And Campbell's Hippocrene is somewhat drouthy.
> Thou shalt not steal from Samuel Rogers, nor
> Commit flirtation with the muse of Moore.
> Canto 1, stanza 205

What was the difference between this and Hone's parodies? Hone noted that at the same time Byron's 'blasphemy' was being sold by the government's publisher, a Birmingham bookseller was facing government prosecution for republishing his *Political Litany*, which also contained a parody of the Decalogue. 'Mr Murray,' Hone commented, 'who is known to be the most loyal, and reported to be the most opulent bookseller in the United Kingdom, and who is an Official Publisher of the Government, actually publishes a Parody of the Ten Commandments of God . . . it remains to be seen, whether the maxim so much vaunted in our Law Courts, that *"force is even handed, and deals with all alike"*, be true or not.'

But in truth the libel laws were political tools, not the protectors of public morals: 'No other man but he who has Government support and Government writers to back him, *dare* publish Don Juan as it now stands. Mr Murray is too "respectable" to fear attack.' Hone concluded his book:

Question: 'Why did not Mr Murray suppress Lord Byron's *Parody* on the Ten Commandments?'

Answer: 'Because it contains nothing in ridicule of Ministers, and therefore nothing that *they* could suppose would be to the displeasure of Almighty God.'

In 1819 the public was most likely to read *Don Juan* in the inexpensive pirated editions issued by Hone and other publishers. They knew that they would not be punished, because the Attorney-General would never involve Murray in a prosecution *ex officio*. It was also certain that 'Don John' would not sue: if the Lord Chancellor believed a work to be blasphemous or seditious, the original publisher lost his copyright. In 1817, Hone and many other publishers had pirated Robert Southey's *Wat Tyler*, a radical poem the Laureate had written in his youth, long before he had become an ardent Tory. When Southey complained, Lord Chancellor Eldon had to warn him that it was seditious and thus he could claim no right over it. By the winter of 1819 Murray was exasperated that his rival publishers were making a fortune pirating his *Don Juan*. He wrote to Byron saying that he would seek an injunction; the poet replied:

My dear Murray – You may do as you please – but you are about a hopeless experiment – Eldon will decide against you – were it only that my name is on the record. – You will also recollect that if the publication is pronounced against on the grounds you mention as *indecent & blasphemous*, that *I* lose all right to my daughter's *guardianship* and *education* – in short, all paternal authority, and everything concerning her – except the pleasure I may have claimed to have had in begetting her.

He was referring to Eldon's decision in a Bill of Complaint against Shelley, in which the poet was deprived of his paternal right over his children on the evidence of his atheistical opinions in *Queen Mab*.[31]

The laws of libel operated in many different and contradictory ways;

if Byron could not be imprisoned or fined, he might be made to suffer in other ways; John Murray lost a fortune because of his hypocrisy. The laws could sometimes work in favour of the anti-government press, especially when they pirated the more contentious works of the Tories: Southey's *Wat Tyler*, a panegyric on the rights of man, was used in the cause of reform, and those that pirated it could not be punished without sending the Poet Laureate to gaol as well. Piracy and parody were closely allied as forms of attack, which, if used wisely, were *too* subversive to be punished under the laws. Hone's *Don Juan Unmasked* was an interesting footnote to his trials, an instance of the law's partiality that complemented his attack on George Canning. It was also another stepping stone in the campaign against censorship: repeated instances of hypocrisy in the administration of justice chipped away at the foundation of the laws.

The trials were a starting point for a long and sustained campaign against the decaying laws. The implications for the press would only become apparent in the next few years of bitter conflict. As Richard Carlile noted of 1818: 'Government evidently sick with prosecutions of 1817! . . . In this year, in London, the Press was free . . . But a skilful general knows that it will not do to be supine whilst a powerful though beaten enemy is near. If success be not followed up, it often ends in being a disaster.'[32]

Images of Resistance

Nicknames for the most part govern the world . . . Nicknames are the talismans and spells that collect and set in motion all the combustible part of men's passions and prejudices, which have hitherto played so much more successful a game, and done their work so much more effectually than reason, in all the grand concerns and petty details of human life, and do not yet seem tired of the task assigned them.

William Hazlitt, 'On Nicknames', the *Edinburgh Magazine*, September 1818.[1]

Throughout 1818 and the first half of 1819 the country was peaceful, the press vociferous and the government seemingly unable to enforce its laws. The days of freedom did not last.

In the late summer of 1819 the newspapers were preoccupied with the radical reformer Henry Hunt's progress to Manchester. Once again food prices had soared; discontent was expressed throughout the country and Hunt was charged by moderate reformists and Tories alike with exploiting the people's misery, particularly that of the hard-pressed and discontented weavers of Lancashire. He was due to address a vast meeting at Manchester on Monday, 16 August. Two days later rumours began to spread that something terrible had occurred.

The full story was not clear. On the morning of 18 August *The Times* came out later than normal, its publication delayed while accurate reports from Manchester were awaited. The hurried stop-press report was sketchy and impressionistic. As far as it knew, the local magistrates had read the Riot Act and called upon the Manchester, Macclesfield and Chester Yeomanry to enforce their order to break up the rally. 'The consternation and dismay which spread among the crowd collected cannot be conceived,' *The Times* speculated. 'The multitude was composed of a large number of females. The prancing cavalry, and the active use of the sabre among them, created a dreadful sense of confusion, and we may add, carnage.' Manchester was in shock. As in London, the full details were hard to ascertain. But in the words of the *Manchester Star*, a 'deathlike stillness pervades the town'.[2]

Eleven people died at the meeting held at St Peter's Fields in Manchester, a tragedy immediately named the Peterloo Massacre and remembered as such ever since. The full story dribbled out over the following weeks and months. The inquests into the deaths and the testimonies of the injured gave a comprehensive scenario and timetable for 16 August. By far the most important publications that appeared on the market were books published by William Hone, *The Whole Proceedings Before the Coroner's Inquest at Oldham, on the Body of John Lees* and the *Report of the Metropolitan and Central Committee Appointed for the Relief of the Manchester Sufferers*. The coroner had tried to hurry through the inquest on John Lees, one of the victims, but the London reformist barrister James Harmer had travelled north to ensure that the hearings were enlisted in the cause of truth – for the country and posterity. It was the only chance to cross-examine witnesses and get the testimonies of weavers and other protesters on the judicial record. For weeks Harmer fought to get his witnesses heard, so that Peterloo could be put into its full context. The rendition of abuses and military cruelty appeared in a long book published by Hone, the most exhaustive and grimly fascinating account of the massacre.

Some eighty thousand men, women and children had gathered at St Peter's Fields that day, dressed in their Sunday best and many carrying richly embellished banners. Witnesses at the inquest recalled the good humour of the families as they gathered round the hustings to hear Henry Hunt address them. There were special constables on duty, and the local magistracy was gathered in a nearby house. At one o'clock they read the Riot Act, commanding the protesters to disburse. None of the witnesses heard the orders or knew they had been given. As the crowd was listening to the speeches, the line of constables parted, and the Manchester Yeomanry cavalry drew up. There was a misplaced sense of camaraderie among the crowd; they shouted out friendly greetings to the soldiers and gave them three cheers. The militia were, after all, volunteers and their well-to-do neighbours. Hunt commanded them to be peaceful. But suddenly the cavalry brandished their sabres and wheeled round the field, surrounding the protesters. They moved in to arrest Hunt and his lieutenants, and then, according to a witness, 'came in galloping, pell-mell, one upon another, with their swords drawn'.[3]

The cavalry charged the crowd with the aim of seizing the much-loved reformist banners, but they hacked and slashed as they went. A cotton spinner later said: 'There was whiz this way and whiz that way: whenever any cried out "mercy", they said, "Damn you, what brought you here?"'. Two yeomen recognised John Thacker Saxton of the *Manchester Observer* in the crowd. 'There is that villain, Saxton,' shouted one; 'do you run him through the body.' Fortunately, the journalist got away with his life. John Lees, a poor weaver, was not so lucky. Joseph Wrigley, one of Harmer's witnesses at the inquest, said: '. . . I saw him receive a cut on the back of his right arm from a sabre; he was parrying off the blows of one of the military, and another came up and cut him; he had his right arm over his head, protecting it with a walking stick.' Lees then tried to hide under the hustings, but the constables saw him and dragged him out. Another witness, Jonah Andrew, testified that he saw them 'beating him with their truncheons severely. One of them picked up a staff of a banner that had been cut with a sword, and said, "Damn your bloody eyes, I'll break your back"; and they struck him for a considerable time with their truncheons and staff of the banner.' John Lees was able to get away from the carnage, but later died of his wounds.[4]

Lord Sidmouth wrote a congratulatory letter to the Manchester magistrates on behalf of the Prince Regent, passing on 'the great satisfaction derived by His Royal Highness from their prompt, decisive and efficient measures for the preservation of the public tranquillity'. The government had had nothing to do with the events of Peterloo. Their swift support for the magistracy and yeomanry, however, disgusted an already shocked country. As E. P. Thompson wrote, 'no authorities have ever acted so vigorously to make themselves accomplices after the fact'. Rather than condemn the brutality of the local troops, the Regent and his ministers gave them full backing. But as Burdett said, the only threat to 'the public tranquillity' had come from the magistrates, the constables and the yeomanry, whose 'prompt, decisive and efficient measures' had been the only sign of violence on that day. The magistrates, the government and their supporters in the press were sent into a flurry of self-justification and downright falsehood. It was claimed that the protesters had flouted the law by refusing to disperse; they had provoked the military and the subsequent injuries had been caused by pressure of an overexcited crowd. The yeomanry, they said, *had* used force, but only in self-defence and only with the flat sides of their swords.[5]

The books brought out by Hone gave the lie to the government. Harmer's stubbornness at the inquest had brought into public view a full description of the violence of the military and the constables, a compendium of horrendous abuses. All witnesses were unanimous in saying that the magistrates had not given the crowd any kind of chance to move away peacefully before the cavalry was sent in. Hone's *Report* of the committee in Manchester, which had been set up to look after the families of the dead and the welfare of the wounded, gave full details of the injuries that the army had inflicted. Of the eleven who died, five had been cut with sabres, one had been shot, three crushed by the cavalry and one had been thrown into a cellar; only one had been crushed in the mêlée. These supposedly violent protesters, killed by the yeomen in self-defence, included two women and one infant. The list of the 421 who claimed relief included 100 women and children and 161 who had been slashed with sabres; the rest had been trampled under the hooves of horses, stabbed with bayonets, cudgelled by the constables or crushed in the press of bodies. The individual accounts make chilling reading. Samuel Allcard, a plasterer: 'right elbow and head cut severely, his finger nearly cut off by the sabre of a Yeoman, thrown down and trampled upon'. Thomas Blinstone, a blacksmith: 'Both arms broken, and much bruised in the body.' The youngest was Edward Lancaster, a boy of eleven, who had been cut by a sabre on the back of his head and his throat had been trodden on by a horse. William Ogden, a seventy-six-year-old printer and a one-time state prisoner had been slashed on the head, wounded in the eye and bludgeoned by the constables.[6]

The personal accounts and sufferings detailed in Hone's two books revolted a country already shocked by such descriptions of military brutality meted out to protesters who had not broken any law. The government had once more shown its partisan application of justice, sacrificing truth to their on-going campaign against reformists. Parliament was due to convene in November. Already it was clear that the government would use the Peterloo tragedy for its own ends. Hunger and discontent would be answered with a further round of repressive legislation. Once again, the press was held culpable for exhorting people to attend public meetings. As *The Times* said, when the government gave the magistracy *carte blanche* to deploy the military against political protesters and the press it would 'sweep away every landmark of our old jurisprudence, and every trace of civil liberty from the soil of the British islands'.[7]

Hone had been propelled once more to the forefront of opposition to the government in the aftermath of Peterloo. He was, in turn, held up as the journalist responsible for the licentiousness of an unbounded press by ministers and as the symbol of free speech by the Whig grandees. The attack had to be renewed, the victories gained at Guildhall made real. The hero of 1817 and, next to Cobbett, the most famous journalist in the country, he had to join the debate as the voice of resistance to censorship. But how could he make his voice heard? How could the anger of the British people be reflected most accurately? Inspiration came one evening a few weeks after Peterloo:

After my trials, the newspapers were continually at me, calling me an acquitted felon. The worm will turn when trodden on. One day, when I had been exasperated beyond bearing, one of my children, a little girl of four years old, was sitting on my knee, very busy, looking at the pictures of a child's book; 'What have you got there?' said I – 'The House that Jack Built' – an idea flashed across my mind; I saw at once the use that might be made of it; I took it from her. I said, 'Mother, take the child, send me up my tea and two candles, and let nobody come near me till I ring.' I sat up all night and wrote 'The House that Jack Built'.

The Political House that Jack Built, a twenty-four-page pamphlet, came out on Saturday, 13 November 1819, a few days before the government introduced legislation to shackle the press further. Hone had found an appropriate means of venting public anger; the country was gripped, and the satire went to fifty-four editions, selling well over 100,000 copies within a few months. Despite its ostensible simplicity –

or triviality, at first sight – it was the most significant publication of the Peterloo period.

The satire was a close parody of the original children's nursery rhyme, starting with a single statement, and accumulating page by page. Each description was accompanied by a cartoon drawn by George Cruikshank. The 'House that Jack Built' is a temple supported by the pillars of King, Commons and Lords, which contains the treasures of 'Magna Charta', the Bill of Rights and Habeas Corpus. But that wealth is threatened by 'Vermin' of courtiers, lawyers, clergymen, borough-mongers and soldiers. The fourth addition to this conflict is the printing press: *The Thing*, which 'in spite of new Acts, / And attempts to restrain it by Soldiers or Tax', will triumph over tyrannising ministers.*

The next in this historical progression is the lawyer, 'The Public Informer, who would put down the Thing', backed by 'The Reasons of Lawless Power': infantrymen, cavalry, cannon and a gaoler. The first six parts of the nursery rhyme refer implicitly to Hone himself, and his battle to establish the press as the guardian of the sacred rights of Magna Carta etc., which are enshrined within the theoretical temple 'that Jack Built'. The second part refers to the situation in 1819. Next to a picture of miserable Lancashire weavers, came the lines:

> These are
> THE PEOPLE
> all tattered and torn,
> Who curse the day
> wherein they were born,
> On account of Taxation
> too great to be borne,
> And pray from relief,
> from night to morn;
> Who in vain, Petition
> in every form,
> Who, peaceably Meeting

---

* 'The Thing' was the way Cobbett referred to the establishment: the overwhelming combined power of ministers, church, army, borough-mongers, sinecurists, the Bank of England, etc. Hone inverts this, mocking the government's contempt for the press and suggesting that the instrument of public opinion will usurp 'The Thing'.

    to ask for Reform,
Were sabred by Yeomanry Cavalry,
who,
Were thanked by THE MAN
  all shaven and shorn,
All cover'd with Orders –
and all forlorn . . .

And 'the man' was the Prince Regent, whom Cruikshank represented as a bloated rake in fancy dress. It is the most memorable image in the parody, one of Cruikshank's most famous caricatures:

THE DANDY AT SIXTY,
 Who bows with a grace,
And has *taste* in wigs, collars,
Cuirasses and lace;
Who, to tricksters, and fools,
Leaves the State and its treasure,
And, when Britain's in tears,
Sails about at his pleasure:
Who spurned from his presence
The Friends of his youth,
And now has not one
Who will tell him the truth;
Who took to his counsels,
In evil hour,
The Friends to the Reasons
Of lawless power;
That back the Public Informer,
 Who
Would put down the *Thing*,
That, in spite of new Acts,
And attempts to restrain it,
By Soldiers or Tax,
Will *poison* the Vermin,
That plunder the Wealth,
That lay in the House
That Jack built.

These lines were a summation of the events in 1819. The Regent had been amusing himself on the Royal Yacht at the time of the Peterloo Massacre, from whence he wrote to congratulate the magistrates who had ordered the troops to attack the protesters at St Peters Fields. Prince George did in fact have a deep love of military uniforms and court pageantry. Although he had been forbidden to serve in the army, he loved all things military, and used to fantasise that he had led Britain to victory at Waterloo, once telling the Duke of Wellington how he had personally defeated Bonaparte. One of George's first acts upon becoming Regent was to appoint himself Field Marshal and design a suitably grand uniform with, it was said, gold braid weighing 200 pounds. The official portraiture of the Regent always depicted him in martial garb and posture. So many medals, so few battles! Amongst the Regent's spurious honours, Cruikshank included a corkscrew: valour in debauchery, not the field.

The friends that the Regent had spurned in his youth were the reformist Whigs whom he had promised power when he was Prince of Wales but had forbidden office when he became Regent. Instead he had turned to the Tories, the men blamed for the tyranny. And they are represented in *The Political House* as the 'Guilty Trio' of Lord Sidmouth, Lord Castlereagh and George Canning, who have perverted Britain, misled the Regent and preside over the treasure that lies in Jack's house. Sidmouth is 'The Doctor of *Circular* fame, / A Driveller, a Bigot, a Knave without shame' in reference to his doctor father, and the infamous Circular of 1817 – the basis for Hone and Wooler's arbitrary arrest and Cobbett's flight to America. Castlereagh, the Foreign Secretary is 'Derry Down Triangle', as he was in Hone's *Political Creed*. Completing the trio is 'the worthless colleague of their infamous power', George Canning, who is dubbed the 'Spouter of Froth' for his florid oratory and jokes aimed at the sufferings of imprisoned reformists.

In a culture saturated with visual information, we are desensitised to the impact of Hone and Cruikshank's satires on the public in 1819. Historians have seen their series of parodies, starting with *The Political House*, as devices to teach reformist arguments to the semi-literate and politically ignorant.[8] But it is the sophisticated, image-weary modern eye that sees them as simply pedagogical tools. They are easy to over-

'The Guilty Trio'

The Doctor [Sidmouth]	Derry Down Triangle	The Spouter of Froth [Canning]
At his last gasp	[Castlereagh]	*With merry descants on a*
– with opium drugged.	*He sold his country.*	*nation's woes. There is a merry*
		mischief in his mirth.

look, which I did the first time I saw them. They should not be dismissed so lightly. What might at first sight appear curiously mild and innocuous was genuinely shocking when they were published. Much later, in 1874, it was remembered that Hone's 'political squibs caught, delighted, and sometimes terrified the public. His *Political House that Jack Built* was so true, that all confessed the truth; so witty, that all laughed at the wit; but it was so "audacious" that steady-going old people thought the end of the world was come if even the most respectable magistrates were to be pulled by the nose, and kicked into the midst of the multitudinous public.' Hone's publications were tellingly called 'squibs', slang for bombs; the term preserves some of the explosive properties of these paper grenades hurled amidst the public. One writer later in the century could find no more expressive word to encapsulate their violence than 'atrocities'.[9]

The function of Hone's satire was to vent popular indignation after
Peterloo and during the enactment of emergency legislation. His work
is impossible to understand isolated from the intense passions at this
time of state-approved repression. They were symbols of people's
anger – the rage of the impotent, of disenfranchised men and women
seeking redress. *The Political House* did not aim to educate or inform or
politicise the masses; simple language does not necessarily infer a simple readership. Hone wanted to provoke laughter – and laughter he
knew from his trials was something people in authority feared. And for
his readers, the cruelty of derisive laughter satisfied their pent-up anger.
Educated and respectable middle-class men and women as much as the
semi-literate could indulge a fantasy of revenge in *The Political House*.
How else could the middle classes express their anger? They could not
vote; they would not go on to the streets. The act of buying one was an
expression of disgust.

Vengeance is inflicted in *The Political House* through contempt.
Simplicity is the key to the satire's success. The deftness of Hone and
Cruikshank's touch, the very restraint of the prose and caricature mag-
nifies the actual crime. Hone chose to parody a nursery rhyme not
because, as some have argued, it was immediately recognisable as a
fundamental text of childhood that illiterate people would understand,
but because that was as much as the political system and the politicians
deserved. Parody worked in a different way than merely making a political discourse uncomplicated: its relationship to the parodied text is the
key to understanding it. As Hone knew from his research, the more
venerable a text that is parodied, the greater the dignity conferred on
the subject of the parody. Taking a nursery rhyme as inspiration makes
explicit the author's feelings about his victims. The government of the
country had become a sad farce, and its Prince *was* like an overindulged
child pampered with toys and baubles (the 'Regent's Bomb', his yacht,
the Brighton Pavilion), stuffed with food, and wont to dress up in grand
uniforms.

The image of the 'Dandy at Sixty' was considered shocking because
it pared the iconography of royalty down to the ridiculous and contemptible, mocking the hollowness of vain pageantry. It warred as much
with the Regent's public image as with the conventional depiction of

him in Whig and reformist satire, where he had been presented over and again as a libidinous old rogue. The 'Dandy at Sixty' does not even have a sexual identity; he is literally the prince that never grew up, never graduated from the nursery. And yet this is the man who presides over a state where innocent protesters are charged by cavalry, there is not enough food to feed the nation and distress is answered with pre-emptive legislation. He chooses ministers that complement his immaturity; the 'Guilty Trio' are feeble and pompous men fit only for walk-on parts in a children's fable, not an overawing junta of tyrannising despots. Had Hone and Cruikshank taken the Regent and his ministers seriously, the effect would have been very different. If they had been savaged as sadists and murderers – if the journalist and artist had adopted the outraged language of the reformist press at this time – the public would not have responded with such alacrity to the satire. *The Political House* sated the public's anger and desire for revenge: George, Sidmouth, Castlereagh and Canning have been made as low and as risible as possible, and the innovation of parodying a child's learning book makes this possible. By treating the country's rulers as vain, stupid, *little* men, Hone inflicted the greatest insult of them all: disdain.

When he explained why he had taken up satire as journalism, Hone quoted the preface of William Gifford's translation of Juvenal: 'The legitimate office of a satirist is to hold up the vicious as objects of reprobation and scorn, for the example of others, who may be deterred by their sufferings; there is in such men a wilfulness of disposition, which prompts them to bear up against shame, and to show how little they regard light reproof, by becoming more audacious in guilt: vice, like folly, to be restrained, must be overawed.'[10] The effect is achieved not by exaggerating the politicians as all-powerful, but by trivialising them and exposing the pettiness of their pretensions. Satire sought to hold up the guilty for punishment on the pillory of public opinion. By traducing them, the satirist and his audience inflict revenge. The laughter is meant to be vindictive, not a joyous release. Hone said that he had unleashed his satires because the political situation demanded it; they were written only 'upon due provocation'.

'Another remarkable "little book" equally solid and ornamental (which we cannot say of its heroes) has appeared from the shop of Mr

Hone . . .' the *Examiner* announced. 'Its caricatures, full of high and huge, if not great personages, are as abundant in meaning, and better drawn than Gillray's – and the letter press is worthy of them.'[11] *The Man in the Moon*, the second satire in the series, appeared two months after *The Political House*, and in it Cruikshank demonstrated far superior skills as a draftsman. Whereas the figures in the first pamphlet are stationary and one dimensional, those in the second are alive with movement and emotional intensity.

The Man in the Moon (which was not written by Hone, but by an anonymous collaborator) adopted a similar simple form to the nursery rhyme, describing a dream of a journey to the Moon where the Regent of 'Lunitaria' has just opened parliament, as the British Prince Regent had just done on Earth. At each state opening of parliament after 1811 Prince George was required to give a formal account of George III's illness. In his satire, the author alludes to the King's mental state in the simple rhyme: 'I grieve to say, / That poor old Dad, / Is just as – bad.' And the satire continues in the same disrespectful style. 'Lunitaria' represents the Regent's ideal land; although the reformers are demanding cheap food, respite from taxes and freedom of speech, the press is silenced, the people kept in check by a strong military, and the 'august' senators continue to profit from the people. Lunitaria's equivalent of Peterloo occurs when the people ask for reform and food. But cold steel takes the place of bread: 'And though the *Radicals* still want food,' the Regent says, 'A few STEEL LOZENGES* will stop their pain, / And set the Constitution right again.'

The image of a miserable people whose hunger pains are ended with the bayonet is the product of a dream. But reality is only a step away from the fantasy. The idea of using a nightmare is effective, because the actual political situation is worse than the visions of a fevered sleep. 'It is the freedom to translate the concepts and shorthand symbols of our political speech into . . . metaphorical situations that constitutes the novelty of the cartoon,' the art historian E. H. Gombrich wrote of satire in general. Political humour fulfils a legitimate role within the political debate; *The Political House* and

---

* A 'Steel Lozenge' was a quack doctor's nostrum at the time.

The Man in the Moon are successful in the 'telescoping of a whole chain of ideas into one pregnant striking image'.[12] Hone's satires do not aim to inform or teach people what is happening; they seek to haunt the public mind with a sequence of powerful, unforgettable images.

Hone's satires triggered a powerful emotional response in the public, which bought his series of pamphlets in the hundreds of thousands for three years. The power of the image was hardly undiscovered territory. In many ways it was considered more corrosively damaging to the public mind than the word. The frontispiece of this book (p.ii) 'The Freeborn Englishman' – certainly a strong image, but not one we might automatically think of as *dangerous* – was described by the Attorney-General as 'indecent' – indecent because it would corrupt public morals and destroy the people's faith in the established authorities. He knew that the blunt, explicit picture could capture the public mind more completely than a journalist's prose. Yet it is wrong to see in late Georgian Britain a universal visual culture with the mass of the population exposed to a panoply of iconography and illustration. There are thousands of paintings, portraits and brightly coloured cartoons that

have survived; we are commonly invited to see the eighteenth and early
nineteenth centuries through the lens of the much-reproduced work of
William Hogarth or James Gillray. But the abundance and quality of the
work can give a misleading impression of the average person's
encounter with the visual. It is the Attorney-General's concern with the
novelty of a cartoon such as John Bull shackled by the libel laws which
is significant. Charles Knight, who as a journalist and publisher from
the 1810s to the 1860s was witness to the great innovations in the printing industry, wrote that before Hone and Cruikshank's collaborations,
book and journalistic illustrations had been mediocre or very expensive. Illustrations accompanying street literature such as ballads, broadsides and news-sheets, were crude and basic. In 1819, most people in
the country had not even seen an example of Hogarth's work; George
Cruikshank, 'the great artist of half a century', was the first to be universally known throughout the country. And most people were first
acquainted with the artist – long before he illustrated *Oliver Twist* –
through his political work for Hone.[13]

Because there was a paucity of good-quality art in popular culture,
the cartoons were doubly effective in fixing themselves in the public
mind. They had an explosive potential that is difficult to appreciate
now. Hone and Cruikshank's achievement was a revolution in technol-
ogy as much as in aesthetics. Their satires were so popular and politically important because they managed to blur the distinctions between
refined and popular humour. In the preceding generation the great
artistic satires had been largely the preserve of the elite. The cartoons of
Gillray and his main rivals, James Sayers, Thomas Rowlandson and
Isaac Cruikshank were undoubtedly works of high genius; but they
were expensive and drawn for a sophisticated metropolitan audience of
political insiders. Every caricature was full of complicated in-jokes, gossip and literary allusions that would only have been understood by the
highly educated. They were predominantly conservative and loyalist in
outlook; radicals were scorned as seditious anarchists eager to pull
down the fabric of the constitution and import the Terror of the French
Revolution to Britain. John Bull was depicted either as a victim or as
the dupe of ministers or radicals; he was only a free agent and stolid citizen when he had to resist the French. The immediate visual sensation

of a satire might have been easy to decode for the 'outsiders' who saw them – but how many *did* see them? The pictures were engraved onto copper plates, which could only withstand around a thousand imprints before they wore out. Later they were hand-coloured, adding to the production costs. They were limited in supply, very expensive, and thus restricted to a wealthy or privileged clientele. Such engraved cartoons could be seen in shop windows, coffee houses, taverns and other public places in London gratis; but the rest of the country did not feel their impact. It was not until 1819 that political satire and caricature found a national market.

Hone was able to keep his satires at a low price because Cruikshank engraved his designs onto block-wood, which, unlike copper, never wore out. Woodcuts had been used for popular illustrations for centuries, but before *The Political House* they were rough and basic. Their heavy, thick lines prevented the representation of detailed facial expression and human emotion. Traditional woodcut illustrations were cheap, and looked it: tawdry, plebeian and emotionally static in contrast to the handsomely embellished copper prints. Cruikshank's woodcuts, however, are full of intricate detail and movement; their fine, elegant lines make them appear at first sight to be engraved on copperplate. A reviewer in the *Examiner* wrote: 'These publications contain much of what is derived from a knowledge of design and the linear development of human passions, and are much above common caricature. They are a link between genuine art and caricature.'[14]

The satires were inexpensive, and sacrificed little of the artistic skill that had made caricature a respectable genre in the late eighteenth century. Some of Cruikshank's work for Hone (most notably in *The Queen's Matrimonial Ladder* and *A Slap at Slop*, published in the next few years) rivals Gillray's finest copperplate designs. The publisher Hannah Humphrey had sold single-sheet Gillray prints for five shillings apiece. Hone and Cruikshank's *Saluting the R–t's Bomb* (1816) cost two shillings. But Hone could sell thirteen Cruikshank woodcut designs in *The Political House*, and twenty even finer ones in *The Queen's Matrimonial Ladder*, for just one shilling. 'The Freeborn Englishman', which worried the government, was first sold in 1819 as a copper-engraved, coloured print. It might not have been seen by many people because of its limited print run; it was brought to the attention of hundreds of thousands – maybe millions – when it was re-done by Cruikshank as a woodblock illustration for Hone in 1821.

Hone wrote, in 1824,

By showing what engraving on wood could effect in a popular way, and exciting a taste for art in the more humble ranks of life, they created a new era in the history of publication. They are the parents of the present cheap literature, which extends in sale of at least four hundred thousand copies every week, and gives large and constant employment to talent in that particular branch of engraving which I selected as the best adapted to enforce, and give circulation to, my own thoughts.[15]

It was a high boast, but Hone was partly justified in making it. Throughout the 1820s, cheap graphic journalism became established, attempting to emulate the high standards of Hone and Cruikshank. The sophisticated woodblock illustration became a staple of popular literature.

In the 1790s and 1800s, the heyday of political caricature, the government could be confident that the worst of satirical jibes would be restricted to a small audience. The power of laughter as a political weapon and the damage an image could do had been taken seriously enough for politicians to bribe caricaturists and dictate their subject matter, and for Canning to award Gillray a pension on the condition he did not depict William Pitt in an unfavourable way. Satirical prints had always been the anomaly in the government's libel laws; it was almost impossible to prosecute caricatured images of politicians and royalty, however offensive they were. The law specified that any painting or printed image that brought the state, the monarchy or public figures into contempt was a criminal libel. But the thought of the Crown having to prove in open court that a cartoon of a fat, immoral, seedy old rake represented the Regent was something at which even the most litigious minister or officious Attorney-General baulked. But it had never been a problem, for at the very worst, satirical invective would be kept within London. It was a different matter when Hone and Cruikshank captured a national market with high-quality and inexpensive artistic satires. Suddenly people who had never felt the impact of the satirical image, which everyone agreed was a deadly effective medium, were exposed to the force of Hone's 'little books'.

On 3 January 1820 *The Times* reported that a copy of *The Political House* had turned up on St Helena in the possession of a passenger on his way to India. This incident was only reported because the man was briefly detained for having it on his person and there was a danger it could have been seen by the British garrison or the exiled Napoleon himself, but the details of this unusual incident hint that the satires were distributed throughout the empire. The standards of workmanship, the cheap price and unprecedented success made them desirable artefacts for all sections of society. As examples of high-quality caricature, they appealed to Gillray's former customers as much as to people outside London who had never experienced the power of visual satire before.

Ministers sought to immure themselves from the public gaze; refusing to engage with the people, they claimed that the only legitimate forum for 'public opinion' was parliament. The libel laws were supposed to protect them from censure and uphold the sanctity of parliament. It was beneath a minister's dignity to descend to the level of the press or even to speak to a wide constituency within the country. A minister like Lord Sidmouth was proud to assert that he represented country gentlemen; to court popularity or justify policies to those outside the small circle of voters, peers and men of influence was considered neither necessary nor constitutionally correct. So for the public, Sidmouth or Castlereagh were just names. The politicians of the 1810s did not have a profile comparable to that of their predecessors. Pitt and Fox became iconic figures and party leaders, recognisable to the public through images on token coins and propaganda prints. Pitt's angular features and piercing gaze, Fox's jowls, stubble and dishevelled clothes were instantly identifiable and carefully cultivated; they were perhaps the first politicians to command widespread recognition. Apart from the Regent and the Duke of Wellington, there were few personalities in politics in the next generation; rarely did the public know a politician beyond what he said in parliament and the acts to which he gave his name.

Cruikshank's group portrait 'The Guilty Trio' in *The Political House* must have been the first representation of the leading ministers that many in the country had seen. Sidmouth, Castlereagh and Canning had been careless of their image; Hone and Cruikshank appropriated it. It is interesting to note, and highly significant, that the 'loyalist' publishers who parodied Hone and published their own satirical pamphlets were forced to imitate the caricatures laid down by their rival. Sidmouth and Castlereagh look exactly the same in some pro-government satires as they do in Hone's books. They had to. How else would the public recognise them? In one 'loyal' satire Castlereagh was shown with the cat-o'-nine-tails that Hone and Cruikshank had given him to remind people of the savagery of punishments in the military when he was Secretary for War. Sidmouth was always depicted as cadaverous and spindly as he was in 'The Guilty Trio'. They could never be drawn as great and good men because the public would not recognise them; pro-government responses to Hone's satires were counterproductive because they reinforced the hostile images developed in *The Political House*.[16]

The ministers did a good job of making themselves ridiculous on their own, providing the ammunition for their caricatures. Hone unearthed and republished in *The Man in the Moon* a poem written by George Canning in 1802 mocking Sidmouth, when the latter had been Prime Minister. Canning dubbed his then political opponent the 'Prime Doctor', and put words into his mouth: 'I flatter'd Pitt; I cring'd, and sneak'd and fawn'd / And thus became the Speaker.' From that job he became Prime Minister: 'My ends attain'd my only aim has been / To keep my place – and gild my humble name!' Cruikshank illustrated Canning's libellous verse, mocking juvenile high political spats.

In Canning's pockets are two pistols labelled 'Challenge'. In 1809, when he was Foreign Secretary in the Duke of Portland's administration, he had intrigued against Castlereagh, then Secretary for War. Castlereagh got wind of his colleague's plots and sent him an angry letter, complaining that his position as a minister had been 'dependent on your will and pleasure'. It was 'a breach of every principle of good faith', Castlereagh said, when members of the cabinet were apparently loyal at the cabinet table but perfidious in private. Their honour as public men dictated that there was little choice but to follow the example of many other politicians, including William Pitt; they fought a duel

'His name's the Doctor'

on Putney Heath in which Canning was slightly wounded in the thigh.

At the end of the poem, Sidmouth was seen in fond embrace with his erstwhile tormentor, George Canning. The 'Guilty Trio' were fully reconciled as members of Lord Liverpool's government. Yet the implication is that their childish disagreements and jealousies end only when outweighed by the attractions of political reward. The caricature of Canning exposing Sidmouth to public derision is one of the funniest in Hone's series of satirical books. But he did not have to think up the situation or the scenario; the ministers had already rendered themselves as ridiculous as possible, proving themselves the 'little men of little minds' that Hone had called them during his trials. If anyone could be accused of debasing politics it was not Hone; by writing silly poems and shooting at each other, ministers of the Crown had set the tone for the satires.

It would take an effort of will to separate the caricature of a minister from reality when there was no other visual representation of him available on the market: when people read his declarations in parliament the image would always be there; whatever dignity the minister might once have commanded automatically as a servant of the Crown was, if not destroyed, at least seriously tarnished. Laughter was a more powerful emotional response than deference: satire was a legitimate political weapon in the reformist armoury. That was why people were shocked by *The Political House* and why the satires were described as 'atrocities' by some: the public were forced to see their rulers for the first time, and they saw them as infantile wretches and delinquents.

Hone called *The Political House* 'A Straw – thrown up to show which way the wind blows'. The satires were symbols of deep anger, bought and circulated as tokens of protest. Their primary role, however, was to explore the limits of free expression. They have been misread as plebeian instruction manuals in politics when Hone's real intention was to use them in the fight against censorship. *The Political House* was published ten days before repressive legislation was introduced to parliament, when Hone would be cited as the man who had opened the Pandora's box of a licentious press. The pamphlets therefore breathed defiance; the act of buying one from William Hone, the victor of Guildhall and the journalist the government hated the most, gave the customer a sense that he or she was engaged in an act of disobedience.

On 23 November 1819, the Regent responded to the crisis. But rather than investigate the Manchester tragedy, he warned the peers and commons: 'It will require your utmost vigilance and exertion, collectively and individually, to check the dissemination of the doctrines of treason and impiety . . . '[17] The government believed that the Peter's Fields meeting had been the first indication of revolutionary action. As in 1817, the reformist press was held responsible for the looming crisis. Lord Liverpool told the Lords: 'The public are every day made acquainted with what parliament is doing, and their deliberations are made the subject of open comment – to such a degree, and to such an extent, as in some measure to influence these deliberations.' The Prime Minister said that this was unprecedented; no government had ever been required to regulate a press with such wide distribution and impunity from prosecution. He dated the changes to the verdicts of Hone's trials:

'whether right or wrong, it materially aggravated the existing evil'. Since that time, he continued, 'seditious' libels had gone unpunished, 'not from the supineness of the government, but from the deficiency of the law as it now exists'. Lord Sidmouth agreed, saying that people believed that the libel laws were unenforceable after the 'remarkable acquittal' of William Hone.[18]

The Home Secretary introduced his notorious Six Acts to the Lords in December, which tightened the coercive power of the state in preventing public meetings and other loci of discontent; two acts dealt with the press: the Blasphemous and Seditious Libel Bills, which would reform laws that he said had been unworkable since December 1817, and a Newspaper Stamp Act, designed to put reformist literature beyond the reach of the people by inflating the price with tax. The Solicitor-General pointed to the three trials (the last significant libel case) and the vast subscription fund that had relieved the defendant's poverty, saying that it 'had had the effect of holding out a hope of impunity to blasphemous and seditious libellers'; since then the press had become ungovernable. Sidmouth's so-called 'Gagging Act' did not propose to find a new way of regulating the press or find a workable criteria for assessing the danger a piece of journalism represented, but to tighten up the existing laws to silence journalists with severe legal penalties. The powers of *ex officio* arrest were made more rigorous. Judges would have the power to confiscate an entire stock of publications they suspected of being dangerous to the safety of the state. A writer or publisher convicted for a second offence of criminal libel would face transportation to New South Wales.

Both houses of parliament agreed that new measures were needed to defend the state. The meagre Whig opposition was all but muted, and it was all Lord Grey could do to implore the Lords to be careful of the step they were poised to take: meddling with the rights of free expression by imposing 'restraints on the press, – restraints now so increased, that I believe they will lead in a short time to the complete extinction of that right; in short, a general code of coercion and force, to which parliament has too readily assented, on the ground that even urgent distress is not to be reasoned with, but to be silenced'.[19]

But for the first time in such a debate, the Whigs had an important precedent. Lord Althorp told the House of Commons, in reference to Hone's trials, that ministers had 'no right to impose fresh restrictions on the press . . . when the sufficiency of the existing restrictions has not been ascertained'. By raising the issue of Hone's victories, the government put itself on dangerous ground. Ministers might point to the acquittal of a low blasphemer as a reason to act, but they were proposing to strengthen laws which had been shown unreliable in operation and intolerable to juries and the public since December 1817. They were contradicting themselves by saying that libellers enjoyed impunity after the trials, but also that the current law still had the capacity to suppress offensive publications. The Whigs would not let them have it both ways. Discussing the growing freedom of the press in 1819, Lord Rossyln told the ministers: 'If such an alteration has taken place after the trial of Mr Hone, it is rather odd to name his acquittal a ground for present measures.' The laws had been made a laughing stock at the Guildhall, but the government was not going to abolish *ex officio* informations, Special Juries or the old and anomalous definition of libel. It was merely intending to strengthen existing laws without considering their flaws. The administration's claim that the law was still as efficacious and thorough as it had always been was ludicrous. Lord Holland said that he had consulted the judicial record and 'on referring to it to see what prosecutions have been instituted during the years after Mr Hone's acquittal, what was the number returned? None.' If the laws still worked, why had they been in abeyance since Hone's trials, the time in which ministers said the seditious press had breached its bounds.[20]

The Whigs warned the government and its supporters that ill-considered legislation, introduced at a moment of panic, would inevitably fail. Lord Grey pointed to the subscription fund that had been raised for Hone. The public had registered its protest against vindictive measures. Hone had exposed the partiality of English justice, and juries – even Special Juries – were now reluctant to do the government's dirty work. In December 1817 three juries had acquitted Hone, not because they agreed with his political views, but because he had been persecuted by hypocritical ministers exploiting unfair advantage. The public was already set against excessive punishment; if the fate of an accused libeller was now to be transportation to Botany Bay, juries would refuse to sanction such a barbarous and unwarranted sentence, even if they believed the accused to be guilty. Yet parliament was still determined to provide measures to silence the press, and the Gagging Act passed the Commons by 190 votes to seventy-two on 21 December 1819.[21]

The problems that journalists faced in 1819–20 were apparently greater than in 1817; the state's new powers increased the danger for publishers and the sense of panic after Peterloo might have been enough to persuade Special Jurymen to convict those blamed for the supposedly imminent conflagration. The signs were ominous; Sir Francis Burdett had been found guilty of libel when he attacked the savagery of the Manchester Yeomanry; Richard Carlile, the editor of the *Republican*, had just been sentenced for blasphemous libel; Henry Hunt the orator and John Wroe of the *Manchester Observer* were in gaol. Pressmen throughout the country were braced for a fresh round of *ex officio* arrests and libel trials. The pessimism was captured in Hone's *Man in the Moon*, where the Regent is seen hand in hand with Satan, the monarchs of the Holy Alliance, bishops and army officers dancing round Liberty's funeral pyre, the flames kindled by a printing press.

The pessimistic tone of the satire is appropriate at this time of uneasiness and suspense; the fantasy of the image is dangerously close to reality. But the very existence of Hone's books proclaims the renewed attempt at censorship a dismal failure; at the very time the Six Acts gain royal assent, hundreds of thousands of copies of his satires are circulating the country with glorious impunity. The freedom and confidence of the press are flaunted in the government's face, defying it to act.

How far could a journalist go in attacking the Regent and the cabinet? Hone knew that the government could never risk bringing him to trial again for writing a satire; the memories of Guildhall were still queasily uncomfortable for ministers and judges. He had a privileged freedom to savage his rulers and the celebrity to draw a vast audience. However far the government pushed its control over the press, the existence of these satires ridiculed those pretensions. The deceptively simple nursery-rhyme format was deployed by Hone to mock the impossibility of ever muzzling the press: it was the *reductio ad absurdum* of censorship. For all the gagging acts that parliament wasted its time passing, journalists could find new ways of expressing their message. And

'The Holy Compact and Alliance'
From *The Man in the Moon*. Liberty burns on the press,
to the delight of the Regent and his allies.

it was ironic that the more the government acted to curtail press freedom, the more outrageous the attack became. Hone could claim that he
had deployed a form of journalism which was both far more savage and
more popular than his accustomed reportage and polemic because the
government had forced his hand by threatening to prosecute reasoned
debate. He was not alone in defying the government; as the Six Acts
came into effect, the press became ever more daring. *The Times*
launched a campaign against the legislation; the provincial press and
the many new *Registers* and other weekly pamphlets savaged the government; public meetings became more frequent. The satires were
symbols of this spirit of resistance. Parodying *The House that Jack
Built* revealed the ridiculous position that the government had forced

'The Pen and the Sword'
Frontispiece of *The Political House that Jack Built*. The Duke of Wellington
tosses the sword of military might onto the scales of justice. Will it outweigh
the power of the pen?

itself into; ill-considered, panicky legislation was answered with the
appropriate contempt. The dreamlike style of *The Man in the Moon*
satirised the absurdities of a situation whereby the government chased
shadows, blundering as it progressed from indignity to indignity.
Wherever Sidmouth looked, whatever gap in the laws he tried to plug,
there would always be a new way of evading his powers. Hone *dared*
the Home Secretary to respond.

The words of the satires are weak without the accompanying cartoons.
In the same way, the pictures taken out of context are meaningless. It
was a genuine collaboration. Hone spent a night writing *The Political
House*. 'In the morning', he remembered, 'I sent for Cruikshank, read it
to him, and put myself into the attitudes of the figures I wanted drawn.

Some of the characters Cruikshank had never seen, but I gave him the likeness as well as the attitude.'

Cruikshank made Hone's pamphlets the great pieces of satirical journalism they undoubtedly are; the illustrations make them works of lasting interest when the words and the passions that inspired them are obscured by time. But the series of pamphlets was not the work of one man. Throughout their long partnership, Hone gave very clear orders about how his words were to be illustrated. Indeed, he wrote the satires with possible cartoons in mind. Their collaboration took place in the Southampton Arms in Chancery Lane, where Hone, Hazlitt, Cruikshank and other members of the literati would spend afternoons playing with ideas, witticisms and ways of representing royalty and politicians.

But for all Hone and Hazlitt's instruction, the artistic brilliance of Cruikshank surpassed their expectations. In Charles Knight's *Passages of a Working Life* of 1864, the scene in the tavern is described:

Three friends – fellow conspirators, if you like – are snugly ensconced in a private room of a well-accustomed tavern. Hone produces his scheme for 'The House that Jack Built'. He reads some of his doggerel lines. The author wants a design for an idea that is clear enough in words, but is beyond the range of pictorial representation. The artist pooh-poohs . . . 'Wait a moment,' says the artist. The wine – perhaps the grog – is on the table. He dips his fingers in the glass. He rapidly traces wet lines on the mahogany. A simple figure starts into life. Two or three smaller figures come out around the first head and trunk – a likeness in its grotesqueness. The publisher cries 'hurrah'. The looker on is silent after the manifestation of a great power. A pen-and-ink sketch is completed on the spot. The bottle circulates briskly or the rummers are replenished.[22]

W. Carew Hazlitt, the essayist's grandson, recalled: 'It was at the "Southampton" that Mr Hazlitt, Mr Cruikshank and Mr Hone used to meet, and discuss the subject for Hone's next squib.' Hone contorted his face, mimicking the caricatures he wanted and Hazlitt would occasionally make 'what he thought was a salient point for illustration' as well. When Hazlitt found it difficult to convey the image in his head, Cruikshank 'got up, and dipping his finger in his ale-glass, traced something in beer on the table. "Is that what you mean, sir?" he asked, and my grandfather assented.'[23]

Hazlitt's eye for detail, his interest in people's idiosyncrasies, tics and distinctive gestures accounts for his involvement in the production of the satires. He was fascinated by distortion and movement – the essays teem with pictorial allusions and an acute sense of 'projection' and organic change. He was himself a painter, and was fascinated by the visual experience of magic-lantern shows. In his 1819 lecture 'On Wit and Humour', Hazlitt said that the success of the humorist consists in a liminal intensity: that moment of 'transition' from known reality to comic distortion, when the idea strikes 'upon the mind more vividly in its loose unsettled state, and before it has had time to recover and collect itself'. A joke or a point of wit has power for the time it imprisons the imagination, and all depends upon the artist or writer's power to sustain the illusion. Particularly successful at this was William Hogarth, whose works 'fill up the void in the mind'.[24]

Hazlitt's description of the powerful, mysterious operation of humour upon the mind in an article written in 1818 suggests why he took such an interest in Hone and Cruikshank's work in 1819-20:

Brevity is the soul of wit; and of all eloquence a nickname is the most unanswerable. It gives *carte blanche* to the imagination, throws the reins on the neck of passion, and suspends the use of understanding altogether. It does not stand upon ceremony, on the nice distinctions of right and wrong. It does not wait the slow process of reason, or stop to unravel the web of sophistry. It takes every thing for granted that serves the nourishment of the spleen. It is instantaneous in its operation . . .

The popularity of Hone's pamphlets suggested that they had achieved this effect upon the public imagination, creating nicknames and images that haunted the mind and fulfilled Hazlitt's criteria of wit as that which shocks preconceived ideas, the blending of distorted image and reality into a monstrous hybrid. Watching these ideas come to fruition was an experience not to be missed. Cruikshank's virtuoso performances in capturing the absurd, the grotesque, the phantasmagoric from the unsatisfactorily expressed imaginations of others must have seemed like a conjuror's trick, the best show in London.

The images in Hone's satires are of course blunt and explicit, sharing little with the intricate word pictures created by Hazlitt. But the very absence of subtle arts in the pamphlets tapped another of the critic's enduring fascinations. In his essays upon popular culture and the national character, Hazlitt frequently returned to the theme of the English love of malice and confident self-expression; he once said that a typical Englishman understood nothing except 'hard words and hard blows'. Arguments had to be settled with violence; a sharp phrase or quick punch was all that was required to satisfy John Bull's anger or soothe his wounded pride. Hazlitt's lecture 'On Wit and Humour' is pregnant with violent words; the 'triumph', 'humiliation' or 'contempt' of laughter inflicts 'punishment' and 'revenge' upon 'hypocrisy' or 'affectation'; as he said, 'some one is generally sure to be the sufferer by a joke'.[25]

There was no better example of this querulous spirit and defiant contempt than in the pages of Hone's satires. A nickname, Hazlitt wrote, 'is a word and a blow': 'It acts, by mechanical sympathy, on the nerves of society.'[26] Describing the British character in the *Examiner* in 1825, he wrote: 'A nickname is to their moody, splenetic humour a freehold estate, from which they will not be ejected by fair means or foul: they conceive they have a *vested right* in calumny. No matter how base the lie, how senseless the jest, it *tells* – because the public appetite greedily swallows whatever is nauseous and disgusting, and refuses, through weakness or obstinacy, to disgorge it again.'[27]

Hazlitt loved the masculine, boisterous, roustabout aspects of popular culture: bloody boxing matches, Indian jugglers, rope-dancers, striking theatrical performances, the fierce competitive spirit of rackets players. Hone and Cruikshank's satires were similarly combative and arresting. The most popular pieces of journalism at this time, Hazlitt could see their progress from the moment of their creation in the Southampton to their impact upon the popular imagination – 'the nerves of society' – as they disseminated from London throughout the country. This was where the public's conception of statesmen and princes was made and nicknames invented; it was the sating of John Bull's need for malicious reprisal and instinct for levelling laughter. Such were the themes that preoccupied Hazlitt's thinking, so it is little wonder that he sought out his friends at their work. The conversation must have encompassed many of the themes that recur in Hazlitt's writing: the power of visual representation, the science of *caricatura*, the stubborn independence of John Bull and the most effective way of shaming Prince George, Sidmouth, Castlereagh and their miserable followers. There is a tantalising hint of it from Patmore:

It has been my lot during the last fifteen years to associate more or less familiarly with a large proportion of the most intellectual men of an age which perhaps deserves to be characterized as the most intellectual that the world ever knew; and I confess that no part of such intercourse has connected itself with more perfectly pleasant recollections and associations than the three or four evenings that I remember to have spent with Hazlitt and Hone, in the little dingy wainscoted coffee-room of the Southampton Arms, in Southampton Buildings, Chancery Lane.

These must have been the great days of Hone's life, the most popular journalist in the country, spending his days in a pub with Hazlitt coming up with wounding jokes and nicknames – 'the spells and talismans' that would inhabit the imaginations of millions when brought to vivid expression by Cruikshank. The issue of the liberty of the press was still undecided in 1820; the satires were popular and as yet unpunished, but no one knew how or when the government would silence it. Yet Hone had had enough. He was engrossed in what he believed to be the greatest work of his life, his *History of Parody*. He announced in the pages of *The Times* on 14 January 1820 that 'claims of a higher order' meant that *The Man in the Moon* would mark the end of an extraordinary period of publishing history.

CORIOLANUS addressing the PLEBEIANS.

'Coriolanus addressing the Plebeians' by George Cruikshank, January 1820. This is
supposedly a loyalist, pro-King satire, but the extraordinary depiction of George IV as
a muscular hero would strain the faith of even the most ardent royalist. The plebeians
are the reformists and radicals. On the far left are Preston, Watson and Thislewood,
radicals under the banner 'Blood and Plunder'. To their right are Richard Carlile, the
editor of the *Republican*, William Cobbett, and the orator Henry Hunt; below them is
the diminutive figure of Wooler conflated with his 'Black Dwarf'. They stand under
the banner of 'Revolution'. Next come the respectable reformists: Major Cartwright
with the sword of universal suffrage, John Cam Hobhouse with the club of eloquence,
Sir Francis Burdett and Alderman Waithman (arms folded). On the far right, looking
truly heroic, and representing the liberty of the press, is William Hone. The King and
Hone stare at each other eye to eye. The journalist carries the greatest weapons the
press has, the bludgeon of 'Parody'. In Hone's shadow is George Cruikshank with his
bag of caricatures. As so often, the artist subverts 'loyalist' satire by glorifying Hone
and standing with him. This print contains valuable portraits of the leading reformists,
and some of the most important men in Hone's life. As Cruikshank represents him,
Hone is the foremost among them, the symbol of a free press.

The Jeers of the World

Lord Erskine: England is a blackguard country.
Richard Rush (US Envoy): A great country.
Erskine: Yes, a great blackguard country; a boxing, fighting
country, and don't you call that blackguard![1]

I think myself of consequence, I have so many enemies.
William Hone, December 1820[2]

'I was told', Hone remembered of the aftermath of the publication of
the *Political House*, 'that, at the Privy Council, soon after it was published, the Prince laid it on the table without saying a word, and that
after he was gone, some one present said, "We have had enough of
William Hone" – and no notice was taken of it.'[3]

The government and the Regent were deeply worried at the success of
Hone's satires. Another prosecution was inconceivable, and the only
option was to answer him in kind. Various hacks were employed to parody Hone's work, coming up with pale imitations like *The Real or
Constitutional House that Jack Built*: there was a 'swarm of rival
"Houses"', which were markedly inferior to the original in style and the
quality of the drawings. *The Loyal Man in the Moon* was patronisingly
dedicated 'To that Truly venerable, and excellent Character John Bull,
Whose Good Humour is proverbial . . . whose Taste in literary matters, is
not very fastidious; who loves a good joke, though sometimes made at his
own expense; but who will never be laughed out of his loyalty, and common sense . . .' But whilst Hone was selling edition after edition in the hundreds of thousands, so-called 'loyal' publishers 'could scarcely sell a
thousand', as one ruefully conceded. 'Even Cobbett, with his denunciation of borough mongers and bank-directors, was little heeded,' Charles
Knight recalled in 1864. 'The pamphlet buyers rushed to Hone . . .

London, and indeed the whole country, had gone mad.' The government response was an emotional, aesthetic and commercial failure. [4]

Shortly after the publication of *The Man in the Moon*, George III died and the Regent came to the throne. George had always been hated for his hard drinking, heavy gambling and inept political intrigues against his father and William Pitt. His wasteful habits had incurred debts of £630,000 in the 1790s, which the Treasury was obliged to pay with public money. The country disapproved of his immoral social life and extravagant fashions. The Duchess of Devonshire described Prince George as a young rake in the 1780s, 'inclined to be too fat' and looking 'too much like a woman in men's clothes'.[5] George III had been celebrated as the incarnation of John Bull: plain-speaking, simply dressed, frugal and patriotic. In contrast, his heir attracted opprobrium as an effeminate, profligate, debauched fop. Even when he became King, the public never lost its antipathy to him.

But he was hated most for the way he treated his wife. George had agreed to marry his first cousin, Princess Caroline Amelia of Brunswick-Wolfenbuttel, in 1793, on the understanding that this act of commitment to the Hanoverian dynasty would be rewarded with the discharge of his uncontainable debts. Lord Malmesbury, who conducted the young bride to England, realised immediately that the marriage would be a failure. Caroline was twenty-six years old, garrulous, indiscreet and something of a tomboy. The Prince prized sophistication, style and gracefulness in women; Caroline had none of these. As they travelled through France to the English Channel, Malmesbury tried to persuade the Princess to wash, but she evidently did not consider such habits to be an attribute of civilised behaviour.

Upon meeting Caroline, George turned to Malmesbury and asked for brandy to help him get over the shock, before seeking solace with his mother; not a word was exchanged. 'My God!' exclaimed poor Caroline. 'Is the Prince always like this? I think he is very fat, and not at all as good looking as in his portrait.' Caroline was in good form at dinner, chatting away in her informal and unaffected manner, making lewd comments to Lady Jersey, the Prince's mistress. George was horrified. Not only did she want the requirements of his fastidious tastes, but he believed that he had married Maria Fitzherbert years before, 'the wife of my heart and soul', as he tearfully said, although their marriage was illegal under the Royal Marriages Act because George III had not given his consent. At the wedding, 'the Prince was like a man doing a thing in desperation; it was like Macheath going to his execution; and he was quite drunk'. He had to be helped down the aisle, and throughout the ceremony he stared at Lady Jersey. When the Archbishop asked if there were any lawful impediments to the marriage, he seemed close to tears. He left with his new wife in stony silence. Later that night, after more drinks, the young bride watched her husband collapse into the fireplace, and pass out.[6]

The Prince found his wife, in his own words, 'filthy' and 'disgusting'; he detected an 'appearance of *evil* in her' when she showed no signs of being a 'novice' in bed. She even complimented him on his natural endowments: how, the Prince asked, could she possibly have any idea of relative size if she was a virgin? The rumours that she had had an affair with a commoner in her homeland seemed to be correct. And if George found his new wife earthy and nowhere near his standards of feminine charm, she was equally unimpressed. In the 1800s Caroline would have affairs with the likes of Admiral Sir Sidney Smith, the painter Sir Thomas Lawrence and George Canning – intelligent and successful men. Her husband fell short of her expectations of manly behaviour: 'He understands how a shoe should be made, or a coat cut, or a dinner dressed and would make an excellent hairdresser but nothing else.'[7]

Within nine months of the honeymoon, Caroline had given birth to their daughter Charlotte, but it was public knowledge that the Prince of Wales had left his wife. Their separation was not formal at first, and Caroline continued to live in Carlton House. He went back to Mrs Fitzherebert in 1800, and Caroline lived a bohemian and enjoyable life in Blackheath. In 1806 George persuaded the Fox–Grenville coalition government to begin a 'Delicate Investigation' into Caroline's private life to find out whether she had given birth to an illegitimate son (a matter of constitutional importance) and to see if there was enough evidence of her adulteries to arrange a divorce. The secret cabinet committee exonerated her of producing a bastard, but were prepared to believe that she had committed adultery, a treasonable offence. The collapse of the Talents ministry in 1807 ended the Prince's hopes of a divorce; the new cabinet under Spencer Perceval dismissed the evidence, and recommended that Caroline be given apartments at court. George was disgusted at the government's support for his wife. Caroline travelled to Italy and the Middle East during the Regency, where her husband believed she was disgracing herself with more men. She was 'the bane and curse of my existence' he railed; she was 'characterised by a flagrancy of abandonment unparalleled in the history of women, and stamped with disgrace and dishonour'. In 1818 he sent a deputation of legal advisers to Italy (the so-called Milan Commission) to find evidence of her misdeeds and depravity. All they could find was unreliable scandal from profit-hungry gossip retailers.

In 1820 Caroline returned to England as Queen. This was her chance to recover her reputation, restore her finances and embarrass her husband. George IV was incensed. He was advised to bribe Caroline to stay out of the country, but would not listen to reason, believing that the courts would have to bow to his wishes as King and grant the blessed relief of divorce. However, he could not go to the ecclesiastical courts because under the rule of 'recrimination' a petitioner citing adultery could not be granted a divorce if he or she had committed adultery as well. George had to instruct his government to pass a Bill of Pains and Penalties to dissolve the marriage and withhold from Caroline all royal privileges.

Caroline had always been popular in Britain, and when she arrived in London, in June, 'The road was thronged with an immense multitude the whole way from Westminster Bridge to Greenwich. Carriages, carts, and horsemen followed, preceded, and surrounded the coach the whole way. She was everywhere received with the greatest enthusiasm. Women waved handkerchiefs, and men shouted wherever she passed.' Over the next few months the country would be engrossed with the divorce proceedings. The King's case rested on the evidence of the Milan Commission, which provided ample proof that when she was in Italy Caroline had been engaged in an open affair with her *major domo* Bartlommeo Pergami (or Bartholomew Bergami, as he was known in Britain). 'No one here has the smallest doubt about the Queen and Bergami,' Byron wrote to Hobhouse from Italy. 'It was as public as such a thing could be.' But, in the words of William Cobbett, the British people 'as far as related to the question of guilt and innocence . . . cared not a straw'. [8]

The hypocrisy of George IV, a bigamist who lived openly with his mistresses, became the defining issue of the whole affair. Although there was no dispute that George had been forced to marry a woman he could never be happy with, few in the country, even his ministers, could condone his vindictive behaviour. The Bill of Pain and Penalties did not allow Caroline's lawyers (the Whig MPs Henry Brougham and Thomas Denman) to cite the King's numerous infidelities. The public was incensed that George was using his unfair advantage to deprive his wife of the justice permitted every other subject under the laws of the land. As the courtier Lady Charlotte Bury wrote, the vocal support of the people was 'a noble proof that the English people *en masse* are a disinterested race, and fear not to espouse the cause of the oppressed, or take the weaker side against the strong and powerful'.[9] Queen Caroline's private life would be exposed to public view, whilst the details of her husband's squalid sex life would be immune from the legal and moral principle of 'recrimination'.

It was an instance of glaring injustice that stank in the nostrils of a majority of Britons, whatever their political principles. There were violent demonstrations throughout the country against the King and the government; wherever the Queen went, she met enormous crowds of supporters. Although she was 'a short, very fat elderly woman with an extremely red face' who was undoubtedly guilty of many of the adulteries alleged in the Bill of Pains and Penalties, the press depicted Caroline as a beautiful and innocent woman who was fighting a debauched old King and his corrupted government. The volume of pro- and anti-Caroline books, pamphlets, ballads, poems and prints was staggering. No other political issue in living memory had inspired such bitterness and division in the country. The reformists manipulated the case into a straightforward battle between justice and the corrupt state. Caroline had to take on the power of the monarchy, a subservient parliament and biased courts. She was emblematic of the struggle for reform. The Queen was not displeased with such a role; as Canning said, she was born with the spirit of opposition.

The country was deluged with commentary and satire from the London press throughout the divorce trial in the House of Lords. The press explored the evidence, and came to differing conclusions; political journalists looked at the implications for the constitution; the satirists venerated or libelled the leading characters according to political prejudice. The array of books and caricatures was astounding; the case was a national obsession.

It was, of course, a perfect opportunity for another satirical book by Hone and Cruikshank. On 20 August 1820, the *Examiner* announced: 'Another of Mr Hone's happy illustrations of public feeling has just appeared called *The Queen's Matrimonial Ladder, a National Toy* . . . We wish to heaven, the government would be as droll at as cheap a rate.'[10]

Hone wrote *The Queen's Matrimonial Ladder*, he claimed, at the behest of Queen Caroline herself. He was researching his *History of Parody* in the Reading Room of the British Museum, when he was approached by some of her 'chief partisans'. 'They urged me to write something for her,' Hone remembered. 'I refused for some time, till at last they said, "The Queen expects it of you"; and I felt I could no longer refuse . . .' This is not implausible. Hone knew both the Reverend Samuel Parr, the Queen's chaplain, and Alderman Matthew Wood, her host in London. Later he would have the chance to meet her.

Hone wrote that when he left the Reading Room, 'Instead of going straight home, I wandered off towards Pentonville, and stopped and looked absently into the window of a little fancy shop. There was a toy, "The Matrimonial Ladder". I saw at once what I could do with it, and went home and wrote "The Queen's Matrimonial Ladder".'[11]

The original toy instructed children in the perfection of marriage, showing a lifetime's progress of idealised conjugal bliss. This was a common pedagogical and advertising form. At this time there was an advertisement for the lottery showing the ascent of a family from the lowest rung of the ladder, the 'Desperation' of poverty, to 'Accumulation' after the wise purchase of a lottery ticket. Hone's pamphlet included a plasterboard ladder which could be glued together to make a toy stepladder, each rung, like the lottery puff and the toy, labelled with a word ending '-ation'. But unlike the original children's

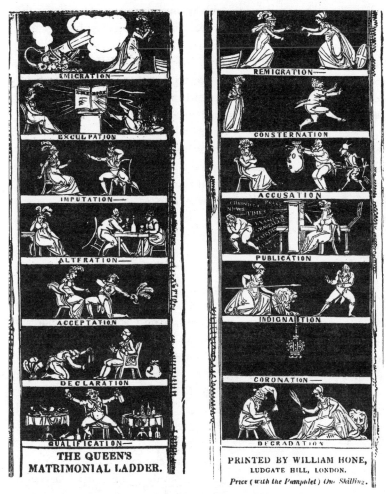

'The Toy Ladder'
Printed on plasterboard so that readers
could assemble the stepladder.

toy and the advertisement, *The Queen's Matrimonial Ladder* goes
down as well as up. The first step, the 'Qualification' for the royal wedding, is George's debt; the marriage is founded on nothing more than
the Prince's profligacy. George climbs the ladder, from the 'Imputation'

against Caroline during the Delicate Investigation, the temporary set-back of 'Exculpation', when Spencer Perceval's defence of the Princess was published, to his eventual triumph, the 'Emigration' of his wife (she is expelled with a blast from 'the Regent's Bomb') – this is the apex of his ladder. However, the route to the bottom of the ladder is marked by his desperate 'Accusation' and the 'Publication' of the details of his sordid life, the 'Indignation' of his subjects, and finally 'Degradation'.

A representation of the toy ladder is depicted in the frontispiece of the book. The Queen sits atop it, *her* apex labelled 'Remigration', the turning point in the King's fortunes when his wife came home and the public rallied to her. The rung of 'Coronation' breaks under his weight, and he lies at the foot, convulsed with the agony and shame of 'Degradation'.

'Qualification'

Every page in the pamphlet describes in verse and illustrates the rungs of the ladder. In the first image, 'Qualification', Cruikshank shows George before his marriage wracked with the searing pain of a hangover. It is Cruikshank's homage to James Gillray's masterpiece, his 1792 caricature portrait of the Prince entitled *A Voluptuary under the horrors of Digestion*.

It is one of the finest examples of Cruikshank's work for Hone, and shows why the satires were considered art as much as political propaganda. In 1823 John Gibson Lockhart (Walter Scott's son-in-law, contributor to the *Quarterly Review* and *Blackwood's*) wondered why a great talent was wasted on mere satire when it could enrich high art: 'Cruikshank may, if he please, be a second Gillray; but . . . this should not be his ambition. He is fitted for a higher walk.'

The caricature is rich in emblems and illusions recognisable from the eighteenth-century satiric tradition. The guttering candles and the bonnet, abandoned by a long-departed and already forgotten female companion, mirror the wretched isolation and melancholy that the artist captures in the Prince's face and posture. He is not languid in the way that Charles II – the Merry Monarch whom George wished to emulate – managed with his decadent court of wits and beauties; the present King is bloated to the point of agonising pain, and youthful *joie de vivre* is extinguished with the flickering candles. The broken wine glass, suggestively placed, hints at impotence – alcohol-induced impotence at that. It contrasts with the scenes of saturnalian debauch depicted on the screen: Silenus rides an ass, and women worship the image of a satyr. But lest the viewer is seduced into believing in the King's virility, the discarded satyr's mask tells us that George's boasts of sexual conquest are part of a sad farce. And with the death of youth and sexual potency and the burden of financial debt comes the last throw, literally it would seem from the playing cards and dice, which have been flung away. The portrait purports to represent the King in the 1790s, when debts and disgrace compelled the feckless gambler to the last resort, Holy Matrimony. But this is the image of the 'Dandy at Sixty' in 1820, not a young and hopeful Prince of Wales.

The power of animation achieved in *The Queen's Ladder* conjures up wonderful images of Hone and Hazlitt in the Southampton contorting their faces and bodies into models for Cruikshank. But the skill of the artist goes far beyond merely depicting a facial expression acted out by his publisher; his characters live, breathe and move off the page. That power of visual expression is shown at its height in 'Qualification'.

The Queen's Ladder outsold even *The Political House*; it was the highest-selling publication during the divorce trial. It first appeared on 15 August, and by the end of the week it had run to twelve printings. According to Hone's advertisement, it was 'The most extensively embellished, and most rapidly selling production ever issued from the press.' Once again, there was a 'blockade of people' in front of the Hone residence in Ludgate Hill eager to read it. This devastating caricature of George IV haunted the public imagination as the image of the persecutor of poor Caroline.

The satire is the *Marriage à la Mode* of the early nineteenth century. Each page charts a different stage in the farce. In the early stages, George is triumphant. Whilst Caroline is left to suckle their daughter Charlotte, the Prince dallies with his harem. He humiliates his wife during the Delicate Inquiry and the publication of his evidence against her; during the Regency, Caroline is forced to leave her daughter and flee the country – she was in exile when Charlotte died in 1817. The early depictions of *The Queen's Ladder* show George triumphant and powerful, and his wife utterly ruined. But when she returns as Queen in 1820, the apex of the ladder, the Regent is made to suffer. When he comes dressed as Guy

'Indignation'
'I am wrapped in dismal thinkings! –'
The King, in *All's well that ends well.*

Fawkes to blow up the Queen with his accusations, the beam of light from the all-seeing eye of the press reveals his criminal act to the world. And 'Publication' inevitably leads to 'Indignation'; the lion of British public opinion awakes and treads on the bag holding the evidence found by the Milan Commission – it contains nothing more substantial than smoke.

The marriage culminates with George's 'Degradation'. The power of the press and his subjects' revulsion has exposed the King as a hypocrite and manipulator of justice. In the end, a fatally crippled George is carted off to the knacker's yard by a seedy and rather mature Cupid, who cries out in the manner of a cheap butcher, 'Cat's meat,' as coronet-wearing cats, hungry for the last pickings of royal profligacy, gather round in expectation.

The Queen's Matrimonial Ladder puts the King himself on trial – but not before the court of venal hirelings and placemen that was to judge Caroline in the Lords. Even before the Bill of Pains and Penalties, the King had been reduced to a figure of scorn and hatred by the press and the people. The satire is not about the marriage or the trial, but about the power of public opinion. The rung of the ladder that is conspicuously absent should have the most appropriate word ending '-ation'. It is, however, taken for granted that the press has achieved the 'Recrimination' denied the Queen by parliamentary justice.

'Cat's Meat!' – *English Cry*

The Lords might swallow the legal nostrum that 'The King can do no wrong', but George IV has been judged by his subjects. Whatever punishment the King can inflict on his wife is nothing compared to 'A mockery that shall never die: The curses of hate and the hisses of scorn'. The power of laughter levels the greatest men in the state however much they try to insulate themselves from the public voice; it is the most fundamental freedom and effective weapon for the disenfranchised. No king can shield himself from 'The laughter of triumph, the jeers of the world'.[12]

Hone's next work was rushed out in response to a particular incident that occurred in the opening weeks of the trial, its hurried expediency evident from the fact that Cruikshank had only enough time for three woodcuts. *Non Mi Ricordo* was a direct attack on the Crown's interference with the evidence of a royal butler during the trial. Teodoro Majocchi was the Crown's key witness, affirming that he had seen Caroline enter Pergami's bedroom, that they had held hands in public, and that the count would 'assist' the Queen when she had a bath. It was devastating for Caroline's case, and during the evidence she could be heard murmuring from her seat, 'Ah, Theodore,' and, throwing her head back, she 'put both her arms akimbo, and looked at him for some time with a countenance which those who saw it said was quite terrific'.

However, Brougham's cross-examination utterly destroyed the butler. Majocchi answered with confidence and clarity all the Attorney-General's questions about the sordid particulars of the Queen's life. But when Brougham asked about minor details of Caroline's household and routine, the butler could only answer *'Non mi ricordo'* – 'I can't remember.' Brougham made him repeat *'Non mi ricordo'* and similar equivocations over two hundred times during his cross-examinations. It was clear that Majocchi had been carefully rehearsed to damn his former mistress by the King's allies. They had forgotten, however, to drill him in details of the more mundane points; his credibility was thus atomised by the Queen's lawyers.

In Hone's *Non Mi Ricordo* the fantasy of recrimination is acted out. The frontispiece shows the King standing at the bar of the House of Lords, where witnesses were examined during the Queen's trial.

George is given the curly black hair of Majocchi, and the bar is transformed into a grill under which he is sweating. Hone turned the King into a witness in the trial, emphasising the close relationship between the Crown and its evidence. The cross-examination of the King reveals the evasions and selective memory of, not just the pawn Majocchi, but the hypocritical state:

> 'Are you married?' – 'More yes than no.'*
> 'Do you live with your wife?' – 'No.'
> 'Why did you marry?' – 'To pay my debts.'
> 'Then why did you part?' – 'Because my debts were paid.'
> ... 'In what light do you consider your oath at the marriage ceremony?' – 'A ceremony.'
> ... 'How much money has been expended on you since you were born?' – *'Non mi ricordo.'*
> 'What have you done for it in return?' – 'More less than more.'
> ... 'How many Wives does *your* Church allow you?' – *'Non mi ricordo.'*
> 'How many have you had since you separated from your own?' – *'Non mi ricordo.'*
> 'Are you a member of the Society for the Suppression of Vice?' – 'Yes' (*with great energy*).
> 'How many bottles a day do you drink?' – *'Non mi ricordo.'*
> 'Do you drink six bottles?' – *'Non mi ricordo.'*
> 'Five Bottles?' – *'Non mi ricordo.'*
> 'How many nights in the week do you go to bed sober?' – *'Non mi ricordo.'*
> 'After Dressing, Drinking, and Dreaming, what time remains for thinking?' – *'Non mi ricordo.'*

At the end of the book Hone included a wanted notice:

---

* This and the following similar answers parody the unusual expressions used by the government's interpreters during the trial. For example, they translated Majocchi as saying: 'Whenever I am on board a ship, I am more unwell than well,' rather than the more accurate translation that he was 'always or almost always sick while on board ship'. The oddities of the translators led many to doubt the veracity of the evidence. Majocchi also answered 'Yes or no' to one question.

Strayed and Missing. An infirm elderly gentleman in a Public Office . . . He is very deaf and very obstinate, and cannot bear to be looked at or spoken to. It is supposed that he has been seduced and carried off by some artful female . . . He is so fond of tailoring, that he lately began a suit that will take him his life to complete. He delights in playing at soldiers, supposes himself a cavalry officer, and makes speeches that others write for him, in a field marshal's uniform . . . If this should meet his eye, it is earnestly requested that he will return to his duty, and he will be kindly received and no questions asked.

Hone and Cruikshank's satire may seem like merely amusing marginalia to the divorce crisis, serving no other purpose than clever illustrations of public opinion. But Hone adopted this mode of expression because he knew it was the most effective means of achieving his journalistic aims. It was no boast that the collective laughter of a nation inflicted the appropriate revenge. The *Loyalists' Magazine*, a periodical launched during the Queen's trial in an attempt to counter the reformist press, fumed:

There never existed a parallel, in the memory of the present age, of such gross abuse and ridicule, such malicious falsehood, as have been mercilessly heaped upon the King by the Radical Press. It is dishonourable to the English character; it is a disgrace to the nation to have borne with it so long. It is not *mere joke!* it is not a question of mere politics! but a *vital question* – whether infidelity or truth, whether revolution or the British Constitution shall triumph?[13]

If the satires had been brushed off with levity or contempt, or simply ignored, by the King and the government, they would have been nothing more than footnotes to the events of 1820. But George was famously susceptible to mockery, and everyone knew it. The Duke of Wellington said that laughter was the only thing the King really feared: 'He cannot bear the company of clever men, for fear of ridicule; he cannot bear to show himself in public, because he is afraid of the jokes that may be cut on his person.'[14] At high points of dissatisfaction he would avoid the excesses of the London press, retiring to the country or his yacht so that he might not see his traduced image and hear the laughter. When forced to London, he would often travel in a coach with Wellington, hoping that the lustre of the field marshal would deter the laughter of the crowd. Cobbett wrote in 1820: 'The gentleman does not dare show himself in London, or indeed, anywhere else . . . He kept himself cooped up in Windsor Forest for nearly two months, and then, all of a sudden we heard of his going on board of ship at Brighton (at which place he was terribly hissed) and out to sea . . . It is a rather melancholy thing to see a King playing at hide and seek in this way.'

The thousands of satires hawked around the country wounded him far more than any other form of criticism; it was personally painful, but also, he believed, a slight to the dignity of the Crown that he was bound by duty to maintain. Every week in the *Examiner* and *The Times*, Hone kept the public informed of the amazing sales of his satires. It was a taunt to the King and his supporters that the images in *The Queen's Ladder* and *Non Mi Ricordo* had captured the public imagination. No other publisher charted the sales of their publications, and Hone did it to humiliate the King. In January 1821 George wrote to Lord Chancellor Eldon: 'As the courts of law will now open within a few days, I am desirous to know the decision that has been taken by the Attorney-General upon the mode in which all the vendors of treason, and libels . . . are to be prosecuted. This is a measure so vitally indispensable to my feelings, as well as to the country, that I must insist that no *further* loss of time should be suffered to elapse before proceedings be instituted.' He continued that satire was foremost in 'those evils of the magnitude of which there can be but one opinion'.

But there was nothing the law officers could do to halt the onslaught of satire. The King had to resort to increasingly desperate measures. When Hone was preparing *The Queen's Matrimonial Ladder*, an important man, whom Hone would never name, visited him and offered £50 if the satire never came out. 'I refused', Hone said, 'and was offered up to £500.' He was right to decline the first offer; the satire would bring in much more when it sold in tens or hundreds of thousands. But £500 was a different matter, close to the kind of profit that Hone and Cruikshank may have made. 'Could you make it £5,000?' Hone asked his visitor. 'Even if you did, I should refuse it.'[15]

According to the accounts in the Royal Archives, George spent £2,600 suppressing prints and articles between 1820 and 1821. The man who visited Hone was undoubtedly Major General Sir Benjamin Bloomfield, Keeper of the Privy Purse and George's private secretary until 1822, who

'The Funeral Pile.' By George Cruikshank, August 1820.

The Tory view of Hone: from the *Loyalists' Magazine*. The reformists have befriended the Queen, and lured her to ascend Hone's 'Radical Ladder' to the peak of the constitutional pillar to seize the crown. As soon as she has served her purpose, she is blindfolded with the Cap of Liberty (a fool's cap), the ladder is withdrawn, and the radicals pull down the pillar; Thomas Wooler – represented as 'the Black Dwarf' – fans the flames of a funeral pyre. Hone looks on in triumph from the top of his famous ladder. But whilst the radicals are depicted as baboon-like creatures, Cruikshank barely caricatures his friend. His political sympathies are not disguised; the artist sides with Hone, and they are together on the ladder.

was sent to induce publishers to sell the plates and copyright of their scurrilous designs. He bribed George Cruikshank with £100 'in consideration of a pledge not to caricature his Majesty in any immoral situation'.[16] The artists gratefully took the money, and continued to satirise George in Hone's books – the images may not have been 'immoral', but their offensive intent cannot be denied. It is a testament to the power of satire at this time that the King himself was prepared to spend so much money on vain endeavours to stem the tide of satire. *The Queen's Ladder* was considered the worst of satires, worth £500 compared to the going rate of between £30 and £100. It was not even seen as innocuous humour, but nothing less serious than 'a preliminary step towards . . . the *last great effort of Rebellion and Infidelity*'.[17]

The *Examiner* believed that the only way of dealing with such an obviously farcical and indefensible case as the Bill of Pains and Penalties was to dismiss it with appropriate derision. British journalists, it said, dignified the King's cause by taking it seriously and debating the constitutional implications. However, their counterparts in the United States treated it with the contempt it deserved: they 'talk of our most religious and gracious King as they would . . . "of a man brought up to a police office for beating his wife!" And the cold-blooded levellers state the various parts of the "case", without any more feeling of the necessity of comment than the English police-reporters would have regard to any low infamy!'[18]

The *Examiner* had nothing but praise for one British journalist, however, the only writer and publisher who adequately reflected the public's incomprehension at the pantomime under way in the House of Lords and found a way of inflicting punishment. 'Mr Hone has served up another relishing dish to the public in the shape of a skit entitled *Non Mi Ricordo*. The present State mockery is the best subject in the world for these laughable satires; and indeed we believe after all they were more effective popular weapons than grave argument.'[19]

Lord Liverpool said privately that the government was 'in a sea of troubles, and God only knows how we are going to get out of them'. In November, when the Bill concluded its third reading with a majority of nine, he stood up to tell their lordships: 'I think it proper to move, that

this Bill be not read now, but be read this day six months,' the polite way
of informing parliament that a bill had been dropped. The press had so
roused the country that any possibility of sending the bill down to the
lower house was unthinkable. It was an unequivocal victory for public
opinion over the wishes of the monarch and the will of a government
previously so hostile to free opinion. Liverpool 'rose and abandoned all
further prosecution of the bill, declaring that he did so on the double
ground of the smallness of the majority, and the strongly expressed
sense of the country against the measure'. When asked why the government had retreated from its victory, Wellington replied 'that the King

'The laughter of triumph, the jeers of the world'
'Consternation', from *The Queen's Matrimonial Ladder*. Even 'Doctor' Sidmouth,
cannot revive the King with 'Essence of Bergami' (administered from a clyster pipe)
from the shock of Caroline's return, the exposure of his own infidelities, and the
laughter of his subjects. The disk hanging above his head is 2/6 – or half-a-crown;
the Queen's appearance and the King's consternation complements the scene on the
tapestry, which depicts a lioness chasing away a braying ass and a herd of stags.
Here, George suffers the mortifying effects of the laughter of his subjects.

was degraded as low as he could be already'.[20]

Richard Rush, President Monroe's ambassador to the Court of St James, detected something of American democracy in the government's decision: 'The Ministry showed great wisdom in surrendering their measure as an offering to public feeling, though they had carried the bill.'[21] Upon hearing the news the country broke into spontaneous rejoicing. Church bells pealed out across the land, bonfires were lit, guns fired, and a mob rampaged through London in time-honoured fashion. The King was incensed; his ministers had obeyed the voice of the people above the commands of the Crown; his royal prerogative was in tatters.

Whose victory was it? For poor Caroline it was but a hollow success. Her reputation had been dragged through the mud when her former loyal servants queued up to give evidence in the Lords that she was a debauched old woman who preferred romping around Italy with young fops to doing her royal duty. When her friends rushed to tell her that the divorce had been abandoned she burst into tears; she had not been acquitted; the government had acted for political motives, not on a matter of right. Many of the lords who voted against the bill did so declaring their belief in the Queen's guilt.

The self-proclaimed winner was the press. When news of the abandonment of the bill became known, Londoners illuminated their windows with candles, as was customary at times of high excitement and celebration. 'London was illuminated, more or less, for three successive nights, under edicts put forth by popular feeling, at the overthrow of the bill,' wrote Rush. 'The streets, the theatres, the highways, gave testimony of the popular joy at the Queen's triumph.'[22] Hone's illumination was one of the most elaborate. Cruikshank painted a transparency, thirteen feet wide by seven feet six inches high, in which Truth reclines on a printing press holding a cap of liberty in one hand, and a portrait of the Queen in the other; the light of truth that emanates from the press scatters the ghoulish figures of the government, who flee into the darkness of night; a Slop Pail (the name Hone gave to the *New Times*, the newspaper Dr Stoddart started after his dismission from *The Times* in 1817) empties its fetid muck into a cast-off crown. The only reference to King George is two ridiculous boots sticking up into the air, labelled with the motto *Honi soit qui mal y pense* – 'Evil to him who evil thinks.'

Above the poster were 1,037 lamps spelling 'Triumph of the Press' and 'Knowledge is Power'. This garish illumination was put up to celebrate the 'Victory obtained by the Press for the Liberties of the People', and appeared again so that the Queen could see it when she went to St Paul's Cathedral to attend a service of thanksgiving.

The triumphalism seemed to be justified. The venom of the press was unprecedented; Sidmouth's 'Gagging Act' of just a few months before was not working. Richard Rush wrote:

That which was perhaps most remarkable throughout the fierce encounter was the boundless range of the Press and liberty of speech. Every day produced its thousand fiery libels against the King and his adherents; and caricatures under the worst forms were hawked about all the streets . . . This tempest of abuse, incessantly directed against the King and all who stood by him, was borne for several months, without the slightest attempt to punish or check it. It may be said to have raged by the permission of the government . . . [23]

The connexion that Hone and many other journalists made between the Queen and the freedom of the press was at all times explicit. Yet Hone was involved with the Queen at a personal level as well. He led a deputation of 138 journalists, printers and compositors to Caroline, and presented 'The Printers' Address to the Queen', signed by 1,345 'letter press printers of London and its environs'. In it, the journalists told the Queen and the country:

In future times, should the page of History record the present era as one in which overwhelming Power combined with Senatorial Venality to crush an unprotected Female, we trust it will also preserve the gratifying remembrance, that the base Conspiracy was defeated by the irresistible force of Public Opinion, directed and displayed through the powerful medium of a Free, Uncorrupted, and Incorruptible British Press.

The Queen replied in like manner: 'The Press is at present the only strong hold that Liberty has left. If we lose this, we lose all. We have no other rampart against an implacable foe.'

Hone got the chance to meet and talk with her at length. He was pleased to hear that she had read his work, and found her a 'frank, open-hearted, unsuspicious woman'. He appears to have been half in love with the woman that he had spent so much of the recent months defending and celebrating. Hone was obviously star-struck, but at the same time he seems to have seen something of himself reflected in the Queen: 'She is shrewd, witty, sarcastic and gay, and so disloyal as to speak what she thinks,' he wrote in a private letter. Her humour was indeed noted. The satirist would appreciate her reply to someone who offered to bring her dinner during a late sitting of the Lords: she would prefer to 'take a chop at the King's Head'. When he met her, Hone found Caroline to be everything he could possibly have hoped. [24]

Hazlitt was shocked that 'the wives and daughters of popular caricaturists' should demonstrate 'that *hankering* after rank and power, which appeared to me to be the base part of human nature'; or, as Lord Holland put it, should display their 'childish love of Royalty'. 'Here were all the patriots and Jacobins of London and Westminster going to pay their homage to the Queen, and ready to worship the very rags of royalty', sneered Hazlitt. '. . . No matter what else she was (whether her case was right or wrong) – it was the mock equality with sovereign rank, the acting in a farce of state, that was the secret charm. That was what drove them mad . . . We in modern times have got from the *dead* to the *living* idol, and bow to hereditary imbecility. The less of genius and virtue, the greater our self complacency.' Even the most contemptuous and iconoclastic of journalists was prepared to play the courtier and become dewy-eyed at the splendour of majesty. [25]

Hazlitt would have been right had the attack on the King been intended as a campaign against the monarchy. But Hone was no republican. The 'Strayed and Missing' notice in *Non Mi Ricordo* earnestly requests the return of a foolish old man so that he might have another chance to occupy the throne with requisite dignity. In *The Queen's Ladder* the public begs George, 'Spurn thy minions – the traitors, who counsel thee banish': the King's troubles stem from his Tory ministers. Thomas Dolby, one of Hone's more successful imitators, treated the Bill of Pain and Penalties as a temporary 'eclipse' of the lustrous rays of monarchy. A parody of the National Anthem in one of his satires captures the general opinion that the Crown will survive the abuses of a single man:

> May one his sceptre sway,
> When he is gone away,

Who'll give us CAUSE to say,
God Save the King.[26]

The Queen was only celebrated when she was the victim of the King's rage. When Liverpool dropped the bill, the interest in Caroline faded away, and by the time of George IV's coronation, in June 1821, the monarchy and the government had regained much of its popularity. Hone's interest in her was confined to the way in which her case affected the relationship between the state and public opinion. There is little to suggest that he was interested in the veracity of the Queen's case. She was only useful to the press as an emblem of the reformist cause; there were few who were prepared to vindicate her dubious claims of injured innocence. When the King was defeated, she ceased to be useful. Few found in this 'plump and coarse' woman the glamour of royalty. People like Hone attended her court-in-exile not because they were besotted with monarchy but to amplify the King's unpopularity and show that, for all the calumny imputed to her, many still regarded her as their true Queen.

In January 1821 Hone published a new satire, *The Political Showman – At Home!* In it, Caroline is no longer the wronged woman fighting the cruel state, but a symbol of the power of the press. The satire shows a printing press anthropomorphised as a circus ringmaster conducting the public through his menagerie of wild animals – the cabinet, Crown lawyers, sundry borough-mongers and members of the royal family. It was celebration of the victory the press had achieved in throwing out the case against the Queen. The ministers, once ferocious wild animals, have been 'tamed' by the press. Hone wrote: '[*The Political Showman*] cost me more labour, and was less popular, than either [*sic*] of my other pieces.'[27] Unlike *The Political House* or *The Queen's Ladder*, this satire did not aim to shock or shame; its punning and whimsical humour contrasted with the bitter reproaches and emotional impact that sustained Hone's journalism during the Peterloo and divorce crises. He had been provoked to attack his enemies with satirical excess; but the anger that gave rise to the campaign abated when the King's bill was withdrawn.

In 1820 a woman entered Hone's shop to buy *The Political House that Jack Built*. She looked up, and saw its author behind the counter.

'Why, indeed, sir, I did not suppose I should *see* you – and I did not expect – (*embarrassed*) – That is, I thought – I expected – I – I –'

'Allow me, madam, to conclude: you expected I had horns and hoofs and a forked tail, and spouted fire?'[28]

When William Hazlitt was in Italy, in 1825, 'the people lifted up their hands when they were shown the caricatures in the "Queen's Matrimonial Ladder", and asked if they were really the likeness of the King?'[29]

The satires had their desired effect; many in the conservative press asked whether censorship could possibly exist if Hone and his fellow satirists' vile libels could go unpunished. The rancour they sparked is evident from a spat in the press in 1821–2 when, William Gifford, editor of the Tory *Quarterly Review*, compared Leigh Hunt, William Hazlitt and William Hone, for him the fuglemen of sedition, to three asses. The *Examiner*'s reply to Gifford reveals some of the impact that Hone's satires had upon the government and the public in the preceding years:

As Messrs. Hone, Hunt, and Hazlitt, are fortunately not at all deficient in the means of reply, the writer of this article has no intention to attempt to do that for themselves; yet there are one or two matters he chooses to strike upon, which may chance to throw out a little light upon Mr Gifford's gloomy endeavour at pleasantry.

And first of Ass The First, Wm Hone – he assuredly must be allowed to be a very singular specimen of this race, partaking little of the dull, submissive, bearing-burthen character of the long-eared tribe, or he never could have caused by his movements such a hubbub and alarm among all the reverend and irreverend orthodox animals in Church and State. He most certainly cannot be of the patient and half starved breed of English asses, but must rather be able to boast of his sprightly and vigorous Spanish blood; or perhaps, which is still more likely, he may be one of the Zebra or 'Queen's ass' tribe, – a wild and hitherto untameable race, as we all know. If these suppositions will not satisfy the inquiring naturalist, he may consult some of the hundred thousand purchasers of the *House that Jack Built*, the *Matrimonial Ladder* and the *Slap at Slop*, who may possibly be able to decide upon the breed and merits of this frolicsome, high mettled, independent, and not to be ridden beast.[30]

Hone achieved enormous fame with his satires. They were an international sensation. For some he was a hero who had mocked the divorce trial out of the House of Lords; for others he personified sedition as a kind of devil. All were agreed that he had influenced the minds of the nation with his unprecedented sales of political invective. The description of the nervous customer shows that the satires fascinated royalists and conservatives as much as the government's enemies. Their devastating ability to capture the public mind is evident from the ways in which people remembered them in succeeding decades

Hone's works left an indelible mark on the consciousness of his contemporaries as few other pieces of journalism have ever done. In the 1840s, William Makepeace Thackeray argued that Hone and Cruikshank had *forced* people to believe that Caroline was 'the most spotless, pure-mannered darling of a princess that ever married a heartless debauchee of a Prince Royal' by the incalculable force of their satire. A whole generation had engrafted on their minds an indelible image of 'the atrocious Castlereagh, the sainted Caroline (in a tight pelisse, with feathers in her hair), the "Dandy of Sixty", who used to glance at us from Hone's friendly windows . . . How we came to believe them!'[31]

A few years later, in 1847, the scholar Dr Robert Shelton Mackenzie wrote an article for the *London Journal* agreeing that people had come to believe the image. He cast his mind back to 1819 and 1820, in an attempt to explain the mysterious power that Hone and Cruikshank had wielded over the country. Mackenzie told his readers: 'We have not seen . . . [the satires] since, but we have a vivid recollection of every one of them.' It was not a critical or historical survey of the works, but an exploration of how memories persisted over time. 'The present generation, examining these things, might wonder at the effect they had upon the public mind; but we can tell them that thousands and ten thousands recollect that the effect was extraordinary. There was a rush and a crush to get them. Edition after edition went off like wildfire. Of some, as many as a quarter of a million were sold.'

The satires achieved legendary status in the nineteenth century long after the circumstances that inspired them faded, because people recalled the way they had infested people's imagination. As late as the 1870s they were still remembered as 'acrid, pitilessly logical and fiercely sarcastic' and the 'severest stings the government had to endure'.[32] If Hone and Cruikshank aimed to destroy the King's reputation for ever, they succeeded. It became impossible to imagine him in any other way than the wounding caricature the two men invented. Dr Mackenzie stressed the universal laughter in Britain at the time: 'It was impossible for any one to avoid laughing at these publications.' And if subsequent generations wondered why, it was because the two satirists had made it impossible to disconnect image from reality: 'Never before nor since was royalty made so ridiculous. The towering wig, the false whiskers, the padded garments, the enormous bulk, the affectation of juvenility by "the dandy of sixty" were all inimitable and not to be mistaken.'[33]

When William Thackeray came to write the history of the four King Georges, he found that he couldn't remember anything about the last except the satirical image: 'But this George, what was he? I look through all his life, and recognise but a bow and a grin. I try and take him to pieces, and find silk stockings, padding, stays, a coat with frogs and a fur collar, a star and blue ribbon, a pocket-handkerchief prodigiously scented . . . and a huge black stock, underwaistcoats, and more underwaistcoats, and then nothing.'[34]

And then nothing. The real George receded, to be replaced by a vacuous yet dangerous clothes horse designed by Hone and Cruikshank: the 'Dandy at Sixty'. Rightly or not, this was all that was left of him. The caricature was thus more expressive and durable than a portrait or a piece of journalism. Indeed, throughout the century the satires entered the mythology of Regency England. Their importance was magnified even beyond the power they actually had; one writer at the end of the century asserted that *The Queen's Matrimonial Ladder* sold over half a million copies. But whether it was a hundred thousand, half a million, two million, or any other notional figure, did not matter; that they had once infested the collective imagination was the memory that endured.

Thackeray, who spent great portions of his adolescence in Hone's Ludgate Hill shop, found that, as with many of his generation, the drawings and character assassinations infected his imagination and entered his soul. This is what makes Hone such an important journalist. His inventions endured in the collective memory of nineteenth-century England, be it Eliza Fenning, 'Doctor' Sidmouth, 'Derry Down Triangle', 'Dr Slop', Lord Ellenborough, Queen Caroline or George IV.

'Doctor Southey's New Vision'

From *A Slap at Slop* (1821). In this, the most wounding of the Hone/Cruikshank caricatures of the king, Robert Southey is mocked for his poem in praise of the late George III, *The Vision of Judgement* (Dr Stoddart is included face down in his Slop Pail – Hone's nickname for his paper the *New Times*). Southey was particularly loathed by the Romantics as a court sycophant, and for his apostasy (in his youth he had written *Wat Tyler*, a hymn to the rights of man), reactionary conservatism, and his immunity from prosecution for blasphemous and seditious libel because he was Poet Laureate and a government propagandist. His praise of the royal family earned him this savage attack and, a few weeks later, Byron's most acerbic political satire appeared, also entitled *The Vision of Judgement. Doctor Southey's New Vision* marks the end of Hone's vicious campaign against George IV, which had so decisively established the image of the King in the public mind.

On Christmas Eve 1820 the *Examiner* wrote of the satires:

We consider them as new features in the history of English publication and politics, and a very entertaining and invaluable portion of that public press, which is at this moment teaching mankind how to separate mere honours, and selfish and intolerant power, from genuine merit and useful government. To Mr HONE is England, and indeed the whole world, indebted for originating this important branch of patriotic publication. He is receiving, as the multitudinous editions of his works gratifyingly shew, the applause of mankind, and we request to assure him that we are not among the least grateful of them.

By 1821 the capricious public had lost interest in the Queen. Hone stopped publishing his satires, believing that the struggle for the liberty of the press had been won. The government and the King had been attacked with impunity in thousands of satires and articles by journalists throughout the country; the bill had been withdrawn in deference to the strong expression of disgust on the part of the people. Caroline had served her purpose; she was quickly forgotten by the press and the public. She died in 1821, a lonely, broken woman.

PART IV

'Bubbles thrown up by the fermentation of society'

13

A Rebellious Will Subjugated

... melancholy, mirth and I are one.
> William Hone to Charles Lamb, 1825

The wildest will that ever rose
To scorn Thy cause, and aid Thy foes,
Is quelled, my God, by Thee.
> From a poem written by Hone on his birthday, 1834

Hone's daughter Sarah said that in 1821 her father was 'tense with nervous excitement'. He had worked without rest since 1819. The most prolific and popular journalist in the country, he had to meet the extraordinary public demand for his work. As he wrote new satires in 1820 and 1821, he was still publishing the later editions of *The Political House*, *The Man in the Moon* and *The Queen's Ladder*; the fifty-first edition of *The Political House* came out in 1821 three years after its first publication, and there would be a further three editions before it came to the end of its run. The pressure was unremitting.

He had suffered apoplectic fits before, but after three years of nonstop labour he had reached complete mental and physical collapse. One day he thought he saw the upper part of his body float along Fleet Street. The next day he saw his disembodied legs walking along in the same place. For many nights he was too afraid to enter his Ludgate Hill home because he thought it 'blockaded from his approach by a dense wall of fire'. Only his sixteen-year-old daughter Matilda could coax him into their house. He suffered from other hallucinations, feelings of agoraphobia, and all the signs of paranoia. One night when he was working in his study he heard the chimes of St Paul's Cathedral strike two in the morning; looking up he believed he saw a 'haggard' and 'ferocious' face staring through a pane at his writing upon the desk, 'as though it chiefly desired to be acquainted with the books that lay upon it'. Later he was to brush off this illusion with some levity, but at the time it must have seemed like a terrifying incubus sent to spy on his work. 'He confided to me', remembered Sarah, 'that his mind was as nearly wreaked as it could be, and his frame as well, solely from the effects of over-work, and ever-present monetary embarrassments.'[1]

It would have been thought that the frequent sales of 100,000 for each book would have made a considerable fortune. But Hone contrived to spend all he could muster on feeding his virulent bibliomania. 'As long as the money lasted,' he remembered, 'I used to go to my cashier for £5 or £10 at a time generally to buy old prints and curious books; at last, asking for money, he said there were no funds. I insisted; "I *must* have the books I have been looking at" – he gave me the last.' In 1820 he pledged his collection for a loan, but when he could not pay it back his books were entered into a hurried sale. The catalogue lists the sad loss of a magnificent library; there were 1,171 books, many old and rare volumes from Britain, France and Italy, some dating from the earliest days of printing, spanning the fifteenth to the nineteenth centuries. There were fourteen folios of prints, and sets of rare books such as the *Harleian Miscellany* (on sale for the bargain price of £24) and *Somers Tracts*. He also had to get rid of his collection of art, which included portraits painted by Highmore and Vaillant, and an original painting of Jeffrey Hudson, dwarf and jester to Charles II. He had to sell the collection of a lifetime when he was at the height of success as a journalist.[2]

Hone was an avowed hater of money, and did not conceal his feckless attitude to it. He had wisely left his finances in his wife and eldest children's hands when he became rich, but even so, the money was spent rapidly. 'I knew him well,' wrote John Britton in his reminiscences of literary London, 'and respected him for warmth of heart, kindness of disposition, and strength of head; but he was most improvident and indiscreet in the money affairs. Had these been placed in the charge of an honest, good accountant, William Hone might have lived to be a rich man, and died a happy one.'[3]

His relationship with George Cruikshank was also at crisis point. In January 1821 he complained that his partner was spending too much time drunk or chasing women to work properly. Hone used to drink late into the night with Cruikshank on occasions, and they had had a riotous late-night and early-morning session just before Christmas.[4] But Hone suddenly lost patience and wanted him to 'foreswear late hours, blue ruin and dollies – all of which united, are unfriendly to certain mechanical motions of the spirit, which I tell George would make him a trustworthy "man of business"'. Cruikshank had no ambition to be a man of business; he responded with 'You be damned,' 'Go to Hell,' and Hone reported, 'He has invited me in rather a dictatorial tone to "Go and teach my Granny to suck eggs!"'

Cruikshank teased him, and wrote a goading letter: 'I was out yesterday and got *wet through & through! My boots let water* & my *mouth let – gin* which made you know *gin & water.*' Hone was tiring of his young friend's drunken games after so many years' indulgence. He wrote an exasperated letter saying: 'The demonic possession is on him even now,' and complained that Cruikshank had turned up requesting that he ask Alderman Waithman on his behalf to dismiss a watch-house keeper with whom he had fought a couple of evenings before – a favour Hone refused to grant. Cruikshank then set about abusing his employer: he 'sent for his pipe, and blew clouds of smoke over me and my books, in my hall of Parody, for a couple of hours, demanded entrance to my wife's bedroom to shave and smarten himself for an evening party, took possession of my best "Brandenburg" pumps, damned me under the denomination of "Old Robin Gray", because I had not a *chapeau bras,* * otherwise decomposed the wonted order of my mind and household and manifested what I had long suspected, that he is by no means friendly to Reform!'[5]

Cruikshank seemed to be on a headlong dive to the gutter in 1821. Hone wrote his mother, 'Whatever of kindness I entertain, and I entertain much, for your son George, has been from admiration of his talents and respect for his honourable disposition. For everything that could diminish either of those qualities, I have expressed to him not only deep regret, but remonstrated with him more severely than any one but a sincere friend, feeling deeply for his best interests and real welfare

---

* 'Auld Robin Gray' was the herdsman-hero of Lady Anne Lindsay's Scottish song 'The bridegroom grat when the sun gaed down' of 1771. Cruikshank was describing Hone as a hapless and romantic, with a hopelessly old-fashioned view of life because he was unable to provide him with a hat *à la mode.*

would venture to do.'[6] In turn Hone received letters from people complaining about the artist's behaviour. Sir John Bowring, the founder of the *Westminster Review*, moaned that Cruikshank 'torments me to death'. He wanted Hone to 'induce him to fulfil his promise – his repeated promises' to either complete a drawing or return the advance. Bowring was exasperated, and told Hone: 'I know you have – or ought to have some influence on him – as anything I say now would perhaps only irritate – not shame him.'[7] Hone had been able to tame and cajole Cruikshank from the time of their first collaborations in 1815, but by now his influence had run out. Their friendship was not completely at an end. Cruikshank continued to illustrate his old friend's books throughout 1821. In 1824 Hone affirmed their intimacy in one of his books: 'Robert Burns had not more kindly feelings when he wrote "Auld lang syne," than I have towards my friend George Cruikshank . . . and though as regards me, his occupation's gone, our mutual esteem is undiminished.'[8]

Hone and Cruikshank drifted apart, not because they had fallen out completely, but because Hone had little work to give to his artist. 'Satire is torpid,' the publisher Thomas Dolby wrote in his autobiography, 'unless hatched into animation by some ruling vice or folly. The more vicious the cause the more stinging the effect. In the case just concluded, the Queen's arrival and treatment excited a strong feeling throughout the country. Satire was awakened into stinging activity; but the public madness subsided before the poor Queen died; the rage was over, and satire became torpid again.'[9]

The rage that engulfed Britain after Peterloo and during the Bill of Pains and Penalties quickly dissipated. And with it went the taste for satire. The King left England to tour his other kingdoms, Scotland, Ireland and Hanover. He spent the rest of his reign secluded in a tiny court at Windsor, rarely seen by the public. If he was never loved, he was never so intensely hated as during the Regency and the first year of his reign. He even agreed to a cut in the civil list, so the charge of monstrous extravagance could no longer be levelled with its former gusto. Lords Sidmouth and Eldon left the cabinet in 1822, the year that Castlereagh declined into depression and committed suicide. The villains of the 1810s, the men who had been set up as the targets of vitriolic satires, were dead or retired in the early 1820s. Their successors never attracted such odium.

The issues that had driven Hone's journalism throughout his career became redundant at this time as well. The post-war depression was over, and the government was able to cut taxes and duties at successive budgets. At the Home Office, Robert Peel reformed the criminal code, abolishing many capital offences. George Canning, as Castlereagh's successor at the Foreign Office, offended the powers of the Holy Alliance with his 'liberal' foreign policy, supporting the national movements in Latin America and Greece. His policies were popular and contradicted the assertions of Hone, Hazlitt and others that Britain had allied herself to continental despotisms. Most importantly, the sinecure issue, which had been at the forefront of reformist politics, ceased to be a problem. By the 1820s, 1,800 public offices had been abolished, at a saving to the taxpayer of £580,000 annually. With the economy in good shape, the government passing piecemeal and constructive reforms, the desire to lash out at the country's rulers with vicious satires abated.

The reformist movement petered out. The fatal flaws that Hone and his fellow writers had identified in the 1810s turned out to be not so dangerous after all. Their constitutional rhetoric, which had galvanised the country throughout the post-war depression, were irrelevant during the prosperity and tranquillity of the early 1820s. The people were not slaves cowering under an arbitrary despotism; Britain was not in a sinister league with continental absolutism. Journalists, writing the first draft of history as it is said, are rarely completely right. The reformist press lost favour when the draconian policies of Sidmouth gave way to greater freedoms.

An unreformed House of Commons could, and did, respond to the disenfranchised. It was capable of dismantling the structure of patronage on its own initiative. Hone wrote in the preface to a revised edition of *A Slap at Slop* that it was becoming 'the fashion for the minority to be polite to the majority'. Thomas Wooler's *Black Dwarf* declined from one of the most popular weekly papers to a beleaguered and forgotten monthly. He was reduced to writing articles attacking his readers for their apathy, entitled 'Present Alarming Trance and Silly Behaviour of that Old and Single Gentleman, John Bull'. In 1824 he closed his paper, commenting, 'It is true, that hundreds of thousands have petitioned for reform; but the event has proved what their enemies asserted, and what the Black Dwarf treated as a calumny, that they only clamoured for bread. And if they were only stimulated by hunger, and the influence of despair and distress, upon the animal passions, they were not reformers, but bubbles thrown up by the fermentation of society.'

Wooler was embittered by the apathy of the British public. He and Hone had believed that the people were as keen as they were for reform, but it proved to be an aberration caused by a temporary economic slump. The post-war economy, the failed harvests of 1816 and 1817, Peterloo and the Queen's trial had excited the population; the reformists and the government had misdiagnosed this as a call for political change. As Wooler said, taking his final bow as a political journalist, 'The majority has decided, in its cooler moments, for "things as they are". The majority must abide the result of its decision. A mere bystander would only waste his breath, by offering unrequested advice; and though words cost nothing, time is too valuable to be always thrown away.' Wooler retired cursing the public for abandoning him.[10]

Hone was more magnanimous in defeat than Wooler. He chided his old friend John Childs for complaining about the quiescent public: 'Don't stand snivelling there, because you can't get people to go a walking with you, but take a walk *by yourself*, as I do, when I have a mind to it, and the more lonely it is, and the fewer I meet, the more I enjoy it ...' He retired as a political writer and satirist in 1822. Two years later he wrote: 'I am neither proud nor ashamed of my productions.' They had served their purpose, and belonged to history. His readers had declared their opinion; politics had changed; there was no point fighting a lost cause. When heavy debt compelled him to republish a collected edition in 1827 he would choose the telling title *Facetiae and Miscellanies*, and wrote: 'My purpose is not a revivification, but a decent funeral: "I come to bury these, sir, not to praise 'em".' The anger had been sapped from politics; satirical invective became a redundant expression of public indignation. The virulence of satire between 1819 and 1821 would not be seen again until the 1960s; later generations were shocked that their forefathers had enjoyed such brutal humour and bilious personal attacks. Hone and Cruikshank's collaboration stood near the end of a long tradition of acerbic political humour. In subsequent years, satire lost its cruel edge and responsive journalistic function. Caricatures resided in magazines like *Punch*, which, though related to Hone and Cruikshank's work, was sapped of the anger that infused Regency satire. In 1840 Thackeray remarked that modern satires 'are a great deal too genteel . . . polite points of wit, which strike one as exceedingly clever and pretty, and cause one to smile in a quiet, gentlemanlike kind of way'. Thackeray railed against the repressed and sterile humour of his generation, which contrasted so strongly with the boisterous spirit of Hone's customers: 'A man who does not laugh outright is a dullard, and has no heart; even the old dandy of sixty must have laughed at his own wondrous grotesque image.'[11]

Hone belonged to an old generation of reformists. The death of Queen Caroline marked a break with their past. His arguments and his satirical style went out of fashion within a few years, leaving him enervated to the point of collapse and disappointed that so much of his effort had been in vain. In 1824 he would inform his readers, quoting Defoe, 'I am weary of strife'. Even his famous sense of humour was waning as he got older: 'If I have wit, "it lies as cold in me as fire in a flint, which will not show without knocking".' Many of the older reformists were silenced, not by the government, but by the vicissitudes of public opinion and economic misfortune. Many of the famous bookshops and newspapers that had been a feature of the later 1810s closed down. Hone was one of the survivors, remaining a prominent journalist throughout his middle age. But he was never to return to politics. He became a successful auctioneer for a while, before turning his mind to antiquarian research and popular literature in a series of books he and many critics regarded as his best works and a great contribution to British culture.

In 1830 Robert Southey, who had been so offended by reformist journalism in 1817, wrote with satisfaction that Hone's opinions had completely changed and, quoting Coleridge, that 'he had become "a sadder and wiser man"'. The Poet Laureate decreed that he would support Hone's non-political literary work, and 'remember nothing more of his earlier life than the ability and presence of mind . . . which he displayed upon his trial'. At the time of the next reformist agitation in the early 1830s, some of the old voices of the 1810s revived traditional reformist rhetoric. But Hone would not celebrate the triumph of reform in 1832, when the ideals of his life became enshrined in a parliamentary act. He had survived the misfortunes of a young bookseller, withstood the rigours of imprisonment and battled against overwhelming powers of the government. Yet a series of personal tragedies and misfortunes crushed his spirit entirely; the story of the country's most popular journalist and hero of the press faded from memory.[12]

It is a commonplace that journalistic careers end in failure; yesterday's newspaper became kindling then as it becomes fish-and-chip paper now. The last twenty years of Hone's life show why he was remembered for something rather different than the fight for freedom of the press by most people in the second half of the nineteenth century.

Hone had been promising the publication of his *History of Parody* since 1819. By the mid-1820s he was still reading in the British Museum. He had been addicted to old and obscure books since his childhood; this passion predated his political awakening. When he could no longer thrive as a political journalist, he began to share some of the gems of literature that he had discovered as an avid reader and researcher with the reading public. In 1820 he published the apocryphal books of the Bible (to the disgust of orthodox churchmen); three years later he issued some of the ancient mystery plays that had been buried in the British Museum. As a political journalist he had attempted to restore the ancient constitution to the British people; from 1820 he reclaimed their ancient literature. With his talent for publicity and ability to engage a mass audience, he turned his love for arcane literature and forgotten history into a commercial success.

Hone's *Every-day Book* came out weekly from 1 January 1825 for two years. In it he set out to record a timeless British popular culture, preserving the skeins of memory that linked men and women with their real and mythic past. Wherever these artefacts of daily life still lived – in oral culture, forgotten books, obsolete ballads, footnotes to history, buildings, tombstones, discarded newspapers, or engrafted upon the landscape itself – he would track them down in dusty libraries, or on investigative journeys throughout the country. Everything was relevant in reconstructing the popular history of Britain, whether it had happened hundreds of years ago, or the day before, or solely in the imagination. No writer was excluded, whether they were drawn from the canon of literature or the hundreds of humbler authors whom society had forgotten.

The week's edition of the *Every-day Book* was divided into seven sections, each entry containing historical events, poems, examples of popular customs and festivals, and other miscellaneous topics relevant to each day. He used the words of Charles Lamb in the first number to elucidate his idea: 'Every man hath two birthdays: two days, at least, in every year, which set him upon revolving the lapse of time, as it affects his mortal duration.' One of these two days is one's actual birthday, but the other is that universal celebration, the first of January: 'the nativity of our common Adam'. But for Hone each day of the year was an anniversary that contained the recollections of the world. People mark out days as an act of communion with their past. 'Our ancestors', Hone wrote, 'were persons of leisure. They appropriated each day in the year to the memory of remarkable persons or events. THE EVERY-DAY BOOK will relate the origin of these three hundred and sixty-five celebrations, with interesting accounts of the individuals and circumstances commemorated.'[13]

Hone's format brought selections of English literature to the public in easily digestible weekly instalments. Each number consisted of thirty-two pages of densely packed text. After twenty-seven months, the *Every-day Book* filled two volumes of 1,700 pages with 320 illustrations, at just fourteen shillings apiece. The anniversary of the laying of the first stone of the Greenwich Observatory on 10 August 1675 allowed Hone to publish for the first time John Flamsteed's original plan for the building based on his 'Scheme of the Heavens'. Every day was overflowing with memories and connexions, or at least provided the opening to explain odd bits of history or folklore – everything from village fairs to an account of Michelangelo's work in the Sistine Chapel. Poets who commemorated certain anniversaries were included: Spenser's descriptions of the months, Byron's poem on the Battle of Waterloo (18 June), Keats's on St Agnes' Day (21 January), and Walter Scott's on Christmas Day, are a few examples. Extracts from Chaucer,

Shakespeare, Jonson, Milton and many other less well-known names were commonly used to illustrate the articles.

Charles Lamb said that Hone's *Every-day Book* had a 'theme as various as the reader's mind'. It is a treasure house of literary and historical information, defying any generalised summation. It has the power almost two centuries after it was first published to draw the reader into a rich world of knowledge stored within the thousands of pages. Trivial facts and accounts of quaint practices jostle with the genuinely fascinating. A random sample from the index of the first volume gives but scant indication of the sheer range: Charles V, emperor and cobbler; Milford, J., his description of Lord Byron's residence at Mitylene; Hindoo festival, Huli; Children, pickled and come to life; Ovid, character of; Falling sickness, in rooks; Niger, the, course of; Sausages, festival of; Civil wars, how commenced in England; Moscow, rebuilt from Grays-inn-lane dustheap; Mary, the rope dancer, her tragic fate; Druids, customs, ceremonies etc.; Henry V, at Agincourt; Kale, where derived; Jonson, Ben, his description of Bartholomew Fair; Julian, emperor, reviver of beards; Naseby, battle of; Drinking, excessive; Learned pig's performance; Livy and his books. Hone's inspiration was Defoe's *Time's Telescope*, and it resembled Isaac D'Israeli's *Curiosities of Literature*, published in 1824. But the *Every-day Book* and its successors, the *Table Book* (1827) and the *Year Book* (1832), were aimed at a different market: middle-class people who wanted to supplement their meagre education.

When he published the first collected volume of the *Every-day Book* at the beginning of 1826 Hone noted in the preface:

Although I confess to have been highly satisfied by the general reception of the *Every-day Book*, and am proud of the honour it has derived from individuals of high literary reputation, yet there is one class whose approbation I value most especially. The 'mothers of England' have been pleased to entertain it as an every-day assistant in their families; and instructors of youth, of both sexes, have placed it in school-libraries ...

This 'ample testimonial', as Hone called it, was, he said, 'the most gratifying reward I could hope to receive'.[14]

But it was still a matter of pride when the books were received with praises from the literary world. The judge, critic and essayist Sir

Thomas Noon Talfourd described his books as 'entertaining and permanently valuable'. In *Blackwood's Magazine* Christopher North said: 'He has deserved well of the naturalist, the antiquarian and the poet.' Robert Southey, whom Hone had attacked in the past as a sycophant to the King and supporter of a vile tyranny, wrote in his *Life of Bunyan* that Hone had 'rendered good service in an important department of literature'. A review of Southey's book said that his tribute to Hone was the only wise remark in an otherwise bad book; the *Books*, the review said, were a benefit to 'the friends of pure English literature' and 'all intelligent men'. In the last two-thirds of the nineteenth century, Hone was remembered primarily as the editor of the *Every-day Book*; it remained a source of miscellaneous information and entertaining reading for decades. Many households had it on their shelves, and even today the various editions can be bought cheaply in second-hand bookshops and market stalls in Britain and America.[15]

The mature Hone was regarded with affection as a gentle old eccentric. Charles Lamb published a poem in the *London Magazine*, 'Quatrains to the Editor of the Every-day Book', beginning,

> I like you, and your book, ingenious Hone!
> In whose capacious, all-embracing leaves
> The very marrow of tradition's shown;
> And all that history – much that fiction – weaves.

And concluding,

> Dan Phoebus loves your book – trust me, friend
> Hone –The title only errs, he bids me say:
> For while such art – wit – reading – there are shown,
> He swears, 'tis not a work of *every day*.

Lamb praised Hone for the 'vast stores of anecdote' he mined for the public's education. Hone replied by writing a well-intentioned poem. He graciously said he was flattered by the compliments of so a great a man; he felt like a 'stricken deer' separated from the common herd. He brushed off the eulogy, saying that any genius he displayed was merely 'Deductions from a strange diversity / Of things not taught within a University'. He attended no 'learned halls' in youth, but it was for him to take the role of teacher and 'persuade the young to think'.

Hone relished the work for his periodical. It gave him the opportunity to reprint nuggets culled from old and forgotten books, the things people would never come across in the course of their general reading. He ransacked dusty manuscripts in the British Museum, local-history books, biographies and ephemera discarded from previous centuries. But the most pleasurable aspect of his new job was the opportunity he got to spend time with Charles and Mary Lamb in the villages surrounding London. In response to Lamb's poem in the *London Magazine*, Hone wrote:

> .... 'Friend Hone' in print is so kind; and then there's such courage, in *public*, to say you dare to encourage my friendship in *private*, I cannot resist a glow of affection for such an assistance towards a poor mortal like me, who only is (and never can be more than) a creeper where others are runners.*
>
> ... There being some sun this May morning, I purpose to shock Miss Lamb and you about 2 o'clock, with a call and an appetite, such as it is, and to eat out my thanks, and excite all your risibility, suavity, compassion and gravity – for melancholy, mirth and I are one.
>
> I'm more than
Yours sincerely,
W. Hone[16]

Lamb contributed essays to Hone's *Every-day Book*, including one on the subject of asses, which Hone entitled 'The Ass'. 'My friends are fairly surprised that you should set me down so unequivocally for an ass as you have done ...' read Lamb's fond rebuke. 'Call you that friendship?' In another letter, he wrote to Hone from Enfield, where he was renting a cottage, begging him to pay a visit and bring the latest copy of the *Every-day Book*, which he could not do without. The letter was posted, but when one of Lamb's friends dropped in shortly afterwards on his way to London, he dashed off an identical note so that it would get to Ludgate Hill sooner, hastening Hone's visit.[17]

Lamb's literary executor, Sir Thomas Talfourd, wrote that the

---

* The grammar in this note has been amended to give some clarity to a hastily written message intelligible to friends but incomprehensible otherwise.

warmth of the two men's friendship could never be recreated because they spent so much time together that letters were unnecessary.[18] The friendship was perhaps the most fulfilling of Hone's life. In 1834, when Hazlitt was dead and he had lost contact with Cruikshank, Hone wrote: 'My friend Charles Lamb is the only man who knows me intimately – all my other intimacies have been with books.' An anecdote told by Hone recalls something of the happy rural life they shared. One evening they were taking a stroll on Hampstead Heath, discussing their slavery to tobacco. In a gesture of confidence known to most nicotine lovers,

We threw our snuffboxes away from the hill on which we stood, far among the furze and brambles below and went home in triumph; I began to be very miserable and wretched all night; in the morning I was walking on the same hill; I saw Charles Lamb below, searching among the bushes; he looked up laughing saying, 'What! You are come to look for your snuffbox too?' 'Oh no,' said I, taking a pinch out of a paper in my waistcoat pocket, 'I went for a halfpennyworth to the first shop that was open.'[19]

In July 1825 Hone wrote an open letter in the *Every-day Book* to a 'Captain Lion', addressed from 'Coleman Cottage'. In old English rural dialect 'lion' was slang for lamb; Charles Lamb lived in Colebrooke Cottage, just off Islington High Street and next to the New River. It did not take much imagination for literary insiders to realise to whom Hone was writing. That summer he had borrowed Colebrooke when Lamb was in Enfield recovering from an illness. In the letter Hone writes that he has escaped the heat of London for cool respite in the countryside. 'I was mistaken,' he complained. 'The malignity of an evil star is against me; I mean the dog star.' July of that year was stifling; Hone escaped up to Islington as soon as he had seen Charles and Mary Lamb off for their holiday: 'That evening I got into a hackney-coach to enjoy your "cool" residence; but it was hot; and there was no "cool of the evening"; I went to bed hot, and I slept hot all night, and got up hot to a hot tea breakfast ...' He continued,

How I got through that hot day I cannot remember. At night, when, according to Addison, 'evening shades prevail' the heat prevailed; there were no 'cool' shades, and I got no rest; and therefore I got up restless, and walked out and saw the Morning Star, which I suppose was the dog star, for I sought coolness and found it not; but the sun arose, and methought there was no atmosphere but burning beams; and the metropolis poured out its heated thousands towards the New River, at Newington; and it was filled with men, and boys, and dogs; and all looked as 'comfortable' as live eels in a stew pan.

I am too hot to proceed. What a summer!

But Hone would not send the letter. He did not want to add to the postal system for compassionate reasons: 'I am told the sight of the postmen in their scarlet coats is not bearable in London; they look red-hot.' Out of sheer lethargy, he writes, he will publish the letter in the *Every-day Book* so that the servant will not have to toil out to a post-box in the midday sun.[20]

The letter was written partly as soft topical satire on the unusually hot summer, attempting to capture the oppressive temperatures in exaggerated repetitive phrases. Yet it was also intended to record something very different. The belt of countryside that encircled London, and the villages it encompassed, had a special place in the city's history. The stream of Londoners that Hone noticed in the heat-induced torpor of July was a characteristic sight.

Islington had always been a popular refuge, a village of pubs, tea gardens and theatres. It was London's favourite resort. In Hogarth's series of engravings *Times of the Day* (1738), the 'Evening' sequence shows a family who have escaped to the fecundity of Sadler's Wells, where Sir Hugh Myddleton's New River system reached its end in the reservoir. In his drawing, the rural bliss of Islington is like the extension of a city street. The family have imported urban manners and fashions, and also their vices. We are told that the pregnant mother has committed adultery by the cuckold's horns that accidentally sit above her husband's head. The children squabble over their material processions. In the background two men sit in a tavern blowing smoke in each other's faces, desperate to re-create the fug of the city.

Hogarth's image of Londoners bringing the city with them to their immediate countryside was a timeless one. When Hone looked up from his 'hot tea breakfast' he saw a copy of the engraving on Lamb's wall. It was a painful reminder that the dog days of summer had ever been thus, 'with the fat hot citizen's wife sweltering between her husband and the

New River, the hot little dog looking wistfully into the reachless warm water, her crying hot boy on her husband's stick, the scolding hot sister, and all the other heats of that ever-to-be-warm-admired engraving'.

'In the annals of the world', Hone wrote in the *Table Book*, 'there have never been such vast improvements as have occurred in the metropolis during the last seven years.' The area of London he loved –

Islington and its environs, Highgate and Hampstead, Kentish and Camden Towns – were about to be built over by property developers. The days when Londoners could temporarily flee their frenetic urban existence were coming to an end. The effect on London, Lamb and Hone were increasingly to realise, would be devastating. Parts of the *Every-day Book* chronicle a city culture about to be lost for ever.

'A walk out of London is, to me, an event,' Hone wrote. 'In my boyhood, I had only to obtain parental permission, and stroll in fields now no more, – to scenes now deformed, or that I have been wholly robbed of, by "the spirit of improvement". Five and thirty years have altered everything – myself with the rest.' He wrote a poem, included here for its sentiment rather than artistic value:

> People methinks are better, but the scenes
> Wherein my youth delighted are no more.
> I wander out in search of them, and find
> A sad deformity in all I see.
> Strong recollections of my former pleasures,
> And knowledge that they never can return,
> Are causes of my sombre mindedness:
> I pray you then bear with my discontent.[21]

In May 1825 he took a walk around Islington to chart the last days of the countryside with George Cruikshank and a couple of others. Cruikshank had discovered sobriety, married, and moved to Amwell Street, a short way from Lamb's Colebrooke Cottage. The first stop was the Pied Bull, a pub on Upper Street, which stood next to a pond where Hone had fished for carp as a boy. It had also been the home of Sir Walter Raleigh, and was about to be demolished to make way for new housing. Hone and his companions went and 'condoled on the decaying memorials of past greatness'. They also went to 'have the gratification of saying hereafter that we had smoked a pipe in the same room that the man who first introduced tobacco smoked in himself'. Cruikshank wanted to smoke the day away in the room where Raleigh had inhaled the first tobacco in England 'so *he* might have been able to smoke the last within the walls that would in a few weeks be levelled to the ground'. Hone and Cruikshank were confirmed nicotine addicts, so it was an act of sincere homage to the founder of their favourite pastime. But they needed alcohol to 'aid' their dutiful smoking, and so numerous pots of ale were bought, followed by wine and port 'at 3/6 per bottle'. When all the beer and wines were gone, Hone made up some punch, and the company drank toasts 'To the immortal memory of Sir Walter Raleigh' and 'Old England', and, as they became drunker, to themselves.

The company emerged from their revelries, no doubt very much the worse for wear, and walked up to Canonbury Tower, another famous monument. The writers Oliver Goldsmith and 'mad' Christopher Smart had rented rooms in the tower 'far from the busy haunts of men'. It commanded an impressive view from its roof overlooking 'open green pastures with uninterrupted views easterly, bounded only by the horizon'. It was an inspiration for poets and a destination for Londoners who climbed the tower to look across the fields towards the mass of spires and chimneys they had left behind. If people in the city were smothered beneath large buildings, unable to comprehend the enormity of London, the view from Canonbury Tower gave them an unique perspective. The New River formed a horseshoe near the building, and a cluster of country tea gardens congregated in the 'prettiest bit on the river nearest to London'. But the slightly inebriated group were looking upon this classic London view for the final time. From henceforth factories and kilns emitting 'flickering fire and sulphurous stench' would obliterate the view. On another walk, through Barnsbury and Caledonian Road, Hone wrote of the pleasures of looking up at Hampstead and Highgate Hills across the open valley. Forty years before, he wrote, 'My childish imagination drew pictures of paradise from the upland horizon of Hampstead and the verdant intermediate scenery which fascinated my young eyes and filled me with indescribable emotions . . . In a few short years', he lamented, 'London will distend its enormous bulk to the heights . . . and nothing will be left to me to admire, of all that I admired.'[22]

The day in Islington was a sad one for Hone and his friends. If the *Every-day Book*'s purpose was to chart the destruction of the best parts of British culture, there was no better way to illustrate it than by a journey to the Pied Bull and Canonbury Tower. When they were buried under suburban streets, where would the memories of history and places of living literary associations exist? Hone's book took on the task of preserving the vanishing memories of the London landscape because 'the dominion of the brick-and-mortar king will have no end'. In a short time the countryside would be built over with 'cages for commercial spirits' – homogeneous housing without any connexion with the historical landscape it colonised.

The laments of the *Books* are among the last and most poignant accounts of the special villages of London, and therefore significant documents in the city's history, written as they were right at the moment of change. The horror that they prophesied did come to pass. The narrow streets and terraces of the suburbs were demonised later in the century as penal colonies for city workers. Dickens wrote of the 'early clerk population of Somers and Camden Towns, Islington and Pentonville', who plodded in solemn dudgeon every morning down St John Street or the City Road to their soulless offices and counting houses. They left their bleak neighbourhoods and became anonymous slaves to the City, neither acknowledging nor being acknowledged by their fellow bondsmen.

The joyous days in Islington did not last long. On 4 April 1826, Hone was arrested for the second time in his life.

'My family is thrust out from Ludgate Hill, and I am in the Rules of the Kings Bench Prison,' Hone wrote to his close friend John Childs, a bookseller from Bungay, in Suffolk. He continued: 'I was transferred hither, after writing a number [of the *Every-day Book*] in the Lock-up House. Since then, I have got out last week's, arranged the Index, so as to make the first volume an immediately productive asset, and have just got the proofs from the printer's, which, when read, will go to press.'

Writers in Hone's age commonly suffered the censorship of government and the harsh laws of bankruptcy. Hone was arrested for the massive debts the *Every-day Book* had incurred as he struggled to keep the cover price affordable for poor families. But he could not carry on indefinitely subsidising his magazine, and when the quarterly bills were due in March he knew his business was fatally crippled. 'How I got through that fearful winter, at what expense of money in fees and costs, and with what wear and tear of mind and loss of spirits, I have no remembrance; my recollection of it is as a long and terrible dream.'

Prior to the inevitable arrest he 'worked like a horse to put the "Every-Day Book" beyond the reach of its destruction, by transferring it to Messrs. Hunt & Clarke, in trust for my creditors'.[23]

The publishing company had just been started in Covent Garden by John Hunt and Charles Cowden-Clarke, a budding writer and friend of William Hazlitt; Hone was never far from the old *Examiner* circle. The plan was that Hone could continue as the editor of the *Every-day Book*, albeit employed by trustees, who would pay his family the 'smallest weekly allowance' while paying off the creditors from the profits of the magazine. The collected volume of the first year of the book was collated, indexed and rushed out for sale within days of the arrest under the name of his new employers.

Hone refused the easy option of giving up work and declaring himself bankrupt. Although he had just 3/6d in loose change in his pocket when he was arrested, and his family were homeless and in 'great distress', he made it clear to his creditors that whilst he had the 'wherewithal' to write and provide for his children he would: 'for I am not a beggar'. 'It is my wish,' he wrote, 'and will be my endeavour to do it, and nothing short of being allowed to make that endeavour, and pay them 20/- in the £, will satisfy me.'[24]

Hone was carried from his home and locked up, writing all the while as if nothing was happening. As a prisoner in the King's Bench Prison, he was required to live within its 'Rules' – a set precinct in Southwark where debtors had to live until they were free from all obligations to their creditors. In effect, it was a penal village, with meat and vegetable markets, pubs and coffee houses. Hone rented a room above the tobacconist's for the first weeks of incarceration, before taking lodgings with his family in a tiny house in Belvedere Place. Most of their furniture had been sold, including the heavy loss of his entire library, including all the books he had purchased for his defence in 1817 and for his proposed *History of Parody*, which, after eight years' hard work, would never come out. The *Every-day Book* continued to appear each week regardless of its editor's reduced circumstances. He had to be thankful, at least, for the small mercy that he was allowed to retain books essential to research.

Submitting to the Rules was not such a bad life compared to the usual horrors of nineteenth-century prisons. Hone could continue his life as a writer and family man without being sent to a cell. He could even apply for what was called a 'day-rule', and leave the confines of Southwark for a few hours. Yet the fact remained that Hone had lost his precious liberty as an independent writer and publisher. For the first time since 1808, when he had begun his journalistic career, he was under external control.

In May he dedicated the first volume of his book to Charles and Mary Lamb, promising never to forget their public support of him, thanking them for their 'sympathy and kindness, when gloom overmastered me; and that your pen spontaneously sparkled in the book, when my mind was in clouds and darkness. These "trifles" as each of you would call them, are scored upon my heart . . .' With friends like these, and a popular work of literature coming out regularly, the future did not seem so dark. By the end of the year he could write that he saw 'daylight through the gloom of [his] late distresses', and if he could struggle on for a little while longer, salvation would be 'at no distant period'; he was content and prepared to 'wait patiently, and endeavour silently'. He played down his apparent loss of liberty: 'As to "being in the world again", I am scarcely out of it than I was at Ludgate Hill. It's true I have not so many friends fluttering about me, but in other respects I am altogether as I was, "except these bonds". I thank God, however, that in this small house we are more comfortable than I could imagine possible.'[25]

The optimism was quickly destroyed, however, when at the beginning of 1827 Hunt and Clarke told him the debts still amounted to £400. It was not to be a temporary loss of fortune, but an indefinite slavery to his creditors; all his writing, for the rest of his life, would be solely dedicated to relieving a bottomless reservoir of debt. The *Table Book* was started in January 1827 amidst what Hone called the 'unhappy crisis of my affairs'.

The latest venture was a monthly rather than a weekly periodical. Hone described it as 'a series of continually shifting scenes – a kind of literary kaleidoscope', aiming to 'annihilate both time and space'. Hone's research was confined to the books he managed to have sent to prison; Charles Lamb continued the work that needed to be done in the British Museum, contributing extracts from the collections of rare plays once kept by David Garrick to each number. They included 'sometimes a scene, sometimes a song, a speech, a passage, or a poetical image, as they happen to strike me'. The gems of literature that lay forgotten in Garrick's folders were republished for the first time. Lamb relished his task, telling Hone, 'Imagine the luxury for one like me . . . of sitting in the princely apartments [the Reading Room of the British Museum] . . . and culling at will the flowers of some thousand dramas! It is like having the range of a nobleman's library, with the Librarian to your friend.'[26]

The *Table Book* was a much more literary enterprise than its predecessor. It republished many old poems, ballads and extracts from rare books. Hone continued to celebrate popular culture, including examples of dialect and street slang alongside the literary content. It was well received among writers and scholars, and contained original pieces written by people like George Dyer among the historical quotations. Mary Novello, who as Mrs Charles Cowden-Clarke became one of the most renowned critics of Shakespeare, recalled that 'To figure in the same volume where dear and honoured Charles Lamb was contributing his selections from the "Garrick Plays" was itself a greatly-to-be-prized distinction.'[27]

The *Table Book* may have been a critically acclaimed work, but Hone struggled through great privations to edit it. The little house in Belvedere Place became insufferable after a year's residence. Southwark was a notoriously unhealthy district in a disease-ridden city. Its water supply was legendarily bad and people were compelled to drink what was pretty much sewage. Hone said it was 'as little inviting as an Irish bog'. Mary Novello visited Hone in Southwark when she was contributing her debut articles to the *Table Book*. She described her journey to Belvedere Place: 'So dingy and smoky were the regions through which we had to pass ere we arrived there, that a morsel of smut found its way to my face and stuck thereupon during the first portion of our interview with Mr Hone.' The effect of the squalid neighbourhood was devastating for the family; in the summer of 1827 Hone reported that 'disease came in upon us, generated by the malaria of this place'.[28]

His daughter succumbed first, catching a fever, and was in 'immediate danger' with inflammation of the lungs. On 10 August Lamb wrote a letter on behalf of his sister: 'We are both exceedingly grieved at dear

Matilda's illness, whom we have ever regarded with the greatest respect. Pray God your next news, which we shall expect most anxiously, shall give hope of her recovery.' But the news was not good; her parents had worn themselves out with 'night watchings'. Hone wrote: 'In the midst of all my wife fell dangerously ill of a fever, and while she was lying helpless in one bed, my daughter was almost a corpse in another – and at the same time the scarlet fever was among five of the young ones.' Hone fell ill himself when he neglected his own health and diet, desperately trying to edit the *Table Book*. He was confined to his bed shortly after, and eventually had to undergo an unspecified operation.[29]

The usual confidence and levity of Hone's private correspondence was replaced with melancholy. Although the family all survived their illnesses, he was all but destroyed. At the end of the year he wrote, 'To say truth, I am o'er wearied with my troubles, and my spirit is too severely wounded to get up when I want it.' It was the lowest point in his life, far worse than the punishment inflicted upon him by Sidmouth and Ellenborough. And misery compounded misery. In October his son Alfred had fractured his skull when he was run over in the Strand; he was brought home showing 'every appearance of mortal termination', vomiting blood for fifteen hours. At the same time Hone's eldest son, William, was serving in the navy, sending his pay home to pay off some of the debts that he had got into. Nothing is known about this William, but it is apparent that he was something of a prodigal son, for Hone commented that the decision to join the navy was an attempt 'to persuade me that the good seed [was] outgrowing the tares'. When Mrs Hone went to collect his pay one day she was told that it had been stopped: 'This mode was feelingly adopted to prepare her the intelligence of his death.' She 'dragged herself home scarcely alive, with a paper indorsed that he died 18th October', to tend her dying Alfred.[30]

At the same time the *Table Book* was not selling as well as the *Everyday Book* had. Lamb told one of his friends: 'Poor Hone's good boy Alfred has fractured his skull; another is returned "dead" from the Navy office; & his Book is going to be given up, not having been answered. What a world of troubles his is!'[31] The readers of the *Table Book*, a work which strongly indicated an editor at the height of his mental powers, would not have realised that he was in fact in the slough of depression. Hone was too good a journalist to allow his mental state to interrupt his public writing. But the tone was very different in private. In December Hone penned an apologetic note to a friend for not having written to any of his correspondents and contributors: 'I have literally been unable.' He continued in a state of unusual but complete gloom: 'You, I am sure, must be aware that "the heart alone knoweth its own sorrows", and that there are times when it can neither make them known, nor bear the weight of ordinary business in addition. I pray you let this be (as it truly is) excuse and apology for seeming neglect. Will and power I have been little of late to connect.'[32]

On Christmas Day 1827 he was forced to write in his paper, 'The next number of the "Table Book" is the last – so wills the public.' Lamb had even stopped writing, and eventually had to get back in contact in April 1828 through Hunt and Clarke: 'I want to hear about Hone. Does he stand above water? how is his son? I have delayed writing to him till it seems impossible. Break the ice for me.' When Lamb was reunited with his friend he would have found that Alfred had recovered, but there was worse news. Another son, John – or Jack, as he was known to the family – had followed his older brother to sea, no doubt to escape his book-obsessed and increasingly depressed father. Hone was incredulous that any of his progeny should want to leave London and pursue active, non-literary careers; he wrote: '[Jack] actually desires "a brush", as he calls it, at fighting! This is a son of mine!' It would have been better for William junior and Jack if they had followed their father into the world of letters. Within months of the first death, it was announced that Jack had plunged to his own from the height of the yardarm of HMS *Gannet*.[33]

In 1828 Hone had finally to admit that writing would never be enough to extract him from a morass of financial disaster. At some point in 1827 or 28, he was approached by Moxhay, a prosperous biscuit supplier to the East India Company, who made mystifying overtures, offering him a job, 'something of a public nature in the city, which his influence and connections in the city can secure'. The plan, undoubtedly, was for Hone to sell off the rights to his books, which would have made an excellent long-term investment for the businessman. Had Moxhay not suddenly appeared in his life, Hone said, 'my spirits must have broken under the conflict'. At least now 'I shall have the prospect of passing a few years with my excellent wife in comparative happiness'. He regretted ever having picked up a pen in the first place, 'for I have had nothing but vicissitudes'; if he had not constantly thought of his children, he said, 'my evening prayers would have been that I might not awake to the miseries of another day'.[34]

But Moxhay could not cope with the Hone debts, which had grown and not abated over the years that he had been in debtors' gaol. Hunt and Clarke had badly mismanaged his literary affairs. Moreover, the book trade at this time was in the midst of depression; many small booksellers and publishers had gone out of business as the market evaporated. The *Table Book* was a commonplace book of high literary accomplishment: gone were the whimsy and quaint anecdotes that had made the *Every-day Book* so popular; and therein lay its commercial failure. Hunt and Clarke followed Hone into debt, and Moxhay withdrew his offer. A deeply frustrated Hone reacted with impotent rage: 'Since my Trials, I have struggled amidst mental infirmities and pecuniary embarrassments for the support of a large family. I had been out-reasoned by sincere friends, desirous of my welfare, into the notions that I could become a man of business, and they persuaded and assisted me, till my unfitness for the position became apparent to them as well as to myself, and I could go on no longer.'[35]

Hone may have wanted to use his wits to rescue himself from his troubles, but as the possibility receded, so did hope: 'My unremitted exertions during more than a year and a half of alternating hope and despondency, have involved me so much deeper that I am without the power of further maintaining my family, or of extricating myself from duress.' In September 1828, two and a half years after he had been taken to the King's Bench Prison, Hone was compelled to give up his stubborn resistance and declare himself bankrupt. The family left Belvedere Place and pestilential Southwark for the tranquillity of Islington.

The rights to Hone's *Books* had finally been sold to Thomas Tegg, a rapacious London publisher, who, like Hone, had ridden the wave of the satire boom before transferring his interests to genteel, mannered social comedies and textbooks. But, unlike Hone, he had made a fortune, managing to buy a mansion in Cheapside, which had formerly been the official residence of the Lord Mayors of London. Tegg advanced Hone £400 to write the *Year Book* along the exact model of the *Every-day Book*.

The *Year Book* would not come out until 1832. In the meantime Tegg employed Hone to compile the *Full Annals of the Revolution in France* [of 1830], a chronological survey of the revolution, from its outbreak to the enthronement of Louis Philippe as a constitutional monarch in September 1830, made up of English and French newspaper articles, letters, personal interviews with eyewitnesses, biographies, reports of debates in the Chamber of Deputies, and historical parallels. Tegg probably chose him as editor because the major theme was the freedom of the French press, and the name William Hone on the title page would have been a selling point. Charles X's Ordinances had legislated against 'the poisoned darts of the press' by closing Parisian newspapers. According to Hone, it was the threat of arbitrary government exemplified in censorship that inspired the bravery of the 'loungers and frequenters of the cafés' (and other supposedly typical Parisians) in confronting the troops. Implied all the way through the book is the lesson of what happens when governments threaten the freedom of public discussion: the people inevitably rebel. As Hone wrote of 25 June 1830: 'The people were induced to maintain their right to the inestimable blessings of a free press, and good government . . . The drums of the National Guard beat "to arms!" The populace answered the calls amid the incessant ringing of the tocsin and the struggle began in earnest.' As a younger man, he might have dedicated a few passages to extolling the principles of free speech; in this work however, Hone chose to be more subtle, keeping the contrast between the freedom of the British press and French censorship merely implicit. And with that Hone finally ended his career as a political writer.

Tegg's £400 investment began to look slightly risky when Hone managed to blow his advance for the *Year Book*, spending most of the cash on renting his house in Islington; 'He is just now in a critical situation,' Lamb told Southey. Hone conceded in a letter published in *The Times*: 'I have lost everything on earth, except my integrity and 10 children.'[36] To prevent Hone once more having to return to the squalor of Southwark, which would have been fatal to the *Year Book*, Tegg stepped in to save him. Yet another subscription had to be advertised for him; the initial contribution from the public was £165, including gifts of £20 each from Tegg and the Duke of Bedford. It was a far cry from the spontaneous national generosity after the trials, but eventually it made enough for Hone to set up as the proprietor of the Grasshopper coffee house in Gracechurch Street in the heart of the city.

It was a bizarre proposition for the great political writer and literary journalist to be serving coffee to city workers. And indeed he was deeply humiliated and resentful at his fall. When Lamb paid a visit just after the Hones took over the Grasshopper in May 1830, he found that his friend had not even bothered to buy any coffee-making equipment, furniture or newspapers. The advertisement 'Good Beds and early Breakfasts' proved to be slightly optimistic. He wrote to Southey from the café commenting on the Spartan arrangements: 'So I am sitting in the skeleton of a possible divan.' He painted a pathetic scene of a coffee shop with an ambivalent host unwilling to provide any refreshments: 'Here his wife and all his children are about me, gaping for coffee customers; but how should they come in seeing no pot boiling . . .?'

Hone would agree with Lamb's rueful comment that 'Those "Every-Day" and "Table Books" will be a treasure a hundred years hence, but they have failed to make Hone's fortune.' It was scant consolation. His spirits were utterly and irrevocably broken. He suffered all the humiliations of a once-famous writer reduced to making breakfasts for workmen; 'hard and appalling work', he called it. 'I have thrown down my pen forever,' Hone told *The Times*, 'and, at fifty years of age, am struggling to enter on a strange drudgery, for the future support of my wife and family.'[37] But however much he wished to give up the pen, he was contractually bound to finish the *Year Book*, and the project became burdensome. Tegg quibbled with the costs he was incurring: 'The expense far exceeds the amount stated by you in the estimate,' he told Hone, and interfered with his editorial decisions. Writer's block plagued him, and he haunted the bar and coffee room of the Grasshopper saying things like, 'I take it I am a doomed man.'[38]

'Mr Hone said he had not looked into a newspaper for four months,' the Cambridge fellow J. Fuller Russell remembered of a conversation in

1833. 'He cared little for passing events, for he knew that the whole frame of society would be dislocated and dissolved. The materials were rotten.'39

Hone was talking of the Great Reform Act, which had recently been passed. The editor of the *Reformists' Register* and the mind behind *The Political House that Jack Built* would have been more than satisfied with the bill's provisions that abolished many rotten boroughs and expanded the franchise; he would have celebrated the victory of public opinion over William IV and the House of Lords. But, at the age of fifty-three, Hone had abandoned all his former political views: 'Ministers had exceeded the wishes of all moderate reformers by their measure ... They had, like Frankenstein, raised a monster which they could not tame ... From that date there ceased to be a government. The disloca-tion of society had risen from the separation of the aristocracy from their dependents, and the dissolution of the paternal relationship for-merly existing between these classes.' Those who remembered Hone as the iconoclastic spokesman of the people, the symbol of discontent, would have been surprised to hear him declare: 'The old Tory, is a gen-tleman who commands respect; but what are modern Tories? – *Whigs*, and Whigs are grubs, door-rugs, fit only to wipe one's feet on!'40

These were not the words of a convert to Toryism, but an embittered old man with no interest in politics. His disavowal of his early life was complete; querulous, depressed and a failure, his natural response was to lash out at his successors in the reform movement and the Whigs who had once been his greatest allies. The freedom of the press and reform had, in the end, brought him no rewards. Every achievement of his life had ended in misfortune and poverty. What did he have to celebrate?

Politics was an unwelcome interruption to a hard life. Moreover, there was a new passion in Hone's life which put everything else in the shade. His unhappiness, he began to believe, was the debt he owed for a 'wayward youth' and a life wasted on 'political frivolities'. What had he achieved but bleak depression, bodily fatigue and the ruin of his family? One day, in the depth of his gloom, he walked into the Weigh-House Chapel, Eastcheap. He had 'not been accustomed to attend a place of worship', but he came out from the sermon with a 'mind dis-turbed, but deeply solemnised'. He found in an instant that 'everything appeared changed – the world and its pleasures, literature and its choicest works had lost their charms'. 'In a very short time it pleased God to break down my self-will,' he told his brother, 'and enable me to surrender my heart to Him . . . I found that I myself had changed, and the mystery of salvation, through the eye of faith, and by the power of grace, a precious truth, by which my rebellious will has been subjugated, and my heart reconciled to God.'[41]

If his life had been a quest for truth – in politics, the beauty of literature, the trappings of secular idealism – it had been utterly futile. The answer had been with him from the day of his birth, embodied in his father, who had but one book, the Bible, and had been blissfully happy. He hadn't made his wife and children's lives miserable with risky court cases, journalistic adventures and the threat of bankruptcy. Never morbidly depressed, he had sought only to be close to his God, and he had died happy. His son, however, had pursued controversy, fame and ephemeral dreams throughout his wretched life, and there was nothing to show for it except a seedy city coffee shop bought through the charity of his friends. Worse still, he had 'detached' his 'dear wife' from her own pious life, and failed to instruct his children with religious knowledge.[42]

The coffee-house venture lasted but three years, during which time one of his daughters ran away from home, another had a nervous breakdown, and Hone suffered the first of a series of paralytic strokes. In 1833 he was bankrupt, the Grasshopper in the hands of his creditors and, as he said, 'I was stripped of every atom I possessed in the world.' Much later Alfred Hone worked out that Tegg had made £412 for every thousand copies he sold of the *Everyday Book* and £206 for the same number of *Table Books*. In the years 1838–9 alone, Tegg sold 80,000 copies of the *Books* for a profit of £37,000. Had Hone not given up the struggle and sold his copyright, he would have paid off his debts with ease and become a wealthy man.[43] As it was, he was given a grant by the Literary Fund after he wrote a humiliating letter of supplication: 'I am too much enfeebled to move about, and my family is in great distress, and I am worried by little claims upon me, and have not a shilling.'[44]

Armed with his newfound faith, he re-entered the world of journalism. In 1834 he joined the staff of the militantly evangelical *Patriot* newspaper as a sub-editor. Hone commuted every morning from the village of Peckham to Bolt Court, back to his old stamping ground of Fleet Street, where the paper was based. After more strokes, Hone moved into the offices, waking each morning at seven and working until midnight; whilst his body was collapsing, the compulsion to write remained undimmed.

In 1836 Hone went for a walk with his youngest daughter, the eleven-year-old Alice, and once more he was struck down: 'We had walked a few hundred yards when my mind became confused, my sight obscured, and I had general indications of oppression of the brain.' Yet he continued to devote every moment of his waning life to the newspaper, receiving just £2 a week as recompense: 'The paper ought to afford more, but it does not.'[45]

The *Patriot* was required reading for nonconformists, the weekly paper dedicating itself to an attack on the Anglican hegemony of religion that forced members of dissenting chapels to pay tithes to churches they never went to. Hone was once again campaigning for reform, but now it was to make life more equitable for religious minorities. Hone sat through innumerable committee meetings and hacked his way through daily newspapers, assembling the facts that would allow his editor to make the case for ecclesiastical reform. His talent for polemical argument, sweeping attack and penetrating caricature was unnecessary; he started his career afresh as a plodding assistant in a newspaper office. The editor, Josiah Condor, described him as 'the very impersonation of indefatigable industry and incorruptible honesty and integrity'.[46]

The staff of the newspaper were little concerned that the elderly man who haunted their offices had once been a great journalist; for them his importance lay in the fact that he was a penitent sinner at last seeking salvation; what he had been before his rebirth as a Christian was quite simply irrelevant. That 'his conscience was awakened to a just sense of man's condition as a sinner', was all that was required of him.

On his birthday in 1837, Hone encountered the Reverend Thomas Raffles in the vestry of the Weigh-House Chapel. The two had met in 1822, when Hone was at the height of his fame as a satirist. 'I am another man,' he told Raffles, and he ripped the flyleaf from his Bible upon which he had written a poem; 'take this as an evidence and memorial of the change.' The poem, entitled 'Lines Written before Breakfast, 3rd June 1834, the anniversary of my birthday in 1780', testified to his complete rejection of his political past:

> The proudest heart that ever beat
> Hath been subdued in me;
> The wildest will that ever rose
> To scorn Thy cause, and aid Thy foes,
> Is quelled, my God, by Thee.
>
> Thy will, and not my will be done;
> My heart be ever Thine –
> Confessing Thee, the mighty Word,
> I hail Thee, Christ, my God, my Lord,
> And make Thy name my sign.[47]

Hone worked as hard as he ever had done for the *Patriot* – grinding, pedantic work. In 1837 he awoke as usual in the offices but found he could not get up to work: 'A spell has bound my faculties.' He was compelled to give up the job for good, and retired to Hampstead and then Tottenham, doing part-time editorial work for the *Patriot*. Two years later, on his fifty-ninth birthday, he suffered another stroke: 'In the morning I found my faculties of expression by tongue and hand impaired – today they are feebler – my powers have been over-wrought. The mind, as mind, is clear and firm. I am only to others seeming idiot – or idiot-like. With great difficulty I scrawl . . . I can neither speak nor write clearly.'[48]

At the height of his career his handwriting was large, bold and confident. After the second incarceration in the King's Bench Prison, it became small and crabbed. By the late 1830s it was the barely legible scrawls of a man hardly able to hold a pen. But, amazingly, considering the havoc of a series of strokes, he published his last book in the summer of 1841. It was a homage to the father he had rejected as a young child. He collected William Hone senior's account of his life as a dissolute youth and early conversion to Christianity. It was the life he should have replicated, following his father's simple pious example. He commented on his father: 'It often seemed that he would be over-whelmed, yet he never suffered from distress.'

The son had looked for answers in philosophy, literature and history, and it had brought misery. 'I willed to be as happy as my Father – but this was impossible,' Hone wrote in his autobiographical notes. 'I concluded that he was happy because he was ignorant. He knew nothing of literature, never read a newspaper, and it was difficult to obtain his attention for more than a few minutes to news or details of great public events . . . he lived by faith and prayer.' Comparing his addiction to reading and politics with his father's tranquil, Godly existence, Hone wrote that they had both been pursuing happiness, but, 'I had sought mine in the frivolities of worldly life, and in books, some of which had ensnared and deluded me.' And at the end of his life, William Hone was left disillusioned:

Sometimes I wished that I, too, had been ignorant – ignorant of the book which had caused me to doubt, and to believe that death was annihilation. I began to question whether my knowledge was of any use. It gave liberty to do as I would, but not the power. I desired to make every being happy and virtuous, but I saw that if I could diffuse all the wealth in the world that its inhabitants could not be *happy* with my knowledge, and I was *sure* they would not be virtuous.

Hone repented his wasted life: atheism, rejection of his loving father, solace in books, political games, and, above all else, the fatal religious parodies – painful reminders of a peccable existence. The consolation was that, for the Victorians, his name was identified with the *Every-day Book* and its successors rather than with the trials or the satires; when the trials were remembered, it was in the context of a sinner's later conversion and repentance. Looking back on his career, he wrote, '. . . I struck out into the gulfstream of Politics, and drifted into its very vortex. There was no happiness for me in that whirlpool . . .' He had nothing to offer God 'but a contrite heart'.[49]

14

That New and Mighty Power

In 1819 the Austrian Frederick von Gentz, a friend of Metternich and supporter of the Holy Alliance, was shocked to find that judges in Britain had no censorial power to place restraints on the press. Compared to Europe, censorship laws in Britain had become confused, even defunct, so that 'the dexterity and ingenuity of the delinquent will enable him to overstep all legal bounds'.[1]

'The public authorities', he continued, 'are assailed by masses of calumny, falsehood and odium, which they are no longer capable of examining, far less of repressing.' And he dated the impotence of state prosecutors in matters of censorship to December 1817:

The case of HONE, the bookseller, in which all that could in scenes of the same sort, be regarded as mortifying to the Government, and encouraging to those who wish to disparage it, was concentrated in one focus, has, at length, made manifest the long since decided victory of the Press of the Populace over the State, and exhibited that victory in features so gigantic, that if the Ministry do not devise some new remedies, or call some new forces to their aid, perhaps the wisest determination would be to renounce, entirely, those criminal prosecutions, and to abandon the Press to its own delirium.[2]

Sidmouth's 'Gagging Act' had been intended to halt the torrent of 'libellous' publications which he believed had been unleashed by Hone's acquittal. Yet in the years that followed, the press existed in almost complete freedom, the degree of its venom both unprecedented and not to be seen again for over a century. The King and the government were powerless to act against a deluge of hostile publications. Sidmouth had promised parliament that the laws of criminal libel, badly mauled by Hone, were still efficacious and capable of keeping the press within reasonable bounds. The furore of the Queen Caroline case proved that he was wrong; the established means of dealing with the press were defunct; the law had been brought into utter contempt by its impotence.

Between 1819 and 1821 journalists wrote with a freedom never experienced and with a self-conscious impunity from the operation of the law. Scarcely a decade before, Cobbett had been imprisoned for criticising flogging in the army and the Hunt brothers for saying that Prince George was not 'an Adonis in loveliness' but a 'corpulent gentleman of fifty'. A decade before that, men had been imprisoned merely for voicing reformist opinions. The savagery of the press after 1819 made those 'libels' of recent memory seem innocuous. The sense of change that many felt in 1820 can be charted in Hone's satires. *The Man in the Moon* was written in January 1820 as the gagging act was being enacted, when the government's new powers were yet to be tested. In the satire, the Regent commands his ministers

> TO CHECK THE CIRCULATION
> OF LITTLE BOOKS,
> whose very looks –
> Vile *'two-p'nny trash'*,
> bespeak abomination.
> Oh! they are full of blasphemies
> and libels,
> And people read them
> oftener than their bibles
> ... go, and be planning,
> Within your virtuous minds, what best will answer
> To save *our* morals from this public cancer.

But by August of the same year, during the Queen's trial, the situation was reversed. The government's legislative energy and persecution of Caroline roused journalists and satirists to the highest pitch of indignation. Despite new acts of parliament, they operated in complete freedom. In *Non Mi Ricordo* George is trapped on the red-hot 'grillery', another of Hone's appellations for the press.

The country lapped up the thousands of satires and personal attacks against the King and the cabinet. The venom of the press reflected the country's anger after Peterloo and during the Bill of Pains and Penalties. Satire was considered the most expressive medium of protest. It also showed in the most vivid way the breakdown in the laws: humour was immune from prosecution. It might seem odd that the freedom of the press in Britain was established during this time and in such a way.

It is perhaps a curiosity of British history that laughter was the spring of liberty. It seems so *trivial*: hardly a motor of change, the stuff of heroic resistance to repression. But laughter is impossible to silence. At the time, it was acknowledged that satire was a way of evading and defying censorship; it had a political function. The press went as far as it did in 1820 because, ironically, the libel laws had the capacity to prosecute moderate criticism, but let the most excessive and violent satires go unpunished. Jeremy Bentham recognised its function in his book *On the Liberty of the Press and Public Discussion* (1821), in which the philosopher advised the Spanish on how they might defeat the censorship that King Ferdinand had imposed upon them:

'Vile Two-p'nny Trash'
From *The Man in the Moon*. Ministers murder Truth and shackle the press, reflecting the unease at the beginning of 1820 when the Gagging Act had just been passed.

By degrees, a sort of language will come into use; a language that will be sufficiently understood for any such purpose as that of giving expression to complaint and indignation, yet will not be sufficiently understood for any such
purpose as that of affording a tenable ground for the infliction of punishment.

Yes: in every apartment defiled by this liberticide yoke, the instrument of
thraldom, the parchment or paper on which it is written, should be hung up on
high; hung up in some spot universally conspicuous, with an appropriate
accompaniment for pointing men's attention to it. By a single glance directed
to this instrument of tyranny, eulogy might be converted into satire; satire
which, be it what it may, can never be too severe.[3]

Musing on the situation in Spain, Bentham was looking at what had
happened in Britain since 1817. His book came from the same printing
press that had issued hundreds of thousands of copies of *The Political
House* and *The Matrimonial Ladder*. Choosing William Hone as his

'The *Fat* in the Fire'
From *Non Mi Ricordo*. The pessimism of early 1820 gives way to
confidence; the press is free, and has the power to inflict pain.

publisher, Bentham made no effort to conceal whom he thought responsible for such a striking change in the balance between the state and the press. The libel laws, for all their savagery and bias in favour of state prosecutors, could not punish satirists. 'Everyone laughed at what Hone had issued,' Dr Mackenzie wrote in 1847. But it was not mere entertainment; the satires 'did the Ministry a thousand times the actual damage' that any conventional piece of journalism ever had done. And the government had to look on while they were savagely mocked, powerless to prosecute the champion of the Guildhall: 'The Attorney-General would have been laughed out of court, had he tried anything of the kind.' The satires were 'the light weapons of ridicule that went through the armour which a heavier weapon could not enter.' The *Loyalists' Magazine*, the King's favourite paper, wrote: 'So effective have been these publications, that they have intimidated the authorities of the land: they have driven back the current of justice in its highest channels!'[4] As a result of the changes he detected, Bentham was able to publish two books he had hitherto suppressed for fear of imprisonment: *Elements of the Act of Packing, as applied to Special Juries* (written 1809, published 1821) and *Truth versus Ashhurst* (written 1792, published 1823).

In 1822 Henry Brougham summed up the changes of recent years: 'To a period of excessive restraint, almost approaching to persecution, succeeded a season of total indifference on the part of the Government and the Law Officers, hardly to be accounted for upon any supposition consistent with the belief that their duty was faithfully and resolutely performed.'[5]

In the aftermath of Hone's trials the press, von Gentz wrote, was in 'neither more nor less than a state of anarchy, occasionally interrupted by the feeble checks of an arbitrary discretion, accidentally roused'.[6] The freedom of the press did not date from Hone's trials, nor did his satires single-handedly destroy censorship. But they symbolised the growing liberty of discussion. It is through Hone's writings, defence in court and the discussions of his victory in parliament that we can get closer to the process by which the laws withered. From the early 1820s things were changing. Prosecutions *ex officio* became sporadic and the Home Office abandoned any pretence that it could regulate the 'licentiousness' of the radical press. The Attorney-General could no longer count on Special Juries to convict the journalists he selected for exemplary punishment. The country was set against political trials; it had seen and read too much of biased judges and unwarranted cruelty in the courts. The full implications of the changes in press prosecutions were little understood in the early 1820s. After a decade, in 1831, looking back at the 'Gagging Act', Thomas Babbington Macaulay told the House of Commons:

In 1819 the Ministers complained of the alarming increase of seditious and blasphemous publications. They proposed a bill of great vigour to stop the growth of the evil; and they carried their bill . . . last year we repealed it: but it was already dead, or, rather it was dead born. It was obsolete before *Le Roi le veut* had been pronounced over it. For any effect which it produced it might as well have been in the Code Napoleon as in the English Statute Book.

And why did the government, having solicited and procured so sharp and mighty a weapon, straightway hang it up to rust? [Macaulay continued]. Was there fewer libels, after the passing of the Act than before it? Sir, the very next year was the year 1820, the year of the Bill of Pains and Penalties against Queen Caroline, the very year when the public mind was most excited, the very year when the press was most scurrilous. Why then did not the Ministers use their new power? Because they durst not: because they could not. They had obtained it with ease; for in obtaining it they had to deal with a subservient Parliament. They could not execute it: for in executing it they would have to deal with a refractory people. This is but one of many instances of the difficulty of carrying the law into effect when the people are inclined to thwart their rulers.

Hone took a leading role in thwarting the government. The Whigs and the government itself were certain that something significant had happened at the Guildhall in 1817. Prosecutions *ex officio* and other oppressive measures against the press did not die out completely in the years after 1819. Richard Carlile, editor of the *Republican*, was indicted and convicted for blasphemy when he republished parts of Paine's *Rights of Man*, and he would serve sentences for other libellous publications in the early 1820s. Booksellers, publishers, journalists and hawkers continued to be prosecuted in 1820 and 1821. The crucial change after December 1817, however, was a revolt among jurymen against harsh punishment and political trials. Hone neither set a legal precedent nor changed a law. What he achieved for the British press was just as important, however. Brougham wrote that censorship had become unworkable when ministers 'greatly exceeded the bounds of moderation and turned men's minds against their persecuting schemes'.[7] This happened in courts throughout the land, in the pages of the national and local papers and the government's tactics. However, in 1817 the case study of the abuses of the libel laws, from arrest to trial, to be found in the pages of Hone's *Three Trials* did more than any polemic, parliamentary speech or legal judgment to expose the government's unfair advantage, hypocrisy and vindictive measures. It was the starting point for popular resistance against the laws.

Hone's trials exposed the injustices of press prosecutions, teaching the public about the corruption of the law. He convinced three juries, and much of the country with his satires, that ministers were 'little men with little minds', that they were actuated by considerations of party advantage, that his and other journalists' trials should be stripped of the 'hypocritical pretext' of blasphemy and sedition when they were prosecuted for political crimes. Sidmouth, Ellenborough, Southey, MPs, clergymen and Tory journalists had spent 1817 trying to convince the country that the freedom of the press threatened the order of society and would inevitably bring revolution. That battle for the sympathy of public opinion and the approval of juries was lost when Hone, supposedly the most dangerous journalist to be found in Britain, threw light on the cant, downright lies and calculated malice of the ministry.

The obvious bias of the law in favour of state prosecutors was threatening to undermine its efficacy when jurors refused to punish journalists who had either already suffered punishment on remand or were likely to receive the excessively harsh sentence of transportation to New South Wales. The people Hone convinced of the inequality inherent in censorship trials were, in the first instance, Special Jurors – the propertied, independent gentlemen whom the government looked upon as the preservers of order. If the ministers recognised the existence of public opinion, it consisted of these kinds of men, the representatives of moderation, morality and decency. Their failure to win over the eminent London merchants and bankers who sat on Special Juries, and Hone's ability to gain their sympathy, rendered prosecutions *ex officio* and trials for criminal libel an unreliable way of confronting the press. The Whig Lords pointed to the subscription fund raised by the country to save Hone from poverty after his trials. It was an indication that public opinion was set against the government's heavy-handed measures when so many people, especially aristocrats, clergymen, merchants and squires, were prepared to give their money to a man bruited the most malevolent libeller in the country. Even if jurors believed that defendants were guilty, they were now reluctant to condone the government's excessive punishments and the injustice of prosecutions *ex officio*; they were not inclined to become the tools of ministers in avowedly political trials. The Attorney-General was forced to concede that, since Hone's trials had become known throughout the country, the public had become resistant to severe measures: 'Is it too much to say, that it is impossible under such circumstances to expect a verdict of guilty against persons prosecuted for a similar offence?'[8]

This is what began to happen in trials throughout the country from 1819. However, had Hone been convicted in 1817, or the government chosen a different victim, the situation in the years between 1819 and 1822 would have been much less friendly for the press. Hone was moderate enough in his political opinions and defence to attract widespread sympathy, even from Tories and those hostile to the press. There were many examples of bravery at this time comparable to Hone's resistance to Ellenborough. Richard Carlile published works that had already been found libellous by juries, and wrote articles he knew would be prosecuted. He acted in defiance of the laws, and gloried in self-immolation for the sake of his opinions. But Carlile was a firebrand and reckless enthusiast. When he was brought to trial in 1819 for blasphemy, he called upon Hone's advice. Hone obliged, but he avowed that he could not support the younger man's views or mode of defence. Carlile did more harm than good in his determination to be gaoled for libel; his writing was violent and reckless, stating the radical case for reform, and invited prosecution. Noble as his refusal to trim his opinions was, this mode of attacking the libel laws was not designed to gain the sympathy of public opinion, and certainly not that of Special Jurors. If the government had restricted its censorship trials to writers like Carlile, it might have achieved greater success; the country would have been persuaded that the more extreme reformist press needed to be curbed, and juries more inclined to convict. But as a writer and defendant, Hone was remembered as moderate and good-natured. The trials made him one of the most famous men in the country, and, for a few years, the most popular publisher. The government had made a rod for its own back, and, as one MP teased the ministers, the trials had 'raised [Hone] (merely by prosecution) from an obscure individual to a man known in every corner of England, Scotland, and Wales . . . '[9] Every satire Hone issued forth was a periodic reminder to the country and government of the days at the Guildhall.

Most realised that the laws had become unenforceable, but some Tories were still convinced that the press was a nuisance that should and could be silenced. Disgusted with the inactivity of the Home Secretary and the Attorney-General, a group of 'loyalists' founded a private prosecution society to fulfil the duty of censorship from which the state had shamefully retreated. Its leading members were men familiar from Hone's career in journalism: Dr Stoddart, Robert Southey and the Duke of Wellington. They raised money to fund prosecutions against reformist journalists, particularly satirists. The Constitutional Association, based in Bridge Street, Blackfriars, had the resources and the backing to emerge as a viable successor to the Crown in press prosecutions.

But it was ridiculed as effectively as the King's deficiencies and Sidmouth's gagging acts. Hone's last satire, *A Slap at Slop*, rendered the Constitutional Association ('The Bridge Street Gang') a laughing stock. Hone took great delight in instancing every example of blasphemy and obscenity that had been issued by the would-be prosecutors. The hypocrisy of journalists and publishers like Dr Stoddart and 'Don' John Murray, who issued libels against reformers and the late Queen and printed works that would have counted as criminal, but who expected their political opponents to be savagely punished, made the Bridge Street Gang one of the most unpopular institutions in the country. Hone accused them of acting 'like the hacknied procuress who, to effect her designs upon innocence, pretends an extraordinary affection for virtue. What shameful pimping to the whiffling understandings of the timid! What artful pandering to pampered bloatedness! What an insolent appeal from the minions of power, and the overgorged feeders upon the public wealth, to their fellow parasites and gluttons!' Hone felt it only fair to warn Dr Slop that he was risking imprisonment or transportation to Botany Bay by breaking the libel laws: 'He must submit to his Political Godfather's public correction . . . If this is not a warning to him, there's no knowing what he may come to.'

Private prosecutions were quickly shown to be as ineffectual as the government's formal censorship. After the publication of *A Slap at Slop*, the Constitutional Association indicted Hone for seditious libels published in *Non Mi Ricordo* and *The Queen's Ladder*; it was Dr Slop's last chance to inflict revenge on his tormentor. The Grand Jury of Middlesex and Westminster did not hesitate to give a verdict of 'not found' on the grounds for indictment. Despite the Association's repeated attempts to bring prosecutions throughout the country and the vast amounts it spent harassing poor publishers, it managed to secure just four convictions, only one of which resulted in a sentence. As early as June 1822 Brougham would brush off 'The Bridge Street Gang' as existing in a 'state of insignificance . . . through the conduct of its agents, and partly through the declared opinion of the public'. As Hone had hoped, the self-appointed inquisitors became laughing stocks. 'While it continued in operation,' Brougham sneered, 'there was nothing absurd or reprehensible which it did not seem ready to attempt.' People were not prepared for the crusade of one set of journalists against another, especially when it had nothing to do with morality or public safety and everything to do with political disagreements and personal vendettas. The days of the loyal jury, which operated on the government's behalf in the 1790s and period 1810-12, were over.

It was this realisation which meant that by the mid-1820s press prosecutions were rare. As Brougham wrote, any attempt to revive the spirit of persecution that had dealt with Cobbett, the Hunts, Burdett Thomas Wooler, William Hone and Carlile would have 'aggravated the mischief complained of, and rendered him who hazarded them in endless difficulties'.[10] In 1829 the Prime Minister, the Duke of Wellington, brought the *Morning Chronicle* to trial when it called him, amongst other things, proud and overbearing and accused him of usurping the power of the Crown. His friend Greville wrote in his diary that the Duke 'would [not] be sorry to adopt any measure which should tend to fetter free discussion, and subject the press to future punishment. But this would be a fearful war to wage, and I do not think he is rash to undertake such a crusade.' He did not have a chance; the mood of the 1820s was entirely different from the first two decades of the nineteenth century. People would no longer believe ministers who attempted to whip up anti-press hysteria or interfere with its freedoms. The juries in Wellington's hesitant crusade either acquitted the defendants or gave qualified verdicts. Even one of those journalists convicted could not be sentenced; Greville wrote: 'Imprisonment will appear to most people too severe a punishment for the offence. The whole press have entered upon this occasion, and in some very powerful articles have spread to every corner of the country the strongest condemnation of the whole proceedings.'[11] As Home Secretary, Sir Robert Peel had tended to shy away from enacting the libel laws. He was not more sympathetic to the free press than Sidmouth, but he knew that he would attract odium and most likely fail if he emulated his predecessor's zeal. In opposition, in 1832, he told parliament that anyone who had any 'official experience connected with the press' would be 'sensible of the danger of a crusade rashly directed against it'.[12]

'Our law of libel is the most absolutely severe that ever existed, so absurdly severe that, if it were carried into full effect, it would be much more oppressive than a censorship,' Thomas Macaulay told the Commons in 1831. 'And yet, with this severe law of libel, we have a Press which practically is as free as the air.'[13]

The theme of William Hone's life in journalism was the gradual co-existence of the harshest libel law in the world with one of the freest presses. The American envoy Richard Rush, who took up his diplomatic post two days after Hone's last trial, noted during his seven-year embassy that if the British press did not have the greatest legal freedom, it certainly enjoyed a latitude amounting to complete impunity. As many acknowledged, the press was free, if not under the laws, in practice and daily example.

Throughout the 1820s politicians were forced to reconsider their attitude to the press. In a letter to Lord Liverpool in 1820, George Canning wrote: '*The State* complains of the Queen's misconduct, which makes her unfit, etc etc. "Eh bien", will the Jacobin say; 'the State complains of the King's misconduct, which makes him unfit" etc.

And can the Government which prosecute the Queen grapple success-fully with this argument?"[14]

It was clear that it could not. The government had no means of engaging with public opinion. It had allowed the press to portray Queen Caroline, a disgraced old woman, as a saintly paragon; its failure to justify the King's case had handed the Whigs and reformists an important victory when public pressure forced Liverpool to drop the Bill of Pains and Penalties. Its popularity had slipped to a nadir and, for a while, the Whigs were convinced that they would be called upon to form an administration. The government's inability to win the confi-dence of parliament and the country had it weakened almost to the point of collapse. Throughout the 1820s, the ministry modified its atti-tude to the press and public opinion.

George Canning had been hostile to the popular press, voting for the Six Acts in 1819 and, in a series of well-publicised speeches a few months later, criticised 'the storms of public commotion' and denied that the people should have 'a direct and daily influence of their tem-porary passions' over the sober deliberations of parliament.[15] Shortly after saying this, Canning resigned from the cabinet because of its treat-ment of Caroline. Whilst out of office he studied the effect the press had in crippling the government. In 1822 the government completely changed character when Castlereagh committed suicide and Sidmouth and Eldon resigned the great offices of state. Canning returned to office as Foreign Secretary and, seeking re-election for his seat, described modern politics. Within two years, he had undergone a conversion in his attitude to the press. He compared it to the recently invented steam ship, 'that new and mighty power'. Just as a writer who did not mention the steam engine would give an incomplete account of nautical science:

So, in political science, he who speculating on the British Constitution, should content himself with marking the distribution of acknowledged technical pow-ers between the House of Lords, the House of Commons, and the Crown, and assigning to each their separate powers ... and should think that he had thus described the British Constitution as it acts and as it is influenced in its action: but should omit from his enumeration the mighty power of public opinion, embodied in a free Press, which pervades, and checks, and perhaps, in the last resort, nearly governs the whole. Such a man would, surely, give but an imperfect view of the government of England as it is now modified, and would greatly underrate the counteracting influences against which that of the executive has to contend.[16]

Such a revolutionary view of the press had more in common with Hone and Wooler than anything normally heard from a cabinet minister. Sidmouth and Ellenborough waged war against this kind of opinion in 1817; had his trial not collapsed, Wooler would have gone to prison for saying the same thing. The essence of Hone's defence, that 'the English government is founded on public opinion; without it cannot exist as a free government – it would be an arbitrary despotism', was considered radical in 1817; less than five years later it was being held up as a constitutional maxim by a minister of the crown. The struggle for the freedom of the press was as much about making the government listen as about destroying censorship. Men such as Robert Southey and Lord Sidmouth had advised that any opinion that came from outside the walls of Westminster or the palace was not to be heeded. This strongly defended view was beginning to become redundant by the 1820s. A minister who claimed that the press had a *legitimate* role in the constitution was indicative of a revolution in attitudes towards the press.

Public opinion was important for Canning's political career. The King hated him because he suspected his minister had once had an affair with Caroline and had left the cabinet on her account. George IV joined the Ultra-Tories in regarding Canning with hostility for his support of Catholic emancipation. Yet he managed to reach the rank of Foreign Secretary and Leader of the House of Commons in 1822 and Prime Minister in 1827, despite the antipathy of the King, because he used public opinion as a base of his parliamentary power. He cultivated 'his' public, claiming: 'A representative of the people, I am one of the people; and I present myself to those who choose me only with the claims of character ... unaccredited by patrician patronage or party recommendation.'[17]

Canning needed 'public confidence' to make real his claims for power. But he also had the vision to realise that the press had attained an influence that no government could ignore. The demands for reform would grow louder every year unless men in power could justify the old

constitution, matching the reformists' sophisticated and convincing
rhetoric with propaganda of their own. In 1822 Lord John Russell
introduced a motion to the Commons calling for parliamentary reform.
In defeating it, Canning gave a brilliant account of the conservative case
against reform, one that ministers had failed to elucidate throughout
the 1810s. Lord Liverpool had once claimed that reform would make
Britain as barbarous as the United States; clearly this was not an expe-
dient or clever answer to the clamour for change.[18] Unlike Castlereagh,
Sidmouth or Liverpool, Canning was prepared to justify the old system
with conviction and verve.

Canning believed in the traditional 'mixed' constitution, and looked
with horror on any suggestion that the people should gain dispropor-
tionate power by electing a House of Commons. Universal suffrage
would upset the perfect balance of the constitution by relegating the
Lords and Crown to mere ciphers. The people should not express their
influence through the ballot box; instead, a free press would provide
them with a voice in the government of their country. 'I contend for a
House of Commons, the spirit of which, whatever be its frame, has,
without any forcible alteration, gradually, but faithfully, accommodated
itself to the progressive spirit of the country . . .' He believed that 'an
interchange of sentiment should take place between the representative
and his constituents'; this was not to be done by 'popular elections' but
by the medium of the press.[19]

Throughout his time as Foreign Secretary, Canning gave British support to the republicans in Latin America struggling against colonial
oppression, to the Spanish and Greek national movements, and he was
ardent in the suppression of the slave trade. In the name of English liberty, he resolutely opposed Britain's former allies, the absolute powers
who made up the Holy Alliance. Unlike no other minister before him,
Canning kept the public informed of all his actions, and he achieved
huge popularity for his 'liberal patriotism'; Britain congratulated herself as the champion of liberties throughout the world. Canning could
claim that the people were guiding policy, that reform was unnecessary
because ministers were the true representatives of the public will.
Greville wrote that 'he was the only statesman who had the sagacity to
enter into and comprehend the spirit of the times, and to put himself at

the head of that movement no longer to be arrested. The march of Liberalism (as it is called) would not be stopped, and this he knew, and he resolved to govern and lead instead of opposing it.' Canning used his position at the centre of politics, and as the representative of the constituency of Liverpool, to speak for sections of the community throughout the country just as Burdett and the Westminster Committee had done in another cause.[20]

The great changes in the relationship between the government and the press became apparent as the 1820s wore on; 'public opinion' was the phrase of the decade. In 1824 the influential political economist of the Edinburgh School, James McCulloch gave a series of lectures to an audience of the greatest politicians and economists in the country, which included several members of the cabinet. He told them of 'The great and increasing influence of public opinion – an influence which gives an impress to all acts of government, and to which, when firmly and deliberately expressed, the proudest minister must consent to bow ...' In 1829, when Wellington attempted to revive Sidmouth's policies, *The Times* was incredulous: 'Why do they discard their natural and most powerful ally? Why resort to the official prosecutor, who never yet in any age saved a feeble ministry from contempt, or added authority to a strong one?'[21]

When Wellington's Tory administration fell, in 1830, even a conservative like Greville put it down to 'a continual series of systematic blunders, and utter ignorance of, and indifference to, public opinion'. And that inability to do as Canning had done, to understand and court the people and the press, was considered 'egregious presumption, blindness, ignorance, and want of political calculation and foresight'. This was a language about, and acknowledgement of, the role of public opinion that had been treated with contempt a decade before.[22]

But as Macaulay said, the House of Commons was 'on the whole, aristocratical in its temper and interest. It was very far from being an illiberal and stupid oligarchy: but it was equally far from being the express image of the general feeling. It was influenced by the opinion of the people, and influenced powerfully, but slowly and circuitously.' The definition of public opinion was always unclear, but most people recognised the qualifications that were necessarily placed on it. McCulloch advised the high political world that 'the public should be well informed on all matters affecting the best interests of the state' before its voice became influential; only those with an advanced knowledge of political science should be counted within the hallowed constituency of public opinion.

Politicians were always vague about what kinds of people or parts of the press made up the public whose opinion they valued. In 1828 W. A. Mackinnon, a Tory MP, wrote: 'The House of Commons . . . does in fact represent the organ of public opinion: it both influences public opinion, and is still more influenced by that feeling.' For him, the historically inevitable rise of an informed, articulate and economically powerful middle class had made the press an influential voice in government.[23] Canning and his followers called upon this notional constituency of the middle classes as the basis of their power within the Commons. His patriotic speeches on the triumph of British liberalism over European oppression were made with this audience in mind, his natural supporters. The liberal Tory and Whig policies of thrift, temperance and humanity appealed to the respectable, rational and polite sections of the community – the prosperous and educated. There was little in 'liberal Toryism' to respond to that part of public opinion which demanded better working conditions, trade unions, humane poor relief and cheaper food. The deep-rooted anxiety about the effect of political journalism upon the uneducated poor had never left the debate. But from the late 1820s this threat was countered, not by prosecution, but by stringent taxation levied on cheap literature – so called 'taxes on knowledge' – which aimed to confine the influence of the press to the moderate and educated members of the community.

Yet notwithstanding the qualifications that must be placed on the emerging power of the press, the new language adopted towards it represents a break with an era of repressive censorship – indeed, the most fundamental moment of change in the history of the British press. When Foreign Secretary Lord Palmerston attacked Metternich for passing censorship laws through the German Diet in 1832, William IV asked his minister whether he really wanted the press in foreign countries 'to become, as it is *here*, the governing power, bidding defiance to the law and to every rule of society?' But the King was chafing against something he knew to be irreversible. Public opinion, Palmerston had told the House of Commons in 1828, was not just a useful means of attracting votes or justifying policies, it was the key to government: 'He who can grasp this power, with it will subdue the fleshy arm of political strength.' And of all powers it was the greatest in the world: 'those statesmen who know how to avail themselves of the passions, and the interests, and the opinions of affairs' achieve influence 'far out of proportion greater than belong to the power and resources of the state over which they preside'.[24]

In his 1828 speech Palmerston told the Commons that those 'who seek to check improvement, to cherish abuses, to crush opinions, and to prohibit the human race from thinking, will find their weapon snap short in their hand'.[25] This had been amplified by Hone eleven years before. Yet the iniquitous laws of criminal libel were not defeated by one man or by a single trial. They were never even repealed. Like so many other laws, they became obsolete when they proved unenforceable. Hone's trials marked the beginning of a revolt against libel trials on the part of jurymen. The consequences played themselves out over a few short years of political crisis. By the 1830s the press enjoyed freedom from legal penalties, and the memories of the bitter conflict of 1817 and 1819 began to fade.

The legal anomaly was acknowledged as a constitutional blessing in 1843 by a House of Lord's Committee set up to inquire into defamation and libel. It concentrated on the law of defamatory libel, stating that criminal libel was no longer relevant. Lord Campbell, the chairman, remarked that he had served as Attorney General for seven years and had brought only one prosecution for seditious libel. During that one trial, he had advised the jury to acquit the defendant. None of the witnesses called to give evidence to the committee (including past and present Lord Chancellors) believed there were any just criteria for drawing up a penal code which could define what was or was not prejudicial to public morals and order. In a landmark ruling, the Lords declared that the laws were 'at present very undefined' and if acted upon 'would seriously fetter the wholesome Liberty of the Press'; but 'from the mildness with which this branch of the criminal law has been administered by successive administrations, and from the liberality of judges and discrimination of juries in modern times, little practical inconvenience has been experienced from the arbitrary doctrines of past ages, though they have never been formally superseded; and the Committee do not find that, as far as public prosecutions are concerned, there is now any complaint from authors or journalists'.[26]

William Hone did not survive to hear the House of Lords declare that the laws he had spent the greater portion of his adult life fighting had dwindled into a lapsed doctrine. The news would probably not have meant much had his life been prolonged for a few months. He had not been able to reap the benefits of press freedom; it was as if his success as a political journalist and satirist had been dependant on having something to fight against. By the mid-1820s, he had become as much a relic of the Regency years as Sidmouth, Castlereagh and the laws of blasphemous and seditious libel.

In June 1842 Hone was showing signs of senile decay. One evening he returned to his home in Tottenham, which was one of a row of identical houses on a terrace. In the twilight, he mistakenly entered the wrong dwelling, and sat down with a group of strangers; it was some time before he realised that he was not among his family. He made to leave, but his neighbours were delighted with the eccentric old intruder. Clearly then, Hone's charm was still there.

'I am going to Tottenham this morning, on a cheerless mission I would willingly have avoided,' Charles Dickens wrote to a friend shortly after. 'Hone, of the "Every-Day Book", is dying, and sent Cruikshank yesterday to beg me to go and see him, as, having read no books but mine of late, he wanted to see and shake hands with me before (as George said) " he went".' Hone and Cruikshank had not seen each other for years, and the final meeting was a fond reconciliation between two close friends. The three men talked together for a long time; Hone clutched Cruikshank's hand, sobbing. An entry in the family diary for 5 October reads: 'Apparently our loved father is rather better, but we are assured by all recent changes that it is but the flickering of the lamp; the end may be sudden when it does come. He is calm and truly happy. George Cruikshank and Charles Dickens saw him today.'[27]

Dickens promised to call again, but by 18 October it was clear that death was imminent. Ellen wrote to Rose: 'His extreme weakness increases daily . . . your dear father is perpetually calm and collected and in a delightful frame of mind – in all his sufferings bearing them with *peaceful patience*, and in his mind enjoying perfect peace.'[28]

Two days later, one of the daughters wrote to a friend: 'My father is gradually sinking – his sun is setting, and it reminds me of such a sunset as we often see at this season, when after a bright and calm day, the glorious luminary sinks serenely to his rest, without a cloud to obscure the last rays of his departing.' He died on 6 November surrounded by his wife and nine surviving children. Dickens and Cruikshank made the journey up to the funeral at Abney Park Cemetery, Stoke Newington, a few days later. In the words of *The Times*, he died from 'increasing infirmities, occasioned not so much by years, as by the unremitting labours of his life'.[29]

Sarah Hone lived to her eighty-fourth year, and was buried alongside her husband in 1864. Abney Park Cemetery is appropriate as the last resting place of William Hone. It was founded in 1840 on unconsecrated land with a non-denominational chapel for the dissenting community of London. It was planned as an informal botanical garden, and by the end of the nineteenth century it had 2,500 different types of shrub, 1,000 varieties of rose, and 100,000 graves. Its owners abandoned it in the twentieth century, and it was finally purchased by the Borough of Hackney in 1979. The happy consequence of neglect is a thirty-one-acre pocket of untamed woodland and wild flowers, rightly cherished as an unique oasis of countryside amid urban sprawl. The roar of traffic from Stoke Newington High Street and Stamford Hill fades to a murmur as the visitor passes the gates, enters the dense wood and walks the narrow avenues and paths; the only sound is birdsong, and on a spring morning the scent of wild flowers and damp moss begins to penetrate petrol-enveloped nostrils.

In his last days, he had a pang of regret that he would die forgotten. But it only lasted a moment; Hone was happy to part from the world reconciled to his God, the sins of his life obscured by time. 'What a place Tottenham is to die in!' he said to one of his daughters; 'who would believe that there could be a place so near London where a man could be buried alive by avoidance, as I have been!'

'My dear father, it is not the place that conceals you,' she replied. 'Once you were on the stilts of popularity – now you are hid in Christ, which is far better.'

'Ah yes, my child! far, far better!'[30]

Notes and References

Abbreviations:
RR – *Hone's Reformists' Register and Weekly Commentary* (2 vols., 1817)
BD – *Black Dwarf* (1817–24)
CW – *Complete Works of William Hazlitt* (ed. P. P. Howe, 1930–34)
1Hansard – *Hansard's Parliamentary Debates*, first series
2Hansard – *Hansard's Parliamentary Debates*, new (second) series.
Hackwood – Frederick William Hackwood, *William Hone, His Life and Times* (1912)
DNB – *Dictionary of National Biography*

Introduction. William Hone

 1 *Yellow Dwarf*, no. 3, 1818.
 2 Add MS 37949 f. 144.
 3 John Foster, *Dickens*, vol. II, pp. 11–13; James T. Fields, *Yesterdays With Authors,* pp. 147–8.
 4 E. P. Thompson, *Making of the English Working Class* (1963), p. 721.
 5 Jeremy Bentham, *The Art of Packing, as applied to Special Juries* (1821), p. 73.
 6 Robert Southey, *Essays, Moral and Political* (1832), vol. I, pp. 419–20. Bentham quoted by Henry Brougham, [review of] 'An Address to the Earl of Liverpool, on the degraded state of the Government Press, and its Supporters', *Edinburgh Review,* June 1822, p. 116. The word 'censorship', which might seem inappropriate and is avoided by historians of this period, was applied to the libel laws by Leigh Hunt and Thomas Macaulay, among others.
 7 *1Hansard*, vol. XXXV, p.1124.
 8 *The Times*, 8 November 1842.
 9 *Evangelical Magazine,* January 1873; *Daily Telegraph*, 20 November 1872.

10 *Notes and Queries*, sixth series, vol. I, pp. 92–3.

11 William Hone, *Aspersions Answered*, p. 61; *Gentleman's Magazine*, January 1843; Henry Crabbe Robinson, *Diaries, Reminiscences and Correspondence* (1869), vol. II, p. 299.

12 Hackwood, p. 67.

13 Philip Stanhope, Earl of Chesterfield, *Letters to his Son*, 9 March 1748; Add MS 40120 ff. 225–6.

14 Add MS 40120 f. 109; Hackwood, p. 322.

15 *Quarterly Review*, July 1821, p. 348.

16 *The Loyalists' Magazine Complete* (1821), p. 133.

17 Add MS 40120 f. 150.

18 *1Hansard*, vol. XXXVII, p. 135; Jonathan Hill, 'William Hone', *British and Romantic Prose Writers, 1787–1832*, p. 137; *The Three Trials of William Hone* (1876), preface by Tegg.

19 *The First Trial of William Hone* (1817), p. 17.

20 *RR*, February 1817, pp. 2–3.

21 *Notes and Queries*, sixth series, vol. I, pp. 171–2.

22 *Ibid.*

23 Hone, *Aspersions Answered*, p. 67; *The Third Trial of William Hone* (1818), p. 21.

24 *The Times*, 22 December 1817.

25 *Notes and Queries*, sixth series, vol. II, p. 284.

26 Add MS 40120 f. 110.

Chapter 1. The Fatal Bookcase

The details of Hone's first twenty years were written by him in the 1830s after his conversion as a way of explaining his atheism; it is probable that they were intended for publication at some later stage. The notes are kept in the Hone Papers in the British Library and are reproduced in Hackwood, pp. 22–63. All quotations in this chapter come from there, unless otherwise indicated.

1 *Quarterly Review*, July 1821, p. 348.

2 Hone, *Aspersions Answered*, pp. 55–7.

3 *Notes and Queries*, sixth series, vol. I, pp. 171–2.

4 Hone, *Aspersions Answered*, p. 54.

5 Add MS 40117 f. 68.

6 Hone, *Every-day Book*, 26 June 1825, vol. I, pp. 857–60. Hazlitt, *The Spirit of the Age* (1825), in *CW*, vol. XI, p. 158n.

7 Hone, *Aspersions Answered*, p. 66.

8 Pauline Gregg, *Free-Born John: The Autobiography of John Lilburne* (2000), p. 397.

9 Add MS 40120 ff. 150–51.

10 Hone, *The First Trial* (1817), pp. 17–18.

Chapter 2. A Parcel of Nobodies

1 Fox quoted in Thomas, *A Long Time Burning* (1969), pp. 136–7.

2 Francis Place, *Autobiography*, p. 180.

3 *Ibid.*, pp. 195–6.

4 Add MS 50746 f. 66.

5 Hackwood, pp. 66, 68.

6 Place, *Autobiography*, p. 198.

7 *Ibid.*, p. 151n.

8 The discussion of Hone, Bone and Tranquillity is based on *The Principles and Regulations of Tranquillity* (1806) and *The Rules and Regulations of an Institution called Tranquillity commenced as an Economical Bank* (1807).

9 See Patrick Colquhoun, *A Treatise on Indigence* (1807), esp. pp. 13, 35, 36, 48, 74–7, 234–41, 284–5.

10 *The Third Trial of William Hone* (1818), p. 20.

11 George Rose, *Observations on Banks for Savings* (1816), p. 35.

12 Joseph Hume, *An Account of the Provident Institution for Savings, Established in the Western part of the Metropolis* (1816), pp. 55–6. *The Third Trial of William Hone*, p. 20.

13 *Modern London* (1804), p. 425.

14 Dr Thomas Rees and John Britton, *Reminiscences of Literary London* (1896), p. 133.

15 *An Exposition of the Circumstances which gave rise to the election of Sir Francis Burdett, Bart.* (1807), pp. 5–7.

16 M. W. Patterson, *Sir Francis Burdett* (1931), p. 40.

17 Hazlitt, *The Spirit of the Age* (1825); in *CW*, vol. XI, p. 140.

18 *An Exposition of the Circumstances*, p. 9.

19 *Ibid.*, pp. 10–11, 15, 17; Cobbett, *Political Register*, 30 May 1807; Thorne, R. G. (ed.), *The History of Parliament: The House of Commons, 1790–1820* (1986), vol. II, p. 271.

20 Donald Thomas, *Cochrane* (2001 edn), p. 114.

21 Add MS 40120 f. 5.

22 Add MS 40120 f. 7.

23 *DNB*; Hackwood, pp. 82–3.

24 *Ibid.*, pp. 85–6.

25 *Ibid.*, pp. 80–82.

26 S. C. Hall, *A Book of Memories of Great Men and Women of the Age* (1871), p. 62.

27 Hackwood, pp. 83–4.

28 *Modern London* (1804), pp. 135–6.

29 Patterson, *Burdett*, p. 246.

30 *A Correct Narrative of Proceedings in the House of Commons relative to the commitment of Sir Francis Burdett to the Tower* (1810), p. 5; Patterson, *Burdett*, p. 246.

31 *A Correct Narrative* , p. 13.

32 Patterson, *Burdett*, pp. 256–7.

33 *A Correct Narrative*, p. 18.

34 Add MS 27850 ff. 188, 189; *A Correct Narrative*, p. 20.

35 *A Correct Narrative*, p. 21.

36 *Ibid.*, pp. 22–3.

37 Add MS 27850 ff. 190, 200.

38 Patterson, *Burdett*, p. 271.

39 Add MS 27850 f. 188. *Examiner*, 8 and 15 April 1810; *A Correct Narrative*, pp. 30–31.

40 Add MS 27850 ff. 228, 233, 235. *Examiner*, 24 June 1810.

41 *Notes and Queries*, fifth series, vol. I, p. 477.

Chapter 3. Hard Truths

1 *Examiner*: Leigh Hunt's preface to the 1811 collected edition.

2 Henry Brougham, [review of] 'An Address to the Earl of Liverpool, on the degraded state of the Government Press, and its Supporters', *Edinburgh Review*, June 1822.

3 *CR*, May 1814, p. 556.

4 John, Lord Campbell, *Lives of the Chief Justices of England* (1874), vol. IV, p. 148.

5 *Ibid.*, pp. 208, 214.

6 *Ibid.*, p. 304.

7 Campbell, *Lives of the Chief Justices*, vol. IV, p. 306; *DNB*; *The Times*, 2 September 1857; Henry Brougham, *Historical Sketches of Statesmen who Flourished in the time of George III* (third series, 1843), pp. 202–3; *Examiner*, 6 December 1812.

8 *Quarterly Review*, vol. LXVI, p. 612.

9 James Routledge, *Chapters in the History of Popular Progress* (1876), p. 395.

10 Edward Smith, *William Cobbett: A Biography* (1878), vol. II, p. 92.

11 G. Wallas, *Life of Francis Place* (1898), p. 117n.

12 *Examiner*, 17 June 1810.

13 *Ibid.*

14 Bentham, *The Elements of the Art of Packing*, p. 72.

15 *Examiner*, 22 March 1812.

16 *DNB*: Leigh Hunt.

17 *Examiner*, 6 December 1812.

18 Trial reports are to be found in the *Examiner*, 13 and 20 December 1812.

19 Charles Knight, *Passages of a Working Life* (1864), vol. I, p.133.

20 J. R. Dinwiddy, 'Bentham's Transition to Political Radicalism, 1808–10', p. 689.

21 Add MS 40120 f. 32.

22 Hackwood, pp. 92–3.

23 Add MS 40120 ff. 20–22.

24 *CR*, January 1814.

25 Roy Porter, *Mind-Forg'd Manacles* (1987), p. 274.

26 Hackwood, p. 93.

27 *CR*, December 1814.

28 The best account of the scandal is to be read in Thomas, *Cochrane*, pp. 211–36.

29 Thomas, *Cochrane*, pp. 213–17.

30 *Ibid.*, pp. 218, 223–4.

31 Campbell, *Lives of the Chief Justices*, vol. IV, pp. 278–81.

32 *CR*, Appendix to the sixth volume of the fourth series, December 1814.

33 *Lord Cochrane's Reasons for Escaping* (1816), pp. 10–13.

34 *Ibid.*, p. 13.

35 *CR*, May 1815, p. 632.

36 *The Report at Large on the Coroner's Inquest on Jane Watson* (1815), p. 43.

37 *Circumstantial Report on the Extraordinary Evidence and Proceedings before the Coroner's Inquest, on the body of Edward Vyse* (1815), pp. 18–19.

38 *Report at Large*, p. 44.

39 *CR*, March 1815, pp. 310–11.

40 *CR*, May 1815, p. 640.

Chapter 4. An Elaborate Investigation

Much of this chapter is based on Hone's book, *The Important Results of an Elaborate Investigation into the Mysterious Case of Eliza Fenning.* All quotations are taken from there, unless otherwise stated. For a discussion that looks beyond Hone's involvement with the Fenning case, see V. A. C. Gatrell, *The Hanging Tree: Execution and the English People*, pp. 353–70.

1 Rolleston, Frances, *Some Account of the Conversion of the late W. Hone* (1853).

2 Gatrell, *Hanging Tree*, pp. 359–60.

3 John Marshall, *Five Cases of Recovery from the effects of Arsenic*, p. 18.

4 *Examiner*, 6 November 1815; *CR*, November 1815, p. 540.

5 *Notes and Queries*, first series, vol. V, pp. 161–2.

6 *Annual Register*, July 1857, pp. 143–4; Gatrell, *Hanging Tree*, pp. 368–9.

7 *Notes and Queries*, tenth series, vol. XII, pp. 68, 115, 138.

8 Gatrell, *Hanging Tree*, pp. 435–6.

Chapter 5. Cursing Made Easy

1 William Makepeace Thackeray, *An Essay on the Genius of George Cruikshank* (republished from the *Westminster Review*, no. LXVI, 1840), pp. 6–7.

2 Hazlitt, *Spirit of the Age* (1825), in *CW*, vol. XI, p. 158n.

3 P. G. Patmore, *My Friends and Acquaintances: being Memorials, Mind-Portraits and Personal Recollections of Deceased Celebrities* (1854), vol. III, p. 74.

4 *London Magazine*, October 1823.

5 John Clare, *John Clare by Himself* (1996), pp. 141–2; Sir Thomas Noon Talfourd, *Memorials of Charles Lamb* (1848), vol. II, p. 171; P. G. Patmore, vol. III, p. 74.

6 Patmore, vol. III, p. 82. *CW*, vol. XVII, p. 261.

7 Patmore, vol. III, p. 80.

8 *Ibid.*, pp. 80, 81–82. Hazlitt, 'On Coffee-House Politicians', *Table Talk*: *CW*, vol. VIII, p. 193.

9 W. Carew Hazlitt, *Memoir of William Hazlitt* (1867), vol. II, p. 312.

10 Add MS 40120 f.131.

11 *CR*, May 1815, pp. 537–68.

12 *The Times*, 7 April 1815.

13 Hone, *A Slap at Slop* (1822 edn), p. 8.

14 Hazlitt, 'Vetus', *Morning Chronicle*, 19 November 1813; in *CW*, vol. VII, p. 34.

15 Hazlitt, 'Illustrations of Vetus', *Morning Chronicle*, 16 December 1813; in *CW*, vol. VII, p. 60.

16 *Ibid*, p. 47.

17 Benjamin Robert Haydon, *Autobiography and Memoirs*, vol. I, p. 213.

18 Hazlitt, 'Illustrations of the *Times* newspaper', *Examiner*, 1 December 1816; *CW*, vol. XIX, p. 177.

19 *Ibid.*, pp. 134–5.

20 *Ibid.*

21 *Ibid.*, 1 December 1816; in *CW* vol. XIX, pp. 153, 182.

22 Quoted in *Buonaparte-phobia: The Origin of Dr Slop's Name* (1820), p. iv.

23 *The History of The Times: The Thunderer in the Making, 1785–1841* (1935), pp. 158–61.

24 Hazlitt, 'On Nicknames', *Edinburgh Magazine*, September 1818; in *CW*, vol. XVII, pp. 48–9.

25 *The Times*, 8 November 1842.

26 Blanchard Jerrold, *The Life of George Cruikshank* (1882), p. 72.

27 *Blackwood's Edinburgh Magazine*, July 1823.

28 *Ibid.*

29 Add MS 40120 f. 150.

30 This version is the one that first appeared in the *Morning Chronicle*, 15 March 1816 and Byron's initial MS; it was later revised, and the authentic version can be read in most modern editions of Byron's poetry.

31 Hone, *A Sketch From Public Life: A Poem Founded Upon Recent Domestic Circumstances* (April 1817).

32 Hone, *The King's Statue at Guildhall, or, French Colouring and French Principles Put Down* (1815).

Chapter 6. Necessary Slaves

1 E. P. Thompson, *The Making of the English Working Class* (1963), p. 659.

2 1*Hansard*, vol. XXXV, pp. 552–4.

3 *Ibid.*, p. 4.

4 *RR*, 1 February, p. 10.

5 1*Hansard*, vol. XXXV, pp. 8, 34–5, 73.

6 *Ibid.*, pp. 121, 130, 250, 315, 317, 319–20.

7 *The Riots in London. Hone's Full and Authentic Account* (1816).

8 *RR*, 15 March 1817, pp. 228–34; E. P. Thompson, *Making of the English Working Class* (1963), p. 659.

9 *Examiner*, 2 February 1817; *RR*, 1 February 1817, p. 12.

10 Thomas Dolby, *Memoirs* (1827), p. 108.

11 *DNB* and *Gentleman's Magazine*, 1853, p. 647.

12 *BD*, 29 January 1817.

13 *BD*, prospectus to the first volume, 1817.

14 *RR*, 15 March.

15 *Examiner*, 16 August 1816.

16 *BD*, 2 April and 4 June 1817.

17 *RR*, 15 March.

18 *RR*, 8 and 15 February, pp. 144–6; 15 March, pp. 250–54; and 9 August.

19 *RR*, 8 February 1817, pp. 35, 47; 16 August 1817, p. 158.

20 *Gentleman's Magazine*, 1852, p. 647.

21 *BD*, 26 February and 3 September 1817.

22 *RR*, 8 February, p. 33.

23 John Wade, *The Black Book* (1820), pp. 4, 115. *Examiner*, 22 December 1816 and *BD*, 5 August 1818 and *passim*.

24 Wade, *Black Book*, p. 36.

25 *BD*, 22 July 1818.

26 *BD*, 9 April 1817.

27 *RR*, 1 February, p. 12.

28 *BD*, 3 September 1817; *Examiner*, 29December 1816.

29 *RR*, 5 April.

30 *BD*, 12 February 1817.

31 *BD*, 8 July 1818.

32 Quoted in Dror Wahrman, *Imagining the Middle Classes* (1995), p. 189.

33 *BD*, 12 February 1817.

34 Robert Southey, *Essays, Moral and Political* (1832), vol. II., p.23.

35 *RR*, 15 February.

36 *RR*, 8 February, p. 35.

37 *RR*, 1 February, p. 2.

38 *RR*, 29 March, p. 290.

39 *RR*, 1 February, p. 3.

40 *1Hansard*, vol. XXXV, p. 818; *Courier* quoted in the *Examiner*, 7 December 1817.

41 *Examiner*, 2 March 1817.

42 *RR*, 8 February and 31May.

43 *RR*, 22 March, p. 286.

44 *RR*, 5 April, p. 321.

45 RR, 5 April, pp. 332–3, 334, 350. Hackwood, p. 129.

Chapter 7. Phantom of the Imagination

1 *BD*, 17 December 1817.

2 *1Hansard*, vol. XLI, p. 1444.

3 *Ibid.*, vol. XXXV, p. 818 and XXXVII, p. 37.

4 *Ibid.*, vol. XLI, p. 344.

5 *Ibid.*, vol. XXXVIII, p. 1110.

6 *New Times*, 5 January 1821.

7 Robert Southey, *Essays, Moral and Political* (1832), vol. I, pp. 132–3.

8 *1 Hansard*, vol. XXXV, p. 510.

9 *Cobbett's Political Register*, 7 and 28 December 1816.

10 Arthur Aspinall, *Politics and the Press*, p. 2n.; Revd Charles Cuthbert Southey (ed.), *The Life and Conversion of the Late Robert Southey* (1850), p. 245.

11 *RR*, 5 April, p. 350.

12 *RR*, 12 April and 21 June.

13 Arthur Aspinall, *Politics and the Press*, p. 45.

14 *RR*, 19 April 1817, pp. 415–16; 26 April, pp. 447–8.

15 *BD*, no. 3, 1819.

16 *Republican*, vol. V, p. 280.

17 Robert Southey, vol. I, pp. 120–21.

18 *1 Hansard*, vol. XXXVI, p. 145; *BD*, prospectus to the first volume, 1817.

19 *1 Hansard*, vol. XXXVI, p.570.

20 Ellenborough 1804; cited in F. von Gentz, *Reflections on the Liberty of the Press* (1819), pp. 26–7.

21 Francis Ludlow Holt, *The Law of Libel*, p. 119.

22 *1 Hansard*, vol. XXXI, p. 396.

23 *Ibid.*, pp. 377–95.

24 *Ibid.*, vol. XXXV, p. 554.

25 *RR*, 7 June 1817, p. 612; F. von Gentz, *Reflections* (1819), p. 14; *1 Hansard*, vol. XLI, p. 741 (Liverpool); *Speeches of the Right Hon. George Canning Delivered on Public Occasions in Liverpool* (1825), p. 267.

26 Wickwar, *The Struggle for the Freedom of the Press* (1928), p. 37.

27 *1 Hansard*, vol. XXXVI, pp. 498, 510.

28 *Ibid.*, vol. XXXI, pp. 395–6.

29 *BD*, 4 June 1817.

30 Bentham, *The Elements of the Art of Packing*, p. 75.

31 *Political Register*, 28 March 1817.

32 C. D. Yonge, *The Life and Administration of Lord Liverpool* (1869), vol. II, p. 298.

33 *Annual Register* (1817), preface.

34 *BD*, 12 March 1817.

35 *Examiner*, 'Liberty of the Press', 7 December 1817.

36 *BD*, 11 June 1817.

Chapter 8. Ellenborough College

1 *RR*, 10 May 1817.

2 *BD*, 14 May 1817.

3 *RR*, 7 June 1817, p. 611.

4 For Hone's first hearing, see *RR*, 10 May 1817.

5 *RR*, 21 June 1817, pp. 680–81.

6 Add MS 38108 f. 189.

7 Hone's account of the spy system comes from *RR*, 12 and 28 June 1817, pp. 705, 723–4, 725–31.

8 *RR*, 28 June 1817, pp. 731–2.

9 Add MS 40120 f. 56.

10 *RR*, 24 May 1817.

11 *RR*, 24 May 1817, p. 557.

12 *BD*, 4 June 1817.

13 *A Verbatim Report of the Two Trials of Mr T. J. Wooler* (1817), p. 5.

14 *Ibid.*, p. 16.

15 *Ibid.*, p. 37.

16 *Ibid.*, p. 35.

17 *Ibid.*, p. 69.

18 *Ibid.*, p. 86.

19 *Ibid.*, p. 89.

20 *Ibid.*, p. 90.

21 *Ibid.*, p. 119.

22 *Ibid.*, p. 143.

23 *RR*, 14 June 1817, p. 642.

24 *RR*, 21 June 1817, pp. 673–9.

25 T. J. Wooler, *An Appeal to the Citizens of London Against the Alleged Packing of Special Juries* (1817), p. 2.

26 *Ibid.*, p. 17.

27 Bentham, *The Elements of the Art of Packing*, pp. 88, 91.

28 Wooler, *Appeal*, pp. 18–19.

29 *Ibid.*, p. 9.

30 *RR*, 26 June 1817; 5 July 1817, p. 737.

31 *Ibid.*, 5 July 1817, pp. 748–9.

32 *Ibid.*, pp. 750–51.

33 *Ibid.*, pp. 761–2.

Chapter 9. The Three Trials
This chapter uses the transcripts of the trials published by Hone in 1817 and 1818; all quotations are from there unless otherwise indicated.

1 *BD*, 17 December 1817.

2 *RR*, vol. II, 25 October, pp. 427–8, 430, 431.

3 Pattern, *Cruikshank*, vol. I, p. 131.

4 *First Trial*, pp. 15–17.

5 *BD*, 3 December 1817; *Examiner*, 7 December 1817; *Annual Register* (1817), pp. 167–171; *Third Trial*, p. 17; *The Times*, 26 November 1817.

6 Hone, *Aspersions Answered*, p. 62.

7 Harriet Martineau, *The History of England During the Thirty Years Peace, 1816–1846* [vol. 1 by Charles Knight], vol. 1, p. 145.

8 Henry Brougham, *Historical Sketches* (third series, 1843), pp. 201, 204, 210.

9 Cambell, *Lives of the Lord Chief Justices*, vol. IV, pp. 284–5.

10 *BD*, 18 June 1817.

11 Henry Crabbe Robinson, *Diaries, Reminiscences and Correspondence* (1869), vol. II, p. 79.

12 *Notes and Queries*, fifth series, vol. I, p. 478.

Chapter 10. Forced into Greatness
1 *The Times*, 22 December 1817.

2 Henry Crabbe Robinson, *Diaries, Reminiscences and Correspondence* (1869), vol. II, pp. 80–81.

3 *Ibid.*, vol. II, p. 78.

4 The Hon. George Pellew, *The Life and Correspondence of the Right Honourable Henry Addington, First Viscount Sidmouth* (1847), vol. III, pp. 236–7.

5 Campbell, *Lives of the Lord Chief Justices*, vol. IV, p. 286.

6 *Examiner*, 21 December 1817.

7 *BD*, 7 and 14 January 1818.

8 *Ibid.*

9 *Trial by Jury and the Liberty of the Press. The Proceeding at the Public Meeting, December 29, 1817, At the City of London Tavern* (1818), *passim.*

10 Keats, *Letters* (1958), vol. I, p. 191.

11 *The Times*, 14 January 1820; *Greville Memoirs*, vol. I, p. 212.

12 Hazlitt, *The Spirit of the Age* (1825), in *CW*, vol. XI, p. 158n.

13 Dr Thomas Rees and John Britton, *Reminiscences of Literary London* (1896), p. 102.

14 Charles Knight, *Passages of a Working Life* (1864), vol. I, p. 245.

15 Arthur Calder-Marshall, *Lewd, Blasphemous and Obscene*, p. 64.

16 Hackwood, p. 182.

17 *1 Hansard*, vol. XXXVII, pp. 28–30.

18 *Ibid.*, p. 64.

19 *Ibid.*, pp. 56–61; *The Times*, 24 December 1817.

20 *1 Hansard*, vol. XXXVII, pp. 134–42.

21 *Ibid.*, pp. 37, 38, 40, 47.

22 *Ibid.*, pp. 134–5.

23 *BD*, 12 February 1817.

24 *1 Hansard*, first series, vol. XXXVII, p. 47 (Folkestone); 60–61 (Holland).

25 *The Times*, 20 December 1817.

26 Add MS 40120 ff. 138 & 140; Howe, *The Life of William Hazlitt*, p. 280.

27 Add MS 40120 f. 110.

28 Add MS 40120 f. 115.

29 Cruikshank's article quoted in Hackwood, pp. 201–3.

30 *Don Juan Unmasked*, pp. 5–6.

31 *Byron's Letters and Journals*, vol. VI, *The Flesh is Frail*, p. 252.

32 *Republican*, vii, p. 676.

Chapter 11. Images of Resistance

1 *CW*, vol. XVII, p. 44.

2 *Manchester Star*, 18 August 1819.

3 *The Times*, 4 September 1819; *The Whole Proceedings of the*

Coroner's Inquest at Oldham on the Body of John Lees (1820), pp. 39, 44, 93.

4 E. P. Thompson, *Making of the English Working Class*, p. 686; *The Times*, 19 August 1819; *The Whole Proceedings of the Coroner's Inquest* pp. 39, 57.

5 Thompson, *Making*, pp. 683–4; *The Times*, 31 August 1819.

6 *Report of the Metropolitan and Central Committee* (1820), *passim*.

7 *The Times*, 30 August 1819.

8 E.g. A. Clarke, 'Queen Caroline and the Sexual Politics of Popular Culture in London, 1820'; M. Wood, *Radical Culture and Print Culture* (1994); and R. Hendrix, 'Popular Humour and the *Black Dwarf*'.

9 *Notes and Queries*, fifth series, vol. I, p. 478; S. C. Hall, *A Book of Memories of Great Men and Women of the Age* (1871), p. 62. Lord Castlereagh described Hone's satires in 1821 as 'atrocious' in their treatment of the King: *2Hansard*, vol. V, pp. 671–2.

10 Hone, *Facetiae and Miscellanies*, p. viii.

11 *Examiner*, 16 January 1820.

12 E. H. Gombrich, *Meditations on a Hobby Horse* (1963), p. 130.

13 Charles Knight, *Passages of a Working Life* (1864), vol. I, p. 244. *The Times*, 8 November 1842.

14 *Examiner*, 24 December 1820.

15 Hone, *Aspersions Answered*, p. 49n.

16 E.g. *The Men in the Moon: or, the Devil to Pay* (1820).

17 *1Hansard*, vol. XLI, pp. 1–3.

18 *Ibid.*, pp. 505, 739–40, 743, 980.

19 *Ibid.*, p. 482.

20 *Ibid.*, p. 981 (Rossyln); 984–5 (Holland).

21 *Ibid.*, pp. 724–35.

22 Knight, *Passages*, vol. I, pp. 245–6.

23 W. Carew Hazlitt, *Memoir of William Hazlitt* (1867), vol. I, p. 300.

24 Hazlitt, *Lectures on the English Comic Writers*: 'On Wit and Humour'; in *Hazlitt*, vol. X, pp. 7, 133.

25 Hazlitt, *Notes on a Journey Through France and Italy* (1824), *CW*, vol. X, p. 241; 'On Wit and Humour', *CW*, vol. XX, pp. 7–8.

26 Hazlitt, 'On Nicknames', *Edinburgh Magazine*, September 1818; in

CW, vol. XVII, pp. 47, 48.

27 Hazlitt, *Notes on a Journey Through France and Italy*, in *CW*, vol. X, p. 246.

Chapter 12. The Jeers of the World

1 Richard Rush, *Memoranda* (second series, 1845), p. 352.

2 Add MS 40120 f. 181.

3 Hackwood, p. 220.

4 *The Radical Chiefs, a Mock-Heroic Poem* (1821); Edgell Rickword, *Radical Squibs*, p. 316; Charles Knight, *Passages of a Working Life* (1864), vol. I, p. 246.

5 Lord Bessborough (ed.), *Georgiana, Duchess of Devonshire* (1955), pp. 289–92.

6 Thackeray, *The Four Georges* (1861), p. 210; Saul David, *Prince of Pleasure*, pp. 163, 165; Aspinall, *Correspondence, 1770–1812*, vol. iii, pp. 122–3; Hibbert, *George IV*, pp. 146–7; Lady Charlotte Bury, *The Court of England under George IV – Founded on a Diary* (2 vols., 1896), vol. I, p. 21.

7 Thackeray, *Georges*, p. 212; David, *Prince*, pp. 169–70; Hibbert, *George IV*, p. 187

8 Charles Greville, *The Greville Memoirs*, vol. 1, p. 28; Patterson, *Burdett*, vol. II, p. 518; Dorothy George, *Catalogue of Political and Personal Satires Preserved in the Department of Prints and Drawings in the British Museum*, vol. X, p. xiii.

9 Lady Charlotte Bury, *Diary of a Lady in Waiting* (1908), p. 273.

10 *Examiner*, 20 August 1820.

11 Hackwood, pp. 236–7.

12 These lines come from a poem in Hone's pirated edition of Byron's verses, *Poems On His Domestic Circumstances* (April 1816). The poem ('Oh Shame to Thee, Land of the Gaul') had appeared anonymously in the *Morning Chronicle* on 31 July 1815. Hone and many others assumed that it was by Byron, and it appeared in many editions of the lord's poetry in the early part of the nineteenth century. Byron denied that it was his. Hone was happy to quote them in 1820, even though he realised shortly after publication of *Poems on his Domestic Circumstances* that they were not by Byron. They clearly

resonated with his kind of journalism, and epitomised his satirical campaign. Hence the title of this book.

13 *The Loyalists' Magazine Complete*, pp. 223–4.

14 Greville, *Memoirs*, vol. I, pp. 236–7.

15 Hackwood, p. 237.

16 Christopher Hibbert, *George IV* (1976), p. 558n.

17 *Gentleman's Magazine*, October 1820, pp. 340–42.

18 *Examiner*, 3 December 1820.

19 *Ibid.*, 3 September 1820.

20 *Ibid.*, 12 November 1820; Richard Rush, *Memoranda* (second series, 1845), p. 345; Greville, *Memoirs*, vol. I, p. 37.

21 Richard Rush, *Memoranda* (second series, 1845), p. 346.

22 *Ibid.*, p. 346.

23 *Ibid.*, p. 347.

24 Hackwood, pp. 240–41; Lady Charlotte Bury, *Diary of a Lady in Waiting* (1908), p. 274.

25 Hazlitt, *Conversations of James Northcote*, in *Hazlitt*, vol. XI, pp. 240–41,

26 *The Total Eclipse: A Grand Politico-Astronomical Phenomenon, which occurred in the year 1820* (1820), p. 5.

27 Hone, *Facetiae and Miscellanies*, pp. vii–viii.

28 *Ibid.*, preface.

29 W. Carew Hazlitt, *Memoir of William Hazlitt* (1867), vol. 1, p. 300.

30 *Examiner*, 6 January 1822.

31 William Makepeace Thackeray, *An Essay on the Genius of George Cruikshank* (republished from the *Westminster Review*, no. LXVI, 1840), p. 11.

32 Frederick G. Stephens, *A Memoir of George Cruikshank* (1891), p. 22; S. C. Hall, *A Book of Memories of Great Men and Women of the Age* (1871), p. 62.

33 Dr Robert Shelton Mackenzie, 'The Artist and the Author', *London Journal*, 20 November 1847.

34 Thackeray, *Four Georges* (1861), pp. 169–70.

Chapter 13. A Rebellious Will Subjugated

1 Hackwood, p. 207; *Every-day Book*, 18 January 1825, vol. I, pp. 123–4.

2 [Hone] *A Catalogue of Ancient and Modern Books, Including many Curious and scarce Articles* (1820).

3 Dr Thomas Rees and John Britton, *Reminiscences of Literary London* (1896), p. 103.

4 Add MS 40120 f. 150.

5 Albert M. Cohen, *George Cruikshank: A Catalogue Raisonné* (1924), pp. xiii–xiv; Pattern, *Cruikshank*, pp. 211–12.

6 Hackwood, p. 190.

7 Add MS 40120 ff. 177–8.

8 Hone, *Aspersions Answered*, p. 49n.

9 Thomas Dolby, *Memoirs*, pp. 149–50.

10 Preface to the twelfth volume of the *Black Dwarf* [1824].

11 Add MS 40120 f. 181; Hone, *Aspersions Answered*, p. 49; Hone, *Facetiae and Miscellanies*, advertisement; William Makepeace Thackeray, 'An Essay on the Genius of George Cruikshank', *Westminster Review*, no. LXVI, 1840).

12 Hone, *Another Article for the Quarterly Review*, p. 32; Hone, *Facetiae and Miscellanies*; Add MS 40856 f. 37.

13 *Every-day Book*, vol. I: Address to the Readers; *ibid.*, 1 January 1825, p. 5.

14 *Ibid.*, vol. I, preface.

15 Sir Thomas Noon Talfourd, *Letters of Charles Lamb*, vol. II, p. 283.

16 Hackwood, p. 269.

17 Talfourd, *Letters* (*1886*), vol. II, pp. 215–16.

18 *Ibid.*, p. 128.

19 Hackwood, p. 274.

20 *Every-day Book*, 14 July 1825, vol. I, pp. 950–52.

21 *Ibid.*, 8 May 1825, vol. I, p. 634.

22 *Ibid.*, pp. 636–42; 26 July 1825, vol. I, pp. 858–63.

23 Hackwood, p. 286.

24 *Ibid.*, p. 255.

25 *Ibid.*, p. 257.

26 Talfourd, *Letters*, vol. II, p. 226, 239.

27 Hackwood, p. 263.

28 *Ibid.*, pp. 264, 284.

29 *Ibid.*, pp. 284–5.

30 *Ibid.*, p. 260.

31 Talfourd, *Letters*, vol. II, p. 218.

32 Hackwood, p. 262.

33 *Ibid.*, p. 260.

34 *Ibid*, p. 285.

35 *Ibid.*, pp. 285–6.

36 *The Times*, 21 May 1830.

37 *Ibid.*

38 Add MS 50746 f. 21.

39 *Notes and Queries*, sixth series, vol. I, pp. 92–3.

40 *Ibid.*, pp. 171–2.

41 Hackwood, pp. 305–6.

42 *The Early Life and Conversion of William Hone . . . A Narrative Written by Himself. Edited by his son William Hone* (1841), p. 44. Hackwood, p. 315.

43 Add MS 40856 f. 62.

44 Dr Thomas Rees and John Britton, *Reminiscences of Literary London* (1896), p.102.

45 Hackwood, p. 329.

46 *Ibid.*, p. 330.

47 *Ibid.*, pp. 342–3.

48 *Ibid.*, p. 340.

49 *Ibid.*, pp. 57, 59, 312

Chapter 14. That New and Mighty Power

1 F. von Gentz, *Reflections on the Liberty of the Press* (1819), p. 37.

2 *Ibid.*, pp. 92, 93.

3 Jeremy Bentham, *On the Liberty of the Press, and Public Discussion* (W. Hone, 1821), p.38.

4 *The Loyalists' Magazine Complete*, p. 234.

5 *Edinburgh Review*, June 1822, p. 110.

6 F. von Gentz, *Reflections* (1819), p. 95.

7 *Edinburgh Review*, June 1822, p. 113.

8 *1Hansard*, vol. XLI, pp. 1439–40.

9 *2Hansard*, vol. VI, p. 1313.

10 *Edinburgh Review*, June 1822, p. 113.

11 Greville, *Memoirs*, vol. I, p.259.

12 Arthur Aspinall, *Politics and the Press*, p. 384.

13 Thomas Macaulay, *Miscellaneous Writing* (1871), vol. II, p. 515.

14 *George Canning and His Times* (1859), p. 307.

15 *Speeches of the Right Hon. George Canning Delivered on Public Occasions in Liverpool* (1825), pp. 294, 285.

16 Rollo, *George Canning* (1965), p. 187.

17 Rede, *Memoir of the Right Honourable George Canning* (1827), p. 358.

18 *1Hansard*, vol. XLI, p. 469.

19 *Speeches of the Right Hon. George Canning Delivered on Public Occasions in Liverpool* (1825), pp. 298, 302.

20 Rollo, *George Canning* (1965), p. 184.

21 James McCulloch, *A Discourse on the Rise, Progress, peculiar Objects, and Importance of Political Economy* (1824), p. 80; *The Times*, 25 December 1829.

22 Greville, *Memoirs*, vol. II, p. 76.

23 A. Mackinnon, *On the Rise, Progress and Present State of Public Opinion* (1828), p. 5.

24 William IV quoted in Anne Somerset, *William IV* (1980), p. 151; *2Hansard*, vol. XXI, pp. 1643–70.

25 *Ibid.*

26 *3Hansard*, vol. LXIX, p. 1229; *Lords Journals*, vol. LXXV (1843), appendix 3, p. 34.

27 Hackwood, p. 345.

28 Add MS 50746 f. 39.

29 Hackwood, p. 346; *The Times*, 8 November 1842.

30 Hackwood, p. 344.

Select Bibliography

Place of publication for all printed works is London, unless otherwise stated

1. MANUSCRIPT SOURCES

From the British Library:

Hone Papers: Add MSS 40108-40122, 40856, 50746: Collections, Correspondence, Notes for an Autobiography, Notes for a History of Parody, MS articles, and Family Papers.

Leigh Hunt Papers: Add MSS 38108.

Place Papers: Add MSS 27808, 27839, 27850, 37949.

2. PERIODICALS AND NEWSPAPERS

All the Year Round
Annual Register
Black Dwarf
Blackwood's Edinburgh Magazine
Cobbett's Political Register
Courier
Critical Review and the Annals of Literature
Dolby's Parliamentary Register
Edinburgh Review
Examiner
Gentleman's Magazine
Guardian
Hone's Reformists' Register and Weekly Commentary
London Alfred
London Journal
London Magazine
Manchester Observer

Manchester Star
Monthly Magazine
Morning Chronicle
New Times
Notes and Queries
Observer
Patriot
Quarterly Review
Republican
Scourge
The Times
Westminster Review
Yellow Dwarf

3. WORKS PUBLISHED, WRITTEN AND EDITED BY WILLIAM HONE

This is not a complete bibliography of Hone's works; readers are referred to Ann Bowden's 'William Hone's Political Journalism, 1815–1821' and the British Library catalogue. The following bibliography cites the works consulted or noted in the writing of this work, and is intended to give an indication of the development of Hone's publishing and journalistic career.

1792

'The Contrast' [published by the Association for Preserving Liberty and Property against Republicans and Levellers]

1805

The Housekeeper's Domestic Library; or, New Universal Family Instructor in Practical Economy

1806

Shaw's Gardener

The Principles and Regulations of Tranquillity; an Institution commenced in the Metropolis for encouraging and enabling industrious and prudent individuals in the various classes of the community to provide for themselves [with John Bone]

1807 *The Rules and Regulations of an Institution called Tranquillity commenced as an Economical Bank* [with John Bone]

1809 [with John Bone, from 331, The Strand] *A Correct Report of the Speech delivered by Sir Francis Burdett . . . in the House of Commons . . . on the conduct of HRH the Duke of York*

First Part of a Catalogue of Books, for 1809 . . . Now on Sale, for Ready Money Only by Bone and Hone

A Full Report of the Proceedings of the Electors of Westminster . . . at a public meeting held in Westminster Hall

The Plan to Reform Proposed by Sir Francis Burdett, correctly reported in two speeches delivered in Parliament . . . To which are added Mr Perceval's objections to the motion

Reasons for Reformation [by Major John Cartwright]

1815 [from 55, Fleet Street – to 1818]

(i) Books, pamphlets and broadsides:

The Account of the Late Mr Whitbread

Bonaparte, His Letter to the Prince Regent of England

Buonaparte-phobia, or; Cursing Made Easy to the Meanest Capacity. A dialogue between the Editor of the 'Times' – My Uncle Toby, & My Father

Circumstantial Report on the Extraordinary Evidence and Proceedings before the Coroner's Inquest, on the body of Edward Vyse

The French Declaration of Rights in 1793

The Important Results of an Elaborate Investigation into the Mysterious Case of Eliza Fenning

The King's Statue at Guildhall

La Pie Voleuse; the Power of Conscience Exemplified [by Charles Phillips]

The Maid and the Magpie

Report at large of the Coroner's Inquest on Jane Watson, shot at Mr Robinson's in Old Burlington Street

(ii) Prints:

Afterpiece to the tragedy at Waterloo [satire engraved by George Cruikshank]

Fast Colours [satire engraved by G. Cruikshank]

Eliza Fenning . . . taken from the life in Newgate [portrait by I. Robert Cruikshank]

Louis XVIII Climbing the Mât de Cocagne [satire engraved by G. Cruikshank]

William Norris as he was confined in Bethlem [engraving by G. Cruikshank produced as evidence to the select committee of the House of Commons]

1816

Authentic Memoirs of the Life and Death R. B. Sheridan

Authentic narrative of escape of M. Count de Lavalette from France

Eloquent Speech at Galway [by Charles Philips]

Eloquent Speech on the Dethronement of Napoleon, the state of Ireland, and the necessity of immediate parliamentary reform [by Charles Philips]

A Full report of the Proceedings of the Meeting, Convened by the Hampden Club, 15th June, 1816

Guy Mannering, the astrologer, or the prophecy of Meg Maerilies the Gipsey

An historical character of Napoleon [with essays by Leigh Hunt, Charles Phillips, and others]

Hone's Interesting History of the Memorable Blood Conspiracy, Carried by S. MacDaniel, J. Berry, J. Egan, and J. Salmon, Thief-Takers, and Their Trials and Sentences, in 1756

Hone's Riots in London: with most Important and Full Particulars, now first published: elucidating the events of Monday, December 2, 1816

Hone's View of the Regent's Bomb, Now Uncovered, for the Gratification of the Public in St James's Park, Majestically Mounted, on a Monstrous Nondescript, Supposed to Represent Legitimate Sovereignty [illustrations by George Cruikshank]

Four Important Trials at Kingston Assizes, April 5th 1816 . . . With a preface, containing thirteen questions to Isaac Espinasse, the prosecutor of Elizabeth Fenning

Letter from Charles Philips

Life of William Cobbett [pirated edition]

The Meeting at Spa Fields . . . Hone's authentic account . . . of all the

Proceedings on . . . December 2nd 1816
The Most Eloquent Speech of Charles Philips
Napoleon and the Bourbons
Napoleon and the Spots in the Sun
On the State of Europe [by George Ensor]
Poems on his Domestic Circumstances [pirated poems by Byron]
Saluting the Regent's Bomb, uncovered on his birthday
A Sketch From Public Life: A Poem Founded Upon Recent Domestic Circumstances
Trial of Lord Cochrane; Lord Cochrane's Reason for Escaping [with portrait]
Two Speeches on the Catholic Question [by Charles Philips]
The Woful Condition of John Bull
The Yacht for the R–t's B-m-b

1817
Another Ministerial Defeat! The Trial of the Dog, for Biting the Noble Lord
Bags Noodles Feast
Bartholomew Fair Insurrection; and the Pie-bald Poney Plot! (Official Account)
The Bullet Te Deum; with the Canticle of The Stone
A Collection of Speeches by Charles Philips
The First Trial of William Hone on an ex officio information
Full Report of the Third Spa-Fields Meeting; With Previous Arrests
Hints to Emigrants from Europe [by the Shamrock Society of New York]
Hone's Reformists' Register and Weekly Commentary [weekly paper]
The Lament of the Emerald Isle [by Charles Philipps]
The Late John Wilkes's Catechism of a Ministerial Member
Napoleon's Appeal to the British People on his Treatment at St Helena
Official Account of the Noble Lords(!) Bite!
Political Catechism
Political Litany; diligently revised; to be said or sung, until the appointed change come, throughout the Dominion of England and Wales and the Town of Berwick-on-Tweed – By Special Command

The Right of the People to Universal Suffrage and Annual Parliaments
The Second Trial of William Hone
The Sinecurist's Creed or Belief; as used throughout the Kingdom Quicunque vult. By Authority
Wat Tyler; a dramatic poem [pirated from the poem by Robert Southey]

1818 [from 45, Ludgate Hill – to April 1826]
The Third Trial of William Hone
The Three Trials of William Hone for publishing Three Parodies
Trial by Jury and the Liberty of the Press. The proceedings at the public meeting, December 29, 1817, . . . for the purpose of enabling W.H. to surmount the difficulties in which he has been placed by being selected by the Minister of the Crown as the object of their persecution

1819
Bank Restriction Barometer
Bank Restriction Note; specimen of a Bank Note – not to be imitated [engraving by G. Cruikshank]
Circumstantial Evidence. Report of the Trial of Elizabeth Fenning
'Don Juan', or Don Juan Unmasked; being a key to the mystery attending that remarkable publication with a descriptive review of the poem, and extracts [selections pirated from the first edition of the first two cantos, with Hone's comments]
A New and Enlarged Collection of Speeches by the Right Hon. John Philpot Curran
Political Essays, with Sketches of Public Characters [by William Hazlitt]
The Political House that Jack Built
Thoughts on the Funding and Paper Systems [by N. J. Denison]

1820
The Apocryphal New Testament, being all the Gospels, and Epistles, and other pieces now extant, attributed in the first four centuries to Jesus Christ, his Apostles, and their companions, and not included in the New Testament by its compliers
Buonaparte-phobia; or the Origin of Dr Slop's Name
A Catalogue of Ancient and Modern Books, including many Curious and

Scarce Articles, together with a Large Collection of Old Tracts

The Form of Prayer . . . for the happy deliverance of Her Majesty Queen Caroline

In Parliament. Dropt Clauses out of the Bill Against the Queen

The King's Treatment of the Queen

The Man in the Moon

Non mi Ricordo &c &c &c

The Prerogatives of a Queen Consort

The Printer's Address to the Queen

The Queen's Case Stated

The Queen's Letter to the King

The Queen's Matrimonial Ladder, A National Toy, with fourteen step scenes and illustrations in verse

Report of the Metropolitan and Central Committee, appointed for the relief of the Manchester sufferers with an Appendix, Containing the Names of the Sufferers, and the Nature and Extent of their Injuries. Also, an account of the distribution of the Funds, and other Documents

The Whole Proceedings Before the Coroner's Inquest at Oldham, On the Body of John Lees, who died of Sabre Wounds at Manchester, August 16th, 1819

1821

An Accurate Report of the Trial of Her Most Gracious Majesty Queen Caroline, before the House of Lords, on a Bill of Pains and Penalties

Memorial of Napoleon

On the Liberty of the Press, and Public Discussion [by Jeremy Bentham]

The Political Showman – At Home! Exhibiting his cabinet of curiosities and creatures – All Alive!

Report of the King v John Hunt

A Slap at Slop and the Bridge-Street Gang

The Right Divine of Kings to Govern Wrong!

A Speech at Dublin

The Spirit of Despotism

Three Tracts relative to Spanish and Portuguese Affairs with a Continual Eye to English Ones [by Jeremy Bentham]

1822

Miraculous Host Tortured by the Jew, under the reign of Philip the Fair in 1290

1823

Ancient Mysteries Described, especially the English Miracle Plays, founded on Apocryphal New Testament Story, extant among unpublished manuscripts in the British Museum

Sixty Curious and Authentic Narratives and Anecdotes respecting Extraordinary Characters: Illustrative of the Tendency of Credulity and Fanaticism

1824

Another Article for the Quarterly Review.

Aspersions Answered: an explanatory statement . . . addressed to the public at large, and to every reader of the Quarterly Review in particular

1825

The Everyday Book, or Calendar of Popular Amusements [weekly periodical; published in two volumes by Hunt and Clarke 1826]

Hone's Popular Political Tracts [published by Hunt and Clarke]

1826 [King's Bench Prison, Southwark]

Facetiae and Miscellanies [published by Hunt and Clarke, a collected edition of satires written between 1819 and 1822]

1827

The Table Book [periodical; published by Hunt and Clarke]

1829 [Newington Green]

Poor Humphrey's Calendar. Wherein are given . . . prophecies concerning the signs of The Times; especially things to come in 1829 [published by Matilda Hone]

1830 [Grasshopper Hotel, Gracechurch Street]

Full Annals of the Revolution in France [published by Thomas Tegg]

Hone's Political Tracts [published by I. Chidley]

The Sports and Pastimes of the People of England by Joseph Strutt [published by William Reeves]

1832

The Year Book of Daily Recreation [periodical; published by Thomas Tegg]

1841 [Church Street, Tottenham]
The Early Life and Conversion of W. Hone, . . . a narrative written by himself, edited by his son, W. Hone [published by T. Ward]
[Hone's autobiographical notes are reproduced in Frederick William Hackwood, *William Hone*, pp. 22–63.]

4. PRIMARY PRINTED SOURCES

Adams, M., *A Parody on the Political House that Jack Built; or the Real House that Jack Built*

Angelo, Henry, *The Reminiscences of Henry Angelo* (2 vols., 1828)

An Exposition of the Circumstances Which Gave Rise to the Election of Sir Francis Burdett, Bart. For the City of Westminster, and of the Principles Which Governed the Committee Who Conducted that Election (1807)

Bentham, Jeremy, *The Elements of the Art of Packing, as applied to Special Juries* (1821)

—, *Plan of Parliamentary Reform, in the form of a Catechism* (Thomas Wooler, 1818).

—, *Truth versus Ashhurst; or law as it is, contrasted with what it is said to be* (1823)

[See works published by William Hone.]

Brougham, Henry, 1st Baron Brougham and Vaux, *Historical Sketches of Statesmen who flourished in the time of George III* (third series, 1843)

—, [Review article] 'An Address to the Earl of Liverpool on the degraded state of the government press, and its supporters', *Edinburgh Review*, June 1822.

Bury, Lady Charlotte, *The Diary of a Lady in Waiting* (ed. A. Francis Stewart; 1908)

Byron, Lord, *Complete Poetical Works* (ed. Jerome J. McGann; 7 vols., Oxford, 1980–1993)

—, *Letters and Journals* (ed. Leslie A. Marchand; 13 vols., 1973–1994)

Campbell, John, 1st Baron, *Lives of the Chief Justices of England from the Norman Conquest to the death of Lord Tenterden* (3 vols., 1874)

—, *Lives of the Lord Chancellors* (10 vols., 1868)

Canning, George, *Speeches of the Right Honourable George Canning Delivered on Public Occasions in Liverpool* (Liverpool, 1825)

Clare, John, *John Clare by Himself* (ed. Eric Robinson and David Powell; Ashington and Manchester, 1996)

Cobbett, William, *Parliamentary History* (1806)

Colquhoun, Patrick, *A Treatise on Indigence; exhibiting a general view of the national resources for productive labour; with a proposition for ameliorating the condition of the poor, and improving the moral habits and increasing the comforts of the labouring people . . .* (1807)

A Correct Narrative of Proceedings in the House of Commons relative to the commitment of Sir Francis Burdett to the Tower (1810)

Croly, The Revd George, *The Coronation. Observations on the Public Life of the King* (1821)

D'Israeli, Isaac, *Curiosities of Literature* (1825)

Dolby, Thomas *Memoirs of T.D. . . . late printer and publisher, of Catherine Street Strand . . . written by himself* (1827)

The Dorchester Guide: or, a House that Jack Built (1819)

Egan, Pierce, the Elder, *Life in London; or the day and night scenes of Jerry Hawthorne, Esq., and . . . Corinthian Tom . . . With thirty-six scenes from real life, designed and etched by I. R. & G. Cruikshank . . .* (1820–21)

Fonblanque, Albany, *England Under Seven Administrations* (3 vols., 1837)

Gentz, Frederick von, *Reflections on the Liberty of the Press* (1819)

The Green Bag: 'a dainty dish to set before a King', a ballad of the nineteenth century, by the author of 'The Political A, Apple Pie' [wrongly attributed to Hone; published by J Robins & Co.]

Greville, Charles, *The Greville Memoirs. A Journal of the Reigns of King George IV and King William IV* (ed. Henry Reeve; 3 vols., 1875)

Hall, S. C., *A Book of Memories of Great Men and Women of the Age. From personal acquaintance* (1871)

—, *Retrospect of a long life from 1815 to 1833* (2 vols., 1883)

Hansard, T. C, *Typographia: an historical sketch of the origins and progress of the art of Printing* (1825)

Haydon, Benjamin Robert, *The Autobiography and Memoirs of Benjamin Robert Haydon* (ed. Tom Taylor; 2 vols., 1926)

Hazlitt, William, *The Complete Works of William Hazlitt* (ed. P. P. Howe; 21 vols., 1930–34)

Hazlitt, William Carew, *Memoir of William Hazlitt with Portions of his Correspondence* (2 vols., 1867)

Holt, Francis Ludlow, *The Law of Libel: in which is contained, a general history of the law in the ancient codes, and of its introduction, and successive alterations, in the law of England . . .* (1812)

Hume, Joseph, *An Account of the Providential Institution for Savings, Established in the Western Part of the Metropolis* (1816)

Hunt, Frederick Knight, *The Fourth Estate: Contributions Towards a History of Newspapers, and the Liberty of the Press* (2 vols., 1850)

Hunt, Leigh, *Autobiography* (ed. Roger Ingpen; 3 vols., 1903)

Knight, Charles, *Passages of a Working Life During Half a Century; with a prelude of early reminiscences* (3 vols., 1864)

Leigh, Samuel, *Leigh's New Picture of London* (1819)

A Letter from a pious and reverend Divine, to his niece, written in the middle of the last century . . . Together with a preface, wherein are introduced, some animadversions on the Trial of W. Hone for blasphemy, and his abettors and subscribers (Oxford, 1819)

The Loyal Man in the Moon (1820)

The Loyalist; or, Anti-Radical; consisting if three departments: satirical, miscellaneous, and historical . . . the history of the radical contest from the Spafield's Riot and Hone's Acquittal to the Queen's elevation on the Radical Ladder (1820)

The Loyalist's House that Jack Built (1819)

Macaulay, Thomas Babbington, *The Miscellaneous Writings and Speeches of Lord Macaulay* (Longmans, 1871)

Mackenzie, Robert Shelton, 'The Artist and the Author', *London Journal*, 20 November 1847.

Mackinnon, William Alexander, *On the Rise, Progress and Present State of Public Opinion in Great Britain and Other Parts of the World* (London, 1828)

Marshall, John, *Five Cases of Recovery from the effects of Arsenic . . . To which are annexed many corroborating facts, never before heard, rel-*

ative to the guilt of Eliza Fenning (1815)

McCulloch, J. R, *A Discourse on the Rise, Peculiar Objects, and Importance of Political Economy* (Edinburgh, 1824)

The Men in the Moon: or, the Devil to Pay (1820)

Modern London; being the history and present state of the British Metropolis (1804)

Nero Vindicated (1820)

The New Pilgrim's Progress; or, a journey to Jerusalem (1820)

Nightingale, J. (ed.), *Report of the Proceedings before the House of Lords on a Bill of Pains and Penalties against her Majesty Caroline Amelia Elizabeth, Queen of Great Britain and Consort of King George the Fourth* (3 vols., 1820)

Oldfield, Thomas Hinton Burley, *The Representative History of Great Britain and Ireland: being a History of the House of Commons and of the Counties, Cities, and Boroughs of the United Kingdom, from the earliest period* (6 vols., 1816)

Patmore, P. G., *My Friends and Acquaintances: Being Memorials, Mind-Portraits, and Personal Reminiscences of Deceased Celebrities* (3 vols., 1854)

Pellew, the Hon. George, *The Life and Correspondence of the Right Honourable Henry Addington, First Viscount Sidmouth* (1847)

Place, Francis, *The Autobiography of Francis Place (1771–1854)* (ed. Mary Thrale; Cambridge, 1972)

Plenipo and the Devil! . . . An Infernal Poem. By the author of The Political House that Jack Built [wrongly attributed to Hone; published by J. Johnston]

The Political 'A, Apple-Pie'; or, the Extraordinary Red Book Versified . . . by the author of 'The House that Jack Built' [wrongly attributed to Hone; published by J. Johnston]

Proctor, Bryan Waller, 'My Recollections of the late William Hazlitt', *New Monthly Magazine* (November 1830)

The Radical Ladder; or, Hone's Ladder and his Non Mi Ricordo explained and applied, the designs of the radicals developed, and their plans traced, a satyrical poem, with copious notes (1820)

Raffles, Thomas, *Memoirs of the Life and Ministry of the Rev. Thomas Raffles, D.D., LL.D.* (1865)

The Real or Constitutional House that Jack Built (1819)

Rede, Leman Thomas, *Memoir of the Right Honourable George Canning, Late Premier of England, with his parliamentary orations* ... (1827)

Rees, Dr Thomas and Britton, John, *Reminiscences of Literary London from 1779 to 1853. With Interesting Anecdotes of Publishers, Authors and Book Auctioneers of that Period* (New York, 1896)

Report from the Committee of the House of Commons, on Madhouses in England (1815)

Rickword, Edgell, *Radical Squibs and Loyal Ripostes, Satirical Pamphlets of the Regency Period, 1819–1821* (Bath, 1971)

Robinson, Henry Crabb, *Diary, Reminiscences and Correspondence* (ed. Thomas Sadler; 3 vols., 1869)

Rolleston, Frances, *Some Account of the Conversion of the late W. Hone* (1853)

Rose, George, *Observations on the Poor Laws, and on the Management of the Poor in Great Britain* (1805)

—, *Observations on Banks for Savings* (1816)

Rush, Richard, *Memoranda of a Residence at the Court of London* (Philadelphia, 1833 (first series) and 1845 (second series))

Slop's Shave at a Broken Hone (1820)

Southey, Charles (ed.), *The Life and Correspondence of the late Robert Southey* (6 vols., 1850)

Southey, Robert, *Essays Moral and Political* (2 vols., 1832)

—, *Life of Bunyan* (1830)

The Theatrical House that Jack Built (1819)

Total Eclipse: A Grand Politico-Astronomical Phenomenon, which occurred in the year 1820; with a series of engravings, to demonstrate the configuration of the planets. To which is added, an hieroglyphic, adopted to these wonderful times (Thomas Dolby, 1820)

Talfourd, Sir Thomas Noon, *The Life, Letters and Writings of Charles Lamb* (1886)

—, *Final Memorials of Charles Lamb* (2 vols., 1848)

Thackeray, William Makepeace, 'An Essay On the Genius of George Cruikshank', *Westminster Review* (June, 1840); republished as a pamphlet, 1840.

—, *The Four Georges. Sketches of Manners, Morals, Court and Town Life* (1861)

Tegg, Thomas (ed. and introduction), *The Three Trials of William Hone* (Leeds, 1876)

The True Political House that Jack Built (1820)

[Wade, J.] *The Black Book* (1820)

[Westminster Committee] *An Exposition of the Circumstances which gave rise to the election of Sir Francis Burdett, Bart. for the City of Westminster, and the principles which governed the Committee who conducted that Election* (1807)

Wooler, Thomas Jonathan, *An Appeal to the Citizens of London Against the Alleged Packing of Special Juries* (1817)

—, *A Political Lecture on Heads, by the Black Dwarf* (1820)

—, *A Verbatim Report of two trials of T. J. W., Editor of the Black Dwarf, for alleged libels . . . Taken in short hand by an eminent writer, and revised by T. J. W.* (1817)

Yonge, Charles Duke, *The Life and Administration of Robert Banks, Second Earl of Liverpool . . . Compiled from Original Sources* (3 vols., 1868)

5. SECONDARY SOURCES

Andrews, Alexander, *The History of Journalism from the foundation of the newspaper press in England, to the repeal of the Stamp Act in 1855, with sketches of press celebrities* (2 vols., 1855)

Aspinall, Arthur, *The Correspondence of George, Prince of Wales, 1770–1812,* (8 vols., 1963–71)

—, *The Letters of George IV, 1812–1830,* (3 vols., Cambridge, 1938)

—, *Politics and the Press, c1780–1850* (1949)

Bain, Alexander, *James Mill: a biography* (facsimile reprint; Tokyo, 1990)

Blunden, Edmund, *Leigh Hunt and his Circle* (1930)

Brewer, John, *The Sinews of Power: war, money and the English state, 1688–1783* (1989)

Bourne, Kenneth, *Palmerston: the early years, 1784–1841* (1982)

Bowden, Ann, 'William Hone's Political Journalism, 1815–1821', (unpublished PhD dissertation, University of Austin at Texas, 1975)

Calder-Marshall, Arthur, *Lewd, Blasphemous and Obscene, being the trials and tribulations of sundry Founding Fathers of today's alternative societies* (1972)

Catalogue of Political and Personal Satires Preserved in the Department of Prints and Drawings in the British Museum (11 vols., 1950: vols. 1–4 by Frederick George Stephen; vols. 5–11 by M. Dorothy George)

Checkland, G. S., 'The Popularisation of Ricardian Economics in England', *Economica*, vol. XVI, no. 61, February 1949

Chew, Samuel C., *Byron in England: His Fame and After-Fame* (1924)

—, 'The Pamphlets of the Byron Separation', *Modern Language Notes*, vol. 34 (March 1919)

Clark, Anna, 'Queen Caroline and the Sexual Politics of Popular Culture in London, 1820', *Representations*, 31 (Summer 1990)

Cohn, Albert M., *George Cruikshank. A catalogue raisonné of the work executed during the years 1806–1877* (1924)

Cole, G. D. H., *The Life of William Cobbett* (revised edition, 1947)

David, Saul, *Prince of Pleasure: The Prince of Wales and the Making of the Regency* (1999)

Dinwiddy, J. R., 'Bentham's Transition to Political Radicalism, 1809–10', *Journal of the History of Ideas*, XXXV, (1975)

—, *Radicalism and Reform in Britain, 1780–1850* (1992)

Donald, Diana, *The Age of Caricature: satirical print culture in the reign of George III* (New Haven, 1996)

Dyer, Gary, *British Satire and the Politics of Style, 1789–1832* (Cambridge, 1997)

Elliott, Robert, *The Power of Satire: magic, ritual, art* (Princeton, 1960)

Fontana, Biancamaria, *Rethinking the Politics of Commercial Society, the Edinburgh Review, 1802–1832* (Cambridge, 1997)

Forster, John, *Charles Dickens* (3 Vols., 1873)

French, James Branthwhite, *Walks in Abney Park* (1883)

Gatrell, V. A. C., *The Hanging Tree: execution and the English people 1770–1868* (Oxford, 1994)

Gilmartin, Kevin, *Print Politics, the press and radical opposition in early nineteenth-century England* (Cambridge, 1996)

Gombrich, E. H., *Meditations on a Hobby Horse and other essays on the theory of art* (4th edition, Oxford, 1963)

Gregg, Pauline, *Free-Born John: The biography of John Lilburne* (1961)

Hackwood, Frederick William, *William Hone, his Life and Times* (1912)

Harling, Philip, 'Rethinking "Old Corruption"', *Past and Present*, 147 (1995)

—, *The Waning of 'Old Corruption'* (Oxford, 1996)

Hatton, Joseph, *Journalistic London, being a series of sketches of the famous pens and papers of the day* (1882)

Hendrix, Richard, 'Popular Humour and the *Black Dwarf'*, *Journal of British Studies*, vol. XVI, no. 1 (Fall 1976)

Hibbert, Christopher, *George IV* (1976 edition)

Hill, Jonathan, 'William Hone', in *British Romantic Prose Writers 1787–1832* (ed. John R. Grenfield; vol. 110 of *Dictionary of Literary Biography* (Detroit, 1991))

Hinde, Wendy, *George Canning* (1973)

Hone, J. Ann, *For the Cause of Truth: radicalism in London, 1796–1821* (Oxford, 1982)

Howe, P. P., *The Life of William Hazlitt* (1922)

Jerrold, Blanchard, *Life of George Cruikshank, in two epochs* (2 vols., 1882)

Jones, Stanley, *Hazlitt, a life: from Winterslow to Frith Street* (Oxford, 1989)

Justman, Stewart, *The Springs of Liberty: the satiric tradition and the freedom of speech* (Evanston, Illinois, 1999)

Laqueur, T. W., 'The Queen Caroline Affair: Politics as Art in the Reign of George IV', *Journal of Modern History*, vol. 54, no. 3 (September 1982)

Luke, Hugh J., 'The Publishing of Byron's *Don Juan'*, PMLA, vol. 80, no. 3 (June 1965)

Macalpine, Ida and Hunter, Richard, *George III and the Mad-Business* (1969)

Martineau, Harriet, *The History of England During the Thirty Years peace, 1816–1846* (1849)

McCalman, Iain, *Radical Underworld: prophets, revolutionaries and pornographers in London, 1795–1840* (Cambridge, 1993)

Morgan, Marjorie, *Manners, Morals and Class in England, 1774–1858* (Basingstoke, 1994)

Nicholson. E. E. C., 'Consumer and Spectator: the public of the political print in eighteenth century England', *History*, 81 (January 1996)

Parry, J. P., *The Rise and Fall of Liberal Government in Victorian Britain* (1993)

Pattern, Robert L., *George Cruikshank's Life, Times, and Art, 1792–1835* (vol. 1, 1992)

Patterson, M. W., *Sir Francis Burdett and his times* (1931)

Paulin, Tom, *The Day-Star of Liberty: Hazlitt's radical style* (1998)

Paulson, Ronald, *Representations of Revolution, 1789–1820* (1983)

Petrie, Sir Charles, *George Canning* (second edition, 1945)

Porter, Roy, *Mind-Forg'd Manacles. A history of madness in England from the Restoration to the Regency* (1987)

Poynter, J. R, *Society and Pauperism: English ideas on poor relief, 1795–1834* (1969)

Rollo, *George Canning, Three Biographical Studies* (1965)

Routledge, James, *Chapters in the History of Popular Progress, chiefly in relation to the freedom of the press and trial by jury 1660–1820* (1876)

Semmel, Stuart, 'British Radicals and "Legitimacy": Napoleon in the Mirror of History', *Past and Present* (May 2000)

Smith, E. A., *George IV* (New Haven, 1999)

Smith, Edward, *William Cobbett: A Biography* (2 vols., 1878)

Smith, Olivia, *The Politics of Language 1791–1819* (Oxford, 1984)

Somerset, Anne, *The Life and Times of William IV* (1980)

Stapleton, Augustus Granville, *George Canning and his times* (1859)

Stephens, Frederick G., *A Memoir of George Cruikshank* (1891)

Stout, G. D., *The Political History of Leigh Hunt's Examiner* (St Louis, 1949)

Thomas, Donald S., *Cochrane, Britannia's Sea Wolf* (1978)

—, *A Long Time Burning: the history of literary censorship in England* (1969)

Thompson, E. P., *The Making of the English Working Class* (1963)

—, 'The State Versus Its Enemies', *New Society*, 19 October 1978

Thorne, R. G. (ed.), *The History of Parliament: The House of*

Commons, 1790–1820 (5 vols., 1986)

[*Times, The*] *The History of The Times: 'The Thunderer' in the making, 1785–1841* (1935)

Wahrman, Dror, *Imagining the Middle Class: the political representation of class in Britain, c.1780–1840* (Cambridge, 1995)

Wallas, Graham, *The Life of Francis Place, 1771–1854* (1898)

Wardroper, *The World of William Hone, a new look at the Romantic Age in words and pictures of the day* (1997)

Wickwar, W. H., *The Struggle for the Freedom of the Press* (1928)

Wood, Marcus, *Radical Satire and Print Culture, 1790–1822* (Oxford, 1994)

Index

Figures in italics indicate captions. 'H' indicates William Hone.

pensions 179, 181, 182, 233, 234, 240, 246
Pentonville, London 26, 362
Perceval, Spencer 59, 73, 79, 318
Percy, Hugh, Earl 51
Pergami, Bartlommeo (Bartholomew Bergami in Britain) 318–19, 327
Peterhouse, Cambridge 74, 75
Peterloo Massacre (1819) 285–9, 294, 296, 304, 307, 337, 348, 350, 377
Philips, Charles 124, 131
Phillips, Sir Richard 49, 60, 71, 86, 211
Piccadilly, London 67
Pied Bull pub, Upper Street, London 360, 361
Pilgrim's Progress, The (Bunyan) 27, 32
Pitt, William, the Younger 19, 33, 35, 46, 213, 233, 300, 302
  'Reign of Terror' 38
  and constitutional reform 39
  and Ellenborough 75
  caricatured 301
  the Regent's political intrigues against 316
Place, Francis 1, 17, 127, 160, 211
  leader of reformist political organisation in London 34
  Pitt's 'Reign of Terror' 38
  tailoring business 39, 42
  on LCS social reform 40–41
  leads the Westminster Committee 51, 56
  Cobbett's trial 77
  and the asylum reform movement 86
  attacks Brougham 161
  and H's subscription fund 270
Plato 31
Plutarch: *Lives* 30
Pole-Tylney-Long-Wellesley, William *175*
Political Register 66, 76, 153, 160, 180, 186–7
Poor Law overseers 42
Poor Laws 10, 43–7, 60, 96, 160, 166
Poor Rates 46
Pope, Alexander iii, 30
  Essay on Man 269
Porter, Roy 88
Portland, Duke of 301, 302
Portman Square, London 68
poverty
  the supposed nature of the poor 41–3
  poor relief 41–4, 47

press, the
  government's campaign against 3, 4–5, 38, 73–4, 76–7, 78, 83–4, 153, 178–9, 183–4, 192–5, 207–10, 224–5, 304–9, 385–6, 390
  laws relating to 3–4, 185, 190–5, 202–3, 213–16, 219–20, 242, 271–6, 304–9, 280–1, 382–4, 386, 392–3
  Bentham on 3, 78, 194, 219, 378–9
  compared to industrial revolution 185–6
  growing freedoms 376–8, 380–1, 387–8, 392–3
  ministers defer to 387–9, 390–2
Preston, Thomas *314*
Privy Council 39, 315
Public Ledger 112
publishers
  prosecution of 33, 73, 381
  arrest of 38, 179, 276
  imprisoned 78
  precarious existence 126
  liturgical parodies pirated 183
  threat of a long prison sentence 193
  threat of transportation 305
Punch 351
Pym, John 60
Pynson, Richard: *Shepherd's Kalendar* 29

Quakers 24, 107, 112
Quarterly Review 8–9, 18, 49, 75, 185, 189, 282, 324, 338

Raffles, Reverend Thomas 373
Raleigh, Sir Walter 360, 361
Real or Constitutional House that Jack Built, The 315
Reasoner 162
Red Lion Square, Holborn 28
Reeves, John 232–3, 241
Reformists' Register (previously *Weekly Commentary*) 154, 158–61, 163, 168, 172, 174, 177, 186, 187, 190, 195, 198, 201, 207, 210, 222–3, 371
Republican 266, 307
republicanism 35
Richards, W.J. ('Oliver') 207–10
Riot Act 285, 286
Robinson, Frederick, MP 95, 97